MW01702739

Principles of Banking

Eleventh Edition

American Bankers Association®

The American Bankers Association is committed to providing innovative, high-quality products and services that are responsive to its members' critical needs.

To comment about this product, or to learn more about the American Bankers Association and the many products and services it offers, please call **1-800-BANKERS** or visit us at our Web site: **www.aba.com.**

This textbook has been approved by the American Bankers Association for use in courses for which ABA certificates or diplomas (formerly American Institute of Banking (AIB) certificates or diplomas) are granted.

American Bankers Association®

Eleventh Edition

Printed in the United States of America
10 9 8 7 6 5 4 3 2 1

Catalog Number: 3010759 ISBN: 0-89982-689-X

Contents

Chapter 6 Lending

Chapter 7 Personal Financial Planning

Exhibit List

Preface

Principles of Banking is an entry-level textbook intended to give those who are new to banking a general understanding of the industry. *Principles of Banking* introduces fundamental banking concepts and principles, the basics of how banks operate as service providers and businesses, their obligation to operate in a safe and sound manner and manage risks, and the responsibilities of bank employees in a customer-focused financial services environment.

OBJECTIVES OF THIS BOOK

- Explain the context, structure, and operation of banks as both service providers and profit-making enterprises that rely on employees to provide customer-focused service
- Describe how the evolution of the U.S. banking system has led to the opportunities and responsibilities of banks and bank employees today
- Explain how banks function as financial intermediaries, contribute to the flow of economic activity, and help the Federal Reserve fulfill its role in managing monetary policy
- Describe the roles of boards of directors, senior management, committees, and employees in the business operations of banks
- Identify the financial statements that banks use and explain banks' business operations, from managing assets and liabilities to maximizing returns on loans and investments, while minimizing expenses and risks, monitoring financial performance, and planning for the future
- Describe deposit products and services, the bank's function in opening deposit accounts, and laws and regulations relating to deposits
- Describe the components of checks as negotiable instruments, types of endorsements, the check payment process, and check fraud schemes
- Explain banking laws and regulations related to payment processes
- Discuss how consumers and businesses bank electronically, how electronic banking is evolving, and laws related to electronic banking
- Identify the types of loans banks offer their customers, the lending process, and laws and regulations pertaining to lending
- Describe what constitutes personal financial planning—the insurance, investment, retirement, and trust products and services banks offer to support their customers' financial plans, and how such services are regulated
- Describe the specialized cash management, insurance, capital markets, trust, employee benefit, and international banking services banks offer to meet the financial needs of their business customers
- Explain how banks build relationships with customers by meeting their expectations, what factors influence customer purchasing decisions, and how both banks and their customers benefit from effective sales and marketing practices

- Discuss methods by which banks protect customer data, identify customers, and authenticate transactions, and describe the various types of fraud against bank customers and how they can protect their privacy and identities
- Explain how banks safeguard their assets and protect the nation's economy by adopting appropriate employee hiring and vendor management practices and remaining vigilant to crimes against banks

INSTRUCTIONAL DESIGN FEATURES

The eleventh edition of *Principles of Banking* contains ten chapters. The text is typeset in a single column and features sidebars that highlight explanatory and interesting information. Graphics and color visually enhance the reading and learning experience. Other notable instructional design features include:

- Learning objectives at the beginning of the chapters
- Chapter introductions that set the stage for topics covered in each chapter
- Charts, illustrations, exhibits, "By the Numbers," and "Did You Know?" callouts that supplement chapter content
- Definitions in sidebars for terms bolded in the text
- Situations that illustrate concepts
- Banker profiles that describe banking career and education possibilities
- Summaries that review each chapter's main points
- Self-check and review questions for testing comprehension
- Answers to self-check and review questions in a separate section at the back of the book
- A glossary that defines terms used in the text
- An index to assist with the location of content

CHANGES TO THIS EDITION

The eleventh edition of *Principles of Banking* contains updated information throughout. New information is provided on such topics as:

- Overall trends in such areas as regulatory evolution, financial services expansion, intensified competition, technological advances, service delivery, and social media use in banking
- U.S. banking system development, including how the banking industry has been affected by recent economic developments and ensuing regulatory change
- Enactment of the Dodd-Frank Wall Street Reform and Consumer Protection Act and its impact on many areas of banking, including consumer lending
- Delivery of bank services via mobile devices such as smart phones and tablets
- Electronic check processing and how technological advances are increasingly moving the United States toward a checkless society

- Developments in perpetrating and combating check fraud
- Virtual banks as an alternative to traditional brick-and-mortar banks and branches, and their competitive and service delivery implications
- Virtual currency, such as bitcoins, and its potential and limitations as a medium of exchange
- Continued expansion of Internet banking, including as a means of furthering consumer lending and investment
- Creation of the Consumer Financial Protection Bureau and its effect on the banking industry with regard to implementing new consumer protections in such areas as mortgage lending
- New developments in many other regulatory and legal areas, including the enactment of the Credit Card Accountability, Responsibility and Disclosure Act and its implications for bank customers with credit card accounts, changes to the Truth in Lending Act and Real Estate Settlement Procedures Act mortgage disclosures, and more
- Demographic and societal trends as they impact banking services, including insurance products, such as health insurance and long-term care insurance, and retirement planning and pension plans
- Bank marketing developments, including new ways of reaching customers through Facebook, Twitter, Flickr, or other social networking services, text messaging, online chats, shopping tools, and so forth
- Banking industry's social responsibility efforts, including promoting financial education and offering products for unbanked and under-banked consumers
- Identity theft and other rising security threats to customer information and the measures banks are using to address those threats
- Latest bank fraud schemes and how banks are responding

Exhibits have also been updated and new exhibits added to illustrate and clarify new material.

CONTENT OVERVIEW

The material presented in *Principles of Banking* has been reorganized into ten chapters that present a logical progression of topics and fall within three key areas: Bank and Employee Responsibilities, Bank Products and Services, and Building and Protecting Relationships.

The eleventh edition begins with an overview of the bank itself and then proceeds to a discussion of the many services that banks offer—from deposit accounts to payment services, electronic banking, lending, personal financial planning, and business and international services. The final chapters look at how banks market and sell products and fulfill their obligation to protect their vital responsibility to customers, shareholders, and the nation.

Bank and Employee Responsibilities

Banks as Service Providers	Chapter 1 considers the role of banks as service providers, meeting the financial needs of everyone from the individual customer to businesses of all types and sizes to local communities and state and national governments. Their employees—bankers—have helped banks fulfill these roles by serving as the special link between banks and their customers. The best bank employees have an understanding of the entire picture of their industry—how banks and their interactions with customers, communities, competitors, and regulators have made the United States into the economic powerhouse it is today.
Banks as Businesses	Chapter 2 explores the bank as a business enterprise. The banking industry is constantly changing, with banks continuing to form, consolidate, merge, and close. Banks range from small banks serving local communities to some of the largest corporations in the United States serving a nation of customers and engaging in global financial services. To remain viable, banks must offer products and services that customers want and, in doing so, prudently manage assets and liabilities in such a way as to generate a profit for shareholders. This chapter examines all these issues, looking at how banks operate as a business and how their performance is reflected in financial reports that show where and how the bank acquired funds, how those funds were put to work, and the results that were achieved.

Bank Products and Services

Deposit Accounts	Chapter 3 focuses on the deposit account, a core bank product. Checking, savings, money market, and time deposit accounts are discussed in this chapter, as are the different ways bank customers can deposit funds. The type of deposit account a customer opens and the way an account is titled determine account ownership, which in turn has a bearing on account opening procedures and federal deposit insurance.

Payments: Cash and Checks	Chapter 4 looks at cash and checks as payment systems. Bank customers not only make deposits, they also move money out of their accounts to make payments. The chapter especially focuses on the check payment function, which continues to transition from paper checks to electronic payments. While paper checks remain common, their physical collection and clearing is almost always done electronically. Regardless of how a check is processed, it is important to know what constitutes a negotiable check that can be properly debited to the account of the check writer and credited to the account of the recipient.
Electronic Banking	Chapter 5 delves further into the world of electronic banking, one in which some banks do not have a physical presence and currency can be virtual. This chapter explores how electronic transactions are processed and the new ways banking is being done electronically by consumers and businesses through such channels as bank websites and the Internet, mobile banking devices, and a wide variety of payment cards.
Lending	Chapter 6 covers consumer and business lending—another traditional core banking function. The chapter looks at the many consumer and commercial loan products that are offered and briefly examines each stage of the lending process from loan application to loan administration and review.
Personal Financial Planning	Chapter 7 explores the basics of crafting a personal financial plan for bank customers and the bank products and services, such as insurance products, investments, retirement vehicles, and trust services that are available to customers to achieve their financial goals. Although banks once simply offered checking and savings accounts and made loans, they now seek to meet the total financial needs of their customers.
Business and International Banking Services	Chapter 8 focuses on the financial products and services banks provide to their business customers. Cash management, insurance, capital market products, trust services, and international banking help businesses of all sizes fulfill their strategic and operational goals.

Building and Protecting Relationships

Building Relationships: Marketing, Sales, and Customer Service	Chapter 9 looks at how banks strive to provide excellent customer service and create and sell products and services that meet customers' needs and expectations. The most successful bank employees and the most profitable banks effectively promote their products and services; the key strategy being to build long-term customer relationships.
Safeguarding Customers and the Bank	Chapter 10 concludes *Principles of Banking* by considering the stewardship responsibilities of banks. Banks have a special duty to protect customer information, safeguard customer and bank assets, deter financial crimes, combat computer attacks, and help protect the nation's financial system.

Acknowledgments

The American Bankers Association extends its gratitude to Nancy Derr-Castiglione who was subject matter expert reviewer for this edition. Ms. Derr-Castiglione (Nancy D-C for short) is an ICB Certified Regulatory Compliance Manager. She is the President and owner of D-C Compliance Services, a regulatory compliance consulting services firm. She has been actively involved with the American Bankers Association and has served on the ABA Compliance Executive Committee, the National and Graduate Compliance Schools Board, and the Editorial Advisory Board of the *ABA Bank Compliance* magazine. In 2001, Nancy was the recipient of the ABA's Distinguished Service Award for service to the regulatory compliance management profession.

The American Bankers Association also wishes to thank David Buzzell for updating the eleventh edition of *Principles of Banking*. Mr. Buzzell is a writer who specializes in banking and business topics and has served as an author for several ABA textbooks and other publications. Mr. Buzzell is a principal in Adeptus Associates in Middletown, MD. Editing was done by Allyn C. ("Allie") Buzzell also a principal at Adeptus Associates. Layout and composition was done by Wendi Calvert, Calvert Creative Design, Lexington, SC.

Sally Spasovski was the project manager for this edition. Sally is a performance and training consultant who has worked with the ABA since 2000. She was co-author of the eighth edition of *Principles of Banking*, and has collaborated with the ABA on many of its course offerings. Sally is located in Tempe, AZ.

The American Bankers Association also extends sincere thanks to the bankers and other team members who reviewed and commented on the previous edition or the manuscript of this textbook. They provided valuable guidance on both content and presentation.

Rita Buchholz, CTFA
Senior Trust Officer
Northwestern Mutual Wealth Management Company
Milwaukee, Wisconsin

Allison Burkholder
Executive V.P./COO
United Bank
Versailles, Kentucky

Michelle Allen Cassel, CFMP
Sr. V.P., Marketing Director
Community Trust Bank
Ruston, Louisiana

G. Jay Francis
Instructor
Keystone Opportunity Center
Souderton, Pennsylvania

Debora A. Lurgio
Controller
Urban Partnership Bank
Chicago, Illinois

Lisa Phillips
Executive Director
Center for Financial Training
Jacksonville, Florida

Karen S. Schellin, CAMS, CFE, CFSSP
Associate Managing Director
Fraud Manager
Talmer Bank and Trust
Kenosha, Wisconsin

Tom Stecher
Education & Curriculum Specialist
Heartland Financial USA, Inc.
Dubuque, Iowa

D. Oliver Swaby
Professor of Accounting,
Economics & Finance
Washington Adventist
University
Takoma Park, Maryland

Kevin J. Thiele
Senior Vice President
Member, Board of Directors
Wahoo State Bank
Wahoo, Nebraska

Banks as Service Providers

1

Learning Objectives

After studying this chapter, you should be able to

- Explain the role of bank employees
- Describe how banks serve customer needs
- Describe the role of banks in their communities
- Identify major bank competitors
- Identify bank regulators and major banking laws and regulations
- Explain the evolution of the U.S. banking system and its role in the U.S. economy
- Discuss future trends in banking

Situation

Customers Matthew and Verna, who immigrated to the United States several years ago, always have wanted a home of their own. Although they have found the house they want, they now need a mortgage to buy it. Another customer, Tamara, has her own successful interior decorating business. She has never worked for a company that offered a pension plan. She would like to set aside a portion of her income for retirement security but is unsure what plans are available for a person in her situation.

Introduction

Banks are unlike any other business. Since the 1700s, going back to the founding of our country, they have occupied a special place in our history. Banks have long contributed to the community, the economy, and the welfare of the nation. Their employees—bankers—have helped fulfill this role by serving as the special link between banks and their customers and communities. To serve customers well and fulfill their community responsibilities, bankers must have a thorough working knowledge of bank products, services, policies, and practices. In a speech to bankers in October 2013, Federal Reserve Board Governor Jerome Powell expressed well the special relationship between banks and their customers and communities:

"[Banking] is fundamentally a local, relationship-based business...bankers live in the localities they serve; their customers are their neighbors and friends. Their direct, personal knowledge of the local economy enables them to tailor products and services to meet their communities' needs."

By meeting community needs, banks have helped make the United States the world's largest economy. On a daily basis, banks must meet the challenges of competitors and the requirements of regulators. Banks must also continually adapt to new ways of doing business. Through it all, banks continue to flourish, and the ties between banks and bankers and the communities they serve have remained strong. As Governor Powell continued:

"Community bankers recognize that their own success depends on the health of the communities they serve...the remarkable resilience of America's community bankers will enable them not only to survive, but also to thrive in the years ahead."

BANK EMPLOYEES

At the center of every banking interaction—whether with a customer or the community, a vendor, a regulator, or a competitor—is the bank employee. The banker's primary responsibility is to professionally represent the bank's interest in every interaction. Bankers must have good judgment, address requests promptly, and follow procedures. The primary attributes of bank employees include:

- **Service**. Customer-focused bankers give customers exceptional personal service, maintain complete confidentiality, and conduct business in a professional manner.
- **Responsibility**. In addition to specific job duties, bank employees are responsible for observing the bank's policies and procedures. They are also responsible to those they report to and for those reporting to them. Most importantly, they are responsible to the bank's shareholders and customers.
- **Trustworthiness**. The strength of the financial services industry depends on how much customers trust their institutions and employees. Because they handle and safeguard the funds and assets of others, banks must uphold the highest standards of business **ethics**. These policies usually are explained in the bank's **code of conduct** (see exhibit 1.1, next page).
- **Professionalism**. In their working relationships with customers, other employees, and managers, the professional attitude and appearance of bank employees set the tone for the entire bank.

ethics—Principles of conduct and judgment that affect business practices.

code of conduct—A formal set of guidelines approved by the board of directors that represents a company's policies for corporate governance and individual conduct.

Bank Employee Careers

As financial products, services, and technological applications expand, so do career opportunities in banking. There will always be a need for employees who enjoy working with customers on a daily basis, such as customer service representatives, tellers, and other front-office staff, but there are many other career opportunities available, ranging from accounting, auditing, and compliance to lending, sales, trust services, human resources, and corporate support. Banks also employ many technology and operations specialists. Also, as banks expand their product offerings, they are employing more people with specialized skills in areas like insurance and investment products.

Bank Employee Training

Banks have a long history of training employees for current and new positions within the bank. In addition to job-specific onsite training, many banks may offer reimbursement for education and training as part of their benefits packages. Employees can access American Bankers Association (ABA) courses through live classes, ABA facilitated online courses and ABA self-paced online training. All courses count toward ABA diplomas and certificates.

Many ABA courses have college-level credit recommendations from the American Council on Education (ACE). Bank employees also can earn bank certifications. The Institute of Certified Bankers, a subsidiary of the American Bankers Association, certifies financial professionals in the areas of wealth management and trust, compliance and risk management, lending, bank marketing, and retirement services.

Did You Know ...

In 1897, the ABA Bureau of Education distributed a pamphlet to educate the public on the role of banks and bankers. *What Is a Bank?* was so popular that over a million copies were distributed the first year.

Source: American Bankers Association

BANKS AND THEIR CUSTOMERS

Approximately 90 percent of all U.S. households have a banking relationship. Almost all commercial enterprises, ranging from sole proprietorships to Fortune 500 corporations, do business with banks.

Exhibit 1.1: Elements of a Code of Conduct

A code of conduct (also known as a code of ethics) establishes bank policies about such matters as employees receiving gifts from customers, serving on public boards, taking outside jobs, and reporting suspicious activities. Most codes of conduct address the following:

- **Personal conduct.** As protectors of other people's money, bankers are held to high standards of employee conduct. Banks are prohibited from employing persons who have committed dishonest acts or who have been convicted of certain crimes. Dishonest and fraudulent activity of any kind is not tolerated.
- **Compliance.** Employees have a personal responsibility to adhere to the many laws and regulations that affect banks. In compliance with the equal employment opportunity law and regulations, for example, an employee must not cooperate in any form of job bias, and employees must report acts that suggest discrimination.
- **Conflict of interest.** As a representative of the bank, every employee is obligated to act in the best interest of the bank, its shareholders, and its customers. Bank employees should avoid situations where personal or financial interests or relationships might influence or appear to influence professional judgment.
- **Accepting gifts.** Employees may not accept money or gifts of significant value from customers or anyone else if acceptance of the gift might cause suspicion of influence or compromise the employee's performance.
- **Outside activities.** Employee conduct, both at work and away, reflects on the bank's reputation and its image in the community. Participating in civic, social, educational, and charitable activities is encouraged. If a question should arise about the activities of an outside organization that an employee supports, the employee should put the bank's interests first.
- **Confidentiality.** Bankers are obligated to exercise confidentiality in all customer interactions. This includes not discussing a customer's financial information with other employees or customers and avoiding the unauthorized use or release of a customer's confidential information. State and federal privacy laws limit how banks may share personal financial information with affiliates and third parties.
- **Purchasing defaulted property.** Employees should not purchase property that has been repossessed or foreclosed by their bank or an affiliate. Such purchases suggest a conflict of interest and bring the bank's reputation into question.
- **Notification of violations.** If a bank is a publicly-held company, its employees are obligated to report suspected wrongdoing of an employee or other insider. Employees who suspect wrongdoing by their institution are ensured protection under whistleblower provisions of banking law.

Did You Know ...

The American Bankers Association recommends that graduating students interested in careers in banking:

- Get to know a local banker
- Develop a career path
- Take advantage of training opportunities

Bankers help customers assess their financial needs and offer appropriate ways to fulfill them. For example, customers' lives are made easier by addressing a college student's need for an education loan, a small business owner's need for a health savings account, or a retiree's need for estate and financial planning services. The many types of products and services for bank customers are discussed in later chapters. However, customers can be generally segmented into five groups.

Basic Product Users

Most households use standard banking products and services. Historically, these have been basic checking and savings accounts. Today, checking and savings accounts have become more segmented. Checking accounts are tailored to the needs of students or senior citizens, for example. Savings accounts can be set up to serve specific customer needs, such as saving for college or paying medical bills. Over the years, the list of bank products used by most households has expanded to include credit and debit cards and small-dollar value certificates of deposit.

High-End Savers

Some customers grow their balances in checking and savings accounts and look to invest their money in other bank savings vehicles. High-end savings products include money market accounts, higher-dollar value savings accounts, certificates of deposits, and other long-term savings products.

Investors

In the past, investors had to set up investment accounts with niche investment banks. Today, banks of all sizes serve the needs of investors, most of whom are engaged with their finances as never before. The Internet has become an important tool for investors to track and manage investments. Banks are serving these customers by making annuities, bonds, mutual funds, and stocks available for investment, and by providing managed money accounts and asset management accounts.

Borrowers

In its simplest terms, traditional banking involves accepting money from those who have it (depositors) and loaning it to those who need it (borrowers). Borrowers represent one-half of this relationship and are critical bank customers. Consumer credit products such as home purchase loans, auto loans, and credit cards represent a significant portion of bank lending. Home equity loans and student loans also serve a growing customer need.

Businesses

Banks have long served the needs of commercial customers. Many of the services offered to businesses are the same as offered to consumers, the difference being that the services are normally larger in size and scope. For example, banks offer a wide array of business checking and savings accounts. For the unique needs of the business customer, banks offer merchant services like check and credit card processing, small business and agricultural loans, dealer financing, cash management services, employer services such as payroll processing, and workplace retirement and benefit plans.

BANKS AND THE COMMUNITY

Banks are convenient places for customers to take care of their financial needs, but banks are much more than mere service providers. Banks improve the quality of life in a community by helping families improve their finances and educate their children; similarly, banks support the growth of the local economy by helping businesses to prosper.

Community Development

By making financial services available in their communities, banks are meeting neighborhood credit and community development needs. Small business and agricultural loans and loans to develop low- to moderate-income housing are examples of how banks directly contribute to the economic vitality of their local communities.

Banker Profile

David Shaw began his banking career as a telephone customer service representative in Charlotte, North Carolina, right after graduating from state college. Using the bank's education benefits, he first obtained his ABA Retail Branch Management diploma in banking and his ABA Supervisor Certificate. Given his demonstrated professional skills, David was promoted first to assistant branch manager and then to branch manager. Keeping his career goals always before him, he continued his studies, partially financed by his bank. Now he has an M.B.A. and a new position as vice president of regional corporate sales. Only in his mid-thirties and newly married, David plans to stay with his bank, explore training and education opportunities, and further his career.

Community Reinvestment Act—A federal law mandating that federal bank regulators regularly evaluate how financial institutions help meet the credit needs of their communities, including low- and moderate-income sections of the community, and publicly rate the bank's performance.

> ***Situation***
>
> Justin opened checking and savings accounts when he graduated from college. Recently he inherited money from his grandmother. Because he is satisfied with the service at his bank, he deposits the money into his savings account there. His banker suggests that he talk to one of the bank's financial counselors, who offers him a mutual fund. Justin inquires about the stock market and is surprised when the financial counselor can help with that too. He is surprised even more when he asks to withdraw money to pay his car insurance bill and is referred to the bank's insurance agency for a quote. Justin leaves thinking how convenient it is to get all of his financial needs taken care of in one place—and with people he knows and trusts.

The **Community Reinvestment Act** (CRA) underscores the integral role banks play in improving the lives of low- to moderate-income consumers and small business owners. In keeping with CRA's goals and objectives, banks are delivering financial services to an increasingly diverse population. For example, banks with branches in low- to moderate-income areas are helping to meet the credit needs of their communities through accessible locations. By providing jobs and generating profits for their shareholders, banks contribute to a vibrant local and regional economy. Many banks also provide services to towns and cities, helping them manage their cash flow and raise capital.

Community Support

Banks support countless charitable organizations through financial contributions and the volunteer help of their employees. Many banks sponsor community events or offer financial education services for the public, such as programs that teach children to save. The ABA helps bankers make their communities better through financial education.

BANK COMPETITORS

Before the 1980s, banks were limited in the types of products and services they could offer. For example, with regard to traditional banking services such as demand deposit accounts, banks competed among themselves. At the same time, banks were restricted from offering products customers desired, such as money market mutual funds that paid higher interest rates than demand deposit accounts.

Today most regulatory barriers between banks and other financial service providers have eroded, and banks must contend in a vibrant and highly competitive marketplace. Those competitors include different types of entities.

Credit Unions

Credit unions offer financial services to members who, by law, must share a common bond, such as being teachers or federal employees. Because credit unions are exempt from federal taxes and often occupy employer-provided facilities, they have minimal expenses and can offer a range of products and services at reduced cost to their members.

Savings Institutions

Savings institutions (also known as savings associations or savings & loan associations) were originally **chartered** to provide mortgage loans to customers. To encourage the flow of deposits into savings institutions, the Federal Reserve allowed them to pay a higher interest rate on deposits than banks until interest rate ceilings were removed for banks in the 1980s. Savings institutions may be stock companies or mutual companies owned by depositors.

Brokerage Firms

Brokerage firms arrange contracts for customers to purchase stocks, bonds, and mutual funds. Their investment products do not carry federal deposit insurance, but the **Securities Investor Protection Corporation (SIPC)** offers their customers some protection against investment loss.

Finance Companies

Finance companies specialize in making small- to medium-sized loans to consumers or small businesses. The most common are personal finance and captive finance companies. Personal finance companies attract the high-risk borrower who may have a negative credit history. Captive finance companies, such as Ford Motor Credit Company, are subsidiaries of manufacturing companies and help sell the company's goods.

Insurance Companies

Insurance companies sell risk protection. These companies accumulate funds received from premiums and place them in relatively risk-free, long-term investments.

Mutual Funds

Mutual funds are organized collections of investment funds. Their sole activity is investing funds, usually in a diversified securities portfolio. Investors buy shares from and sell them back to the fund, either directly or through a stock exchange.

Money Market Funds

Like mutual funds, money market funds invest in portfolios of securities, but only in short-term instruments, typically with a three-month average maturity. Their investments include certificates of deposit, commercial paper, banker's acceptances, and U.S. Treasury bills. A checking account option may allow investors to write checks, usually of $500 or more, against their shares. Electronic transfers also are allowed.

Mortgage Companies

Mortgage companies specialize in financing loans backed by real estate.

Money Service Businesses

These are companies that cash checks for consumers for a fee and also provide remittance transfer and other money services. Many **unbanked** consumers use these companies.

BANK REGULATORS

As providers of financial services to consumers, farmers, businesses, and government entities, banks have a responsibility to the public to carry on their business with integrity and to protect the public trust. Therefore, banking is among the most highly regulated of business enterprises. There are five regulators with the authority to supervise bank activities.

Securities Investor Protection Corporation (SIPC)—A non-profit membership organization created by the Securities Investor Protection Act of 1970 to provide financial protection to customers of failing brokers or dealers who are members. In the event a member firm becomes insolvent, SIPC will liquidate the firm's assets and pay off account holders up to a specified maximum amount.

charter—A document issued by a federal or state supervisory agency granting a bank or other financial institution the right to do business.

unbanked—People who do not have a relationship with a bank or similar financial institution and generally rely on cash or money orders to receive or make payments.

Did You Know ...

There are more credit unions in the United States than commercial banks. At the end of 2012, there were 6,155 banks, 987 savings institutions, and 6,819 credit unions.

Source: Federal Financial Institutions Examination Council

bank holding company—A corporation that owns or controls one or more banks.

nonbank subsidiary—An entity owned by a bank holding company that offers nonbank products and services.

savings and loan holding company—A corporation that owns or controls one or more savings and loan associations or savings institutions.

state bank—A bank that is chartered by a state to provide financial services (as opposed to a national bank).

Edge Act corporation—Established under the Federal Reserve Act, a corporation that is a bank subsidiary for either foreign trade-related banking or foreign investment.

agreement corporation—A corporate subsidiary of a bank engaged in international banking and finance.

regulation—An official rule or set of rules having the force of law. Regulations are issued by government agencies and are based on, and designed to implement, a law enacted by a legislature.

national bank—A bank that is chartered by the federal government to provide financial services (as opposed to a state bank).

federal savings association—A thrift institution that is chartered by the federal government to provide deposit services and extend credit for homes and other goods and services.

Federal Reserve System (Fed)

The Federal Reserve System, often called the Fed, is the central bank of the United States. It therefore has a central role in the banking system and the economy. The Fed is responsible for supervising and examining all **bank holding companies**, their **nonbank subsidiaries**, and their foreign subsidiaries; **savings and loan holding companies; state banks** that are members of the Fed and their foreign branches and subsidiaries; and **Edge Act** and **agreement corporations** through which U.S. banks conduct operations abroad. Besides issuing **regulations** for these types of institutions, the Fed rules on merger and branching applications of state-chartered member banks and holding companies.

The Fed is operated under regulations, policies, and guidance adopted by the Board of Governors of the Federal Reserve System, commonly known as the Federal Reserve Board.

Office of the Comptroller of the Currency (OCC)

A bureau of the Treasury Department, the OCC is responsible for chartering, examining, and supervising **national banks** and **federal savings associations**. All applications for national bank and federal savings association charters, all requests for opening new domestic or foreign branches or offering new services, and all mergers or acquisitions involving national banks or federal savings associations must have OCC approval. The agency issues regulations governing bank investments, lending, and other activities.

Federal Deposit Insurance Corporation (FDIC)

The FDIC provides federal deposit insurance for insured depository institutions. To promote the safety and soundness of insured depository institutions, the FDIC also identifies, monitors, and addresses risks to the Deposit Insurance Fund (DIF), which insures depositor accounts.

In addition, the FDIC supervises and examines state-chartered commercial banks that are not Federal Reserve System members (called "nonmember banks") and state-chartered savings associations. The agency also has the authority to examine other FDIC-insured institutions for deposit insurance purposes.

Consumer Financial Protection Bureau (CFPB)

The CFPB was established by the Dodd-Frank Wall Street Reform and Consumer Protection Act to help protect consumers in the financial services marketplace. The CFPB's main focus is making sure that consumers have all the information they need—and that they can understand the information—when making financial decisions for themselves and their families.

As part of the Dodd-Frank Act's reorganization of bank supervision and oversight, the CFPB inherited responsibility for the consumer protection laws and regulations from the Federal Reserve Board. Among the CFPB's functions are to:

- Write rules to implement the consumer protection laws for all financial institutions
- Enforce compliance with the consumer protection laws and regulations by large financial institutions and **nonbank financial companies** (Note: The Federal Reserve Board, FDIC, and OCC continue to oversee consumer compliance by small and mid-sized banks under their jurisdictions.)
- Watch for and address unfair, deceptive, and abusive acts or practices that harm consumers
- Promote financial education
- Oversee the student loan market
- Monitor financial markets for new risks to consumers
- Enforce laws that prohibit discrimination and unfair treatment of consumers in mortgages and other financial transactions

nonbank financial company—A financial institution that does not have a banking license but is allowed to provide most banking services.

Federal Register—A daily publication of the federal government that contains, among other material, proposed and final regulations adopted by federal agencies.

State Banking Departments

Each state has its own banking department responsible for chartering, supervising, and examining state-chartered banks within the state. Applications for state charters are submitted to the banking department, and banks must pass qualifying tests. If a proposed new bank desires membership in the Federal Reserve System and the FDIC, its application must be approved by those agencies as well. State banking departments also examine the branches and agencies of foreign banks operating in their state.

Bank Regulations

Banking laws and regulations protect the U.S. banking system, respond to changing financial market conditions, and protect consumers. When the U.S. Congress or a state legislature passes banking-related laws, the regulatory agencies reporting to the executive branch of government are directed to formulate regulations to implement the laws. A regulation is more specific than the law and contains more explanatory material, such as procedures that banks can follow to ensure compliance. It also has the force of law.

When an agency writes a regulation, it first studies the history of the law to determine the intent of Congress. Then it drafts the regulation, which is published in the **Federal Register** for public comment. After the comment period passes, the agency takes the comments into consideration and publishes a final rule.

Final regulations published in the Federal Register are incorporated into the Code of Federal Regulations (CFR). The CFR codifies regulations by title and chapter numbers. Of the 50 titles, Title 12 applies to regulations issued by agencies that oversee banks and banking.

Did You Know ...

The Dodd-Frank Wall Street Reform and Consumer Protection Act reorganized the system of supervision for savings and loan associations. The Office of Thrift Supervision was abolished, and supervision of all federal savings associations went to the Office of the Comptroller of the Currency. Supervision of state-chartered savings associations went to the Federal Deposit Insurance Corporation, and supervision of savings and loan holding companies went to the Federal Reserve Board.

Did You Know ...

In 2012, the United States had a gross domestic product (GDP) of over 15.6 trillion dollars. China has the second largest economy in the world with a GDP of about 8.3 trillion dollars. The next largest world economies are those of Japan, Germany, and France.

Source: World Bank

DEVELOPING THE PUBLIC TRUST: A BRIEF HISTORY OF BANKS AND THE U.S. ECONOMY

By the 1920s, the United States had become the largest economy in the world, surpassing Great Britain. Nearly 100 years later, it remains the largest economy. Achieving this distinction was no accident—it was fueled by a banking system that today finances not only our country's economic growth but also much of the economic development around the world.

The brief history that follows illustrates how banks and their interactions with customers, communities, competitors, and regulators have made the United States into the economic powerhouse it is today.

THE EARLY BANKING SYSTEM

Banking in the 1700s and 1800s bore little resemblance to banking today. The financial system then was fledgling and very unreliable. Depositors, mostly local businessmen, had no assurance that money left in a bank would be there when they wanted to withdraw it—or that it would have the same value. For example, two merchants from different areas of the country might have difficulty completing transactions because neither had faith in the other's bank.

However, after a series of legislative milestones, the U.S. banking system evolved from the chaotic, unstructured, and unregulated days of the 1700s to the creation of the Federal Reserve System in 1913, which formed the foundation of the safe and sound banking system of today (see exhibit 1.2).

CENTRAL BANKING

Early in the nation's history, the banking system consisted of a large number of unrelated and unregulated banks with no nationwide system for clearing checks. Thus, the public never had full confidence in the banks where they deposited their

Exhibit 1.2: Milestones in the Evolution of U.S. Banking

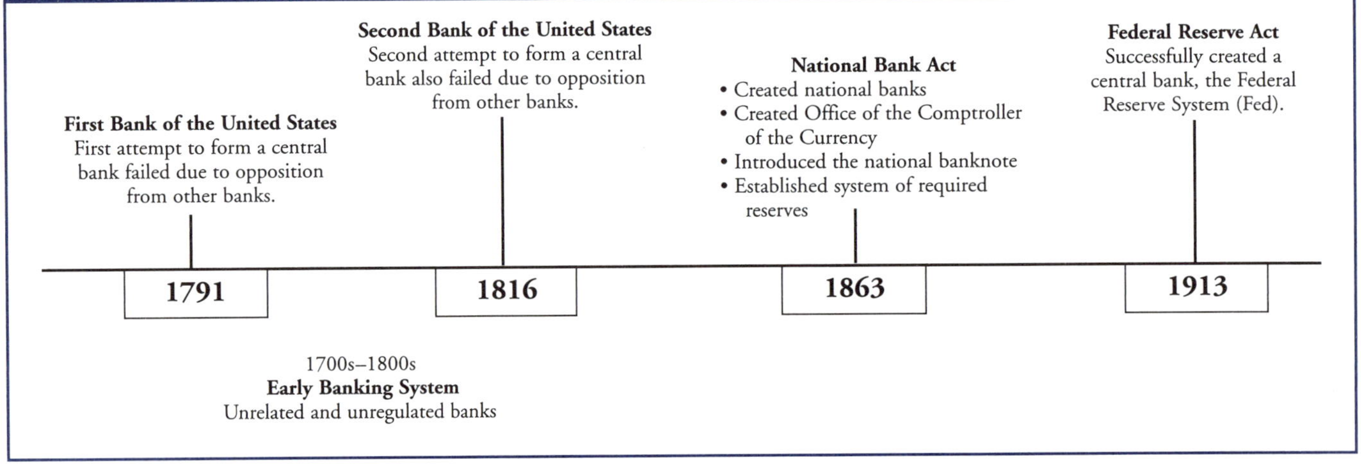

money. There was also no common currency—banks would issue their own notes, which were often easily counterfeited (see exhibit 1.3).

Congress tried to address this problem by authorizing a new central bank that had the direct involvement of and backing from the federal government. Opened in Philadelphia in 1791, the First Bank of the United States restored the public's faith and confidence in banking. However, the banks whose notes were redeemed for coin and currency issued by the new bank opposed it so strongly that Congress refused to renew the charter. The bank closed in 1811.

Without a central bank, many of the old banking problems recurred, including poorly operated and undercapitalized banks, limited access to credit, and lack of faith in the currency. In 1816, Congress responded by creating the Second Bank of the United States, but it met the same fate as the First Bank for basically the same reasons.

Dual Banking System

By 1862, the U.S. banking system and the economy in general were in serious trouble. In 1863, Congress passed the National Bank Act. The act set up a new state and federal banking system in the United States. It contained provisions

Federal Reserve Act, 1913

National check clearing system
- Twelve Federal Reserve districts
- Reduced float
- Faster check collection

Decentralized reserves
- Reserve requirements
- Bank reserves kept within each Federal Reserve district

Federal Reserve notes
- Local control over banks' Federal Reserve notes
- Notes backed by Federal Reserve assets of securities and gold
- Basic form of U.S. currency today

Exhibit 1.3: A Common Currency

Banknote Issued by the Bank of Morgan, Georgia, 1857

Although colorful and artistic, early banknotes were easy to counterfeit and their issuance could not be easily controlled.

Source: Photo courtesy of the Smithsonian Institution, National Numismatic Collection

National Banknote, 1902

National banknotes brought uniformity to America's currency.

Source: Photo courtesy of the Smithsonian Institution, National Numismatic Collection that created the OCC and national banks; introduced a national **banknote**; and established a **reserve requirement** to meet depositor withdrawals.

Today, the OCC, which is headed by the Comptroller of the Currency, charters national banks and federal savings associations. Like state banks, national banks and federal savings associations are owned privately. The addition of national bank charters to the existing state bank charters created a **dual banking system**. To distinguish national from state banks, the former are required to include the word "national" in their name—for example, Union National Bank and Trust Company—or add the words "National Association" (abbreviated as "N.A.") to their name, as in Liberty Bank, N.A. Federal savings associations must have the word "federal" in their names.

banknote—Currency issued by a bank promising to pay the amount of money designated on its face when the note is presented to the bank.

reserve requirement—A mandate that each bank set aside a portion of its cash assets against its outstanding deposits. Today reserve requirements are managed by the Federal Reserve as part of its monetary policy duties and apply only to the deposits in transaction accounts.

dual banking system—The banking system in the United States today in which a bank may be chartered by either a state or the federal government.

pyramided reserves—The reserve patterns of banks before the Federal Reserve System was authorized. Smaller banks would place their reserves in larger banks, which would then place their reserves and those of the smaller banks in money center banks such as those in New York City.

buying on margin—Using borrowed funds to buy assets such as stock.

The Federal Reserve System

Although the National Bank Act went a long way toward restoring confidence in the banking system, some weaknesses remained: an inadequate nationwide check collection system, an inflexible currency, and **pyramided reserves**. These were addressed in the Federal Reserve Act of 1913, which created the Federal Reserve System (see exhibit 1.4).

The Great Depression

Creation of the Federal Reserve System restored public confidence in the banking system and gave a powerful boost to the economy. By the 1920s, national prosperity and optimism were high, and the stock market soared. Investors were convinced that the stock market would continue to rise. No one wanted to be left out; people who did not have funds to invest in the stock market simply borrowed from banks, paying for a percentage of their investment with their own money and financing the rest—a practice called **buying on margin**. The stock bought was used as collateral for the loans.

On October 28, 1929, the stock market crashed, triggering the most severe economic depression this country has ever experienced (see exhibit 1.5, page 14). The Great Depression lasted 12 years in the United States, during which time unemployment reached 25 percent. Unable to collect on loans, many banks became bankrupt and closed their doors. By 1933, over 8,300 commercial banks (about half the banks in the nation at the time) had failed.

The causes of the Great Depression were many, including easy credit that led to speculative investing and an absence of deposit protections so that, when a bank failed, customers lost their money and had no recourse.

In the 1930s, Congress enacted several laws to reform the banking system and address the factors believed to have contributed to the stock market crash. Three acts in particular—the Banking Act of 1933, which contains sections referred to as the Glass-Steagall Act; the Securities Exchange Act of 1934; and the Banking Act of 1935—had a great influence on the banking business and, in some cases, still do (see exhibit 1.6, page 14).

Exhibit 1.4: Problems Solved by the Federal Reserve

Problems with the 1863 National Bank Act	*Federal Reserve Act of 1913 Solutions*
Difficulties with Check Collection The check collection system was slow, complicated, and obstructed by poor communication systems. Checks could take weeks to travel coast to coast for posting and payment. Collection and transportation costs were deducted from the face amount. Checks were returned unpaid (sometimes months later) because accounts had closed or funds were insufficient. When larger money center banks served as clearing centers, checks had to travel through a number of banks before reaching their destination.	**National Check Clearing System** The Federal Reserve accepts checks for clearing at its processing center. This center routes checks to the paying banks, those on which the checks are drawn. Federal Reserve Banks offer check clearing, collection, and return-item services to banks; they are allowed by law to charge fees for these services.
Inflexible Currency The money supply, which was tied to the number and value of government bonds, could not expand with the economy. A national bank only could issue notes when it could buy bonds to pledge as security. When the economy expanded, the federal government received more tax revenue, which allowed it to pay its bond debt and reduced the ability of national banks to buy bonds and issue more banknotes. The money supply contracted when it needed to expand to support the needs of the economy.	**Federal Reserve Notes** Federal Reserve Banks issue Federal Reserve notes. Because the notes do not have to be backed by specific government securities, the limitations of the old national banknotes are eliminated. Today, Federal Reserve notes are the basic form of U.S. currency; they are backed by the assets held in Federal Reserve Banks, as well as by the taxing authority of the U.S. government.
Pyramiding of Reserves Having national banks hold their own reserves led to instability and bank panics. Smaller banks used larger city banks as depositories for reserves. City banks, in turn, placed their own and their depositors' reserves with larger money center banks, such as those in New York City. The result was a concentration of **pyramided reserves** in the money center banks. Money center banks used deposited reserve funds to make short-term loans, usually to brokerage firms. When smaller depositing banks needed to withdraw reserves to meet obligations, the money center banks had to raise funds quickly by calling in loans. Payment delays led to bank panics.	**Decentralized Reserves** The 12 Federal Reserve districts also solved the problem of pyramiding reserves: The Federal Reserve Board has the authority to set and change reserve requirements as needed, within limits. Besides keeping their reserves as cash in their vaults, banks can keep them in the Federal Reserve Bank for their district. Bank reserves are thus spread across the country rather than centralized in one or a few locations.

Social Change and Consumer Protection

The Great Depression ended with the start of World War II, when manufacturing geared up and people returned to work to meet the demand for military equipment and supplies. Banking reforms enacted by Congress helped keep the financial system sound and functioning.

The decades after the Great Depression were marked by restrictive regulations that limited bank competitiveness. Nevertheless, there were several innovations in

Risks of Buying on Margin

- Stock decreases in value.
- The value of stock as collateral for a margin loan decreases.
- Bank issues "margin call" to borrower.
- Borrower must put up more money, or
- Bank sells (liquidates) the collateral.
- Liquidation drives down the stock value more.
- The market decline worsens.

Exhibit 1.5: The Great Stock Market Crash: Dow Jones Industrials (June 1929 to May 1933)

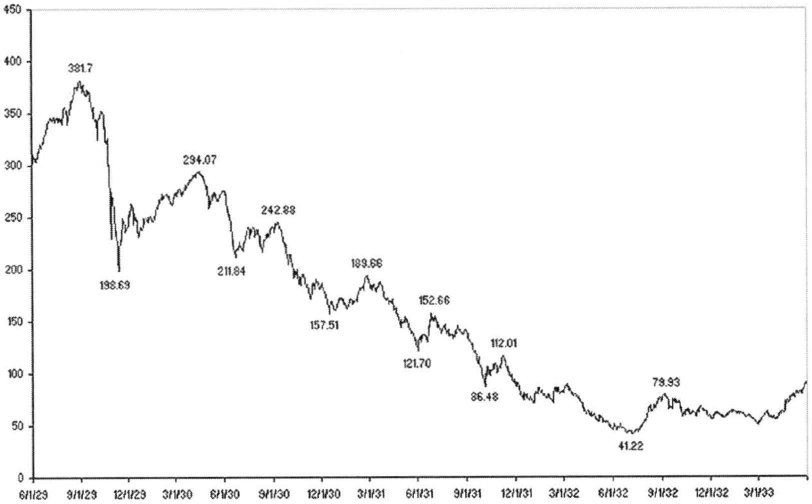

Source: Chartingstocks.net

Exhibit 1.6: Banking Law Arising Out of the Great Depression

Banking Act of 1933 (contains sections referred to as the Glass-Steagall Act)

- Prohibited banks from paying interest on demand deposits
- Raised the minimum capital requirements of national banks
- Prohibited banks that were members of the Federal Reserve System from underwriting securities and affiliating with organizations dealing in securities
- Allowed the Federal Reserve Board to forbid member banks to use reserve credit for speculative purposes
- Created the Federal Deposit Insurance Corporation (FDIC) to protect depositors at FDIC-insured banks

Securities Exchange Act of 1934

- Gave the Federal Reserve authority to set margin requirements (all loans made by banks that accepted securities as collateral were subject to the margin requirements)

Banking Act of 1935 (also called the Federal Deposit Insurance Act of 1935 and amended the Banking Act of 1933)

- Set standards for operations at FDIC member banks
- Gave the FDIC authority to examine member banks to ensure that they comply with the standards
- Empowered the FDIC to take action to reduce the possibility of troubled banks failing
- Authorized the FDIC to pay depositors if an insured bank fails

credit and investment products to meet marketplace demands—innovations that continue to this day (see exhibit 1.7).

Along with these innovations came social change. Before 1968, little if any federal law protected consumers in their dealings with banks and other financial institutions. Consumer protection was a state responsibility.

The 1968 Consumer Credit Protection Act, of which Title I is the Truth in Lending Act, was a turning point. The act requires all lenders to make meaningful disclosure of their credit and leasing terms so that consumers can compare loan terms. Since then, Congress has enacted a host of other consumer protection laws (see exhibit 1.8, next page).

Exhibit 1.7: Innovations in Banking in the 20th and 21st Centuries

1946	First drive-in banking service offered by Exchange National Bank of Chicago
1947	First lockbox installed by First Chicago Bank
1952	First bank credit card issued by Franklin National Bank, New York
1960	Magnetic ink character recognition (MICR) technology helps automate check handling
1961	First negotiable certificate of deposit is offered by First National City Bank (now Citibank) to selected corporate customers
1966	First truly paperless point-of-sale (POS) system instituted by Hempstead Bank in Syosset, New York, in 32 retail establishments
	Bank of Delaware pilots debit card*
1969	Automated teller machines (ATMs) introduced by several banks
1972	Automated Clearing House (ACH) payment mechanism established as an electronic alternative to the traditional paper-based check collection system
	City National Bank of Columbus, Ohio, marketed a card with a debit feature
1974	Telephone bill payment services initiated by the savings and loan industry
1980	Home banking infrastructure was first developed, laying the groundwork for Internet banking
1994	Banks began to create a presence on the World Wide Web
1999	Mobile banking and payment initiatives began, with widespread deployments in Europe and the United States a few years later
2000	Electronic signatures gained legal validity for consumer transactions, breaking down a barrier to e-commerce
2001	Electronic bill payment and presentment systems went online
2003	A new negotiable instrument, the "substitute check," was created by law to support digital imaging of checks and electronic check payment processing
2007	Several major banks launched social networking sites to reach customers
2010	Cell phone point-of-sale purchases

*Source: Kansas City Federal Reserve Bank

Exhibit 1.8: Consumer Protection Laws

Since the late 1960s, Congress has enacted a broad range of laws to protect consumers in their financial transactions with banks. These laws include the following:

- Americans with Disabilities Act
- Bankruptcy Abuse Prevention and Consumer Protection Act
- Bank Sales of Insurance Act
- Community Reinvestment Act
- Consumer Leasing Act
- Controlling the Assault of Non-Solicited Pornography and Marketing Act (CAN-SPAM Act)
- Credit Card Accountability, Responsibility and Disclosure (Credit CARD) Act
- Dodd-Frank Wall Street Reform and Consumer Protection Act
- Electronic Fund Transfer Act
- Equal Credit Opportunity Act
- Expedited Fund Availability Act
- Fair and Accurate Credit Transactions Act
- Fair Credit and Charge Card Disclosure Act
- Fair Credit Billing Act
- Fair Credit Reporting Act
- Fair Debt Collection Practices Act
- Fair Housing Act
- Federal Trade Commission Improvement Act
- Financial Privacy Act
- Flood Disaster Protection Act
- Home Equity Loan Consumer Protection Act
- Home Mortgage Disclosure Act
- Real Estate Settlement Procedures Act
- Right to Financial Privacy Act
- Telemarketing and Consumer Abuse Protection Act
- Telephone Consumer Protection Act
- Truth in Lending Act
- Truth in Savings Act
- Service Members Civil Relief Act
- Women's Business Ownership Act

NOW account—An interest-earning transaction account against which check-like instruments (negotiable orders of withdrawal) may be drawn.

money market deposit account (MMDA)—A type of savings account created in 1982 that pays a market interest rate and gives account holders limited check-writing privileges.

affiliate—A business organization sharing with another organization some aspect of common ownership and control, such as interlocking directorates, stock ownership, or parent company.

Leveling the Playing Field

Beginning in 1980, the tight rein on banking powers began to relax as Congress enacted a series of laws that gave banks more freedom to compete. In 1980, the Depository Institutions Deregulation and Monetary Control Act was enacted. This law redefined banking powers to allow financial institutions to offer new products. For example, savings and loan associations (S&Ls) and credit unions were permitted to offer credit cards, commercial loans, and trust services. Restrictions on the interest rates that banks could pay on checking accounts were phased out, allowing the introduction of **NOW accounts** (negotiable order of withdrawal accounts), which are interest-bearing checking accounts, also known as "interest checking."

Two years later, the Garn-St Germain Depository Institutions Act of 1982 was passed. This law allowed banks and other depository institutions to offer **money market deposit accounts** (MMDA). The law also preempted state laws that restricted state-chartered banks and other lenders from offering alternative mortgage products (such as adjustable-rate mortgages).

Another law that broke down regulatory barriers was the Riegle-Neal Interstate Banking and Branching Efficiency Act of 1994. This law allowed interstate banking across the country. **Affiliate** banks within bank holding companies could function as branches for each other. National banks could operate branches by acquiring banks in other states.

New Opportunities

Even though regulatory barriers were tumbling down, many bankers still felt that Congress had not gone far enough in deregulation to allow banks to compete against brokerage firms and other providers. The Glass-Steagall Act, passed after the Great Depression, still prohibited banks from underwriting securities and paying interest on demand deposits.

A new chapter in banking, one in which opportunity became the operative word, was ushered in with the enactment of the Gramm-Leach-Bliley Act (GLBA) in late December 1999. The GLBA (also known as the Financial Services Modernization Act of 1999) repealed key provisions of the Glass-Steagall Act and gave banks the tools they needed to compete.

Banks, securities firms, and insurance companies could now enter each other's businesses and affiliate with each other. As a result, banks were permitted to offer a full complement of financial services, from loans and deposits to life insurance and mutual funds. With fewer competitive constraints and more opportunities to look for profit, banks also became leaders in applying technological advances, such as the Internet, mobile devices, and social networking, to better deliver financial services and fulfill their customers' needs. Banks could also offer these products and services through holding company affiliates or financial subsidiaries.

New Responsibilities

While the GLBA opened up new doors for banks in providing financial services, allowing them to catch up with the demands of their customers, the U.S. economy and society at large continue to evolve, creating new financial issues and assigning banks new responsibilities.

Financial Privacy

Besides providing new business opportunities for banks, the GLBA also imposed new obligations to protect customer financial information. The expansion in the types of products and services that banks could offer brought with it an increase in the exchange of consumer financial information. GLBA protects financial privacy by assuring customers that their personal information will not be shared with third parties without their permission.

Information Security

Although banks have had to maintain anti-money-laundering programs since 1987 and have been required to report suspicious activity since 1996, the USA PATRIOT Act extended these obligations to other types of financial institutions in 2001. The precipitating event was the terrorist attacks of September 11, 2001, with Congress acting swiftly to broaden the intelligence-gathering powers of law enforcement agencies in an effort to prevent future attacks. The USA PATRIOT Act places responsibilities on financial institutions to track and prevent the illegal transfer of funds by, for example, implementing customer identification programs and expanding the requirements for reporting suspicious activities, including possible terrorist financing schemes, to the government.

identity theft—A crime involving the possession of identifying information not lawfully issued for the possessor's use, or the attempt to access the financial resources of another person through the use of illegally obtained identifying information.

recession—A period of significant economic slowdown, often defined as a decline in the gross domestic product over two or more consecutive quarters.

corporate governance—The manner in which directors, management, and auditors handle their responsibilities to shareholders.

mortgage-backed security—An investment instrument that is backed by mortgage loans as security.

subprime loan—A loan made to a borrower who does not qualify for prime market interest rates because of credit problems or other deficiencies. A subprime loan charges a higher interest rate and/or greater fees.

With the rise of electronic banking, **identity theft** became an even greater problem. In 2003, the Fair and Accurate Credit Transactions Act was passed to help curtail identity theft, improve consumer access to their credit reports, enhance the accuracy of credit reports, and limit the sharing of certain consumer information.

Investor Protections

In the late 1990s, accounting irregularities and corporate mismanagement on the part of executives and directors of a few major companies caused investors to lose confidence in the companies they were investing in, causing stock prices to plummet and triggering a major **recession**. These management irregularities demonstrated weak **corporate governance**.

To restore investor confidence in publicly held corporations, Congress passed the Sarbanes-Oxley Act of 2002 (SOX). The law imposed new responsibilities on company executives, directors, audit committees, and accounting firms. The SOX requirements were modeled after the annual audit requirements that already applied to insured depository institutions such as banks.

SOX applies to public companies, those that issue stock to the public. After SOX was enacted, the federal banking agencies issued guidelines and regulations that applied SOX-like requirements to all banks, whether publicly or privately owned, in addition to the existing annual audit requirements.

Consumer Debt

Because of the ease with which consumers could obtain and use credit cards, many Americans in the early 2000s found themselves deeply in debt, subject to high credit card fees and often unable to keep up payments on their outstanding credit card debt. Congress reacted to the growing consumer card debt burden by passing the Credit Card Accountability, Responsibility, and Disclosure (Credit CARD) Act in 2009.

The Credit CARD Act contains several consumer protections, including requiring creditors to provide expanded written notice to consumers before changing the interest rates or terms of a credit card account. The Credit CARD Act also expanded the protections on gift cards and other types of prepaid cards.

The Financial Crisis and Great Recession

In 2008, a serious financial crisis triggered a deep and prolonged economic recession. This time much of the blame was assigned to financial institutions and what some critics called an inadequate system of financial regulation that had failed to adequately supervise the largest, most complex financial institutions and their investments.

The Great Recession was years in the making, but was ultimately sparked by risky mortgage lending practices and speculation in real estate and **mortgage-backed securities**. Housing lenders had, over time, greatly relaxed their lending standards. **Subprime loans**, once rare, became prevalent and a specialization of some mortgage lenders. As a consequence of this easy credit, home prices soared, fueling even more buyer speculation and enticing lenders to further relax their credit standards. This produced a so-called housing bubble—an artificial inflation of prices.

When the housing bubble burst, the real estate industry was not the only one to suffer. These risky mortgages were packaged and sold to investors as mortgage-backed securities. It was only after the housing bubble burst, however, that the worth of the underlying assets—the value of the houses securing the loans—was exposed as overinflated. Investment companies that traded in mortgage-backed securities went bankrupt or were sold for pennies on the dollar. Financial institutions that purchased these securities also suffered losses. Several major banks and securities firms had to be acquired by healthier entities.

To address the risks and abuses in the financial marketplace that led to the financial crisis and recession, Congress passed the Dodd-Frank Wall Street Reform and Consumer Protection Act in 2010. The Dodd-Frank Act is the most comprehensive financial reform legislation enacted since the Great Depression. Among other things, the Dodd-Frank Act:

- Reorganizes the bank oversight framework and expands its reach to include large nonbank financial companies whose activities have an impact on the U.S. financial system
- Requires banks to set aside more capital so they can better withstand financial stress
- Mandates changes in the federal rules that govern mortgage lending
- Requires large debit card issuers to reduce the fees they charge for processing consumer transactions at the cash register
- Creates a new federal agency, the Consumer Financial Protection Bureau
- Mandates changes in mortgage foreclosure processing procedures
- Directs large banking organizations and financial companies to write orderly resolution plans in the event they become insolvent
- Eliminates the prohibition against paying interest on demand deposits (imposed by the Banking Act of 1933)

The law is still being implemented under rules issued by the CFPB and the banking regulators. Some of the rules include exceptions for community banks, which did not contribute to the behavior that led to the financial crisis but still suffered the consequences. Despite these exceptions, community banks have been greatly affected by the Dodd-Frank Act and many of its implementing regulations.

As this history of banking in the United States demonstrates, there will always be financial peaks and troughs and, as a result, banking law and regulation periodically expand and contract. After the financial crisis, a period of re-regulation began as the federal government sought to control financial risk-taking (especially by the largest, most interconnected financial companies), protect consumers from abuses, and make the U.S. financial system safer and more transparent.

For a chronology of major banking legislation in the 20th and 21st centuries, see exhibit 1.9 (next page).

Did You Know ...

The text of the Dodd-Frank Wall Street Reform and Consumer Protection Act is 2,319 pages.

Exhibit 1.9: Chronology of Major Banking Legislation

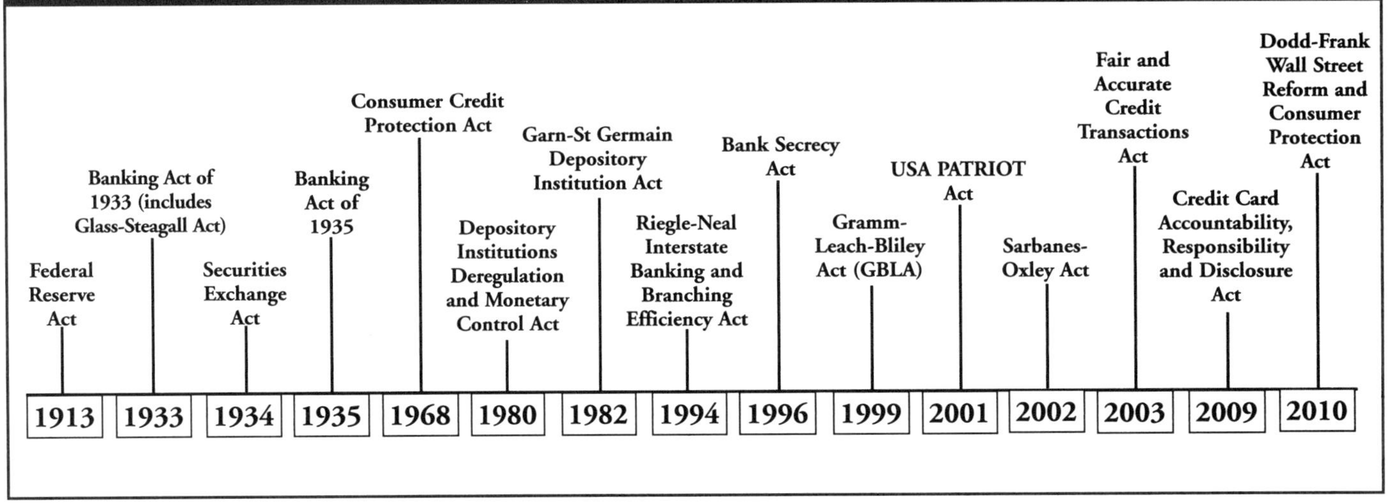

THE FUTURE OF BANKING

After more than two centuries of contributions to the U.S. economy, what does the future hold for the banking industry? Many industry analysts believe that:

- Regulation will continue to evolve.
- Services will expand.
- Competition will continue.
- Technological innovations will multiply.
- Branches will become smaller and more innovative.
- New ways will be found to target and reach customers.

Regulatory Evolution

Government regulation may increase in areas like national security and bank safety and soundness; and the direction of regulation is uncertain in other areas, like technology and product offerings. This will present challenges and opportunities for banks. Federal and state regulators will continue to seek to minimize risk in the banking system through regulation and oversight while recognizing the critical role banks play in promoting financial stability and economic development through innovative products and services.

Financial Services Expansion

Banks will continue to offer more premium and fee-based services. The fees earned from these many services may be equal to or exceed interest income earned from such products as loans and investments. Consumer and business preferences will continue to change, requiring banks to broaden their services—for example, by developing new market instruments to satisfy investment demand. Changing demographics, such as a U.S. population that is growing older and more diverse, will also compel banks to rethink how they market and deliver services.

Continued Competition

Nonbank competitors will make further forays into traditionally bank-dominated businesses, such as payment systems, deposit gathering, and lending. For many users of financial services, the distinctions between banks and their competitors will blur. Banks must strive to remain the one-stop, full-service provider of financial and finance-related services for consumers and businesses.

Technological Advances

Automation—electronic delivery and maintenance of bank services and related operations—will keep banks at the forefront of change. Shifts from employee-driven to technological solutions will continue. Automation and electronic services will expand into more areas of banking, transforming U.S. society into one that is increasingly cashless as wallets give way to personal computers, tablets, and smart phones as the favored means for paying bills, checking bank account balances, transferring funds, and making investment decisions. These advances, together with the pervasive use of automated teller machines (ATMs) and card-based transactions, will have profound implications for the traditional delivery of bank products through brick-and-mortar branches. Even complex services like financial planning will find more automated solutions to lower the cost of delivery where there is high volume.

Smaller, More Innovative Branches

Although banking has increasingly migrated to ATMs, personal computers, cell phones, and the like, many customers still prefer the convenience of visiting their local branch and interacting in person with their banker. Because of this, branches may never disappear, but they may get smaller. Too many routine transactions are moving to other channels and costs are too high to support the extensive network of branches of the past. In lieu of the traditional stand-alone brick-and-mortar branch, banks will continue to open smaller branches located in places like stores and cafes.

Online and Social Media Marketing

Banks are continually exploring ways to reach new customers. Marketing dollars will shift from traditional media to online and social media. Online marketing and social media such as Facebook and Twitter offer banks the opportunity to more precisely target customers and to better analyze the results of their marketing efforts.

SUMMARY

- Bank employees serve bank customers in many capacities. They retain customer confidence by conducting their duties responsibly and ethically. Bank employees are professional in attitude, appearance, and work habits. Individuals with these attributes will find that banking offers a wide variety of career opportunities with great potential for advancement.

Did You Know ...

By July 2013, 61 percent of U.S. adults who use the Internet were banking online. At the same time, 35 percent of mobile phone owners used their phones for banking.

Source: Pew Research Center

- Most Americans have a banking relationship, and banks serve a wide variety of customers. These customers can be grouped based on their general needs as standard product users, high-end savers, investors, borrowers, and businesses. Successful bank employees know both their bank's products and their customers' needs—and match them.
- Banks benefit their communities in many ways, from offering the public a full range of financial services to financing community development activities and supporting charitable activities.
- The financial services marketplace is very competitive. Besides banks, major financial service providers include credit unions, savings and loan associations, brokerage firms, finance companies, insurance companies, mutual funds, money market funds, mortgage companies, and check-cashing firms.
- Because of their important economic role, banks are highly regulated. There are five bank regulators: the Federal Reserve System, Office of the Comptroller of the Currency, Federal Deposit Insurance Corporation, Consumer Financial Protection Bureau, and state banking departments. To one degree or another, these bank regulatory agencies have supervision and examination powers, issue regulations, approve charters and expansion requests, authorize new activities, and promote safety and soundness by, for example, offering deposit insurance through the FDIC.
- The banking system in the United States has been evolving for more than 250 years. The industry has gone from a completely decentralized and unregulated system in the 18th century to one of the most highly regulated sectors of the economy in the 21st century. As with the U.S. economy, the banking industry has had its share of ups and downs, but the U.S. economy remains the largest in the world, and banks are by far this country's largest provider of financial services.
- The future of banking remains bright but challenging. Banking in the future may include further deregulation of restrictions on what services may be offered; continued expansion of the financial services available to customers; intensified competition in financial services; continued technological advancements in product delivery and operations; a shift from brick-and-mortar branches to smaller branches placed where consumers congregate such as retail establishments; and new approaches to target and reach customers via online marketing and social media.

Learning Check

SELF-CHECK AND REVIEW

1. How do banks contribute to their communities?
2. What five government agencies regulate bank activities?
3. Why is the National Bank Act of 1863 important in relation to dual banking? Does dual banking still exist today?

4. What were some of the causes of the Great Depression that began in 1929?
5. Explain why easy credit, as exemplified by subprime lending, led to tighter credit, both of which helped trigger the Great Recession that began in 2008.
6. What are some trends in banking today?

Banks as Businesses

2

Learning Objectives

After studying this chapter, you should be able to

- Explain how banks, by functioning as financial intermediaries, are central to the U.S. economy
- Discuss how the Federal Reserve determines and applies monetary policy in the economy
- Describe a bank's organizational structure
- Identify bank assets and liabilities and explain how they are managed to achieve bank objectives
- Identify the primary sources of bank income and expenses
- Explain how banks maximize loan and investment returns and fee income
- Identify typical performance measures in banking and how they are used in budgeting to achieve bank objectives

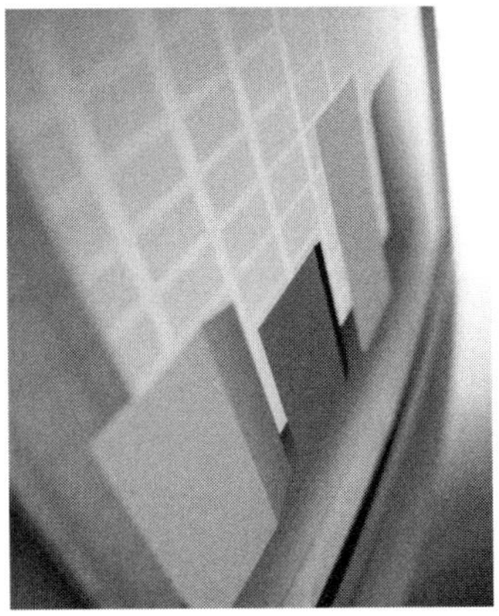

financial intermediary—A financial institution that facilitates the exchange of funds between savers and spenders by taking in funds from savers and then lending those funds to borrowers and investors.

monetary policy—The management of a nation's money supply by a central bank, such as the Federal Reserve, to ensure the availability of credit in quantities and at interest rates consistent with specific economic objectives.

discount operations—A tool of monetary policy in which banks borrow funds from the Federal Reserve. These loans, priced at the discount rate, help reduce liquidity problems for banks and maintain stability of financial markets.

Introduction

Banks have a unique role in the national and international economy because they manage money. As financial intermediaries, banks transfer money from one party (depositors) to another (borrowers). They also create money through the lending process; funding for new loans is deposited into demand deposit accounts, which increases the amount of money in circulation. These new demand deposit balances become the funds used for new loans to consumers, businesses, and the government.

In many other respects, banks are like any other businesses. They are responsible to their shareholders, as well as their customers, with an obligation to meet corporate and social responsibilities.

As with other businesses, banks also manage their assets and liabilities to produce a profit. As businesses, banks report their performance through financial statements and ultimately in an annual report to investors, customers, employees, and regulators. These statements and reports demonstrate the performance of a bank and its employees. They show where and how the bank acquired funds and put them to work, and the results it achieved.

BANKS AS FINANCIAL INTERMEDIARIES

Financial intermediaries accept funds from customers who want to save or invest and lend funds to customers who want to borrow. Many entities function as financial intermediaries, such as savings banks, credit unions, and even nonbank companies, such as American Express and General Electric. Nonetheless, commercial banks are still the main source of loans to businesses and, thus, are central to the money creation function in the economy.

The Fed's Management of Bank Loans and Deposits

Traditionally, banks differed from other financial intermediaries in that only banks could "create" money by making loans that generated new checkable deposits—still the core medium of exchange in the U.S. economy. That is why the Federal Reserve (the Fed) primarily uses the nation's banks to implement **monetary policy** and keep the financial system stable.

Control of the U.S. money supply is the primary duty of the Fed. It must ensure that the money supply does not outpace the needs of the economy. The Fed can shape the economic environment by taking specific actions to influence the flow of money and credit. It has three tools it can use: reserve requirements, **discount operations**, and **open-market operations**. The Fed's application of these tools has a great effect on bank loans and deposits, and thus on bank business operations (see exhibit 2.1).

Exhibit 2.1: Federal Reserve Tools and Their Effects

Reserve Requirements	Increase	Rarely used because its effects can be too disruptive; decreases the money supply
	Decrease	Stimulates the economy by increasing the supply of loanable funds; rarely used
Discount Operations	Increase Discount Rate	Can have moderately fast effect on banks and economy. Borrowing can lead to a reduction in the money supply when inflation is becoming a problem
	Decrease Discount Rate	Has opposite effect during economic slumps when the Fed wants to expand business activity
Open-Market Operations	Purchase Securities	Immediate, powerful effect on the economy; increases money supply available for purchases by crediting the reserve accounts of banks
	Sell Securities	Tightens credit by reducing the money supply in times of rising inflation

Source: Amaury Betancourt, Loan Review Examiner

Reserve Requirements

As the institution responsible for maintaining the stability of the financial system, the Federal Reserve tries to ensure that the deposits created by the nation's banks are neither too much nor too little for the needs of the economy. It does this by controlling the amount and cost of the reserves banks have available to lend to their customers.

By changing the reserve requirement, the Federal Reserve decreases or increases the amount of money a bank has available to lend and influences the money supply in the economy. For example, if the Federal Reserve were to raise its reserve requirements from 10 to 20 percent, a bank holding $100,000 in deposits would only have $80,000, not $90,000, to make new loans.

To build reserves, banks are free to compete for customers with each other, against other financial intermediaries, and in other markets. At this level, the Federal Reserve is only concerned about the total amount of reserves available in the overall banking system, not about the reserves held by individual banks. To meet a reserve deficiency, banks can market themselves to attract more deposits or borrow from another bank through **federal funds** transactions.

Federal funds transactions, typically occurring overnight, adjust the reserves of the two transacting banks on the Federal Reserve's account books. The rate charged, known as the federal funds rate (or fed funds rate), is set by the banks, not by the Federal Reserve. The Federal Reserve does, however, announce the target federal funds rate and influences the rate by increasing or decreasing reserve requirements and, thus, reserve availability. By doing so, the Federal Reserve aligns the federal funds rate with its monetary policy goals.

Discount Operations

The Federal Reserve is the lender of last resort for banks that have a short-term need for funds. By raising or lowering the rate it charges on its loans to banks—known as the discount rate—the Federal Reserve can reduce or expand business

open-market operations—The purchase and sale of U.S. Treasury and federal agency securities by the Federal Reserve to influence the growth of the nation's money supply. They are the principal means by which the Federal Reserve implements monetary policy.

federal funds—Excess reserves that banks deposit at Federal Reserve Banks and are made available for other banks to borrow, generally for a very short period of time such as overnight.

Federal Discount Rate Versus Federal Funds Rate

Federal discount rate
The rate the Federal Reserve charges on its loans to banks

Federal funds rate
The rate banks charge one another for overnight loans of reserve funds held at Federal Reserve Banks

Banker Profile

While he was earning his undergraduate degree in finance, Evan Sharmin took an internship with a large Dallas bank that rotated him through different departments, including investments and auditing. His math skills and analytical abilities were so impressive that, on graduation, he was offered a job in the bank investments section of the asset management department. Evan continued his studies, getting his ABA Bank Financial Management Diploma and attending ABA conferences and, eventually, the ABA's Stonier Graduate School of Banking. Today, he is vice president and manager of the bank's investments.

prime rate—The interest rate a bank offers its most creditworthy customers and the base rate used to set interest rates for other loans.

lending and investment spending in the economy. To increase lending, the Federal Reserve might lower the discount rate, thereby lowering the cost of funds to banks and encouraging borrowing and, thus, business growth and activity. To decrease lending, the Federal Reserve might raise the discount rate, thereby increasing the cost of funds to banks to discourage borrowing and slow the growth of the money supply.

Open-Market Operations

The Federal Reserve's most powerful monetary control tool is the open-market operations conducted by the Federal Reserve Bank of New York for the Federal Open Market Committee (FOMC). The FOMC directs the Federal Reserve Bank of New York to buy or sell government securities in the open market through selected dealer firms. The Federal Reserve's purchase or sale of government securities immediately increases or decreases the money supply and affects the availability of short-term credit.

When the Federal Reserve Bank of New York buys securities from banks, it increases the amount of cash and reserves on deposit with the Federal Reserve. The banks that sold the securities thus have more reserves to lend, either in their own communities or in the federal funds market. This, in turn, causes interest rates to decline. As the money is lent, it turns into new deposits that can be re-lent, multiplying the effect on credit in the economy.

If the Federal Reserve Bank of New York sells securities, bank reserves will decline—the banks get the securities and the Federal Reserve gets their reserves—so banks will not have as much to lend. When this happens, the federal funds rate, the **prime rate**, and other bank lending rates rise since the supply of money available has decreased.

Sometimes FOMC policy may conflict with bank goals. For example, loans are bank assets, but when inflation is increasing, the FOMC wants to restrain bank lending to hold down credit-induced buying. In this situation, the FOMC will drive up market interest rates, forcing banks to raise the interest rates on the loans they make. In this environment, businesses and consumers are less likely to borrow money. Rising interest rates also generate paper losses on securities held in bank portfolios that were bought when rates were lower.

On the other hand, in recessionary times when there is less demand for loans, the FOMC may provide banks with additional reserves they can lend and drop interest rates to stimulate loan demand. Declining interest rates also increase the value of securities that were bought at higher rates, which can be very helpful for a bank's profitability, considering that securities tend to be a major component of most banks' assets.

THE BANK AS A BUSINESS ORGANIZATION

A bank may be publicly owned or closely held. A publicly owned company sells stock to the public. Buyers of the stock are called shareholders. A closely held (also known as a privately held) bank is owned by a limited number of individuals or a family.

If the bank is a **corporation**, shareholders elect a **board of directors** to be the governing body of the corporation. Directors are ultimately responsible for the bank's operations, regulatory compliance, and performance, including profitability—and can be held liable for their actions. Directors appoint the bank's executive officers. The board of directors usually functions through committees, such as audit, compliance, risk, credit, trust, corporate governance, and compensation committees.

The board of directors, headed by the chairman of the board, is responsible for the policies that guide the bank. The bank's president, typically the chief executive officer, is responsible for applying those policies and supervising operations. Another top executive is the chief operating officer (COO), who is responsible for overseeing the day-to-day activities of the bank. Depending on the size and scope of the bank, various departments or divisions may be created and specific employees assigned responsibility for functional areas. Exhibit 2.2 illustrates how a typical bank is organized.

corporation—A business organization treated as a legal entity and owned by a group of shareholders (stockholders). The shareholders elect the directors, who serve as the governing body managing the corporation's affairs.

board of directors—The governing body of a corporation ultimately responsible for its financial performance, consisting of individual directors elected by the shareholders.

Exhibit 2.2: Typical Commercial Bank Organization

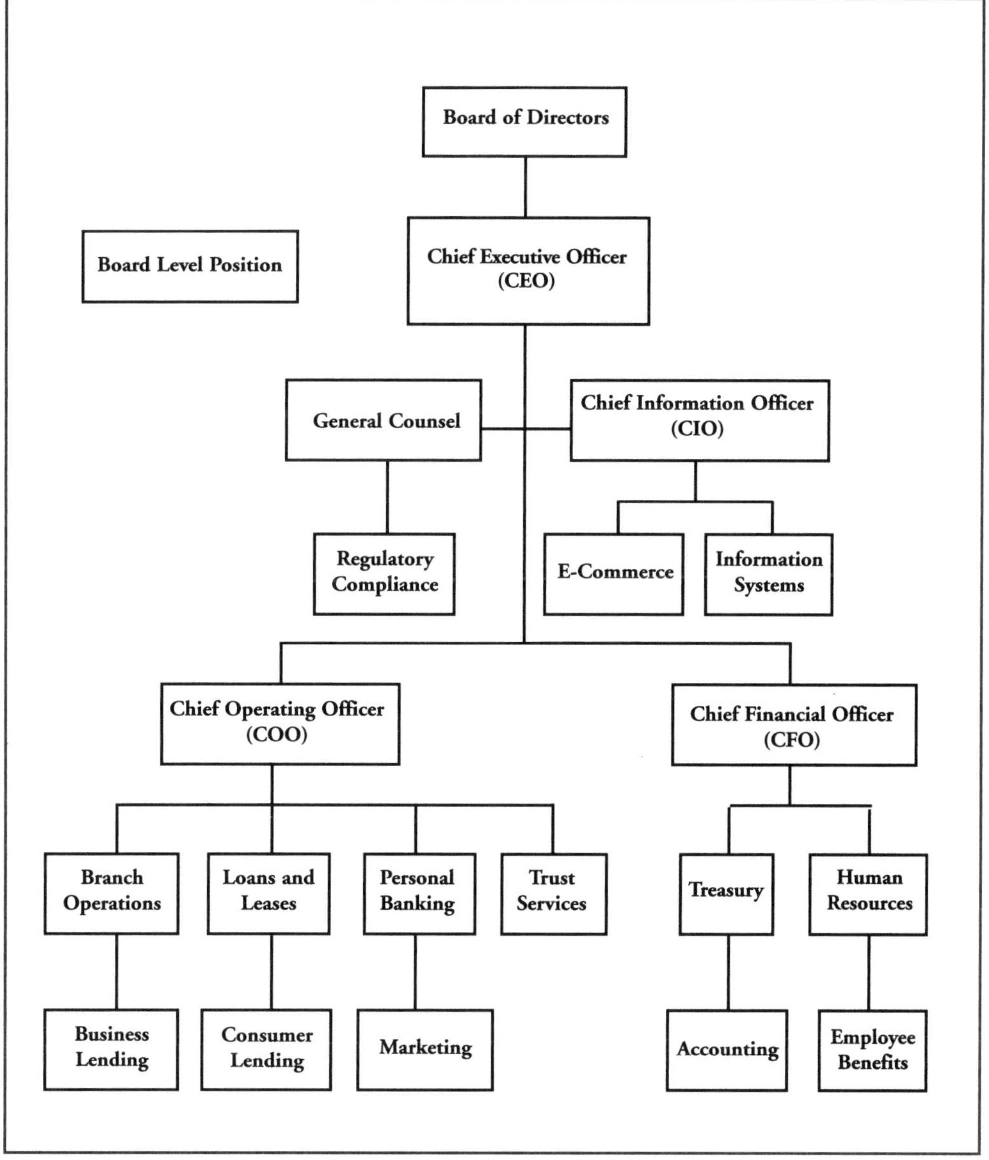

Although titles may vary, a typical bank has the following division of functions:

Department	*Function*
Accounting and Finance	Organizes, records, and reports all transactions that represent the financial condition of the bank, including how efficiently and profitably the bank is operated
Audit and Loan Review	Makes sure the bank is safe from risks such as internal and external fraud and underperforming loans
Commercial or Business Banking	Delivers loan, deposit, and payment services to businesses
Compliance	Ensures that all bank staff and departments are in compliance with banking laws and the associated regulations
Consumer Banking	Delivers loan, deposit, and payment services to individuals
Funds Management	Balances the bank's needs for liquidity, safety, and income
Human Resources	Recruits, trains, compensates, and supports bank employees
Information Systems Operation	Delivers information to the bank and its customers; processes transactions by using mainframes, computer networks, personal computers, the Internet, and other electronic media; and keeps the necessary equipment functioning
Insurance	Provides insurance services for consumers and businesses
International	Services the bank's international consumer and business needs, such as letters of credit and foreign exchange services
Electronic Banking	Provides banking services over the Internet or other electronic delivery channels

Marketing and Sales	Identifies potential customers, learns what they want, and devises strategies for promoting and delivering the bank's products and services to its market area
Trust	Administers trusts and trust-related activities for individuals and businesses
Wealth Management	Provides personalized service to valued high-net-worth customers

Did You Know ...

Approximately 94 percent of all banks are community banks—generally defined as banks with assets of less than $1 billion.

Source: FDIC, Community Banking by the Numbers

Bank and Financial Holding Companies

A bank may be organized as a bank holding company (BHC), which is a company that has control over one or more banks or other BHCs. A bank does not have to be large to choose this organizational structure. BHCs may engage in financial activities through nonbank subsidiaries that banks themselves are not allowed to engage in, such as securities brokerage and underwriting stocks and bonds. Some of the specific services of BHCs include issuing credit cards, providing trust services, offering general and portfolio investment advice, providing management consulting services, servicing loans, acting as a general insurance agent in small towns, providing community investment services, and providing financial counseling, tax planning, and tax preparation services to consumers.

The Gramm-Leach-Bliley Act authorized financial holding companies (FHCs). FHCs are allowed to engage in the same activities as BHCs, but they can also have affiliations with banks, insurance companies, brokerage firms, and securities dealers under a common ownership. Thus, FHCs can offer customers a complete range of financial services, such as providing administrative and other services to mutual funds, owning shares of a securities exchange, acting as a certification authority for digital signatures, providing check cashing and wire transmission services, providing management consulting services on nonfinancial matters, and organizing, sponsoring, and managing a mutual fund subject to ownership limitations.

BHCs and FHCs may own banks in more than one state, which facilitates interstate banking. A BHC that meets certain eligibility requirements may apply for FHC status.

Bank Structural Change

For three decades, the number of banks in the United States has steadily declined. The decline has not been due to large-scale customer migration to other financial service providers, nor has it been due to bank failures alone. The banking industry historically has been profitable, and usually more new banks (**de novo banks**) are started each year than are closed.

Banks are, however, undergoing continual change, with banks being opened, closed, acquired and renamed, and merged. For example, from 1984 through 2011,

de novo bank—A bank that has been in operation for five years or less. Commercial banks operating for five years or less that convert to Federal Reserve membership are subject to the de novo bank application and supervision standards.

Did You Know ...

Double-entry bookkeeping is the foundation of modern accounting. It was developed in the 1400s by Italian merchants to keep track of how their businesses were doing. In double-entry bookkeeping, debits are listed on the left side of the page and credits are listed on the right side. The totals on both sides of the page are added up, and if everything is done correctly, the totals match. Italian Renaissance man Luca Pacioli, author of the first major book on accounting, advised, "If the totals did not match, then that would indicate a mistake in your Ledger, which mistake you will have to look for diligently with the industry and intelligence God gave you."

the total number of banks declined by more than one-half, with most of the decline attributable to consolidation among smaller banks (see exhibit 2.3).

Through mergers and acquisitions, banks eliminate duplication of efforts and operations and, thus, can become more profitable. They take advantage of economies of scale by:

- Reducing or eliminating departments that perform the same tasks
- Closing branches that are in close proximity and combining their services in one location
- Using data processing centers that support the larger volume of the combined banks

Banks also combine forces to enter new geographic areas and expand market share. Through mergers and acquisitions, banks can extend their reach across state boundaries and around the world.

Although the trend is toward the formation of large regional and nationwide banks, community banks still play a significant and important role in the economy and, in fact, far outnumber large banks, as shown in exhibit 2.3. Community banks are especially well suited to relationship-based personal services and financial products that require extensive knowledge of the customer, such as lending to small businesses and farms. De novo banks often focus on a unique service delivery channel, such as the Internet, or concentrate on a special market segment, such as business owners or the affluent.

Exhibit 2.3: Banking Industry Consolidation, 1984–2011

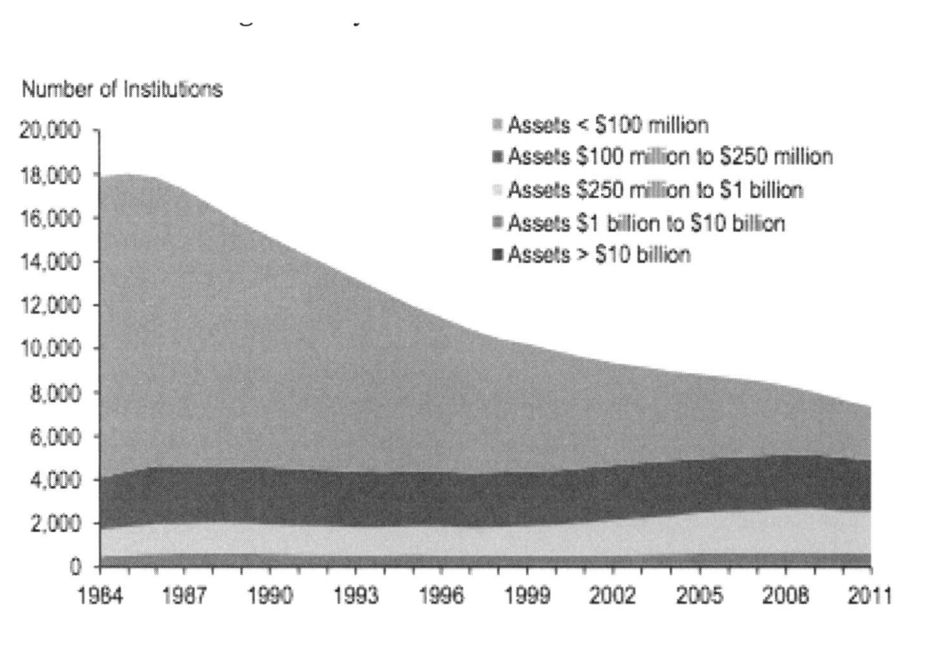

Source: Federal Deposit Insurance Corporation

BANK ASSETS AND LIABILITIES

Just as the Federal Reserve manages the nation's funds to achieve its monetary policy objectives (and, in so doing, affects banks and their business objectives), banks manage their funds to achieve their business objectives. Bank funds are their assets and liabilities. The most important and largest bank assets are loans and investments; its most important liabilities are its customers' deposits. Banks have other assets and liabilities as well, all of which are reported on a bank's statement of condition.

STATEMENT OF CONDITION

The statement of condition, more commonly called the balance sheet, is prepared as of a specific date; for example, December 31 of a given year (see exhibit 2.4, next page). It is a snapshot of total bank assets, liabilities, and bank capital (**equity** or net worth) on a given day. An asset is anything of value the bank owns or is owed; a liability is anything a bank owes. For example, loans owed to the bank by borrowers are assets. Deposits owed by the bank to depositors are liabilities.

Major categories of assets listed on the statement of condition are:

- **Cash on hand and due from other banks**—coin and currency held in the vault, checks in process of collection, and balances with other banks and the Federal Reserve
- **Investments**—includes obligations of the federal government and its agencies, obligations of state and local units of government, and stock in the Federal Reserve if the bank is a member
- **Loans and lease financing**—all indebtedness to the bank, usually subdivided by category
- **Fixed assets**—real estate owned by the bank, as well as furniture, fixtures, and equipment
- **Other short-term assets**—for example, fed funds sold and securities purchased under an agreement to later resell them

Major types of liabilities that appear on the statement of condition include:

- **Deposits**—customer deposits subdivided into demand, savings, time, domestic, and global deposit accounts
- **Taxes payable**—all federal, state, and local taxes due
- **Dividends payable**—dividends to shareholders that have been approved by directors but not yet disbursed
- **Other short-term liabilities**—for example, fed funds purchased and securities sold under an agreement to be repurchased later

Depending on the size and scope of bank operations, other assets and liabilities may be listed in order of **liquidity**. Being the most liquid, "cash and due from banks" is the first asset shown and "deposits" is the first liability listed.

equity—The investment interest of all shareholders in a corporation, equaling the excess of assets over liabilities and including common and preferred stock, retained earnings, surplus, and reserves.

lease financing—A specialized area of finance dealing with renting property owned by a lender, financing the leases of a company engaged in rentals, or financing the purchase of an item to be leased out by the borrower.

liquidity—(1) The ability of a business to meet its current obligations or to take advantage of new investment opportunities, such as a bank's ability to cover withdrawals, pay for operating expenses, or make loans; (2) the quality of an asset that makes it readily convertible to cash without significant loss.

Balance Sheet Versus Income Statement

Statement of condition (balance sheet)
A detailed list of a company's assets, liabilities, and capital (equity) on a specific date

Profit and loss statement (income statement)
Summary of revenue, expenses, and net income earned by a company during a stated period, such as a quarter or a year

Exhibit 2.4: Consolidated Statement of Condition

Assets		**December 31**	
(In thousands of dollars)	20XY	20XX	Change
Cash and due from banks	$ 1,649,334	$ 1,332,586	$ 316,748
Overseas deposits	458,313	460,396	(2,083)
Investment securities:			
U.S. Treasury securities	881,081	982,654	(101,573)
Securities of other U.S. government agencies and corporations	199,318	243,420	(44,102)
Obligations of states and political subdivisions	738,813	396,948	341,865
Other securities	88,278	92,032	(3,754)
Total investment securities	1,907,490	1,715,054	192,436
Trading account securities	14,846	66,140	(51,294)
Fed funds sold	168,600	108,450	60,150
Loans (net of reserve for loan losses and unearned discount)	9,715,728	8,074,132	1,641,596
Direct lease financing	147,860	134,472	13,388
Premises and equipment, net	133,506	132,320	1,186
Customers' acceptance liability	372,835	248,271	124,564
Accrued interest receivable	133,840	123,719	10,121
Other real estate owned	34,332	13,668	20,664
Other assets	103,939	131,711	(27,772)
Total assets	$ 14,840,623	$ 12,540,919	$ 2,299,704

Liabilities and Stockholders' Equity		**December 31**	
(In thousands of dollars)	20XY	20XX	Change
Demand deposits	$ 3,543,141	$ 2,937,065	$ 606,076
Savings deposits	3,585,808	3,485,886	99,922
Savings certificates	1,635,215	1,391,107	244,108
Certificates of deposit	1,827,420	1,601,707	225,713
Other time deposits	424,592	313,811	110,781
Deposits in overseas offices	1,468,003	722,950	745,053
Total deposits	12,484,179	10,452,526	2,031,653
Fed funds borrowed	897,189	924,501	(27,312)
Long-term debt	44,556	43,766	790
Acceptances outstanding	373,022	249,088	123,934
Accrued taxes and other expenses	142,756	122,064	20,692
Other liabilities	171,904	122,890	49,014
Total liabilities (excluding subordinated notes)	14,113,606	11,914,835	2,198,771
Subordinated notes:			
8.25% capital note to Wells Fargo & Company, due 20XZ	25,000	25,000	—
4.5% capital notes due 20XZ	50,000	50,000	—
Total subordinated notes	75,000	75,000	—
Stockholders' equity:			
Capital stock	94,461	94,461	—
Surplus	300,036	251,512	48,524
Surplus representing convertible capital note obligation assumed by parent corporation	10,065	14,589	(4,524)
Undivided profits	247,455	190,522	56,933
Total stockholders' equity	652,017	551,084	100,933
Total liabilities and stockholders' equity	$ 14,840,623	$ 12,540,919	$ 2,299,704

insolvent—A position where liabilities exceed assets, resulting in the party being unable to meet its debt obligations.

Unless a bank is **insolvent**, its total assets are greater than its total liabilities. The excess of assets over liabilities show in the capital accounts, also called shareholder equity or net worth. A fundamental equation in accounting states that total assets must equal total liabilities plus net worth. In other words, if all of a bank's liabilities were paid by using assets, what is left would be its net worth. The standard equation is:

Assets = Liabilities + Net Worth (Shareholders' Equity)

Managing Assets and Liabilities

Managing bank funds is far more complex than just making sure the rates charged for loans are higher than the rates paid for deposits. When crafting a strategy to manage its funds, every bank takes many variables into account. Most banks use a funds management strategy that is applied simultaneously to assets and liabilities. Because this is so important, banks usually have an Asset and Liability Management Committee (ALCO) that is responsible for this function.

The ALCO monitors the cost of deposits and the income from loans. Its goal is to manage bank assets and liabilities so that shareholders achieve the maximum possible long-term gain while allowing the bank to meet the needs of its customers. Accomplishing this feat requires balancing three objectives: liquidity, safety, and income.

Liquidity

Liquidity is important because a bank must have enough money available when depositors want to make withdrawals. When it is suspected that a bank is **illiquid**, depositors will rush to withdraw funds. This has triggered bank panics and failures in the past.

The need for liquidity is tied to both the deposit and the lending functions. Liquidity enables a bank to meet customer loan demand and respond to the credit needs of its community.

Every bank operates with the expectation that, over time, fund inflows will approximate outflows. Normally, new deposits arrive at a bank each day as checks and orders for withdrawals are being honored.

However, over time, if fund inflows and outflows do not match often enough, liquidity problems can build up. High loan demand (because of low interest rates or other market factors) and low deposits (because funds are being diverted to stock or other investments, or people stop saving) can cause a "credit crunch." In a credit crunch, banks find it difficult to meet the legitimate borrowing needs of their customers.

Reserves, classified usually as primary and secondary, help prevent liquidity problems. Primary reserves include cash on hand, demand deposit balances at **correspondent banks**, and reserves kept at the Federal Reserve. Because the funds support daily operations, they are available immediately and thus highly liquid.

Secondary reserves are the highest-quality investments permitted by law, such as Treasury bills. They earn interest but can be converted to cash quickly. They are a back-up source of liquidity because they must be sold to be converted to cash.

Although a bank must stay liquid, it cannot afford to overemphasize liquidity by keeping large amounts of currency in its vaults. Because excess reserves reduce the percentage of deposits available for lending, they lower income from loans. Therefore, while recognizing the primary importance of liquidity, a bank also recognizes two other obligations in its program of funds management: safety and income.

Did You Know ...

Although there are now more credit unions in the U.S. than commercial banks, banks play a much larger role in the nation's economy, holding more than $13 trillion in assets at the end of 2012. Credit unions and saving institutions reported combined assets of a little over $1 trillion.

Source: Federal Financial Institutions Examination Council

illiquid—Deficient in assets that can be quickly used to meet current obligations.

correspondent bank—A bank, often a larger bank, that maintains an account relationship or engages in an exchange of services with another, usually smaller, bank. Sometimes called upstream correspondent bank. The bank that uses the services is the respondent bank.

Situation

Joan has a $5,000 certificate of deposit that will mature soon. She has decided to reinvest the money in another certificate of deposit and wants the highest rate of return possible. She is not certain if her bank's rates are competitive with the current market. Joan plans to shop around for the best rate and, if necessary, will move her money to another bank.

Safety

Depositors must be confident that their money is safe. Although deposits are insured by the Federal Deposit Insurance Corporation (FDIC) up to $250,000 (per depositor, per insured bank, for each account ownership category), banks must protect the deposits entrusted to them by avoiding unnecessary risk. Prudent lending practices, appropriate loan loss reserves, and strong corporate governance minimize fraud and mismanagement and help protect depositors.

Banks must strike a balance, however, and not be overcautious. A bank that aimed at maximum safety by avoiding all risk would make few loans and invest only in instruments that yield little income. This results in neglecting the legitimate credit needs of its customers and community and losing interest and fee income, thus minimizing the return to shareholders.

Income

The third objective of funds management is income. If liquidity and safety were the only factors a bank had to consider, it could keep most of its assets in cash held in its vault and make only those loans that carry an absolute minimum of risk. However, if a bank did this, it would fall far short of its income needs.

U.S. banks are not owned or directly subsidized by the federal government. Banks are owned by their shareholders, and thus earning a profit for those shareholders is of primary importance. A bank that repeatedly operates at a loss soon loses the confidence of its depositors, its shareholders, and the public.

Throughout U.S. financial history, banks that chose to maximize short-term income at the expense of liquidity and safety were forced out of business because their practices were unsafe. Although there may be a short-term gain in profits, unduly lowering credit standards will, in the long run, be fatal to a bank when weak loans cannot be collected and must be charged off for a loss. Income, like liquidity and safety, can never be considered alone.

Matched Funding

For years, bank management concentrated primarily on traditional assets such as loans. Managers were not as concerned about the source of the funds—primarily customers' deposits—that were used to purchase assets. Today, however, because customers have a wide variety of options for depositing their money, managing the liability side of banking has become equally important.

Banks work hard to attract new depositors and keep them. Periodically, every bank must decide how much it needs in funds, where to acquire additional funds, and how much it is willing to pay for funds in a competitive market.

One of the largest expenses for banks is the interest paid to depositors. A challenge for bankers is to ensure that interest paid is less than the interest received on loans. The difference between the two is known as net interest income (or loss). Each bank's net interest income is important to its efforts to meet payments, generate profits, and grow.

Applying the principle of **matched funding**, short-term loans are funded with short-term deposits and long-term loans with long-term deposits. A 15-year mortgage

matched funding—An asset and liability management technique in which assets are financed with liabilities of the same maturity or duration.

loan to purchase a home is funded by, for example, long-term certificates of deposits. A short-term loan or an adjustable-rate loan that is repriced as market rates change is funded with demand deposits.

Matched funding is applied not to individual loans but to the entire loan portfolio. For this reason, banks are careful to maintain a balance in the types of deposits they attract and the types of loans they make.

Did You Know ...

During the Bank Panic of 1907, anxious depositors around the country lined up outside banks in the hope of withdrawing their cash. Some enterprising people earned as much as $10 a day holding places in line for weary depositors. Depositors of New York's Knickerbocker Trust Company, which would fail, were so desperate to withdraw their money that Knickerbocker tellers paid out more than $8 million during a three-hour run. Only with the intervention of J.P. Morgan and other financiers and businesspersons (including John D. Rockefeller, who deposited $10 million of his own money in New York's financial institutions) was enough liquidity injected back into the banking system to stem the panic.

Source: Federal Reserve Bank of Boston

BANK INCOME AND EXPENSES

How effectively a bank manages its assets and liabilities determines the income it earns and the expenses it incurs. The difference between a bank's income and expenses is its profit. Income, expenses, and profit are reported on a profit and loss statement.

Profit and Loss Statement

At the end of every **fiscal year**, banks prepare a profit and loss statement (also called an income statement) that details their financial performance for that given period of time. The bottom line of a profit and loss statement lists the net income. Positive net income is termed a "profit"; negative net income is termed a "loss". Banks, as with all for-profit enterprises, must consistently report a profit on the bottom line to remain viable.

fiscal year—The 12-month period selected by a business or government as an accounting period, at the end of which the books are closed and profit or loss determined. It may correspond to the calendar year.

The profit and loss statement lists all categories of income and expense (see exhibit 2.5, next page). The following major sources of bank income are typically listed in order of size and importance:

- Interest and fees earned on loans (loan income)
- Interest and dividends earned on investments (investment income)
- Fees, commissions, and service charges (fee income)

The major items of expense, also listed in order of size and importance, are:

- Interest paid on deposits (deposit interest expense)
- Salaries, wages, and benefits (employee expenses)
- Occupancy and equipment expense (occupancy expense)
- Taxes (federal, state, and local) (income tax expense)

Loans Versus Investments

As mentioned, there are three sources of bank income: loan income, investment income, and fee income. Before looking at all three, it is important to understand the distinctions between loans and investments.

Bank loans and investments differ in several basic ways. First, loans take priority over investments. By law, banks must meet the credit needs of customers and their communities by lending money to individuals, businesses, governments, and other banks. Investments, on the other hand, are made chiefly to generate income. The fact that banks contribute to the general well-being of a community by buying the community's notes or bonds is secondary to the income objective. Investments are made after the demand for loans has been met.

Exhibit 2.5: Consolidated Profit and Loss Statement

Interest Income (Thousands of dollars)	December 31 20XY	20XX
Interest and fees on loans	$ 823,415	$ 693,463
Interest on fed funds sold	6,429	3,496
Interest and dividends on investment securities:		
U.S. Treasury securities	69,938	59,883
Securities of other U.S. government agencies and corporations	16,520	25,228
Obligations of states and political subdivisions	22,504	15,846
Other securities	7,067	7,268
Interest on overseas deposits	24,394	37,658
Interest on trading accounts securities	4,419	3,478
Direct lease financing income	33,371	32,560
Total interest income	1,008,057	878,880

Interest Expense (Thousands of dollars)	December 31 20XY	20XX
Interest on deposits	463,733	414,832
Interest on fed funds borrowed and repurchase agreements	35,193	33,019
Interest on other borrowed funds	17,751	12,882
Interest on long-term debt	21,232	19,079
Total interest expense	537,909	479,812
Net interest income	470,148	399,068
Provision for loan losses	41,028	46,379
Net interest income after provision for loan losses	429,120	352,689

Other Operating Income (Thousands of dollars)	December 31 20XY	20XX
Trust income	21,635	19,649
Service charges on deposit accounts	25,511	24,254
Trading account profits and commissions	(268)	1,690
Other income	43,797	23,324
Total other operating income	90,675	68,917

Other Operating Expense (Thousands of dollars)	December 31 20XY	20XX
Salaries	168,085	145,746
Employee benefits	41,028	32,126
Net occupancy expense	34,919	31,636
Equipment expense	20,648	19,234
Other expense	94,331	68,317
Total other operating expense	359,011	297,059
Income before income taxes and securities transactions	160,784	124,547
Less applicable income taxes	73,484	61,076
Income before securities transactions	87,300	63,471
Securities gains (losses), net of income tax effect of $(1,233) in 20XY and $48 in 20XX	(1,020)	40
Net income	$ 86,280	$ 63,511
Income per share (based on average number of common shares outstanding):		
Income before securities transactions	$4.03	$3.16
Securities transactions, net of income tax effect	(.05)	
Net income per share	$3.98	$3.16

Second, banks negotiate directly on loans but only indirectly on investments. In making loans, banks and borrowers agree on the amount, purpose, maturity, interest rate, and other conditions, and banks investigate borrowers' **creditworthiness**. In contrast, banks make investments indirectly through bond dealers or underwriters, and the issuers may not know the purchasers. Banks may also rely, but not solely, on rating services to determine investment quality and risk.

Third, banks invest in **securities** to diversify their risk, ensure that assets are productive, and perhaps reduce taxes. Diversifying holdings between loans and investments helps to keep income stable. Securities can be converted to cash easier than loans can be called or paid off, and some investments, such as municipal bonds, provide tax relief, which increases bank earnings.

Fourth, loans and investments present different kinds of risk. The chief risk concern with loans is **credit risk**: will the borrower repay the loan? Investments typically present less credit risk. With U.S. government securities, there is no credit risk because the federal government guarantees repayment. There is very little credit risk when a state, county, or city guarantees debt securities because such issuers can raise taxes to repay the obligation. The difference between the credit risk of bank loans and investments is reflected in the rate of return or yield on investments. In general, investments produce less revenue than loans.

With investments, the chief concern is **market risk**. When a holder wishes to sell a security, market conditions and the desirability of the security determine its market value—the seller cannot control it. The risk is that the market value at the time of sale may be less than the price the bank initially paid to purchase the security. Although U.S. government securities carry no credit risk, like other investments they do have market risk. With respect to loans, market risk comes into play only for loans secured by **collateral**, such as stocks. If the value of the stock decreases, the collateral securing the loan may not be sufficient to repay the loan should the borrower default.

creditworthiness—The ability and willingness to repay a debt, largely demonstrated by the borrower's credit history.

securities—financial instruments such as stocks (equity securities) or bonds (debt securities) that have value and are easily bought and sold between parties.

credit risk—The risk that the borrower cannot or will not repay a loan with interest as scheduled.

market risk—The risk that the market value of a security or other asset will decrease because of interest rate changes and other market conditions.

collateral—Specific property or other assets pledged by a borrower to secure a loan. If the borrower defaults, the lender has the right to sell the collateral to liquidate the loan.

Loan Income

Interest and fees earned on loans is a primary source of bank revenue. Therefore, choosing the interest rate for each loan is important. The interest rate for a particular loan is usually based on the cost and availability of funds, risk factors of the borrower, the term of the loan, and market interest rates.

Cost of Funds

The basic source of loanable funds is customer deposits. Deposits cost the bank the interest it pays on them and the costs of processing, such as teller and check clearing services. Banks monitor the cost of funds to determine the interest rate to charge on loans.

Availability of Funds

The Federal Reserve controls the nation's supply of money and credit by raising or lowering reserve requirements and the discount rate. In addition, purchases and sales of government obligations, as directed by the FOMC, directly affect the availability of loanable funds.

Risk Factors

The interest rate charged on loans is affected by the bank's perception of the risk of loss. Banks also evaluate risk according to the type of loan. Unsecured loans, such as credit card loans, are higher risk than secured loans, such as mortgages or home equity loans. If a borrower defaults on a secured loan, the collateral backing the loan can provide an alternative source of repayment.

Loan Term

The term of the loan (amount of time before the loan is repaid) affects the interest rate charged. The longer the term, the higher the risk that the borrower's credit standing will deteriorate and jeopardize repayment. The cost of deposits also becomes less certain over time. To offset these risks and costs, banks usually charge higher rates for long-term loans than for short-term loans.

Market Interest Rates

The interest rates in the financial markets is another important factor. Historically, interest rates have fluctuated substantially, but in recent years they have been stable and low (see exhibit 2.6). Several market rates are used:

- **Discount rate**—This is the interest rate the Federal Reserve charges banks for short-term use of its funds.
- **Prime rate**—This is the base rate a bank will charge. Prime rate, or sometimes below-prime rate, loans are reserved for the bank's most creditworthy customers. Rates on other loans are set at a certain percentage above prime rate (such as prime plus 1.25 percent). The prime rate is variable; it is adjusted as the cost and availability of funds change.

Exhibit 2.6: Comparison of Prime and Fed Funds Interest Rates, 1960–2012

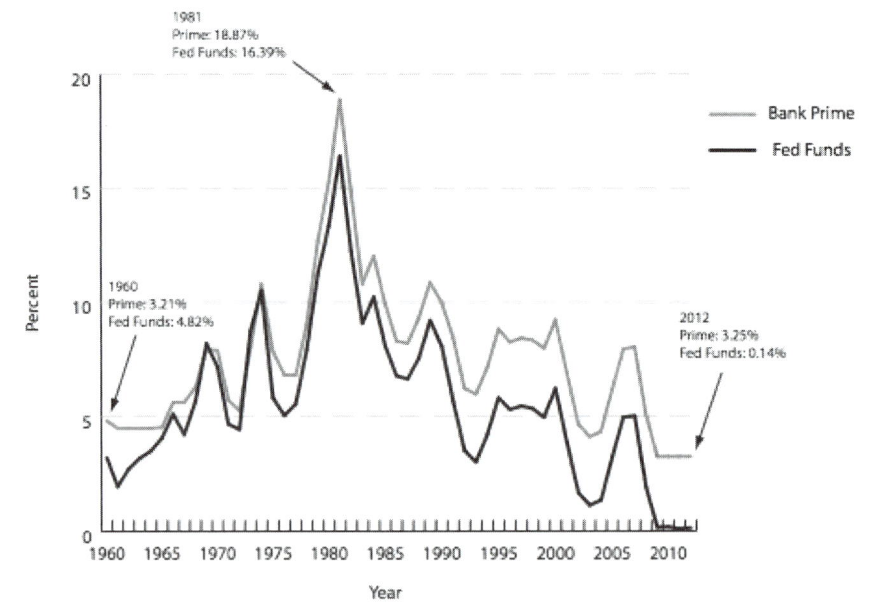

Source: Federal Reserve Statistical Release, H-15 Selected Interest Rates, Historical Data

- **Fed funds rate**—This is the rate one bank charges another for overnight use of reserve funds to bring reserves up to requirements. Exhibit 2.6 shows the relationship between the fed funds and prime rates and the rates paid on six-month certificates of deposit and Treasury bills.
- **LIBOR rate**—The London Interbank Offered Rate is an international money market rate that represents the average rate offered by banks for interbank placement of Eurodollars. Banks add percentages above LIBOR to set the interest rate on a given loan.

Investment Income

Another important source of revenue is the income banks earn on investments. Investment income is derived from interest and **dividend** payments. Banks diversify their investments—choosing from a variety of instruments with different maturities—to achieve a balance of liquidity, safety, and income.

Banks are also limited by regulation in the percentage of their capital they can invest in the securities of any one issuer, except for the U.S. government.

Many states require banks to pledge U.S. government securities to ensure protection for deposits in public fund accounts beyond the coverage provided by the FDIC. Similarly, many states require bank trust departments to use as reserves federal and state bonds to protect the pension, trust, and profit-sharing funds they manage.

A typical bank investment portfolio consists almost exclusively of four types of holdings: U.S. Treasury securities, U.S. agency securities, state and municipal bonds, and miscellaneous investments.

dividend—Payments made by a corporation to its stockholders. The payments are based on a percentage of the corporation's after-tax earnings and are usually made quarterly.

Consumer Price Index—A measure of the average change over time in the prices paid by consumers for selected goods and services. It represents whether prices are rising or falling in the U.S. economy and, thus, whether there is inflation or deflation.

U.S. Treasury Securities

U.S. Treasury securities are the most acceptable collateral for Fed loans to banks because they are backed by the full faith and credit of the federal government. These include:

- **Treasury bills**—With maturities of less than one year, these securities are readily marketable and have limited market risk.
- **Treasury notes and bonds**—Longer-term securities, they have maturities of between 2 and 10 years, in the case of Treasury notes, and 30 years, in the case of Treasury bonds. They are marketable but bear more market risk than Treasury bills.
- **Treasury Inflation Protected Securities (TIPS)**—With 5-, 10-, and 30-year maturities, these securities protect investors against inflation because the principal increases with the **Consumer Price Index**. When TIPS mature, the investor is paid the inflation-adjusted principal or the original principal, whichever is greater.

U.S. Agency Securities

Unlike Treasury securities, which are liabilities of the U.S. government, U.S. agency securities are liabilities of U.S. government agencies and U.S. government-sponsored enterprises. They are guaranteed or protected by the U.S. government, and they yield higher interest than U.S. government obligations of the same maturity. Banks invest in two types of agency securities:

- **Mortgage-backed agency securities**—These obligations are issued by U.S. government agencies or U.S. government-sponsored enterprises such as the Government National Mortgage Association (Ginnie Mae), the Federal National Mortgage Association (Fannie Mae), or the Federal Home Loan Mortgage Corporation (Freddie Mac).
- **Nonmortgage-backed agency securities**—These obligations are issued by other U.S. government agencies or U.S. government-sponsored enterprises such as the Export-Import Bank, a government agency that provides financing to American businesses that export goods to other countries.

Did You Know ...

FDIC-insured institutions earned nearly $252 billion in noninterest income in 2013.

Source: Federal Deposit Insurance Corporation

State and Municipal Bonds

Banks also invest in bonds issued by any government or government agency other than the U.S. government—for example, state, city, county, town, or school district. Although backed by the taxing power of the issuer, they have some credit and market risk. Income is exempt from federal income taxes and sometimes state and local taxes. These investments represent a bank's commitment to the community.

Miscellaneous Investments

Banks also invest in a variety of nongovernment securities. These investments carry more credit and market risk than government obligations. These include:

- **Banker's acceptances**—These investments are drafts or bills of exchange that banks accept as liabilities by pledging their credit on behalf of customers.
- **Negotiable certificates of deposit**—These certificates of deposit (CDs) can be sold before maturity and have a $100,000 minimum denomination. Rates may be negotiated with depositors. To be attractive investments, CD rates need to be higher than rates on Treasury bills and commercial paper with the same maturities.
- **Commercial paper**—This is the short-term unsecured obligations of large, financially sound corporations, both foreign and domestic. There is no collateral except a firm's good reputation. Companies issue commercial paper, instead of borrowing from a bank, to raise short-term funds.
- **Corporate debt**—Investments in corporations in the form of bonds can provide a good source of income. Banks are permitted to invest in investment-grade securities—that is, bonds that have a high credit quality rating and present a low risk of default.

Fee Income

The financial services marketplace is competitive. Although banks used to be the only source of deposits and loans, customers can choose from a variety of financial service providers today. As a result, banks must seek other opportunities to earn income. Fee-based income has transformed many traditional commercial banks into diversified financial service providers. Income from fees is an important component of **noninterest income**. Exhibit 2.7 lists some sources of fee income. Banks improve fee income in three ways:

- Increasing fees to cover the cost of service—for example, raising check processing fees to reflect the risk of paying checks returned for nonsufficient funds
- Charging for previously free services—for example, charging for a copy of a statement
- Entering into fee-based services—for example, offering credit and debit cards, securities processing, international payments, private banking, investment management, and fiduciary services

noninterest income—Income a bank derives from sources other than interest, for example, fees and service charges, trading income, and investment securities gains.

certified public accountant (CPA)—An accountant licensed to practice public accounting. To earn this title, a person must pass the Uniform Certified Public Accountant Exam and meet other requirements established by each state for education and experience.

audit—An official examination and verification of accounts and internal controls, usually by an independent accountant, to determine whether financial information is accurate and prepared in conformity with generally accepted accounting principles (GAAP).

EVALUATING BANK PERFORMANCE

The information reported in a bank's financial statements, such as the statement of condition, the profit and loss statement, the annual report (see description on page 44), and the statement of cash flows (see description on page 45), can be used to obtain a good picture of a bank's financial health—how profitable it is and how well it has used its assets and liabilities to earn that profit. This financial information also provides the raw numbers for calculating common measures of performance, thus allowing meaningful comparisons between financial reporting periods and among peer banks and other financial institutions. Information in prior financial reports also provides the starting point for determining subsequent years' budgets.

Public companies must have their financial statements prepared by an independent **certified public accountant** (CPA). To satisfy the requirement of independence, a CPA cannot be an employee of the company being **audited**.

Exhibit 2.7: Sources of Fee Income

Deposit Account Fees
- Monthly account fees
- Overdraft and NSF fees
- Early withdrawal fees
- Stop payment fees

All Other Service Fees
- ATM fees
- Safe deposit boxes
- Money orders
- Cashier's and traveler's checks
- Renting bank property

Fiduciary Trust Services
- Trust department revenues

Insurance and Securities
- Insurance brokerage
- Providing insurance
- Securities brokerage and selling
- Handling securities of others
- Securitization

The Annual Report
The annual report is management's summation of the bank's achievements over the course of the year. It describes management's perspective on the past year, including significant achievements, and presents objectives for the future. It also includes information about the bank's financial position and business performance. Many banks post their annual reports on the Internet. An annual report has four main components: promotional information, analysis, financial statements, and an audit report.

- **Promotional information**—Promotes the company to investors using photographs of the bank at work, reports of employee contributions and achievements, and nonfinancial statistics, such as contributions to the community
- **Analysis**—Discusses management's business strategies and how they played out in the previous year
- **Financial statement**—Sets out the numbers that reflect performance, such as the income statement (usually with comparisons to previous years)
- **Audit report**—A written statement by outside accountants attesting to the integrity of the financial reports provided

Accountants base their work on generally accepted accounting principles (GAAP). GAAP ensure that the information accountants report in different financial statements meets similar requirements to ensure comparability. GAAP are continuously being refined to accommodate:

- Innovations in the ways credit is extended and debt financed
- Innovations in the ways accountants calculate and present financial information
- Legal considerations, such as changes in tax laws

Of the organizations that develop GAAP, the most important is the Financial Accounting Standards Board (FASB), which has been authorized by the Securities and Exchange Commission (SEC) to establish accounting standards for public companies. GAAP is widely used by private companies as well. The American Institute of Certified Public Accountants (AICPA) establishes professional standards for CPAs in implementing GAAP.

Financial Information Users

The information in a bank's financial statements and reports is important not only to management and the board of directors, but also to shareholders and investors, banking regulators and other government agencies, employees, and other banks.

Shareholders and Investors

Shareholders and investors are interested in a bank's financial data because the information can have an immediate effect on stock value. For example, if reported earnings are higher than expected, the value of bank stock usually rises. If the financial data suggest that a bank is performing poorly, the stock value typically falls.

Bank Regulators

Regulators examine bank financial reports because the information helps reveal the true financial condition of a bank. Regulators are particularly interested in verifying the adequacy of a bank's capital. Banks are required to file regular financial reports with their banking regulator.

Other Government Agencies

In addition to reporting financial information to their primary regulator, banks are required to report to other federal and state agencies on a whole range of issues relating to taxes, investments, loans, and many other transactions that affect line items on balance sheets and income statements. The agencies to which banks report include the Internal Revenue Service (IRS) and, for certain banks and bank holding companies, the SEC. Small community banks are exempt from reporting financial information to the SEC.

Most publicly traded companies file quarterly reports (Form 10-Q) and annual reports (Form 10-K) with the SEC. For most companies, the Form 10-K must be filed within 60 days after the bank's fiscal year. The financial information required is typically more detailed than is presented in a company's annual report.

Employees

The financial information produced by a bank affects its employees. Many take pride in the financial results of their organization and are interested in how their bank compares with competitors. Their salaries, bonuses, benefits, and compensation may be tied directly to bank performance. In addition, many banks maintain executive compensation plans that are based on performance, including performance in relation to bank peers.

A primary goal of both management and employees is to increase shareholder value by ensuring that bank financial results are positive. Attaining financial goals helps motivate employees, especially if the bank has a profit-sharing plan that gives the employees a stake in the bank's financial results. Some banks are entirely employee-owned.

Other Banks

Banks seeking to expand through merger or acquisition closely evaluate the financial reports of other banks. Potential acquirers are looking for bargains. If its performance ratios suggest operational inefficiencies, a bank could be a prime candidate for acquisition. The potential acquirer may be able to reduce expenses or take advantage of economies of scale to turn a lackluster bank into a top performer.

Banks judge their own performance relative to their peers as well as to their own goals. One way they do this is by **ratio analysis**.

Performance Measures

While the bottom line—net income—gives a number to a bank's profitability, it is not necessarily a true measure of its performance. A bank with $10 billion in assets should be expected to generate more net income than a bank with $100 million in assets. For this reason, management, investment analysts, state and federal regulators, and shareholders use measures such as ratios to evaluate bank financial performance.

Financial Ratios

Financial ratios are calculated by comparing one entry on a financial statement to another. For example, earnings and other items from the income statement may be compared to assets or capital on the balance sheet. Analyzing these ratios can reveal much about bank profitability and financial performance. Current financial ratios also can be compared to those of previous periods to determine whether or not performance is improving.

But financial ratios offer only one perspective on a bank's financial strength. To get a thorough understanding of a bank's performance, the local economy and the bank's management strategy also must be considered. Therefore, management often compares the bank's financial ratios to those of other banks in similar circumstances—its **peer group**. The peer group might include a few banks with similar amounts of

The Statement of Cash Flows

The statement of cash flows illustrates a bank's sources and uses of cash over a period of time. It details the bank's financing, investing, and operating activities. The statement of cash flows can give bank managers and owners a more complete understanding of where the bank's money came from and how it was used.

To illustrate how the bank funded its business activities and to reconcile changes in cash and liquid assets for a given period, the statement of cash flows uses information from two balance sheets and one income statement for the period, such as a fiscal year.

Bank management uses information from the statement of cash flows to draft financial strategies by anticipating changes in balance sheet items, such as a decline in deposits, and determining how the bank would fund itself if those changes actually occurred.

ratio analysis—A technique for analyzing a financial statement that examines the relationships between certain values reported in the statement.

peer group—In banking, a statistical grouping of banks that have similar characteristics, such as asset size. Each bank is compared to other banks in the group.

Situation

The Jayson Investment Group manages the pension fund for ACME Corp., a manufacturing business with more than 3,000 employees. Mr. Jayson is thinking of investing in several bank stocks. He has read their annual reports and other financial data and has set up a meeting with senior management and auditors to discuss future projections. If Mr. Jayson is satisfied with the banks' prospects, he will invest a large sum of money for the ACME Corp. pension fund.

assets that operate in the bank's local market, or a larger number of similar-sized banks in a broader region.

Return on assets, return on equity, the capital ratio, net interest income, and earnings per share are among the most common ratios used to measure performance. Their formulas and what they measure follow:

- Return on assets (ROA) = Net profit ÷ Total assets x 100
  Measures how well a bank uses assets to produce income
- Return on equity (ROE) = Net profit ÷ Total equity x 100
  Measures the rate of return achieved relative to funds invested (equity)
- Capital ratio = Capital ÷ Assets x 100
  Measures bank stability and strength; the capital account absorbs losses not covered by current earnings and loan loss reserves
- Net interest income = Interest earned – Interest paid
  Defines the difference between interest earned on loans and interest paid on deposits; the higher the amount, the greater the profit if other expenses are constant
- Earnings per share = Net income ÷ Average number of shares of stock outstanding
  Establishes income goals, such as $4 per share; earnings per share is compared with the market price of a stock to determine value in the market

By The Numbers

Return on Assets

$$\text{Return on assets ratio} = \frac{\text{Net profit}}{\text{Total assets}} \times 100$$

What is the ROA for a bank with assets of $532,400,000 and net profit of $7,986,000?

$$\mathbf{1.5\% = \frac{7,986,000}{532,400,000} \times 100}$$

By The Numbers

Return on Equity

$$\text{Return on equity ratio} = \frac{\text{Net profit}}{\text{Total equity}} \times 100$$

What is the ROE for a bank with total equity of $57,043,000 and a net profit of $7,986,000?

$$\mathbf{14\% = \frac{7,986,000}{57,043,000} \times 100}$$

By The Numbers

Capital Ratio

$$\text{Capital ratio} = \frac{\text{Capital}}{\text{Assets}} \times 100$$

What is the capital ratio for a bank with total assets of $2.54 billion and capital of $153 million?

$$\mathbf{6.02\% = \frac{153,000,000}{2,540,000,000} \times 100}$$

Exhibit 2.8 shows key financial ratios for the banking industry as a whole. Exhibit 2.9, page 48, shows the trend in ROA and ROE for the banking industry over the past three decades.

Budgeting and Planning

Good financial performance is not achieved automatically. Bank management must plan carefully, set earnings objectives, and structure the balance sheet to achieve its goals.

The Budgeting Process

The budget is management's financial plan for attaining its goals. Although budgeting varies from one bank to another, the basic concept is the same: establishing a financial plan at least for the coming year and perhaps for the next three to five years.

Most banks base their budgets on amounts spent the previous year. For

Exhibit 2.8: Financial Ratios for the Banking Industry, 2013

Ratio	Percentage	Used to Measure
Performance Ratios		
Net interest margin	3.25	Difference between amount of interest earned and amount of interest paid out
Noninterest income to earning assets	1.95	Amount of fee earnings
Noninterest expense to earning assets	3.24	Operations overhead cost
Loan and lease loss provision to assets	0.21	Amount of protection against nonpayment of troubled loans
Net operating income to assets	1.05	Sustainable rate of earnings
Return on assets	1.07	Profitability relative to assets
Return on equity	9.60	Profitability relative to equity
Net charge-offs to loans and leases	0.69	Losses from nonpayment of loans and leases
Loan and lease loss provision to net charge-offs	56.99	Amount of protection relative to actual loan losses
Efficiency ratio	60.53	Ability to control costs and expenses
Condition Ratios		
Earning assets to total assets	88.39	Assets put to productive use
Loss allowance to loans and leases	1.75	Amount of protection against nonpayment of loans
Loss allowance to noncurrent loans and leases	66.09	Amount of protection against nonpayment of troubled loans

Source: Federal Deposit Insurance Corporation, *Quarterly Banking Profile, Fourth Quarter, 2013*

example, a bank may establish a goal that noninterest expense will not exceed noninterest expense in the previous year by more than 2 percent.

It is difficult to budget for interest income and expense because a bank must project not only loan and deposit volumes but also interest rates and the effect rates will have on interest income and expense. Budgeting is not an exact science, but a properly prepared budget offers a blueprint for the future.

Budget Variances

Unforeseen circumstances cause variances from the budget. An expenditure may be incurred earlier than expected, or business volume may be higher. Banks usually do not adjust the budget once it is in place. Instead, for example, they offset negative variances in income with cost reductions.

Variances that cannot be offset, such as large loan charge-offs, are documented because they will have a negative effect on profitability.

Exhibit 2.9: Banking Industry ROA and ROE

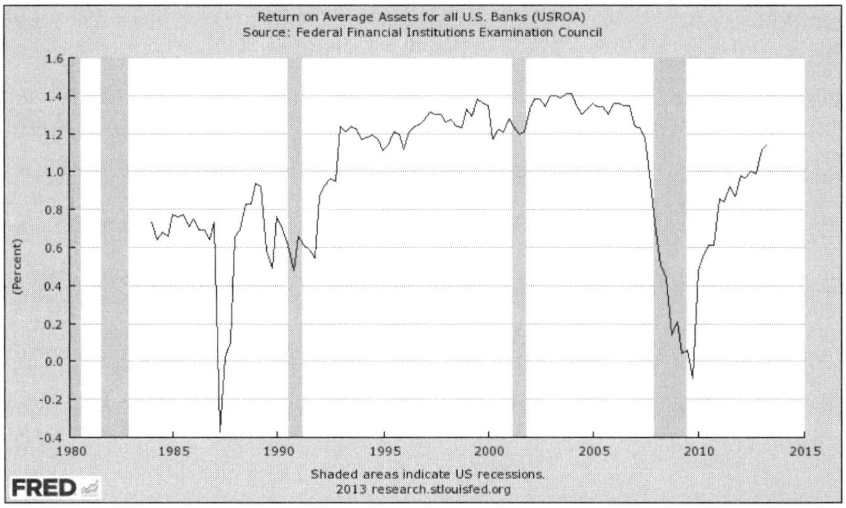

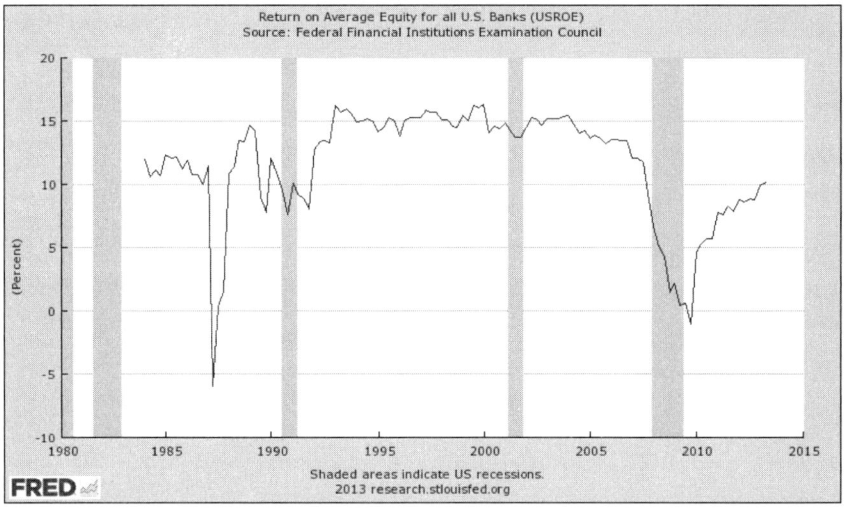

Source: Federal Financial Institutions Examination Council

SUMMARY

- In their role as financial intermediaries, banks accept deposits from consumers and businesses and make them available to borrowers. As such, they are central to the money creation function in the United States. The Federal Reserve (the Fed) is responsible for managing the nation's money supply. The Fed implements monetary policy in three ways: setting reserve requirements, managing its discount operations, and conducting open-market operations. Open-market operations are the Fed's most powerful tool. The Federal Open Market Committee decides whether to purchase or sell government securities in the open market and sets the federal funds target rate.

- Most banks are corporations owned by shareholders. A bank may be closely held by a limited number of individuals or a family, or publicly held by investors. Shareholders appoint the board of directors, and the board's committees oversee management on behalf of the shareholders. The bank's chief executive officer is the lead member of management. Typically, a bank is organized into departments, each responsible for a specific area of operations—for example, consumer banking, human resources, or marketing. Some banks are organized as bank holding companies or financial holding companies. New banks may be formed (de novo banks), and established banks may consolidate, merge, and close.

- The statement of condition, or balance sheet, lists all of a bank's assets, liabilities, and shareholder equity as of a specific date. An asset is anything of value a bank owns or is owed; a liability is anything the bank owes. A bank's assets are equal to its liabilities plus net worth. A bank's asset and liability management practices are key to its success. In managing its assets and liabilities, banks strive to strike a balance between liquidity, safety, and income, and to fund short-term loans with short-term deposits and long-term loans with long-term deposits.
- The profit and loss statement, or income statement, covers bank operations over a certain length of time such as the quarter, the fiscal year, or the calendar year. It shows all revenues and expenses and the resulting profit or loss.
- To maximize its return on loans and investments, banks must manage both credit and market risk. Because interest income is a primary source of bank revenue, choosing the right interest rate to charge for loans is important. Factors influencing interest rates are the cost of funds, funds availability, risk factors, and the loan term. As a starting point for setting rates, banks look at market interest rates, such as the discount, prime, and fed funds rates, and LIBOR.
- Banks also seek to diversify their investments. The investment portfolio of a typical bank consists of U.S. Treasury and agency securities; mortgage-backed securities issued by Ginnie Mae, Fannie Mae, Freddie Mac, and other U.S. government agencies or U.S. government-sponsored enterprises; nonmortgage-backed agency securities; and miscellaneous investments such as banker's acceptances, negotiable CDs, commercial paper, and corporate bonds.
- A bank's financial information is of interest to many parties, including shareholders and investors, bank regulators, government agencies, employees, and other banks. Net income is only one, and not necessarily the best, measure of financial performance. Return on assets, return on equity, the capital ratio, net interest income (or loss), and earnings per share are among the many ways that a bank's strength can be evaluated over a given period. Using ratios, a bank can compare its performance with its own past performance or with peer group banks. In addition to financial performance measures, many banks establish other types of performance objectives to measure the productivity and quality of specific bank units or employees.
- Good financial performance is not achieved automatically. Bank management must plan carefully, set realistic earnings objectives, and structure the balance sheet appropriately. The budget is the financial plan for attaining the goals set by management.

Learning Check

SELF-CHECK AND REVIEW

1. How does the Federal Reserve manage the money supply?

2. Why does the Federal Reserve need to manage the money supply?

3. Some banks have experienced losses while others have remained profitable. Who ultimately is accountable for a bank's poor financial performance?

4. What is a bank's largest asset? Its largest liability? Its largest income and expense items?

5. Why is accurate financial data so important to bank shareholders and investors? To federal and state regulators? To customers?

6. What would be the consequences if a bank overemphasized liquidity to the detriment of other factors in funds management? What would be the consequences of overemphasizing safety at the expense of liquidity and income?

7. What is the difference between the discount rate and the prime rate?

8. What is the net worth of a bank that has the following assets and liabilities?

	(thousands of dollars)
Cash on hand	$45,400
Investments	$76,600
Loans (net of reserve for loan losses)	$224,300
Fed funds sold	$35,800
Fixed assets	$18,900
Other assets	$12,200
Deposits	$312,700
Fed funds purchased	$68,600
Other liabilities	$4,300

9. What is the net profit or loss of a bank reporting the following revenues and expenses?

	(thousands of dollars)
Interest and fees on loans	$253,700
Interest and dividends on investments	$22,100
Interest paid on deposits	$158,800
Salaries, wages, and benefits	$70,300
Taxes	$11,000

Deposit Accounts

3

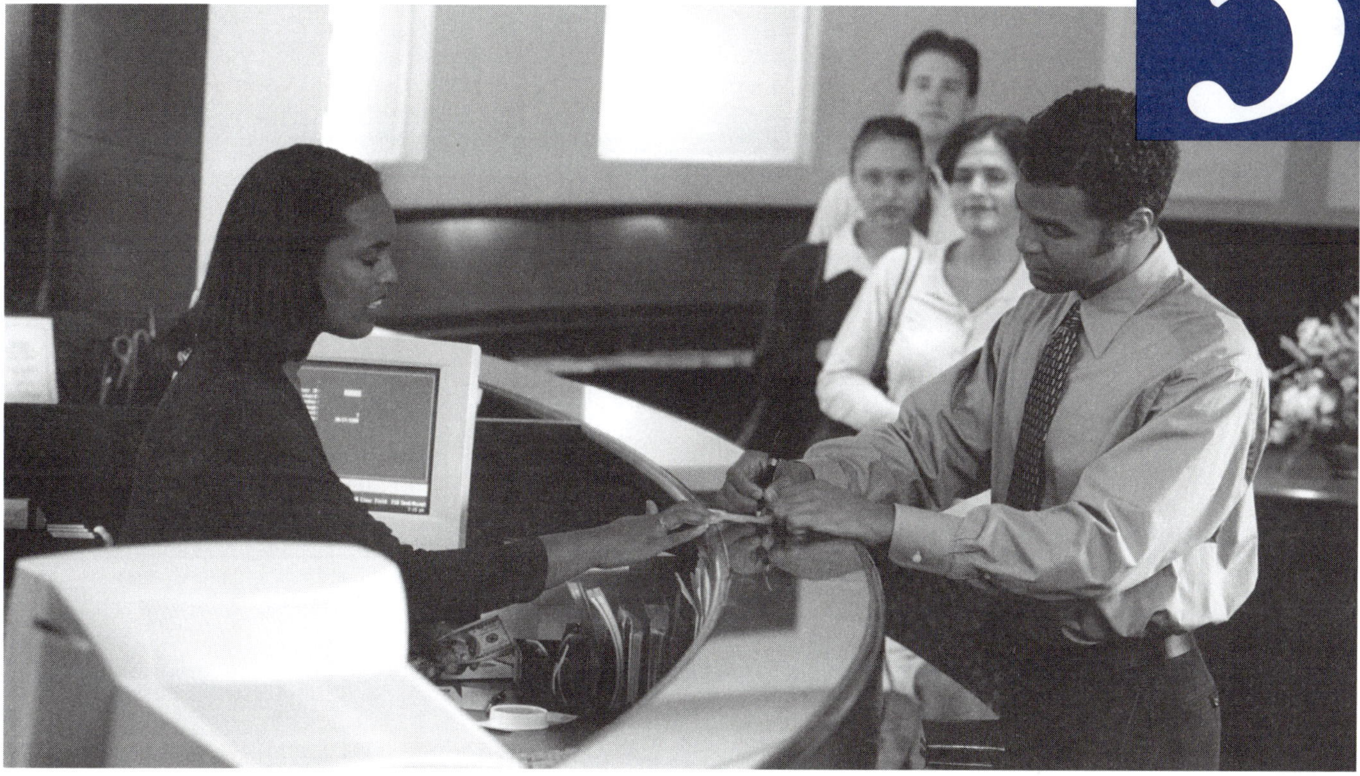

Learning Objectives

After studying this chapter, you should be able to

- Discuss the deposit function
- Describe common deposit accounts banks offer
- Identify deposit-related services for retail and business customers
- Describe types of account ownership
- Explain requirements for opening deposit accounts
- Describe banking regulations for deposit products and services
- Discuss federal deposit insurance coverage

Introduction

Checking, savings, money market, and time deposit accounts are traditional "core" deposit products that banks offer to their customers. Banks use funds generated by deposits to maintain liquidity and to make loans and investments. In turn, loans and investments generate income that enables banks to pay interest on certain types of deposits. Along with deposit products, banks also feature services, such as online banking, to make it more convenient for customers to manage their financial affairs.

Whether the owners of deposit accounts are consumers, businesses, or government entities, account titling and identification are important. Bank regulations, policies, and procedures address consumer protection and legal concerns. Because the deposit function is important not just to customers but also to the economy, bank regulations address reserve requirements, electronic fund transfers, funds availability, and account disclosures—all of which affect a bank's relationship with its depositors.

THE DEPOSIT FUNCTION

The deposit function is the basic banking activity of accepting customers' checks, currency, or other financial instruments for credit to their accounts. Without deposits, banks would not have enough funds to lend. Lending, in turn, brings in funds to allow banks to pay interest to depositors (see exhibit 3.1).

Billions of dollars are deposited in and withdrawn from banks each day in the form of cash, paper checks, and electronic transfers. The total dollar amount of checks deposited is greater than the amount of coin and currency deposited. However, while consumers and businesses continue to use paper checks for making and receiving payment, electronic payment methods are rapidly becoming the method of choice. Regardless of the form, bank deposits are central to the nation's economy.

Exhibit 3.1: A Bank's Relationship with Depositor and Borrower

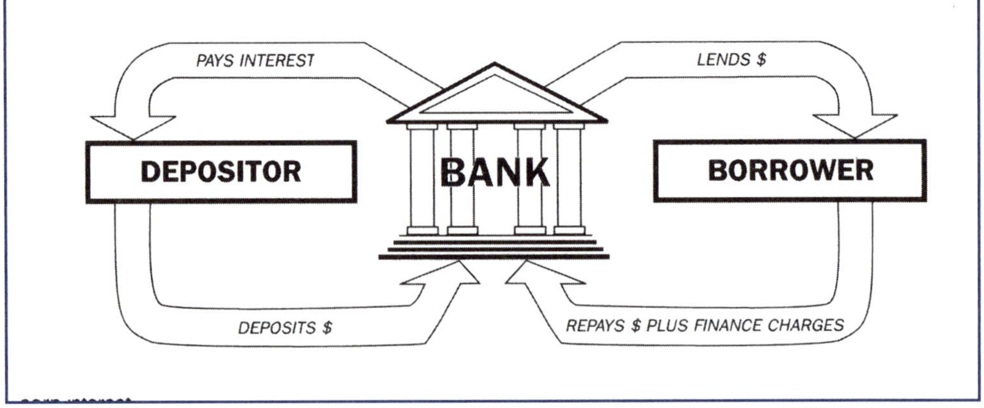

Money Supply

As discussed in chapter 2, the Federal Reserve (the Fed) sets monetary policy with the goal of keeping the U.S. economy stable—neither growing too fast, which might cause inflation, nor growing too slowly, which might cause a recession. The Fed achieves its monetary policy objectives by carefully managing the nation's money supply, of which the most important component is bank deposits. Thus, from an economic standpoint, bank deposits, and how the Fed controls them through such tools as reserve requirements and open-market operations, determine the growth of the economy.

The Federal Reserve uses a variety of money supply measures to predict and control the pace and direction of U.S. economic activity. The most important measures are M1 and M2 (see exhibit 3.2).

M1

M1 consists of funds that are readily accessible for spending, including:

- Currency and coin circulating outside the U.S. Treasury Department, Federal Reserve Banks, and the vaults of commercial banks
- Traveler's checks of nonbank issuers
- Demand deposits in commercial banks—except those due to domestic or foreign commercial banks, certain foreign official institutions, and the U.S. government—less cash items in the process of collection

Exhibit 3.2: Components of the Money Supply

		Amount* (in billions of dollars)	
M1			
	Currency and coin	$1,171.8	
	Traveler's checks	3.4	
	Demand deposits	1,078.5	
	Other checkable deposits in commercial banks	259.8	
	Other checkable deposits in thrift institutions	218.0	
	Total M1		**$ 2,731.5**
M2			
	M1	$2,731.5	
	Savings deposits at commercial banks	6,185.2	
	Savings deposits at thrift institutions	1,042.0	
	Small denomination time deposits at commercial banks	388.4	
	Small denomination time deposits at thrift institutions	137.5	
	Retail money funds	628.3	
	Total non-M1		**$ 8,381.5**
	Total M2		**$11,113.0**

*Seasonally adjusted, in billions of dollars

Source: Federal Reserve Statistical Release, Money Stock Measures—H.6, February 2014

- Other checkable deposits (OCDs) consisting of negotiable orders of withdrawal (NOW) accounts and automatic transfer service (ATS) accounts at depository institutions, share draft accounts at credit unions, and demand deposits at thrift institutions

M2

M2 includes M1 and adds these near-monies:

- Savings and money market accounts at banks and thrifts
- Time deposits at depository institutions with minimums of less than $100,000, except individual retirement accounts (IRAs) and Keogh accounts
- Balances in retail money market mutual funds, less IRA and Keogh balances

As can be seen, bank deposits comprise most of M1 and M2.

Aside from the broad, essential economic role of making funds available for lending and as a means for the Federal Reserve to manage the nation's economy, bank deposits fulfill two important objectives for customers: they offer a safe and convenient place for their money.

Safety

Banks are responsible for safeguarding customer deposits at all times and ensuring that funds are available for withdrawal. By law, banks must operate in a safe and sound manner. Through their investment and lending policies, banks ensure prudent use of customer deposits. Bank policies also establish practices to honor legitimate requests for withdrawals and ensure that creditworthy borrowers have access to bank loans. When an unauthorized withdrawal occurs on a customer's account, the customer's funds are protected when proper steps are taken to notify the bank.

Customer deposits are insured up to federal deposit insurance limits. Deposit insurance comes into play when a bank fails, there is no buyer for the bank, and there are not enough funds to pay depositors. The Federal Deposit Insurance Corporation (FDIC) manages the Deposit Insurance Fund (DIF), which protects customer deposits.

Customer Convenience

Customers value convenience. By maintaining branch offices and branches in grocery stores and other retail locations, banks make it easy for customers to deposit money. Banks also offer extended banking hours, drive-up windows, and automated teller machines (ATMs). ATM service has been one of the great advances in customer convenience. Through linked ATM networks, customers can access their accounts worldwide for cash withdrawals. Not only do ATM machines provide convenience for customers, they also reduce transaction costs and allow banks to offer round-the-clock service.

Banks also deliver deposit account services through other electronic means. The majority of banks now offer services through the Internet, from opening accounts to paying bills. Mobile banking services have become especially popular, and among the services offered is mobile deposit, which offers the convenience of depositing paychecks and other payments directly to the customer's account from anywhere a mobile device, such as smart phone, can be used. Other payment methods include electronic fund transfers (EFTs), such as direct deposits and **point-of-sale** (POS) transactions conducted, for example, with debit cards.

DEPOSIT ACCOUNT PRODUCTS

Banks offer a wide variety of deposit products and services to meet customer needs, but before considering deposit account products and services, it is important to understand the differences between transaction, savings, and time deposit accounts.

Types of Deposit Accounts

Customers may deposit money in a checking, savings, or time deposit account. Money is deposited into checking accounts with the intention that funds will be withdrawn soon to pay bills and meet expenses—that is, engage in transactions. Checking accounts, or transaction accounts as they are also known, are **demand deposit** accounts. Until recently, demand deposit accounts generally were not permitted by law to pay interest. However, checking-like accounts that pay interest, known as negotiable order of withdrawal (NOW) accounts, have been authorized for more than 30 years. Savings and time deposit accounts also pay interest, usually at a higher rate than demand deposit accounts, but there are limits on funds withdrawal. As a result, savings and time deposit accounts are for customers who do not need immediate access to funds.

Demand Deposit Transaction Accounts

With demand deposits, the total amount on deposit is payable "on demand" and may be converted into coin and currency as soon as the deposited funds are available as mandated by bank policy. For example, a customer with a balance of $100 in a checking account can write a check for that amount and present it to a teller to immediately obtain $100 in cash. In 2010, the Dodd-Frank Wall Street Reform and Consumer Protection Act eliminated the legal prohibition on paying interest on demand deposit accounts, although most banks still do not pay interest on such accounts.

Interest-Earning Transaction Accounts

Traditionally, checking accounts existed only at commercial banks as demand deposits. However, in the late twentieth century, thrift institutions, credit unions, and brokerage firms began competing aggressively with banks for checking accounts. Thrift institutions and brokerage firms introduced interest checking. Credit unions offered **share drafts**, which are similar to checks.

When the Depository Institutions Deregulation and Monetary Control Act was enacted in 1980, commercial banks were able to offer NOW accounts. Withdrawals are made using check-like forms. Because NOW accounts earn interest, banks have the legal right to require a seven-day notice before any withdrawal, although they rarely do. NOW accounts may be offered only to individuals, certain nonprofit organizations, and governmental entities.

point-of-sale (POS)—A device used to transfer funds from a bank account to a retailer to pay for purchases.

demand deposit—Funds that a customer may withdraw from a bank with no advance notice, usually by writing a check or using an ATM.

share draft—A bill payment device offered by some credit unions. Members of a credit union can write these check-like instruments against their savings share accounts.

Did You Know ...

In 2005, the personal savings rate for Americans reached a historic low at 2.6 percent, and it was not much better in 2006 and 2007. However, the recession of 2008-2009 caused many Americans to rethink their savings habits, and the savings rate doubled between 2009 and 2012. Nonetheless, personal savings remained low compared to the 1960s and 1970s, when the savings rate always exceeded 10 percent of income.

Source: Federal Reserve Bank of St. Louis

By The Numbers

The Savings Rule of 72

The Rule of 72 helps savers know how long it takes to double the money they have on deposit. Simply take the interest earned on the deposit and divide 72 by that number. The result is roughly the number of years it will take for the balance to double, without taking into account inflation.

For a 5 percent interest rate, calculate as follows

$$72 \div 5 = 14.4$$

It will take 14.4 years to double the balance without any further contributions, if there is no inflation.

Savings and Time Deposit Accounts

Savings accounts differ from demand deposit transaction accounts because technically they cannot be withdrawn on demand. As with interest-earning transaction accounts, banks can require a seven-day notice of withdrawal. In practice, few do. Unlike interest-earning transaction accounts, certain types of transfers are limited to six per month (checks, preauthorized transfers, and electronic transfers to third parties). Savings accounts, like checking accounts, have no maturity date. Deposits and withdrawals can be made on any day.

Time deposit accounts, such as certificates of deposit, have specific maturity dates, starting at least seven days from the date of deposit. When a time deposit is withdrawn before maturity, an interest penalty is generally imposed. Banks pay interest on both savings and time deposit accounts; typically they pay a higher interest rate for longer-term deposits.

Ratio of Transaction Accounts to Savings and Time Deposits

The ratio of transaction account deposits to savings and time deposits is important to banks for two reasons. First, a bank has to meet reserve requirements for transaction accounts. Second, the turnover rate for transaction account deposits is higher than for savings or time deposit accounts.

Every deposit accepted from a customer is a liability—not an asset—for the bank. The deposit is an obligation that the bank must repay at some future date. Deposits are typically the largest percentage of liabilities on bank balance sheets. At the same time, as the bank's raw material, these deposits are the primary source of funds for banks to put to profitable use as loans and investments. Because time deposits with stated maturities remain with the bank longer than demand deposits, these funds generally are used for longer-term bank loans and investments. High-turnover demand deposit funds are put to short-term use.

Common Deposit Account Products

Some of the more common products offered to consumers and businesses include checking accounts, savings accounts, certificates of deposit, and retirement accounts.

Checking Accounts

A checking account is a demand deposit transaction account that offers check-writing privileges. Depending on the account, banks may require a minimum balance to avoid a service charge and allow unlimited check-writing privileges. Most checking accounts offer a **check debit card** and **ATM card** as well, allowing customers to make payments and withdrawals at POS facilities and ATMs.

Some checking account types are marketed to select groups, such as students and senior citizens. Checking accounts may also be tailored to specific needs of

check debit card—A plastic access card that enables the cardholder to purchase goods or services or withdraw cash online through a point-of-sale terminal and offline upon signing a receipt. The transaction cost is debited from the cardholder's deposit account. The card, which may be used for ATM transactions as well, may carry a VISA or MasterCard logo.

ATM card—A plastic access card that enables the cardholder to withdraw cash through an ATM and that, in some retail locations, can be used for point-of-sale transactions after a personal identification number (PIN) is entered. The cost of the transaction is debited from the cardholder's bank account.

bank customers, including basic checking accounts that provide fundamental services at a minimal fee; premier checking accounts that offer extra benefits such as free money orders or traveler's checks; and checking accounts with enhanced identity theft protection measures, such as ID theft insurance and credit monitoring and alerts.

Checking accounts are also tailored to the business customer. A business checking account is usually a demand deposit account that can offer services such as night deposit, merchant services, and cash management services. Detailed statements are provided to help business customers organize transaction activity. In exchange for these services, a monthly service charge is applied. Alternatively, a charge for each deposit ticket processed and check deposited and paid is applied unless a specified average daily balance is maintained.

Did You Know ...

In 1909, the Carlisle Trust Company, Carlisle, Pennsylvania, started the first Christmas savings club. Merkel Landis, the bank's treasurer, originated the idea.

Source: American Bankers Association

Savings Accounts

Statement savings accounts pay interest on deposits periodically, often monthly or quarterly. However, Fed Regulation D limits certain savings account transactions to six per month. These include transfers to third parties by automatic, preauthorized, or telephone transfers, or by check, debit card, or the Internet. Unlimited withdrawals may be transacted at the teller window, by mail, or at an ATM. Once the withdrawal limit has been reached for those applicable transactions, a bank may either charge a fee or prohibit the withdrawal. With any type of withdrawal, the bank may legally require seven days of notice.

The number of deposits is not limited. Statements are rendered monthly when there is electronic transaction activity on the account.

Savings accounts are also offered to businesses. These are typically interest-earning accounts used to accumulate funds for anticipated bills, such as quarterly tax payments.

Savings Clubs

Savings clubs are a special-purpose savings account generally used for end-of-year holiday purchases, to pay off high credit card bills due in January, or to save for purposes like a vacation.

Money Market Deposit Accounts (MMDAs)

MMDAs, first introduced by brokerage firms, pay a higher interest rate than savings accounts because the rate of interest is tied to current money market rates. However, MMDAs have a higher minimum monthly balance requirement than do savings accounts. Monthly transfers to third parties are limited to six. In-person withdrawals are unlimited. Legally, a bank may require seven days of notice before a withdrawal.

Business MMDAs, like MMDAs offered to personal customers, pay a higher interest rate than a corresponding savings account, allow six preauthorized and automatic transfers and checks per month to third parties, and may require seven days of notice before a withdrawal. Business-related banking services may be attached to the account.

Did You Know ...

Savings balances can grow substantially because of compound interest. For example, a customer purchasing a 5-year, $10,000 certificate of deposit with a fixed interest rate of 3.5 percent, compounded quarterly, will have, when the CD matures, accumulated $1,909.44 in interest.

Certificates of Deposit (CDs)

A CD is a time deposit with a fixed maturity, usually seven days to five years, and a fixed interest rate tied to the maturity and the purchase amount. Withdrawals before maturity incur a penalty charge. CDs that have a minimum denomination of $100,000 or more are called jumbo CDs. Whether they are purchased by individual customers or businesses, CDs are for those not needing immediate access to their funds.

Retirement Savings Accounts

These accounts help individuals and the self-employed save for retirement by making deposits to traditional IRAs, Roth IRAs, or simplified employer plan IRAs (SEP-IRAs). Contributions to IRAs and SEP-IRAs are tax-deductible and the earnings are tax-deferred.

Education Savings Accounts

There are generally two types of education savings accounts: Section 529 College Savings Plans and Coverdell Education Savings Accounts (ESAs). Section 529 plans are so named because they are authorized by Section 529 of the Internal Revenue Code. Both types of accounts allow families to save for educational expenses by making contributions that earn tax-deferred interest, although contributions are not tax-deductible. A major difference between the plans is that Coverdell ESAs can be used to pay for K-12 education expenses and higher education expenses, while Section 529 plans are limited to higher education expenses only. There are also differences in contribution limits, withdrawal limits, and income limits for contributors.

Did You Know ...

The individual retirement account (IRA) was created in 1974 by the Employee Retirement Income Security Act (ERISA). IRAs were originally limited to employees who were not covered by a qualified employer-based retirement plan, and the maximum contribution was $1,500.

Health Savings Accounts

A health savings account is a tax-deferred savings account that must be used for paying medical expenses. Contributions are tax-deductible annually up to 100 percent of the required deductible of an individual's high-deductible insurance plan. Distributions are made according to plan guidelines, normally involving a withdrawal request form, check, or debit card, and are excluded from an individual's gross income as long as funds are used for defined medical care.

Concentration Accounts

Designed for businesses, a concentration account is a central account for all deposits not invested. Deposits from other accounts or from other financial institutions are gathered, usually electronically, and deposited in the concentration account, which is then used to fund a disbursement account.

Disbursement Accounts

Also for businesses, a disbursement account is usually a zero-balance account funded by the concentration account when payments must be made. Any excess funds at the end of the day are transferred to the concentration account.

DEPOSIT-RELATED SERVICES

Banks provide many services to support deposit accounts, such as facilitating deposits, processing deposits once they are made, and giving customers access to their money and account information.

Options for Depositing Funds

Customers have many options for easily depositing funds to their checking and savings accounts.

Automated Teller Machines (ATMs)

An ATM is a convenient way to make deposits and collect cash from an account, inquire about balances, and transfer funds between accounts. Access to these services only requires an ATM debit card, a check debit card, or a smart card.

Computers and Mobile Devices

Computers and mobile devices, such as smart phones and tablets that have wireless connectivity to the Internet, are rapidly becoming a preferred way of accessing bank deposit account services to check balances, deposit payments, and transfer funds.

Branch Locations

Whether inside the bank or at a drive-up window, bank employees at branch offices offer personal service and convenience, which some customers prefer when making a deposit.

Night Depositories

A night depository is a locked, secured safe into which a business customer places deposits. The customer is given a key or card to access the night depository after the bank is closed. Deposits are processed at the beginning of the next business day. Small businesses most often use this service.

Direct Deposit

Direct deposit is an electronic banking service that allows depositors to have periodic payments—such as paychecks, Social Security checks, regular dividend payments, and annuity or pension checks—automatically credited to a specified deposit account. Direct deposits are processed through the **automated clearing house (ACH)** payment system.

Payroll Cards

A payroll card is a deposit account access card much like an ATM or debit card. Employers have banks set up accounts, or subaccounts, of a company's payroll account, for employees. Instead of issuing paper checks or using direct deposit to employee accounts, employers have banks issue payroll cards to employees, who use the cards to withdraw funds at ATMs and make purchases at POS terminals. Some payroll card services also offer convenience checks and electronic bill payment.

Did You Know ...

The Coverdell Education Savings Account is named after Senator Paul Coverdell (R-GA), who sponsored legislation to provide favorable tax treatment for accounts set up by families to pay their children's educational expenses. The accounts, originally called Education IRAs, were renamed in honor of Senator Coverdell, who died in July 2000 while still serving in the Senate.

automated clearing house (ACH)—A clearing facility operated for the convenience of banks in a particular region, generally through the regional Federal Reserve Bank. An ACH electronically processes interbank credits and debits.

Automatic Transfer Services (ATS)

This service allows for the automatic transfer of funds from, for example, a savings account to a checking account to cover checks and prevent **overdrafts**. By prior arrangement (preauthorization), banks move funds from the savings to the checking account when checking account balances are too low to pay incoming checks or electronic debits.

overdraft—A negative (minus) balance in a customer's checking account resulting from the paying (posting) of items for an amount greater than the account's available balance.

Electronic Fund Transfers (EFT)

EFT is a service that allows funds to be transferred to and from deposit accounts electronically rather than physically. EFT can be handled by telephone or through the Internet.

Remote Deposit Capture

Remote deposit capture uses imaging technology and EFT. Checks received at business locations are scanned to create an image or an ACH data transmission, which is then transmitted in encrypted form over the Internet to the bank for deposit. A customer needs a personal computer or mobile electronic device, such as a smart phone, an Internet connection, and a check scanner or camera.

Did You Know ...

More than 420,000 ATMS are located in the United States.

Source: U.S. Government Accountability Office

Wire Transfers

Deposited funds can be transferred electronically from the account of one financial institution to the account of another—for example, between affiliates of a bank holding company, between unaffiliated financial institutions, or between a financial institution and another entity, such as a Federal Reserve Bank. This service is often used to move large amounts of money.

Mailed Deposit Services

Deposit by mail is an option for customers who are away from home or do not want to go to the bank or an ATM. Customers complete deposit slips, endorse checks, and mail both to the bank.

Courier and Armored Car Services

When large amounts of cash or valuable securities need to be transported, personal couriers or armored cars offer a convenient and secure alternative to picking up and making deposits.

Did You Know ...

Effective March 1, 2013, all Americans receiving federal benefits, such as Social Security, were required to do so by direct deposit.

Source: Social Security Administration

Types of Deposited Items

Banks are responsible for collecting funds on most items deposited into accounts and for making them available to customers. Banks act as agents for customers and, depending on the type of item deposited (see exhibit 3.3), collect the funds.

Coin and Currency

Coin and currency usually do not require collection. Businesses may use bank courier and armored car services to deliver coin and currency to banks. Most customers deposit coin and currency to their accounts, and the bank typically makes funds available that day or on the next business day. There are expenses relating to these

Exhibit 3.3: Characteristics of Deposited Items

Cash Items	Noncash Items
• Give customer immediate, provisional account credit • Create float (time lag between account crediting and collection) • May be payable on demand • Must not have documents attached • Must not carry special instructions or require special handling • Inexpensive: can be processed in bulk • Payable in U.S. funds	• Give customer delayed (deferred) credit • Do not create float (account not credited until collection is completed) • May or may not be payable on demand • May have documents attached • Require special individualized handling; may carry specific instructions • Are more expensive to handle • May or may not be payable in U.S. funds
Example • Checks	**Examples** • Promissory notes • Drafts with attached documents • Clip coupons for municipal bonds • Checks drawn on banks outside the United States

deposits: teller salaries for handling and processing, cost of shipping excess cash to the Federal Reserve, fraud prevention, and protection of coin and currency when stored at the bank. Business customers, such as large grocery stores (though not individuals or small businesses), may be charged a fee for bank handling of coin and currency deposits.

Cash Items

Cash items, like cash, are often made available to the customer before the bank has collected those funds. A cash item is, for example, a check in U.S. currency that flows through the collection process without special handling. Banks may make cash items available immediately, and they must make cash items available no later than a schedule set by federal regulation.

Noncash Items

Noncash items require special handling; they cannot be processed in bulk. A draft that cannot be paid unless an auto title is attached is an example of a noncash item; so is a foreign check that must be converted to U.S. dollars. Upon receipt of noncash items, a teller either enters them for collection or sends them to a special department for processing.

Accessing Funds and Account Information

Customers have a variety of options for accessing funds and account information. They may go to a branch to ask the teller, call their bank's call center, or use ATMs. Internet banking, debit cards, and stored-value cards such as payroll cards have become popular alternatives to writing checks and in-branch banking.

In recent years, Internet banking has grown rapidly as more customers use their computers, tablets, or smart phones to access personal and business account information, including balances, transaction history, and statements. Often both consumer and business customers can reconcile their accounts online, authorize fund transfers, buy certificates of deposit, open deposit accounts, and apply for loans.

OWNERSHIP OF DEPOSIT ACCOUNTS

Ownership of a deposit account determines what documentation the customer must present to open an account. It also determines the type of account that may be opened and the account's title, both of which determine the rights, obligations, and liabilities of the parties to the account. Exhibit 3.4 shows the two general types of deposit account ownership: consumer and business.

CONSUMER ACCOUNT OWNERSHIP

The types of consumer account ownership are individual, joint, and fiduciary.

Individual Accounts

An individual account is opened for, and owned by, an individual. The individual is the sole owner of the account, and no other person has any rights to it. When the individual dies, the account normally becomes part of his or her estate. Sometimes the individual may want to give someone else the authority to sign checks or make other decisions for the account. This can be accomplished through a **power of attorney**.

Powers of attorney vary depending on the wishes of the individual account owner (the **principal**). A general power of attorney gives unlimited authority over the account to the person designated. A special power of attorney limits the authority to a specific duty or function for a limited period. For example, a customer may give someone a power of attorney for a checking account so that bills can be paid; but not for a savings account or certificate of deposit. A power of attorney ceases at the death of the person who grants it.

Joint Accounts

A joint account is opened in the names of, and owned by, two or more individuals. Establishing identification is just as important in opening joint accounts as it is in opening individual accounts. Joint account holders should be present to sign the signature card. In most circumstances, the account agreement holds each account holder responsible for the transactions on the account, including overdrafts.

Joint accounts can be held either in joint tenancy with full right of survivorship or as tenancy-in-common. Most banks require joint accounts to be established as joint tenancy with full **right of survivorship**.

Exhibit 3.4: Account Ownership

Consumer	Business
• Individual	• Sole Proprietorship
• Joint	• Partnership
• Fiduciary	• Corporate
	• Public Funds
	• Unincorporated Organization

Situation

On her way home from work on Monday, Liz withdraws $100 in cash from one of her bank's ATMs. On Tuesday, she goes into the bank and deposits her $700 paycheck at the teller window. On Thursday, she stops at the kiosk in the bank lobby and authorizes a $406 payment on her auto loan. Later that evening, Liz sits down at her home computer and accesses her bank account through the Internet. She checks her balance and prints out a statement of the activity on her account. All the transactions she made that week appear on the statement.

power of attorney—A legal document that authorizes a person named as an agent (attorney-in-fact) to act on behalf of another person (the principal).

principal—The person or company that appoints another (an agent) to act on his or her or its behalf.

right of survivorship—The right of surviving tenants to take full possession of specific assets, such as account funds, upon the death of other tenants, without establishing an estate but subject to state laws.

Joint Tenancy with Rights of Survivorship	*Tenancy-in-Common*
Bill Wiltshire **or** Peggy Wiltshire	Bill Wiltshire **and** Peggy Wiltshire
Word "or" separates the names of the account holders.	Word "and" separates the names of the account holders.
Only one signature is required on the check. Either account holder may make deposits, write checks, make withdrawals, transfer funds, access the account electronically, stop payment on checks, or close the account.	In many circumstances, account holders must act together. Both signatures are required for withdrawal from the account. Requires more monitoring. Bank verifies that all account holders sign checks or withdrawal slips. If checks are paid with only one signature, bank could be liable to the account holders who did not sign.
Surviving owners have rights to all of the funds.	Upon the death of one account holder, the remaining holder is entitled only to his or her share in the account. The decedent's share may be inherited by a third party.

Fiduciary Accounts

A **fiduciary** account is opened by a representative for the benefit of another person. Examples are trust accounts, estate accounts, guardianships, and custodial accounts.

Trust Accounts

A simple trust account, for example, is opened by a mother and father "in trust for" a minor child. When opening the account, the bank obtains identification from the representatives (the parents) as if it were opening an account for an individual.

Estate Accounts

An estate account is established for an estate of a decedent and requires specific documentation, often a document issued by the probate court appointing an individual as the personal representative or executor of the estate.

Guardianship Accounts

A guardianship account is set up by a court-appointed guardian to manage funds intended for a ward, a minor, or an incapacitated person. A guardianship account requires substantial documentation. Laws vary by state, but in general, a guardianship account may only be opened with court documentation, and often withdrawals may be made only by a court order. These accounts usually require special handling by experienced bank officers.

In all cases, this type of fiduciary account has a representative (such as a guardian) and a **beneficiary** (such as a minor child) or person for whose benefit the account

fiduciary—An individual, bank, or other party to whom specific property is turned over under the terms of a contract and who acts for the benefit of another party on a basis of trust and confidence.

beneficiary—(1) The party legally entitled to receive the proceeds of an annuity, insurance policy, letter of credit, trust fund, retirement account, or will, either from an appointment, assignment, disposition, instrument, or contract; (2) in the context of electronic fund transfers, the term used in Article 4A of the Uniform Commercial Code to refer to the person to be paid under the payment order.

Situation

A retired couple is planning to take a long vacation in their new recreational vehicle. They have arranged to have their pension checks automatically deposited into their checking account and want to give their daughter the ability to pay bills and otherwise manage the account while they are away. However, they also want to be able to get money from the account while they travel. They give their daughter power of attorney over their checking account and revoke the power of attorney when they return from their trip.

partnership agreement—A legal agreement stating the contributions each partner has made to the business, the nature of the business, and the proportions in which each partner will share in profits or losses.

partnership resolution—A document containing language certifying that the name of the partnership is exactly the same as the one provided to the bank and listing who is authorized to write checks and sign for loans on behalf of the partnership.

is held. The accounts take many different forms and require different types of documentation, depending on the fiduciary relationship.

Custodial Accounts

A custodian, typically an adult such as a parent or a guardian, can create and manage a custodial account for the benefit of a minor. Before the minor may make transactions, approval from the custodian is required.

In the case of business relationships, a custodial account may be created to manage the retirement funds for employees of a business. Usually the investments are limited to mutual funds or other similar investments with regulated companies.

The custodian account relationship also describes the role of banks when they hold securities on behalf of institutional investors.

Business Account Ownership

The types of business account ownership are sole proprietorship, partnership, corporation, public funds, and unincorporated organization.

Sole Proprietorship Accounts

A sole proprietorship account may be opened in the name of the proprietor (the person owning and operating the business) or in a trade name. "Trading as" (t/a) or the phrase "doing business as" (d/b/a) may be used. For example, if Tabatha Thompson owned a business called The Gift Shop, the account would read "Tabatha Thompson d/b/a The Gift Shop."

When a proprietorship is operated under the individual's own name, a bank requires identification, references, and signature cards to open the account, just as in the case of an individual. Often there is no way to distinguish a sole proprietorship from the individual who is the owner. However, when any name other than the individual's name is used, the connection between the owner and the fictitious trade name should be established legally. The proprietor provides the bank with the legal registration form required by the state. This may be a business certificate, a fictitious name registration, or a certificate of registration of trade name.

A sole proprietor has the right to open an account, make deposits, stop payments, and manage the account. Checks payable either to the owner or to the proprietorship may be deposited to the account. The proprietor can authorize another individual as a signer on the account, but this person would not have the same rights to the account as the owner.

Partnership Accounts

A partnership account may be opened under the names of the individual partners or under a trade name. Partnerships are businesses operated by two or more individuals that are not incorporated.

Depending on the terms of the **partnership agreement**, any one partner may be empowered to act for the others: one partner's actions are legally binding on the others. In opening an account for a partnership, a bank requires it to submit a **partnership resolution** with signatures from all partners authorized to act on behalf of the partnership. The bank also obtains a copy of the partnership agreement and, if the partnership operates under a trade name, maintains a copy of the business certificate on file.

Corporation Accounts

A corporate account is opened in the name of the corporation, which is the owner of the account. The bank legally interacts with the corporation, not the stockholders, directors, or officers. A corporation is identified by its legal name, which usually must include "Corporation," "Incorporated," or "Limited," or an abbreviation of one of those terms.

A corporation—like an individual, sole proprietorship, and partnership—is a legal entity, but the similarity ends there. The corporation cannot act independently; it must act through representatives. Stockholders, who own the corporation, elect the board of directors. The board of directors, which is the governing body of the corporation, is responsible for conducting the corporation's business. The board establishes who can open and operate a bank account on behalf of the corporation.

To verify authority to open an account, the bank requires and maintains on file a certified **corporate resolution**. The bank keeps on file the names, titles, and signatures of persons who are authorized to transact business on the corporation's behalf. This file is updated with new signature cards as new people are given authority or a previous authority is terminated.

corporate resolution—A document filed with a bank that defines the authority given to the corporation's officers and specifies who may sign checks, borrow on behalf of the corporation, and otherwise conduct business and issue instructions to the bank.

Besides knowing who can transact business for the corporation, banks keep records on the authority limits of each signer. The president, for example, may have unlimited authority, but the vice president of finance may only have the authority to sign checks up to a specific amount. Depending on the resolution, it may be necessary for several people to sign checks for certain amounts. The following is an example:

Individual		*Combined (any two)*
Vice President	$5,000	$10,000
Comptroller	$5,000	
Secretary	$5,000	

Unlike an individual or a partnership account, neither a corporate account nor the operation of the corporation is affected by the death of a stockholder, officer, or director.

Government or Agency Accounts

A unit of federal, state, or local government opens a public funds account to receive and disburse funds on behalf of communities and citizens. The unit of government officially appoints the banks with which it opens accounts. Federal, state, and local laws usually prescribe the procedures for setting up public funds accounts.

Documentation generally consists of signature cards listing authorized signers and an official letter or notice appointing the bank as a depository, which is typically issued by the head of the government unit. By law, amounts in accounts that exceed

FDIC insurance limits are secured by specific segregated assets held by the bank. For federal agencies, these assets are usually U.S. Treasury securities.

Unincorporated Organization Accounts

Banks open deposit accounts for all sorts of unincorporated organizations, such as churches, bowling leagues, soccer teams, class reunions, and charitable relief funds. Although these are not businesses in the traditional sense, banks usually treat them as business accounts.

Signature cards are required when an account is opened for an unincorporated organization, and so is a taxpayer identification number (TIN), even if the organization does not pay taxes and is not designated formally as a nonprofit organization under tax laws. Each situation dictates what additional letters, forms, agreements, or special documents should be obtained. The bank's attorney, compliance officer, and policy and procedures manual should be consulted when establishing accounts for such organizations.

Banker Profile

Dan Kelly joined his community bank in West Virginia when he was discharged from the Army. He started as a teller, working at one of the bank's three branches. He also started taking courses for professional development through his local training provider and earned an ABA General Banking Diploma. Meanwhile, Dan continued his education and earned his bachelor's degree in business administration. After taking more ABA courses, particularly in accounting and lending, he was picked for his bank's management trainee program and then promoted to vice president of the bank's main branch. That was 15 years ago, and Dan continued his studies, earning his Certified Financial Marketing Professional certification through the Institute of Certified Bankers. Today, Dan Kelly is an executive and regional retail manager for a national bank's West Virginia market.

OPENING A DEPOSIT ACCOUNT

A customer must open an account before the bank can accept items for deposit. The account-opening process entails much more than filling out forms. The bank must:

- Establish the identity of the person opening the account
- Determine that the person has the legal capacity to open the account
- Ensure that the person is authorized to open the account

By opening an account, a bank enters into a contractual relationship with the account holder and assumes risk. There is the risk that the customer will write checks for more than the amount in the account. There is also the risk that deposited items will be returned. No matter what kind of account is opened, the same advice applies: know your customer!

Establishing Identity

To protect against loss and misuse of funds, a bank must establish the identity of the person opening the account. But how can the bank truly verify identity? Unfortunately, there is no completely foolproof way. Forgers can counterfeit driver's licenses, auto registrations, credit cards, and other forms of identification. A passport is often regarded as ideal identification, but not everyone has a passport, and passports are subject to fraud as well. Bankers must use good judgment and evaluate the identification that is offered according to the bank's customer identification procedures.

Customer Identification Program

The USA PATRIOT Act, enacted after the terrorist attacks of September 11, 2001, requires financial service providers, including banks, to set up a customer identification program (CIP) for new accounts. The legislation's intent is to stop terrorists from using the U.S. financial system to launder money and finance crimes.

A bank's CIP must be written and incorporate reasonable procedures to:

- Collect identifying information about individuals and entities opening an account, such as name, date of birth (for individuals), address, and TIN
- Verify customer identification
- Determine if a customer appears on any government agency lists of known or suspected terrorists
- Maintain records of the information used to verify a customer's identity

A taxpayer identification number is as follows:

For individuals	***For business organizations and nonprofit entities***
Social Security number (SSN)	Employer identification number (EIN)

The act also specifies minimum standards for acceptable identification documents, verification procedures, and record keeping.

Evaluating Capacity and Authority

Banks want to attract new business, but they must be selective in opening accounts. A bank is not obligated to open an account if the potential customer fails to meet its requirements.

Capacity

Before opening an account, a bank determines that the person opening the account has the legal capacity to do so. This means that the person or organization is recognized under the law as a legal entity with the right to open an account.

Most people have the capacity to open accounts, but a person who is considered a minor or incompetent normally does not. Although minors can have checking accounts, the accounts are co-owned or otherwise guaranteed by a responsible adult. Organizations also are required to provide proof that the corporation, partnership, or unincorporated organization exists.

Authority

The person opening the account is asked to prove authority to open and use the account. Individuals opening accounts in their own names need to prove their identity. Those opening accounts on behalf of other individuals, estates, corporations, or partnerships must present official documents that establish their authority to act for the other parties.

BANK DEPOSITS REGULATION

The federal government enacts laws to protect banks and the consumers and businesses that establish deposit relationships with them. Federal bank regulators supervise and enforce these laws. State banking authorities also may supervise and enforce laws that define the deposit relationship.

When Congress passes a law, it usually delegates rulemaking and enforcement authority to a banking agency such as the Federal Reserve Board. The Dodd-Frank Wall Street Reform and Consumer Protection Act (Dodd-Frank Act) transferred rulemaking authority for the Fed regulations implementing the consumer protection laws to the Consumer Financial Protection Bureau (CFPB). The laws that apply to deposit functions were among those transferred to the CFPB and include Regulation E, which implements the Electronic Fund Transfer Act; and Regulation DD, which implements the Truth in Savings Act. The Fed retained Regulation CC, which implements the Expedited Funds Availability Act.

Another regulation that applies to bank deposits is the Fed's Regulation D, which governs reserve requirements for depository institutions. Finally, all bankers should be aware of the FDIC's deposit insurance protection requirements.

Electronic Fund Transfers

The Electronic Fund Transfer Act, implemented by Regulation E, establishes the rights, liabilities, and responsibilities of parties to electronic fund transfers (EFTs). EFTs subject to Regulation E include direct deposit of paychecks and Social Security payments, ATM transfers, debit card purchases, telephone bill payment services, and banking transfers initiated through the Internet, including making deposits, transferring funds between accounts, and paying bills.

Regulation E requires disclosures related to EFTs, including recurring credits to deposit accounts. For example, if a third party does not notify the customer when a recurring preauthorized credit, such as a direct deposit, has or has not been made as scheduled, the bank must do so or provide a telephone number to the customer to call for more information. Regulation E also outlines the consumer's and bank's respective responsibilities for reporting and resolving disputed or erroneous EFTs (such as unauthorized transfers) and for servicing payroll cards.

Expedited Funds Availability

Regulation CC implements the Expedited Funds Availability Act. Generally, the same availability schedule is applied whether the funds are deposited through a teller or an ATM. Depending on the time of the deposit and the location of the ATM, however, funds deposited may take longer to be available than if they were deposited with a teller. Banks must alert customers to their funds availability policies. The notices must be posted where customers making deposits can see them, including in the teller area and at all ATMs, but the notice is not required at drive-in teller windows.

The following types of deposits are generally made available on the first business day after the day of deposit (next-day availability):

- Cash deposited in person
- Electronic payments received for deposit
- U.S. Treasury checks deposited in an account held by the payee
- U.S. Postal Service money orders deposited in person into an account held by the payee

- Federal Reserve Bank and Federal Home Loan Bank checks deposited in person into an account held by the payee
- State or local government checks deposited in person into an account held by the payee if the payee is in the same state as the payor
- Cashier's, certified, or teller's checks deposited in person to an account held by the payee
- Checks drawn on an account held by the drawee bank (on-us checks)
- First $200 of any check deposited in one day

Although Regulation CC refers to "next-day availability," it really means that deposits must be made available for withdrawal by the consumer by the next business day. So, if a customer deposits a check on Saturday, that check is considered deposited on Monday (actual business day of deposit) and would have to be available by Tuesday, which is the next business day after the day of deposit. Saturday and Sunday are not business days unless the bank is open to the public for carrying on substantially all of its banking functions on those days. None of the federal holidays are business days either.

Regulation CC does allow banks to postpone funds availability in some cases. Exceptions include deposits in excess of $5,000, redeposited checks, checks deposited into accounts of repeat overdrafters, situations when there is a reasonable doubt of collectability, emergency conditions, or checks deposited by a new customer.

Truth in Savings

The Truth in Savings Act, implemented by Regulation DD, requires banks to give customers the information they need to compare deposit account features. The law applies to consumers opening deposit accounts. It does not apply to business deposit accounts, including accounts held by individuals as sole proprietors. Regulation DD requires banks to use one of two methods to calculate interest: the daily balance method or the average daily balance method.

Daily balance method — The application of a daily periodic rate to the full amount of principal in the account each day

Average daily balance method — The application of a periodic rate to the average daily balance in the account for the period. The average daily balance is determined by adding the full amount of principal in the account for each day of the period and dividing that figure by the number of days in the period

annual percentage yield (APY)—A rate reflecting the total amount of interest paid on a deposit account, based on the interest rate and the frequency of compounding for a 365-day period.

When a customer opens a savings account, the bank must disclose the interest rate, **annual percentage yield (APY)**, frequency of interest compounding, minimum balance requirements, fees, transaction limits, and other important information. The act requires periodic statements of the APY, amount of interest earned, fees imposed, and length of statement period. Customers must be given advance notice of changes in terms that would affect the account, such as the APY, fees, or maturity dates.

Calculating Annual Percentage Yield (APY)

By The Numbers

APY = 100x[(1+Interest/Principal)(365/Days-in-term) -1]

A bank pays $25.80 in interest for a $1,000 12-month certificate of deposit. Using the general formula above, the APY is 2.58%.

APY=100x[(1+25.80/1,000)(365/Days-in-term)-1]

APY=2.58%

Or, using the simple formula above (because the term of an account without a stated term is deemed to be 365 days):

APY=100x(25.80/1,000)

APY=2.58%

Reserve Requirements

The Federal Reserve Act requires **depository institutions** to keep a certain percentage of their assets on reserve with the Federal Reserve. Regulation D, Reserve Requirements for Depository Institutions, sets the reserve requirements for transaction accounts and nonpersonal time deposits. Regulation D defines such deposits and requires depository institutions to make periodic reports of total deposits to the appropriate Federal Reserve Bank.

This regulation also sets withdrawal penalties on time deposits and transaction limits on deposit accounts such as savings and money market deposit accounts.

depository institution— A financial institution that obtains funds mainly from deposits by the public. Commercial banks, savings and loan associations, savings banks, and credit unions are all depository institutions.

FDIC Insurance Protection

The FDIC was created in the midst of the Great Depression during a time when thousands of banks were closing, resulting in customers losing all of the money they had deposited in the banks. To restore public confidence in banks and provide reassurance that deposits were safe, the FDIC began offering $2,500 in deposit insurance coverage. If an FDIC-insured institution fails, depositors can withdraw funds up to the insured amount, which is backed by the U.S. government. That amount of deposit coverage was periodically increased over the years and, by 1980, had reached $100,000 per depositor. To shore up consumer confidence during the financial crisis in 2008, the deposit insurance limit was raised temporarily to $250,000, and the Dodd-Frank Act made this amount permanent in 2010.

The FDIC insures only deposits at banks and savings associations that pay premiums to the Deposit Insurance Fund. Insured banks must display an official sign at teller windows, night deposits, and ATMs. However, it is important to note that FDIC insurance covers only certain products that banks offer.

Did You Know ...

In 1933, over 4,000 banks failed in the United States. In that year, President Franklin D. Roosevelt delivered his first radio-broadcasted fireside chat, during which he said, "After all, there is an element in the readjustment of our financial system more important than currency, more important than gold, and that is the confidence of the people." Measures taken to stabilize the banking system and his chats to boost public confidence helped. In 1934, only nine banks failed.

Covered by FDIC insurance

- Checking accounts
- Savings accounts
- NOW accounts
- Money market deposit accounts
- Certificates of deposit
- IRA retirement accounts

Not covered by FDIC insurance

- Stocks, bonds, municipal bonds, and other securities
- Mutual funds
- Annuities
- Insurance products (automobile and life insurance)
- U.S. Treasury bills, bonds, or notes
- Safe deposit box contents

Insurance coverage is based on where the deposits are held and how the accounts are titled. For example, deposits in separate branches of an insured bank are not separately insured, but accounts of the same depositor in two different insured banks are separately insured. For purposes of calculating the insured amount, both principal and accrued interest are included. For example, if a depositor purchases CDs from one bank totaling $250,000, and the CDs accrue interest of $10,000, only $250,000 of the $260,000 would be covered.

How accounts are titled determines the current coverage. As a result, it is possible for a customer to benefit from FDIC insurance for a total amount that is more than $250,000 at one insured bank. Finally, the amount of coverage is determined by type of ownership and how deposits are allocated within those types of ownership. FDIC insurance covers a number of account ownership categories (see exhibit 3.5).

When two banks merge, some depositors may end up with balances that are too high to be fully insured by the FDIC. To address this situation, FDIC deposit insurance rules provide a six-month grace period for depositors to reallocate the deposit amounts. For time deposits, the grace period is the greater of six months or the maturity date.

To help bankers and depositors understand coverage rules, the FDIC has a website devoted to the subject at http://fdic.gov/deposit.

Situation

Matt is co-owner of three joint accounts at First National Bank. The accounts are in the amounts of $300,000, $200,000, and $100,000. Because there are two owners for each account, Matt's interest in each account is presumed to be half the balance in each account. To determine Matt's level of insurance coverage, his interest in all the joint accounts must be added together. Thus, his total interest in the three joint accounts is $300,000, half of the $600,000 total value of the accounts. His insured interest is $250,000, and $50,000 is uninsured.

SUMMARY

- Individuals and businesses deposit billions of dollars daily in the nation's banks. Bank deposits—in the form of cash, paper checks, and electronic transfers—are the main components of two measures of the money supply, M1 and M2, which are measured and managed by the Federal Reserve to help direct U.S. economic activity.
- Through the deposit function, banks provide a safe place for customers to keep money and an economical way to pay for transactions. Deposit account services are easily accessible by customers through bank branches, ATMs, and the Internet.
- Banks offer a wide variety of deposit products and services. Deposits may be placed in checking, savings, or time deposit accounts. Customers make checking account deposits because they intend to withdraw the funds soon to pay bills and

Exhibit 3.5: FDIC's Deposit Insurance Ownership Categories and Coverage

• Single Accounts (owned by one person)	• $250,000 per owner
• Joint Accounts (owned by two or more persons)	• $250,000 per co-owner
• Certain Retirement Accounts (includes IRAs)	• $250,000 per owner
• Revocable Trust Accounts	• $250,000 per owner per beneficiary up to 5 beneficiaries (more coverage available with 6 or more beneficiaries subject to specific limitations and requirements)
• Corporation, Partnership and Unincorporated Association Accounts	• $250,000 per corporation, partnership, or unincorporated association
• Irrevocable Trust Accounts	• $250,000 for the non-contingent, ascertainable interest of each beneficiary
• Employee Benefit Plan Accounts	• $250,000 for the non-contingent, ascertainable interest of each plan participant
• Government Accounts	• $250,000 per official custodian

Source: Federal Deposit Insurance Corporation

The standard maximum FDIC insurance amount is allocated

- Per depositor
- Per insured depository institution, not branch
- Per account ownership category

meet expenses. Customers generally place funds in savings and time deposit accounts if they do not need the funds immediately.

- Deposit account products offered to consumers include personal checking accounts, savings accounts, savings clubs, money market deposit accounts, certificates of deposit, retirement savings accounts, education savings accounts, and health savings accounts. Deposit account products offered to businesses include checking and savings accounts, concentration accounts, disbursement accounts, certificates of deposit, and money market deposit accounts.

- Customers enjoy a number of deposit-related services, including ATMs, the teller window, night depository, direct deposit, payroll cards, automated transfer service (ATS), electronic fund transfers (EFT), wire transfer, mailing deposits, and courier or armored car services. Electronic access to deposit accounts and services via personal computers, smart phones, and other mobile devices is widely available.

- Bank customers can deposit funds in a variety of forms: coin and currency, cash items, and noncash items. Banks must accept cash items, such as checks in U.S. currency, and certain noncash items, such as checks in foreign currency.

- The type of deposit account a customer opens and how the account is titled determine the ownership of the account, what identification is required, and what documentation is necessary to establish capacity and authority to open the account. An individual, more than one person (joint ownership), or an individual in a fiduciary capacity may open consumer accounts. Examples of fiduciary accounts are trust, estate, and guardianship accounts. Sole proprietorships, partnerships, corporations, public agencies, and unincorporated entities may open business accounts.

- Bank employees must exercise caution in opening accounts and ensure that the customer gives the bank proper identification. Before opening an account, the bank must determine that the potential customer has legal capacity and authority to do so. The USA PATRIOT Act establishes minimum standards for customer identification.

- A number of federal laws and regulations apply to deposit products and services offered by banks, among them Regulation E, which implements the Electronic Fund Transfer Act; Regulation CC, which implements the Expedited Funds Availability Act; Regulation DD, which implements the Truth in Savings Act; and Federal Reserve Regulation D, Reserve Requirements for Depository Institutions.

- The Banking Act of 1933 created the FDIC and provided $2,500 in coverage for deposits maintained in insured banks. Today, that coverage is $250,000. FDIC rules determine how deposits are insured by the Deposit Insurance Fund. Coverage is based on where the deposits are held and how they are owned. The FDIC publishes on its website information for depositors and bankers that explains its insurance.

SELF-CHECK AND REVIEW

Learning Check

1. Why are deposits important to banks?

2. What are the basic differences and similarities between a checking account and a savings account?

3. How do automatic transfer services benefit a customer?

4. What deposit account would you recommend to a customer who wants to earn interest and would like the option of writing a small number of checks (no more than six) every month?

5. How can customers make deposits into their accounts without going to the bank?

6. How do account transactions differ for joint accounts held in joint tenancy versus those held as tenants-in-common?

7. When a deposit account is opened, why is it important for a bank to establish the authority of the customer to use the account? What three steps does the bank take to accomplish this?

8. What types of deposit transactions are covered by Regulation E?

9. Connie has a single checking account containing $10,000, a single savings account containing $30,000, and a single certificate of deposit in the amount of $35,000. She also has three joint accounts containing $200,000, $110,000, and $90,000, respectively. Because there are two owners for each of the joint accounts, her interest is half of those balances. What is her insured amount? How much is uninsured?

Payments: Cash and Checks

4

Learning Objectives

After studying this chapter, you should be able to

- Discuss the use of cash in payments and its care and distribution
- Describe the components of a check and a negotiable instrument, including the types of bank checks and endorsements
- Discuss developments in the electronic processing of checks
- Explain the check payment process
- Identify major check fraud schemes
- Explain banking laws and regulations related to check payment processes

Introduction

Throughout history, people have used many items to facilitate the exchange of goods and pay for services, among them brass rings and shark's teeth, salt bricks and precious metals. In today's society, cash, in the form of coin and currency, and checks are the more traditional forms of payment.

Payments are made through both simple, traditional processes and through electronically sophisticated systems. The payment system consists of instruments and procedures used to transfer money, make payments, and settle debts for consumers, businesses, and governments. Legislation and related regulations govern payment processes to protect the economy, the banking industry, businesses, and consumers.

cash—(1) Money in the form of bills or coins; (2) money on hand or in the bank.

medium of exchange—Currency or other financial instrument used to facilitate transactions between parties.

dual custody—A security technique that uses two or more individual parties operating together to protect sensitive functions, information, or assets. Both are equally responsible for physically protecting materials in vulnerable transactions. Neither party may access or use the materials independently. Also known as dual control.

CASH AS A PAYMENT SYSTEM

In its simplest sense, **cash** is a country's legal tender—the coin and currency the government declares to be used as a **medium of exchange**. As such, it can be exchanged for goods and services, the settlement of a debt, and in other financial transactions.

Cash is one payment system in our economy that everyone uses to some degree. Minting, printing, and distributing coin and currency begins with the U.S. Treasury Department's Bureau of Engraving and Printing for currency and the U.S. Mint for coins. After it is produced, cash is processed through the Federal Reserve System to consumers (see exhibit 4.1). For banks that are not members of the Federal Reserve System, correspondent banks serve as the intermediary connection.

United States Legal Tender

In the United States, legal tender is known as Federal Reserve notes. The 12 Federal Reserve Banks put notes into circulation pursuant to the Federal Reserve Act of 1913. The value of notes in circulation is enormous—more than $1.15 trillion in 2013, of which the greatest amount in circulation is the $100 bill ($889 billion), followed by the $20 bill (more than $148 billion). Member banks obtain notes from the Federal Reserve Bank in their district. The district Bank then charges the individual member bank's Federal Reserve account for the cost of the notes.

Federal Reserve Banks obtain the notes from the Bureau of Engraving and Printing, which they pay for producing the notes. The notes are then liabilities of the Federal Reserve and obligations of the U.S. government. Each Federal Reserve Bank holds collateral, chiefly U.S. securities, equal in value to the notes it receives. Since 1933, the notes are not redeemable in gold, silver, or any other commodity. Because they are legal tender, Federal Reserve notes, which are the U.S. currency, are essentially backed by all the goods and services in the U.S. economy.

Today's currency is safer and more secure than ever. Every seven to 10 years, the design of U.S. currency is changed to protect against counterfeiting. The recent

Exhibit 4.1: U.S. Cash Distribution System

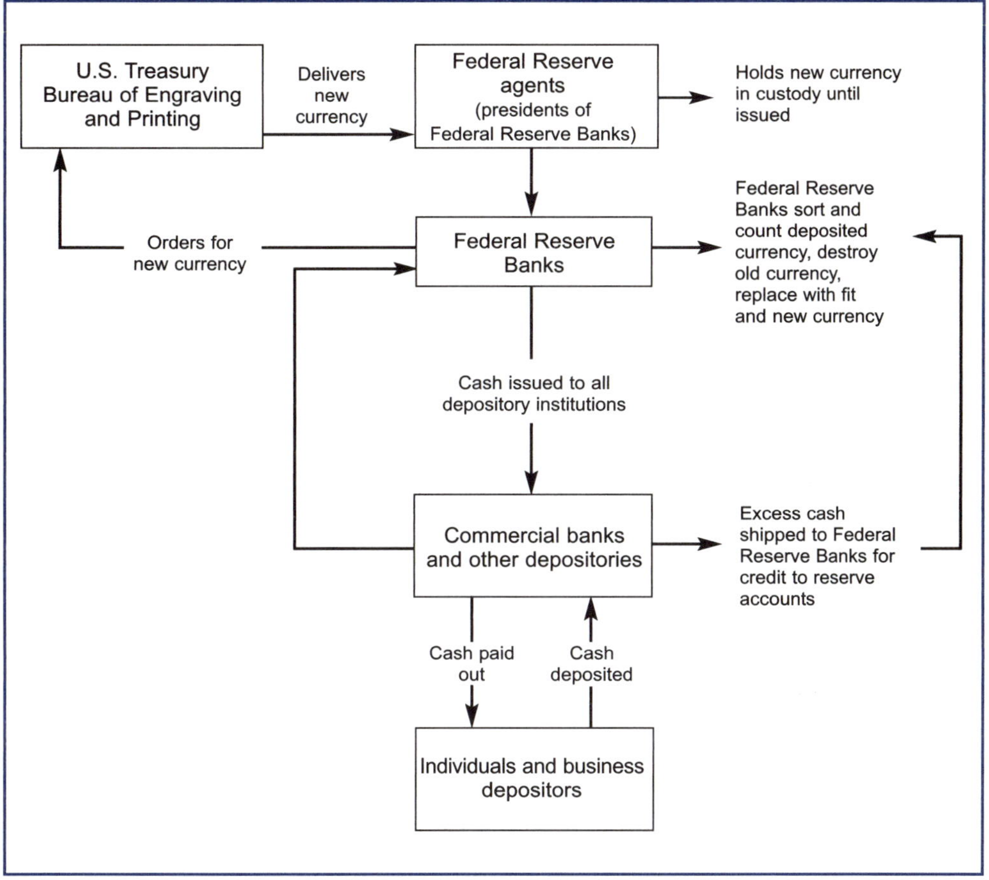

series started changing in 2003 with the new $20 note (or bill, as it is popularly called), followed by new $50 and $10 bills. A redesigned $5 bill was released into circulation in March 2008, and the redesigned $100 bill went into circulation in October 2013, with the latest security features, including a 3-D security ribbon.

For all the bills, the most noticeable difference in their redesigns is the subtle mix of background colors, which add complexity to the bill and make counterfeiting difficult. Because different background colors are used for different denominations, they can be more easily distinguished.

Damaged Coin and Currency

Coin and currency shipments are received by the Federal Reserve Banks using a **dual custody** procedure. Federal Reserve Banks value notes by their face amounts and coins by weight. When Federal Reserve Banks receive cash, it is processed through high-speed sorting machines. These sorting machines separate mutilated and suspected counterfeit currency, which is removed from circulation.

Suspect currency is sent to the U.S. Secret Service. Federal Reserve Banks destroy mutilated currency—notes that are torn, weak, limp, written on, missing a portion, or otherwise damaged—on behalf of the U.S. Treasury.

Coins have a life span of about 30 years. Uncurrent coins (those that are worn but recognizable and machine-countable) are redeemed by Federal Reserve Banks and returned to the U.S. Mint for disposition. Mutilated coins (those that are bent,

Did You Know ...

The U.S. Mint was created in 1792. Before that, a variety of foreign and colonial coinage was used for currency. Mostly, however, a barter system was used, with colonists trading livestock, produce, wampum (Indian beads made from clam shells), and other goods.

Source: U.S. Mint

Did You Know ...

U.S. coins are no longer made of precious metals such as gold or silver. The penny is copper-plated zinc. The nickel consists of copper and nickel. The dime, quarter, and half dollar are clad with a cupronickel alloy made primarily of copper and nickel. The coin's core is copper.

Source: U.S. Mint

chipped, and not machine-readable) are redeemed only through the U.S. Mint facility in Philadelphia, Pennsylvania. All uncurrent and mutilated coins received by the U.S. Mint are melted and reused to manufacture new coins.

CHECKS AS A PAYMENT SYSTEM

Convenient as money is, to be useful in many transactions it has to be converted to forms other than coin and currency. For example, a utility bill is more easily paid by check, credit card, or electronic transfer.

A **check** drawn on a demand deposit account was, for many years, the most popular alternative to coin and currency. Until electronic transactions became more prevalent, U.S. consumers, businesses, and government entities used checks to make the vast majority of commercial and personal payments, as measured by dollar volume. Billions of checks worth trillions of dollars are still processed annually.

Nonetheless, according to the Federal Reserve, the number of checks written by U.S. consumers declined by more than one billion from 2009 to 2012. This drop reflects the fact that consumers are turning to alternative bill payment methods, such as debit cards. Another factor in the declining use of checks has been online bill payment. In 2012, account holders paid an estimated 2.5 billion bills through online banking websites or with mobile bill-payment applications.

Although checks as a payment mechanism are being replaced by the use of electronic forms of payment, checks still remain popular because they are one of the most convenient and flexible methods of payment. A person or business can transfer money to another person or business simply by filling in blank spaces on a check. A completed check tells a bank how much money should be transferred, when, and to whom. There are rules and practices that govern check negotiability, check processing, and the liabilities of the parties to the transaction.

check—A draft on an account in a bank that the owner of the account signs to direct the bank to pay a certain amount to the payee.

Uniform Commercial Code—A set of laws adopted by states to govern commercial and financial transactions between parties. Many states add their own amendments to the basic code.

negotiable instrument—An unconditional written order or promise to pay a certain sum of money. The document must be easily transferable from one party to another by endorsement and delivery or delivery alone. Every negotiable instrument must meet all requirements of Article 3 of the Uniform Commercial Code.

endorsement—A signature (other than the signature of the maker, drawer, or acceptor) typically made on the back of the instrument, such as a check, for negotiating the instrument, restricting payment, or transferring liability of the instrument to another party.

Uniform Commercial Code

The **Uniform Commercial Code** (UCC) consists of a set of laws drafted by the Uniform Law Commission, previously known as the National Conference of Commissioners on Uniform State Laws. Individual states can decide whether to adopt these uniform laws. The purpose of the UCC is to provide uniformity in how states treat commercial transactions. The UCC consists of 11 articles (Articles 1 through 9, plus 2A and 4A) that have been adopted by all 50 states, except that Louisiana has not adopted two of the articles, Articles 2 and 2A.

UCC Article 3 provides standards for negotiable instruments, describes obligations of all parties to a transaction, and sets rules for presentment of a negotiable instrument. UCC Article 4, Bank Deposits and Collections, describes the responsibilities of banks in the check collection process.

Elements of Negotiable Instruments

A check is a **negotiable instrument** involving three parties: the person writing the check (the drawer), the person to whom the check is written (the payee), and the bank that holds the checking account (the drawee) (see exhibit 4.2).

For drawers, the check is a convenient way to pay for goods, services, or other obligations. For payees, the expectation is that checks will be exchanged for cash at a teller window or credited to their bank accounts. Both parties take for granted the collection process and the governing laws.

As negotiable instruments, checks are governed by the legal requirements of UCC Article 3. To satisfy the requirements of negotiability, checks must be:

- Payable to bearer or to order
- An unconditional order or promise to pay
- For a fixed amount of money
- Payable on demand or at a definite time
- Written and signed

Did You Know ...

An estimated 18.3 billion checks were paid in 2012, having a total value of $26.0 trillion and an average value per check of $1,420.

Source: 2013 Federal Reserve Payments Study

Payable to Bearer or to Order

A negotiable instrument is payable to bearer or to order if the word "bearer" or "cash" is used or if it otherwise indicates that the person in possession of the instrument is entitled to payment. A check can be payable to an identifiable person and, once it is **endorsed** by that person, becomes a bearer instrument (see (1) of exhibit 4.3). Thus, any person in possession of an instrument payable to bearer is the holder of the instrument and may present it for payment.

Negotiable instruments are

- An order or promise to pay
- Payable to bearer or to order of
- Payable without conditions
- Payable for a specific, fixed, amount of money
- Payable on demand or at a definite time
- In writing and signed by the drawer

Exhibit 4.2: Parties to a Check

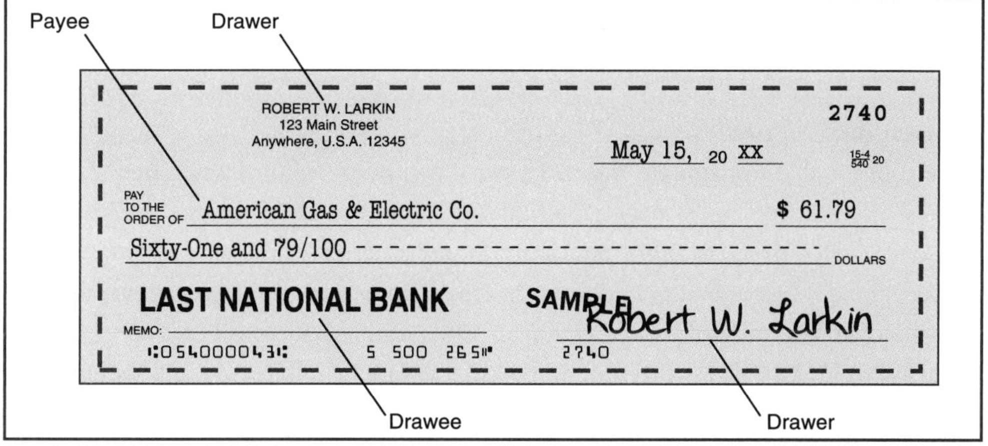

Exhibit 4.3: Elements of a Negotiable Check

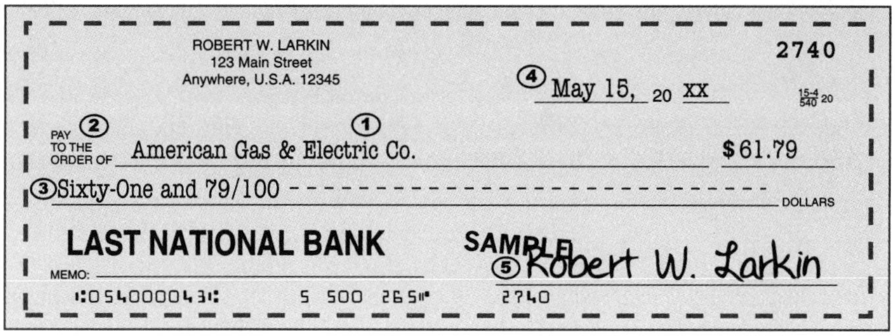

(1) payable to order of or bearer
(2) unconditional order to pay
(3) fixed amount of money
(4) payable on demand or at a definite time
(5) written and signed

Unconditional Order or Promise to Pay

A negotiable instrument is an unconditional order or promise to pay. Checks contain a written order to the bank to pay the amount of the check to the payee. This order cannot depend on any conditions—it must be unconditional (see (2) of exhibit 4.3). For example, a check may not contain the statement: "If he paints the house, pay to the order of Leonard." An instrument that carries a condition to payment is not a negotiable instrument.

Fixed Amount of Money

The unconditional order or promise to pay must be for a fixed amount of money (see (3) of exhibit 4.3). The amount, which can be in U.S. dollars or a foreign currency, must be specified clearly in monetary terms on the face of the instrument. It may not be stated in terms of something of value that could be converted to money, such as one ounce of gold, even though the value of one ounce of gold can be easily determined. In cases where the written amount does not coincide with the numeric amount, UCC Article 3 stipulates that the words control numerals unless the words are ambiguous, in which case the numerals control.

Payable on Demand or at a Definite Time

The date stated on the check determines when it is payable (see (4) of exhibit 4.3). A check may be postdated (date is in the future) or antedated (date is prior to when the check is written). If a check is not dated (either intentionally or unintentionally), the date of the check is considered to be the date it is presented for payment—in other words, the check is payable on demand.

Written and Signed

To be a negotiable instrument, the check must be in writing and signed by the drawer (see (5) of exhibit 4.3). A negotiable instrument signed by a signature machine or stamped with an individual's signature is considered valid, as are "identifying marks" like Xs. Some banks may have specific procedures for these signature types and may arrange for solutions ahead of time, often calling on the services of a **notary public** to witness the drawer putting the identifying mark on the check.

notary public—A public officer who acknowledges or otherwise attests or certifies documents as authentic, usually under an official seal.

Other Types of Checks

Besides personal and business checks, banks provide cashier's checks, teller's checks, certified checks, money orders, and traveler's checks for certain transactions.

Cashier's Check

Cashier's checks are issued by and drawn on a bank. Thus, the bank is both the drawer and the drawee. Often banks use cashier's checks to pay their own obligations or to pay out loan proceeds. Banks may also sell these checks to customers who have been asked to provide payment using a bank's official instrument.

Teller's Check

A teller's check is like a cashier's check but is issued by one bank and drawn on another. The issuing bank's obligation for these checks is the same as for cashier's checks. In other words, even if the purchaser decides it does not want to pay, once a bank issues a teller's check, it is obligated to honor the check.

The payer bank supplies teller's checks and maintains the blank check stock, reconciles the teller's check account, stores the paid checks, and provides service to both the customer and the issuing bank.

Certified Check

A certified check is accepted by the bank on which it is drawn. Essentially, it is a depositor's check stamped with the word "certified" and a signature and date. The original order to pay becomes the bank's promise to pay. Thus, certified checks are legal liabilities of the bank.

Typically, a customer presents the personal check to be certified. The bank sets aside the funds for the check, debits the customer's account, and credits a "certified checks outstanding" account. The bank then places an official bank stamp and signature on the check. The magnetic ink character recognition (MICR) line is covered by the certified check account number or mutilated so it will not pass through the customer's account.

> **Situation**
>
> Franco and Lena are closing on a house tomorrow. To protect against the check being dishonored, the mortgage company will not accept a personal check for the closing. Franco and Lena do not want to bring a large amount of cash to the settlement, so they purchase a cashier's check to pay for the down payment and closing costs.

Money Order

A money order is an order for payment of a specified sum of money to a designated party. Money orders are issued by many post offices and retail establishments, and some banks offer them as a convenience to their customers. Money orders are similar in many respects to certified checks. A customer requests a money order in a specified amount, and the bank debits the customer's account and prints the money order in that amount. To discourage counterfeiting, money orders are imprinted with check-writing equipment on paper with security features such as watermarks and security strips. The party that the money order is payable to is paid funds in the amount printed on the order.

Traveler's Check

A traveler's check is so named because it is used when traveling, especially abroad or where bank checks or credit or debit cards may not be accepted. It functions much like cash but is protected against loss and theft. A traveler's check is drawn on a bank and is payable on demand to the payee. A traveler's check does not require the holder to present it to the drawee bank for payment.

ELECTRONIC CHECK PROCESSING

Technological advances are increasingly moving the United States toward a checkless society. However, while paper checks remain common, their physical collection and clearing process may soon become obsolete. In fact, nearly all checks are now cleared electronically.

This transformation in check processing has occurred because, in 2004, a new negotiable instrument was created to help overcome the obstacles to fully electronic check processing. The Check Clearing for the 21st Century Act—commonly known as "Check 21"—created the **substitute check** (see exhibit 4.4, next page).

substitute check—A paper reproduction of the original check drawn from an electronic file that contains an image of the front and back. It bears the full MICR line as allowed by industry standards for such checks, conforms in paper stock and dimensions to the standards, and can be processed through automated check systems.

Exhibit 4.4: Recognizing Substitute Checks

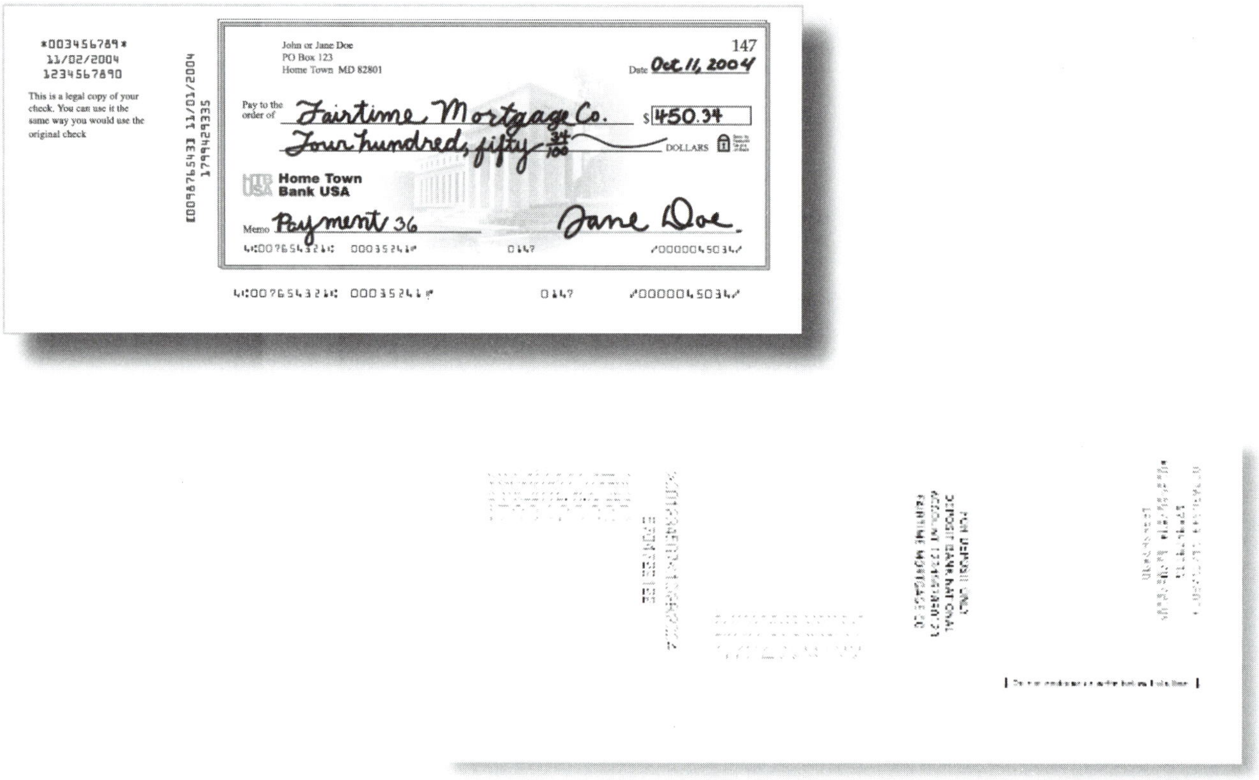

Source: Board of Governors of the Federal Reserve System

Did You Know ...

In 2003, before Check 21 was enacted, paper checks were processed by the Federal Reserve Banks at 45 locations. As a result of Check 21, paper checks are now processed at only one location in Cleveland, Ohio.

Source: Federal Reserve Bank of New York

A substitute check is a special paper copy of the front and back of an original check that is the legal equivalent of the original. Previously, to collect a check electronically, every bank in the collection process had to agree to do so. Otherwise, the original paper check had to be presented to the bank on which it was drawn. This changed after Check 21. The law allows banks that wish to process checks electronically to do so provided that, in the process of collecting checks, if a bank insists on receiving a paper check, that bank is provided with a substitute check created from the electronic image file.

A substitute check is the legal equivalent of its original for all purposes, provided the check:

- Contains an image of the front and back
- Conforms to industry standards, including MICR (with some exceptions) and physical characteristics of a check
- Is suitable for automated processing
- Accurately represents all information on the original check
- Bears the following legend: "This is a legal copy of your check. You can use it the same way you would use the original check."

- Includes all endorsements
- Includes identification of the party creating it

Using the Check 21 process, a bank converts the paper check into an electronic file (see exhibit 4.5). The bank that converts the check into an electronic file is the **truncating** bank. The electronic file, rather than the physical check, is transferred through the Federal Reserve System. The original paper check is usually destroyed by the truncating bank.

truncation—The process of removing the physical paper check from the processing flow.

If a bank somewhere along the processing chain does not exchange checks electronically, or if a customer wants a copy of the check, the electronic file can be converted back into a paper item at any point. That paper item is the substitute check, and it is the legal equivalent of the original paper check. It can be processed through high-speed check processing equipment and is acceptable for all legal purposes.

Check imaging fosters innovation in the check clearing system without mandating that checks be received in electronic form. Creating a substitute check makes it possible for banks to truncate checks at any point in the collection process, regardless of state laws or agreements that may otherwise require delivery of the original paper check. Banks do not have to truncate checks for their own customers, but they must accept substitute checks from banks that do truncate. When customers receive a substitute check in their monthly statement or when they request a copy of a check, they also must accept a substitute check as the legal equivalent of the original check.

Exhibit 4.5: Check 21 Conversion Process

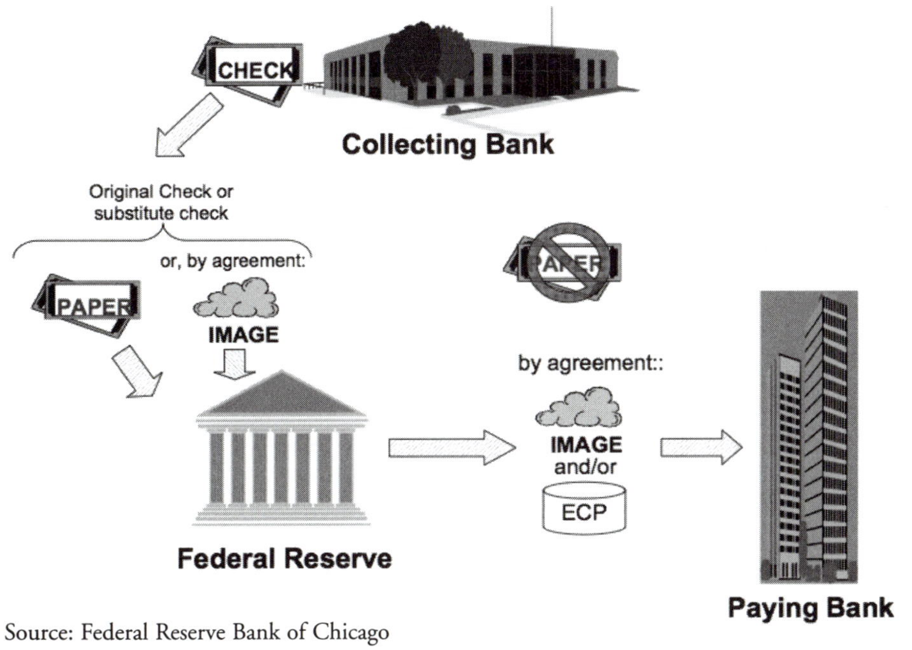

Source: Federal Reserve Bank of Chicago

Did You Know ...

Most checks continued to be deposited in paper form, but the number of checks deposited as electronic images is steadily increasing. About 17 percent of checks are now deposited as electronic images, compared with 13 percent in 2009.

Source: 2013 Federal Reserve Payments Study

THE CHECK PAYMENT PROCESS

The payment process starts when a check is transferred from one person or company (the drawer) to another person or company (the payee) (see exhibit 4.6). The drawer authorizes the transfer by signing the check, usually in the lower right corner. Presentation of the check to a bank for payment (drawee) starts a collection process that results in the transfer of money from the drawer to payee. During this process, the party that holds the check at any given point has legal protections as the holder in due course.

The Drawer

The first stage in the check payment process begins when the drawer writes a check on his or her account payable to bearer, cash, or an identifiable person.

Checks Payable to an Identifiable Person

Negotiation of a check payable to an identifiable person requires endorsement by that person and delivery or transfer of the check. An identifiable person is an actual person or a legal entity, such as a corporation.

Exhibit 4.6: Check Payment Process

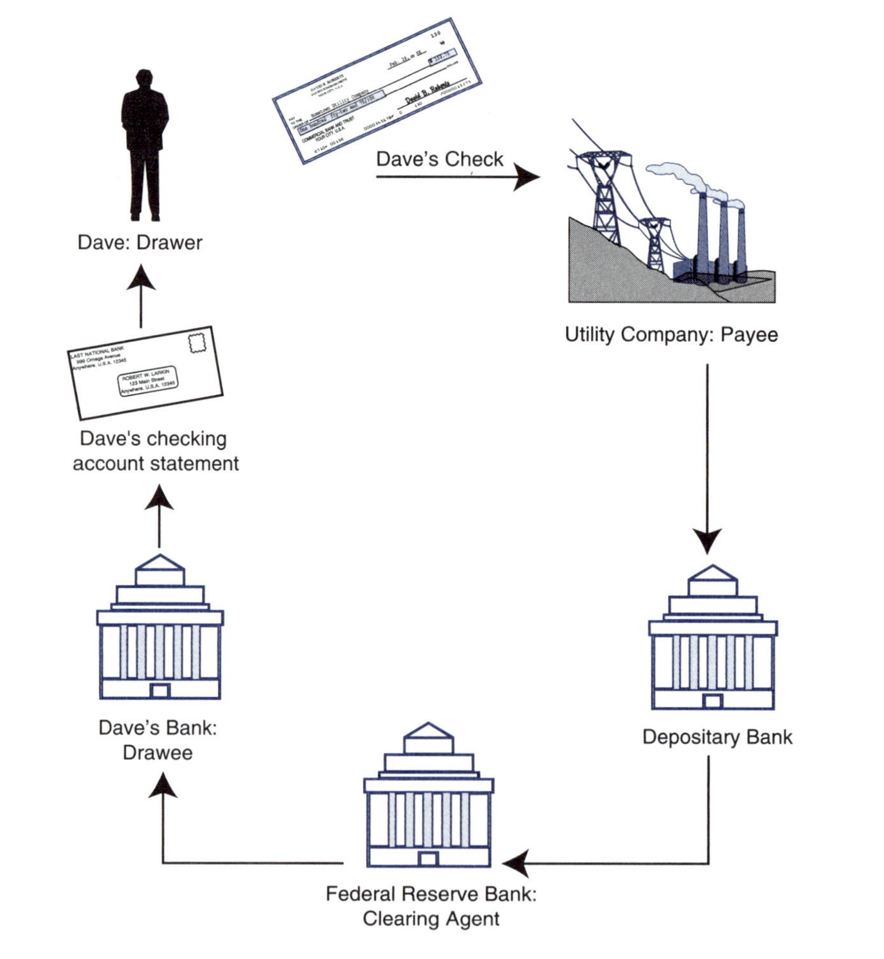

The check payment process begins when a check is written by the customer (drawer) on his or her bank account and ends when the check amount is debited from the customer's account and recorded in the account statement.

If the endorsement of the payee is forged, the negotiation is invalid. A bank that takes a check with a forged endorsement is subject to a claim directly from the payee or from the bank the check is drawn on (drawee).

Checks Payable as "And" or "Or"

A check payable to joint payees (Bill and Betty) requires the endorsement of both payees. If one payee did not endorse the check and did not benefit from the proceeds, he or she may file a claim against the bank or the other payee. However, if the check is payable to one or the other payee (Bill or Betty), either can negotiate the check.

Checks Payable to Bearer

Instead of being made payable to an identifiable person, checks can be made payable to "cash" or "bearer." Negotiation is by delivery alone and does not require an endorsement. Thus, any person in possession of an instrument payable to bearer is the rightful holder of the instrument.

If the bearer takes the check to a teller to obtain cash, most banks would require the check to be endorsed so as to identify the person to whom the cash was given. If the endorsed check is dishonored, the endorser, after being given timely notice, is obligated to take the check back.

The Payee

After the drawer writes the check, the next step is for the payee to accept it. The payee can transfer the check to another person, convert it to cash, or deposit it to an account in a **depositary bank**. What the payee intends to do with it depends on how the check is endorsed. The payee endorsement area is confined to the top inch and a half of the back of the check. The principal types of endorsements are blank, special, and restrictive.

depositary bank—The bank in which a check is first deposited. The bank also may be the drawee if the check is drawn on, payable at, or payable through the bank.

- A *blank endorsement* (or an endorsement in blank), the most common endorsement, is the signature of the payee. A check endorsed in blank becomes a bearer instrument that may be negotiated without another endorsement and may be used for any purpose.

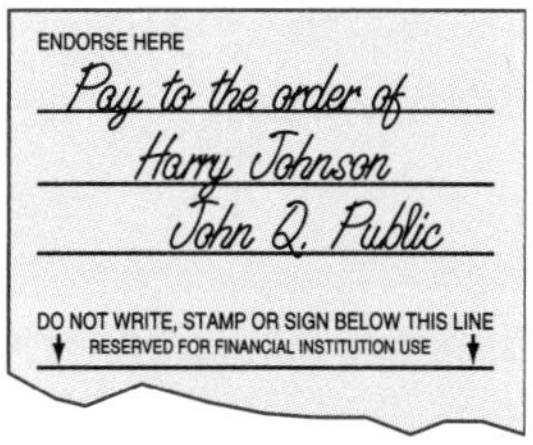

- A *special endorsement* names another designated person. The endorsement may state "Pay to the order of," and then the payee signs under that statement. Only the designated person can negotiate the check. A special endorsement may be used when the payee is mailing the check to another person.

- With a *restrictive endorsement*, the payee or other holder restricts the purpose for which a check may be used. The most common restrictive endorsement, used for depositing an item to an account, is "For Deposit Only." Any use other than for deposit to an account is prohibited.

The endorser may cancel any endorsement, including a restrictive endorsement, by deleting it or scratching through it and endorsing the check in another manner. The deletion, however, should bear the payee's or holder's initials.

Holder in Due Course

holder—A person who is in possession of a negotiable instrument and who is entitled to receive payment of the instrument.

on-us check—A check deposited or otherwise negotiated at the bank on which it is drawn.

The person in possession of a check is the **holder**. As checks proceed through the check processing system, they come into the possession of businesses, banks, and Federal Reserve Banks. Individuals, businesses, and banks can accept a check as a negotiable instrument without being liable for any claims and defenses if they possess the check as a holder in due course.

A holder becomes a holder in due course by showing that, at the time the check was transferred, the holder paid value for it, took it in good faith, and had no notice of any defenses against payment or other claims to the check.

- *For value* means something of value has been given in exchange for the check. A teller giving cash to a customer for a check has given something of value.
- *Good faith* means that the holder has acted honestly and fairly when accepting the check and believed the check was not legally defective in any way.
- *Without notice* means the holder takes the check without notice of any defect, defense, or claim against the payment of the check. A clear defect, such as lack of a signature or an altered amount, is considered notice. A stolen check is an example of a check that has a defense against payment.

Holder in Due Course
One who holds a negotiable instrument, such as a check, and who takes the instrument:
- For value
- In good faith
- Without notice that it is overdue or dishonored
- Without knowledge that it has unauthorized signature or is altered
- Without knowledge of claims to the instrument
- Without knowledge of defense against payment

Bank-Provided Endorsement

Under Article 4 of the UCC, the bank automatically becomes a holder of an unendorsed instrument when it is accepted for deposit to the account of the payee or other holder or is cashed for the payee or holder. The bank becomes the holder of the instrument for all purposes, having become a holder in due course.

A bank can still supply a missing endorsement. If a customer failed to endorse an item and the item itself did not require the payee's personal endorsement, the bank could endorse it, stating "For deposit to the account of the within named payee." This endorsement usually is stamped on the item at the time it is deposited. The bank typically supplies the endorsement when items are received for deposit through the night depository, the mail, or an automated teller machine.

The Drawee

Continuing with the check payment process, after the depositary bank accepts the endorsed check, it is cleared for presentment to the drawee. The drawee is the bank that holds the drawer's account and pays the check.

Most people think a check is being cashed when it is presented to a teller. However, there are important differences between paying and cashing a check.

A bank is obligated to its own customers to pay a check drawn on it that is properly payable. When a person presents an **on-us** check to a teller, it is deposited in an account or paid over the counter. In either case, the teller is making final payment on the check. However, if it is paid or accepted by mistake, the check is deemed not to have been paid or accepted in spite of final payment.

Because making final payment on an on-us check is a risk for the bank, it is important that the teller examine the check and the account on which the check is drawn to ensure that:

- The person presenting the item is properly identified
- There are no **stop payments** on the check or holds on the account
- Sufficient funds are available in the account to cover the check
- It is not post-dated—that is, dated for payment at some future time

To inspect a check for these attributes, a teller can perform both visual and nonvisual tests (see exhibit 4.7).

Online systems now allow tellers to view an image of the bank's record of the customer's signature to compare it to the actual signature on the check. This helps reduce the incidence of forged signatures. To ensure that the funds are available when the posting process is completed later that day, many banks also place a teller's hold on the funds when the check is paid.

A bank may pay a check on a customer's account only if the check is properly payable. Under UCC Article 4, a check is properly payable if it is authorized by the customer and is in accordance with any agreement between the customer and the bank.

stop payment—An order by a depositor to the bank (the drawee) to not pay a previously issued check or item.

wrongful dishonor—Failure of the drawee to pay a properly payable check.

Wrongful Dishonor

A bank is required to honor a check that is properly payable. If it fails to do so, the bank could be liable to the customer for **wrongful dishonor** of the check. A bank that wrongly dishonors a check could be liable to the payee for both the amount of the check and any consequential damages incurred as a result of failing to pay the check. Unless the bank has an overdraft agreement with a drawer to pay a check that results in a negative balance in the account, it is not liable when it dishonors a check that would overdraw the account.

A bank is liable for wrongful dishonor if it:

- Fails to pay an item drawn on sufficient collected funds
- Pays a check that is subject to a stop payment order and then dishonors other checks that would otherwise have been paid

Situation

Ben Watson presents a Pebble Bank teller a check for $3,000 that, in addition to stating "payable to the order of XYZ Company," also notes that the drawer "promises to protect the asset securing the payment." Although the additional wording is not typical for checks received for payment, the teller pays it. The additional wording is acceptable under UCC Article 3.

Exhibit 4.7: Visual and Nonvisual Tests for Inspecting a Check

Nonvisual Elements

- Has a stop payment order been placed on the check?
- Has a hold been placed on the account?
- Is there sufficient available balance to cover the check?
- Is the account balance available to the drawer?

Visual Elements

- Is the item an actual check drawn on the bank?
- Is the signature genuine and authorized?
- Has the check been altered?
- Is the check properly dated?
- Is the check properly endorsed?

Paying Versus Cashing a Check

- *Paying a check*: giving cash in exchange for an on-us check
- *Cashing a check*: giving cash for a check drawn on another bank

- Places a hold order on the wrong account pursuant to an attachment order or Internal Revenue Service levy and then dishonors checks presented for payment
- Mistakenly applies funds against an obligation not owed by the depositor, leading to the dishonor of checks
- Closes its depositor's account without giving reasonable notice of the closure and dishonors checks that were outstanding before the account was closed

Cashing Checks

A teller cashes a check by giving cash in exchange for a check drawn on another bank. Cashing checks presents a greater risk than paying checks. When cashing a check, the teller can verify only whether the check has not been altered and was properly endorsed and dated. For example, if a check is stale—that is, a check, other than a certified check, that is presented for payment more than six months after its date—a bank is not required to honor the check, although it can choose to honor the stale dated check (as long as the bank does not have reason to suspect that the drawer does not want the check paid).

Although there is additional risk in cashing a check, banks generally do so for at least two reasons. First, the person presenting the check usually has an account with the bank. Second, the drawer may have other relationships with the bank, such as loans.

Clearing Checks

Almost all checks processed today are cleared as electronic check images. For banks, the savings in clearing time and expense are enormous because, unlike the clearing process with electronic items, accepting paper checks for payment required that each check be proofed, encoded, captured, sorted, and transported to the bank on which the check was drawn. Today, the manual handling of checks has been almost eliminated. Instead banks process the checks they receive electronically.

As discussed earlier, on-us checks are deposited at and drawn on the same bank. Interbank checks are deposited at and drawn on different banks.

Clearing on-us checks is a direct process of the bank making the appropriate entries on its books by debiting the drawer's account and crediting the depositor's account. In the case of interbank checks, banks have several ways in which they receive payment for checks deposited with them (see exhibit 4.8):

- Present the paper checks or transmit images of the checks directly to the drawee
- Forward the paper checks or images of the checks to a correspondent bank for collection
- Exchange checks, in paper or electronic form, with a group of banks participating in a clearinghouse arrangement
- Forward the paper checks or images of the checks to a Federal Reserve Bank for collection

Did You Know ...

In 2009, interbank checks, which are checks that are deposited at and drawn on different depository institutions, accounted for about 74 percent of the checks paid that year. The remaining 26 percent of checks were on-us checks, which are deposited at and drawn on the same depository institution.

Source: Federal Reserve Bank of New York

Exhibit 4.8: Check Clearing Process

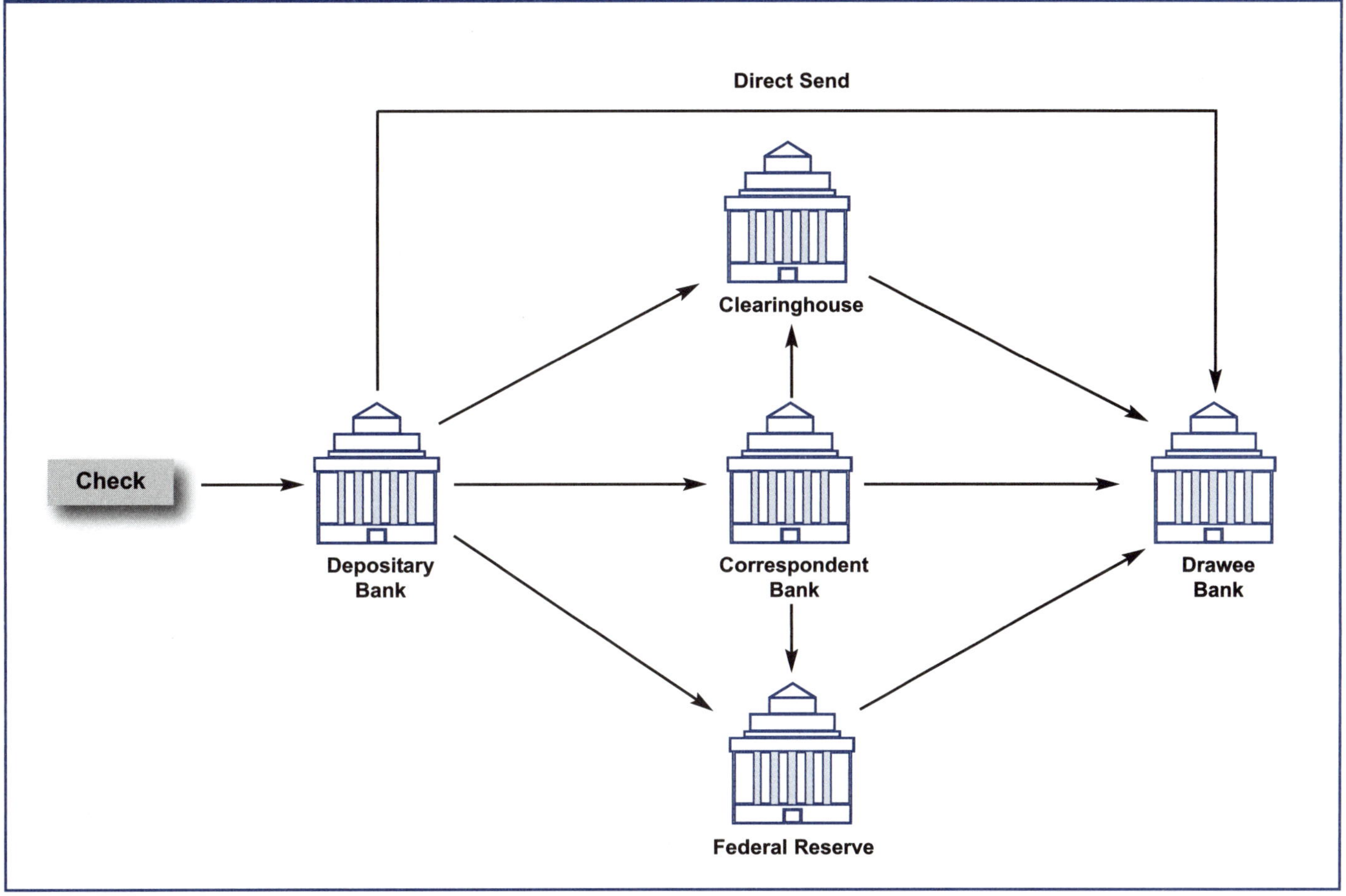

Smaller banks usually either deposit checks for clearing with a Federal Reserve Bank or with a correspondent bank. Larger banks deposit exclusively with a Federal Reserve Bank or use a combination of methods to clear checks.

Check deposits are received as either bundles of paper checks called **cash letters** or, more commonly, computer files of imaged checks called image cash letters. When cash letters or image cash letters are deposited, the Federal Reserve account of the depositing bank or its correspondent bank is credited. The Reserve Banks debit the Federal Reserve account of the drawee bank or its correspondent bank when the checks drawn on the drawee bank are presented to that bank for payment. A drawee bank may choose to receive checks drawn on it in image files or in paper form. If the drawee bank elects to receive check presentments in paper form, it will most likely receive substitute checks. The drawee bank then charges the accounts of the customers who wrote the checks in accordance with its account agreement.

cash letter—An interbank electronic or paper transmittal form, resembling a deposit slip, used to accompany cash items sent from one bank to another.

Posting Checks

Posting is the process of adding deposits to an account balance and subtracting checks and other withdrawals from that balance. Usually, deposits and other credits are posted first, then debits are posted.

Checks rejected from the normal posting process require special handling. These are commonly referred to as exception items. Checks may require special

nonsufficient funds— An expression indicating that a check or item drawn against an account exceeds the amount of funds available in the account. Commonly called an "NSF" or overdraft.

hold—A restriction on the payment of all or any part of the balance in an account.

handling for a number of reasons: **nonsufficient funds** (NSF), an uncollected balance so that there are insufficient funds, a stop payment order on the check, or a **hold** placed on the account.

Each exception item requires an action. If a check is to be returned to the depositary bank, it is either charged back (debited) to the customer's account, or if it was returned for NSF, it is redeposited and sent back through the system for payment.

A bank might place a hold on a customer account for many reasons. If the account is used as collateral for a loan made by the bank to the customer or the bank has received a court order to freeze the funds, the bank may decide to place a hold on the account. A bank may also place a hold on a specific check deposit because, for example, it has reason to doubt whether the check will be collectible, the check is for a large dollar amount, or the customer has a history of repeatedly overdrawing the account.

Whatever the reason, checks drawn on an account on which a hold is placed must be rejected, examined, paid, or returned. If a bank places a hold with the intention of not honoring checks drawn on specific deposits, the bank must meet the requirements of Federal Reserve Regulation CC, Availability of Funds and Collection of Checks, which implements the Expedited Funds Availability Act.

By The Numbers

Reconciling a Bank Statement

Statement Balance + Deposits - Checks = Checkbook Balance

Today is April 5th, and your checkbook shows an account balance of $254.75. You've just received your bank statement dated March 31 that shows an account balance of $360.90. On April 2nd, you made a deposit for $200.00 and wrote two checks in the amounts of $125.00 and $181.15. Does your bank statement balance reconcile with your checkbook balance?

Statement Balance 3/31	**$360.90**
ADD Deposit 4/2	**+ $200.00**
SUBTRACT checks 4/2	**-$125.00**
	-$181.15
TOTAL	**$254.75**

Yes, your bank statement and checkbook balances reconcile.

Statement Rendering

When a customer receives a statement in the mail or online listing the previous month's checking account deposits and debits, the check payments process has come full circle.

An account is assigned a statement cycle date—the date on which the statement is produced. On the statement, the bank prints the date each check was paid, the amount, and the check number. Customers can use this information to reconcile their account with their own records.

CHECK FRAUD

Although fewer checks are used for payments today, check fraud remains a major cause of financial loss for banks. One of the reasons is that, when check fraud occurs, the losses can be great. The average value of a check written today exceeds $1,000. Payments by other means are typically in smaller amounts. Criminals continue to find novel ways to defraud their victims. The broad term "check fraud" encompasses a variety of schemes, including counterfeiting and alteration, closed account fraud, and check kiting.

Check Counterfeiting and Alteration

Counterfeit checks are bogus checks drawn on valid accounts or valid checks that are presented with fraudulent identification. Banks are expected to detect counterfeit checks and are responsible for paying checks only as originally drawn. Passing a counterfeit check often begins with the counterfeiter stealing a blank check, retrieving a discarded canceled check, or removing a check used to pay a bill from a mailbox. A personal computer, software, scanner, laser printer, or high-resolution photocopier may be used to counterfeit checks as well.

Checks can be **altered** by removing the payee's name or dollar amount but leaving the authorized signature. Information on the check can be erased through check washing—that is, removing details from a check with a solvent so that the payee's name, dollar amount, check serial number, or date can be changed, but the authorized signature is kept.

altered check—A check on which a material change, such as the dollar amount, has been made.

Closed Account Fraud

Closed account fraud involves one or more checks being written against an account that is closed. This scam is also known as paperhanging. In a closed account fraud scheme, checks are not physically altered, but the account information is no longer valid. This type of fraud generally relies on the float time involved in interbank transactions. For example, a check is deposited into a new account at a different bank through one or more ATMs operated by other banks. The float time between the ATM deposits and the checks drawn on the closed accounts reaching the issuing bank for payment allows the criminal to withdraw funds from the new account.

Did You Know ...

In July 2012, the chief executive of a major foods product company and his co-conspirators were charged by the U.S. Department of Justice with fraudulently inflating their company's earnings through an international check kiting scheme in which they kited approximately $750 million worth of checks not backed by sufficient funds through various banks in the United States and Canada. The victimized bank lost approximately $26 million that the defendant and his co-conspirators had withdrawn before the bank discovered the scheme.

Source: U.S. Department of Justice

Check Kiting

Check kiting begins with a criminal opening several checking accounts in different banks. The criminal then writes checks to transfer funds from one account to another. Transfers occur so frequently that actual funds do not exist in a given account when a check is written. At this point, the customer usually disappears with more money than originally deposited. By using float time, check kiters create fraudulent balances.

Bank Efforts to Combat Check Fraud

Vigilant tellers and other bank employees are one of the best defenses in the war against check fraud. Knowing some of the indicators of check fraud helps bank employees thwart fraudulent transactions. To identify a bogus check, bank employees inspect the items for the following:

- Check lacks perforations, is stained or discolored, or has an odd "feel." Most check paper has the same weight and texture.
- Check number is missing, does not change, is out of sequence with already paid checks, or is low (between 100 and 500). Ninety percent of returned checks have low check numbers. Low check numbers indicate a recently opened account and, therefore, a possibly more risky check.
- Additions to the check are handwritten.

- Customer's address or bank's address is missing.
- There is evidence of erasures or alterations.
- MICR numbers are missing or are shiny. Fraudulent checks often substitute regular toner or ink for magnetic ink.
- MICR encoding does not match the check number, the bank district, or the routing symbol in the upper right-hand corner of the check.
- Word "VOID" appears across the check.
- Check lacks an authorized signature.

Vigilance can also prevent closed account fraud. Banks should place special holds on checks drawn on accounts that have been inactive for some time and advise customers to destroy checks from closed accounts and notify the bank when they intend to close an account.

Technology and software are also helping banks stem losses from check fraud. Check 21 has reduced float time, making it more difficult for check kiters to exploit processing delays. For example, check imaging deters check kiting because check clearing and settlement do not require a time-consuming physical inspection before payment. The reduction or absence of physical checks from the payment system reduces opportunities for check fraud as well.

positive pay—A bank service that pays a business's checks only if they match the check data on an electronic list of issued checks that the business sends to the bank.

Software, such as that used to support **positive pay**, is helping tellers detect duplicate check numbers and numbers that appear out of sequence and to compare signatures to detect fraud.

LAWS AND REGULATIONS

In addition to Articles 3 and 4 of the UCC (discussed earlier in this chapter), several laws and regulations govern the use of paper and electronic checks. Federal bank regulators supervise and enforce these laws and regulations.

Collection of Checks and Funds Transfers

Collection of Checks and Funds Transfers, Regulation J, covers check collection and returns, cash and noncash items processed through Federal Reserve Banks, and funds transferred through Fedwire. Its purpose is to provide holders in due course with the rules for collecting and returning items and settling balances.

Expedited Funds Availability Act

Regulation CC implements the Expedited Funds Availability Act that requires depository institutions to make funds deposited into transaction accounts available for withdrawal on a set schedule. The availability of the deposited items is based on the type of check (government, cashier's, or personal). Certain types of deposits, such as cashier's checks deposited into an account of the payee in person and the first $200 of any check deposited, must be given next-day availability.

Banks may hold funds beyond the general funds availability schedule under certain safeguard exceptions, including funds in excess of $5,000 and funds from checks the bank has reasonable cause to believe are uncollectible. If a bank invokes an exception, it must notify the customer in writing.

Regulation CC requires the depositary bank to ensure that its endorsement is in the proper location on the check; that the customer does not interfere with the area designated for the depositary's endorsement; and that the depositary accepts a returned check, even if delayed, because of improper placement of the endorsement or a customer obscured the endorsement.

Regulation CC was amended to include rules for Check 21. These rules require banks to:

- Educate customers about substitute checks and provide special customer notices in certain situations
- Provide warranties and indemnities to protect parties handling substitute checks
- Establish a process by which customers may receive an expedited credit of amounts paid if they believe a substitute check they received was incorrectly charged to their account

Banker Profile

Tameka Smith is a young married mother with two elementary school-aged children. She wants to earn a living, but she also wants to be available to care for her children. Her teller job at the local community bank allows her to achieve both objectives. She works 30 hours per week during the school year, and her bank hires college-age floating tellers so that Tameka and other parents can take time off during the summer to be with their children.

In addition to being an excellent teller, winning a customer service award, and participating in the national Teach Children to Save program for her children and others, Tameka is taking professional development courses like Principles of Banking from the ABA to better understand her job, the bank, and the banking industry.

SUMMARY

- Cash is the one type of payment everyone still uses today. Coins are minted by the U.S. Mint, and currency is printed by the U.S. Bureau of Engraving. Coin is returned to the U.S. Mint facility in Philadelphia, Pennsylvania, for disposition. The Federal Reserve Banks also collect and destroy damaged currency as a service to the U.S. Treasury.
- A check is a negotiable instrument involving three parties: the person writing the check (drawer), the person to whom the check is written (payee), and the bank that holds the checking account (drawee). Uniform Commercial Code (UCC) Article 3, Negotiable Instruments, and Article 4, Bank Deposits and Collections, establish the legal requirements for checks as negotiable instruments. Negotiable instruments are payable to the bearer or to order, contain an unconditional promise to pay a fixed amount of money on demand or at a definite time, and are written and signed by the drawer.
- Besides personal and business checks, banks provide cashier's checks, teller's checks, certified checks, money orders, and traveler's checks.
- Electronic processing of checks came to fruition with the Check Clearing for the 21st Century Act (Check 21). Check 21 created the substitute check. Banks in the clearing and payment chain can truncate the paper check by converting it into an electronic image file for transfer. If necessary, the electronic version of the check can be reconverted back into a paper substitute check. The substitute check is the legal equivalent of the original paper check. Because of Check 21, banks have switched to full electronic check processing.
- The check payment process begins when a drawer writes a check on his or her account at a bank. The person who takes possession of a check is the holder. After the check is written, the next step in the check payment process is for the payee

to accept the check. Individuals, businesses, and banks can accept checks without liability for claims and defenses if they are a holder in due course. What the payee intends to do with the check depends on whether the endorsement is blank, special, or restrictive.

- The endorsed check is then accepted by a depositary bank, which also endorses it. A bank is required to honor a check that is properly payable. Failing to do so could make the bank liable to the customer for wrongful dishonor. A bank will pay an on-us check and may cash a check drawn on another bank, which carries more risk.
- Once a check is accepted by the depositary bank for cash, payment, or deposit, it is processed for collection. Paper checks, bundled into cash letters, and imaged checks, bundled into image cash letters, are cleared through the selected clearing arrangement (direct presentment, correspondent bank, clearing house, or Federal Reserve Bank).
- After clearing, checks are posted to customer accounts, either adding deposits to an account balance or subtracting checks and other withdrawals from that balance. Checks may be rejected for posting for many reasons, such as nonsufficient funds in a checking account, and require special handling. The final step in check processing is rendering statements for customers showing the previous month's checking account deposits and debits.
- Check fraud is a major cause of financial loss for banks. It encompasses a variety of schemes, including counterfeiting, closed account fraud, and check kiting.
- In addition to UCC Articles 3 and 4, laws and regulations that govern the bank payment process are the Collection of Checks and Funds Transfers, Regulation J; and Expedited Funds Availability Act, Regulation CC.

Learning Check

SELF-CHECK AND REVIEW

1. What law governs the requirements that make a check negotiable? What are those requirements?
2. Who are the parties to a check?
3. What is the difference between a blank endorsement and a special endorsement? Discuss when each is used.
4. What are the differences between a cashier's check, a teller's check, a certified check, and a traveler's check?
5. What are some examples of checks that might be rejected from the normal posting process and require handling as exception items?
6. What is dual custody? Provide an example of when it is used.
7. What are at least three signs of a fraudulent check?

Electronic Banking

5

Learning Objectives

After studying this chapter, you should be able to

- Explain how electronic banking and the electronic funds transfer systems have evolved
- Describe processes for transferring funds electronically
- Describe electronic banking services commonly used by consumers
- Identify electronic banking services used by businesses
- Explain provisions of the laws and regulations that affect electronic banking services

Introduction

Chapter 1 traced the history of U.S. banking back to colonial times, nearly 300 years ago. The history of electronic banking is much shorter. In fact, it is so brief that, less than 50 years ago, the simplest way for a bank customer to obtain cash was to visit his or her bank in person. There were no automated teller machines. The machines did not arrive until 1969, and it would be many more years before ATMs were within walking or driving distance of most Americans.

More than 20 years after that, it took the development of the Internet to bring electronic banking to the masses. Once the Internet was introduced in the early 1990s, electronic banking quickly became the preferred method of banking for millions of Americans, especially the younger generations who have no memory of the day when there were no ATMs.

Today, every household that has a computer or any person who carries a smart phone or tablet can check account balances, make deposits, pay bills, find ATMs and branches, or have an online conversation with a personal banker. Electronic banking has forever altered the financial services landscape by enabling banks to improve efficiency and offer the 24/7/365 service customers have come to expect.

Did You Know ...

More than half (51 percent) of smart phone owners used their device for mobile banking in 2013.

Source: Federal Reserve Board, *Consumers and Mobile Financial Services*, March 2014

THE DEVELOPMENT OF ELECTRONIC BANKING

The term "electronic banking" encompasses all the technologies that allow customers to perform banking transactions electronically without visiting a brick-and-mortar institution. Terms commonly used in connection with electronic banking include personal computer (PC) banking, Internet or online banking, virtual banking, home banking, remote banking, telephone banking, and mobile banking. Electronic technology provides many of the services consumers and businesses now take for granted, from electronic fund transfers, including direct deposit, to credit card payments and online bill payments.

The Roots of Electronic Banking

Banks constantly strive to deliver better service. For several centuries, payments had to be made in person or by mail, or delivered on foot, by horse, or by ship. Improvements to transportation—trains, cars, trucks, and planes—helped speed mail delivery. The most significant advances, however, came with the advent of electricity and related wired technology. The telegraph, telex, and telephone allowed transactions to be conducted rapidly across continents and oceans.

With these developments and the continued inventiveness of both science and business, the 20th century brought more improvements to speed the delivery of banking services and bank operations. Today's innovations in check processing build on imaging technology that converts document information into digitized formats that computers can read—technology that was state of the art just a decade or so ago and, in fact, was derived from other technologies also considered amazing in their day.

For example, since the early 1960s, all banks have processed checks by reading the **magnetic ink character recognition** (MICR) symbols printed on the lower edge of checks. The MICR symbols are printed with special ink that is magnetized through an iron oxide compound contained in special MICR toners. The MICR line is read by a bank's reader/sorter machine, which picks up the magnetized ink and activates it in the machine's electromagnetic field. Once the ink is activated, the machine can then read the MICR line on the check, validate the check, and deposit it into, or withdraw it from, a bank account.

New imaging technology takes the check reading process one step farther. The entire image of the check is captured through scanning, stored as an electronic record, and then transmitted for processing. Check imaging now occurs not only at banks but also at commercial operations such as retail stores and business accounting offices.

magnetic ink character recognition (MICR)—Numbers printed in magnetic ink near the bottom of the front of a check to facilitate automated processing. The position and content of the MICR line are governed by industry standards. MICR encoding includes the bank's routing number, the customer's account number, the number of the check, and often the amount of the check.

MICR Line

Trends in Electronic Banking

Having reviewed the past and looked at the present, one might naturally ask what lies ahead for electronic banking. From all indications, it will grow increasingly popular with banking customers, and banks will continue to find ways to tap its potential. For example, consumers using electronic bill payment services report significantly greater satisfaction with their banks compared to customers who do not use this service. Consumers appreciate the convenience, due-date reminders, assured on-time payments, and environmental benefits. They are also more likely to recommend their bank's online bill payment services to family members and friends and are less likely to switch providers.

These rising levels of satisfaction are encouraging banks to deliver better services, often by blending personal service with the speed and convenience of electronic banking.

Virtual Banks and Virtual Currency

Almost all banks have websites as well as brick-and-mortar branches, although some banks, known as virtual banks, have only websites and do business solely on the Internet. The success of Internet banking services beginning in the 1990s led to the development of virtual banks. The first fully operational virtual bank began operations in 1995. Virtual banks are also known by other terms, including direct banks, cyber banks, and Internet banks (as distinct from Internet or online banking, which is banking done through the Internet regardless of the type of bank).

Did You Know ...

In the late 1950s, the Stanford Research Institute came up with the idea of imprinting an MICR line on every check as a way to provide a uniform standard for tracking checks. Until then, individual banks often had their own tracking system, which could create confusion when a check from one bank was deposited into an account at another bank. The American Bankers Association worked with Stanford Research Institute on the adoption of MICR technology, helping make it the industry standard.

Sample List of Internet-Only Banks

- Ally Bank, www.ally.com
- Bank of Internet USA, www.bankofinternet.com
- First Internet Bank, www.firstib.com
- Simple Bank, www.simple.com
- VirtualBank, www.virtualbank.com

Customers can connect to virtual banks at any time via any device that offers an Internet connection. Virtual banks only operate online; they have no physical branches. Customers make deposits primarily through direct deposit and automatic transfers from accounts at other financial institutions. Withdrawals are made online, by telephone transfer, or by card.

Because virtual banks do not have the traditional banking infrastructure of physical branches, their operating expenses are lower. These savings can be passed on to the customer in the form of savings accounts with higher interest rates or loans with lower interest rates, for example. On the other hand, customers of virtual banks do not enjoy some of the conveniences of banks with branches. There is no option to visit a bank's branch office to make a deposit or to speak in person with a bank employee.

For both traditional and virtual banks, a major challenge is how to provide excellent personalized services along with convenience. Although customers are demanding new ways to access products and services, they also expect seamless delivery of, and access to, a bank's products and services—and consistent service across all delivery platforms. In addition, like all banks, virtual banks must comply with the banking laws and regulations, including consumer financial protections.

Currency may also be virtual. Just as virtual banks have no physical brick-and-mortar presence, virtual currency is intangible—while it functions like currency as a medium of exchange, it exists only in the electronic world. One example is Bitcoin, a peer-to-peer payment system in which bitcoins are the currency used to purchase goods and services or exchanged for other currencies. Participants purchase and exchange bitcoins using software on a personal computer, mobile device, or web application. Transactions among participants are facilitated by Bitcoin exchanges, which rely on technology and networks to record and verify payments. As financial intermediaries, Bitcoin exchanges function like banks, with the critical difference being that bitcoins, like other virtual currency, are not legal tender, as are coins and Federal Reserve notes. Because virtual currency is not recognized by the U.S. government or any other jurisdiction, users do not have the same legal protections and may be subject to losses. In one recent case, computer hackers are alleged to have stolen more than $400 million in bitcoins, causing the bankruptcy of a Bitcoin exchange.

Mobile Banking

Mobile banking is banking done through the Internet with a wireless device, such as a **smart phone** or **tablet**, instead of a personal computer. Although relatively new, mobile banking is rapidly developing as an avenue for performing financial transactions. Mobile banking is especially popular with younger customers, ensuring that banks will continue to focus their efforts on developing and expanding this service delivery channel. According to a March 2014 survey report by the Federal Reserve Board on consumer use of mobile financial services, nearly 40 percent of those age 29 and younger used mobile banking in 2013, compared to about 34 percent of those ages 30–44, 21 percent of those ages 45–59, and 7 percent of those age 60 and older. Mobile banking is clearly the wave of the future.

smart phone—A mobile phone enabled to access the Internet.

tablet—Handheld computer devices, with screens typically larger than smart phones but smaller than laptop computers, and using a touchscreen rather than a keyboard and mouse.

With mobile banking, a connection between the customer and the bank can be made in several ways. One way is for the customer to use a smart phone to connect to the bank's web server. Alternatively, the customer may be given a special access telephone number to dial, with the bank acting as the Internet service provider. Once connected, the customer enters a request using the keypad on his or her mobile device.

More recently, banking by smart phone is being offered via text messaging (also called short messaging service or SMS). Text-based mobile banking, which is growing in popularity compared to the older, browser-based method, allows a bank customer to request and receive account information by sending and receiving text messages on a mobile phone. For example, to request an account balance, the user might text "BAL" and send the message to his or her bank.

Mobile apps, using the Android platform or the iPhone or iPad, are also rapidly growing in popularity. This type of mobile banking is distinct from either browser-based or text messaging, although text messaging can be combined with either type.

Mobile banking provides many of the services online banking provides, such as viewing account balances or transferring money between accounts. Banking via mobile devices may also offer such interactive benefits as information notification and alerts prompting the customer to view balances, see whether checks have cleared, and receive email messages about deposits and other changes to accounts or payments due.

Mobile banking presents additional security and privacy issues, however. Smart phones and tablets are small and easily lost or stolen, making it even more important that protective measures, such as access codes and passwords, be used to access account information or perform transactions.

Did You Know ...

Nearly 70 percent of all mobile banking users checked their account balances before making a large purchase in 2013, and half of them decided not to purchase an item as a result of seeing their account balance or credit limit.

Source: Federal Reserve Board, *Consumers and Mobile Financial Services*, March 2014

PROCESSING ELECTRONIC TRANSACTIONS

Widespread usage of the Internet and the continued development of computer networks and devices have accelerated the growth of electronic banking. Processing financial transactions requires sophisticated electronic banking systems that enable funds to be moved quickly and securely.

EFT AND ACH

Electronic fund transfer (EFT) systems and services are indispensable for modern banking. An EFT is any transfer of funds initiated through an electronic terminal, telephone, or computer that instructs a financial institution to either credit or debit a customer's account.

electronic fund transfer (EFT)—A transfer of money from one bank account to another that is initiated through an electronic terminal, telephone, computer, or magnetic tape.

Banks use EFTs to borrow funds from each other, invest daily surplus funds, settle clearing balances in the check collection process, and provide instantaneous transfer services for depositors. Examples of EFT consumer services include automated teller machine (ATM) transfers, direct fund deposits or withdrawals, and transfers initiated by telephone, point-of-sale (POS) terminals, debit cards, and electronic check transactions.

Many of these services are provided by the Automated Clearing House (ACH) network, which is responsible for processing such services as online bill pay, direct

Types of ACH Payments

- Direct deposit of payroll, Social Security, and other government benefits, and tax refunds
- Direct payment of consumer bills such as mortgages, loans, utility bills, and insurance premiums
- Business-to-business payments
- E-checks
- E-commerce payments
- Federal, state, and local tax payments

Source: NACHA—The Electronic Payments Association

originating depository financial institution (ODFI)—The term adopted by NACHA—The Electronic Payments Association to refer to the bank that receives payment instructions from the originator and then forwards those instructions (entries) to the automated clearing house (ACH) operator.

receiving depository financial institution (RDFI)—The term adopted by NACHA—The Electronic Payments Association to refer to the bank that receives automated clearing house (ACH) entries from the ACH operator and then posts them (either as credits or debits) to the accounts of its depositors, the receivers.

deposit, and direct debiting. ACH has proved to be a viable, faster, and more cost-effective alternative to paper check processing. NACHA—The Electronic Payments Association (formerly the National Automated Clearing House Association) governs the ACH network and is responsible for issuing rules for its use. According to NACHA, the ACH network grew by more than 5 percent between 2012 and 2013. During the fourth quarter of 2013 alone, 4.5 billion transactions representing almost $10 trillion were processed.

Banks, corporations, individuals, and governments use the ACH to make recurring payments, such as payroll deposits, less expensively and more conveniently than by paper checks. Banks process customers' credit and debit information, which they then forward in batches to either a Federal Reserve Bank or the ACH network. Customers use the ACH to authorize payments of insurance premiums, mortgages, loans, and other recurring bills.

The bank originating the ACH transaction is the **originating depository financial institution** (ODFI); the bank receiving the transaction is the **receiving depository financial institution** (RDFI). Once the customer directs the ODFI to originate the transfer (using a preauthorized transfer), the transaction is batched with others and sent to the ACH. The ACH sorts, settles, and sends credits and debits to the RDFI to credit or debit the specified accounts (see exhibit 5.1).

Fedwire, CHIPS, and SWIFT

The two major wholesale EFT systems that banks use to borrow from each other, invest daily surplus funds, settle clearing balances, and give better service to depositors and borrowers are the Fedwire Funds Service and the Clearinghouse Interbank Payments System (CHIPS). The Society for Worldwide Interbank Financial Telecommunication (SWIFT) is an international messaging network used by financial institutions.

Fedwire Funds Service

The Fedwire Funds Service—the Federal Reserve's EFT network—is used for transfers of reserve account balances of depository institutions and U.S. government and federal agency securities, almost all of which are in electronic form only. Fedwire also is used to transfer certain third-party payments—usually those that are large-value and time-critical—to bank customers. Clearing systems, such as CHIPS, also may engage Fedwire for settlement purposes.

Many banks use Fedwire. In 2013, more than 134 million transfers were originated over the Federal Reserve's network at a total value of more than $713 trillion (averaging $5.31 million per transfer). Fedwire funds transfers are processed individually rather than in batches like ACH transfers. Each transaction is processed in seconds.

A related Federal Reserve service is the Fedwire Securities Service, which provides safekeeping, transfer, and settlement services for securities issued by the U.S. Treasury Department, federal agencies, government-sponsored enterprises, and certain international organizations. Federal Reserve Banks act as fiscal agents for these entities.

Exhibit 5.1: Process Flow for Preauthorized Payment

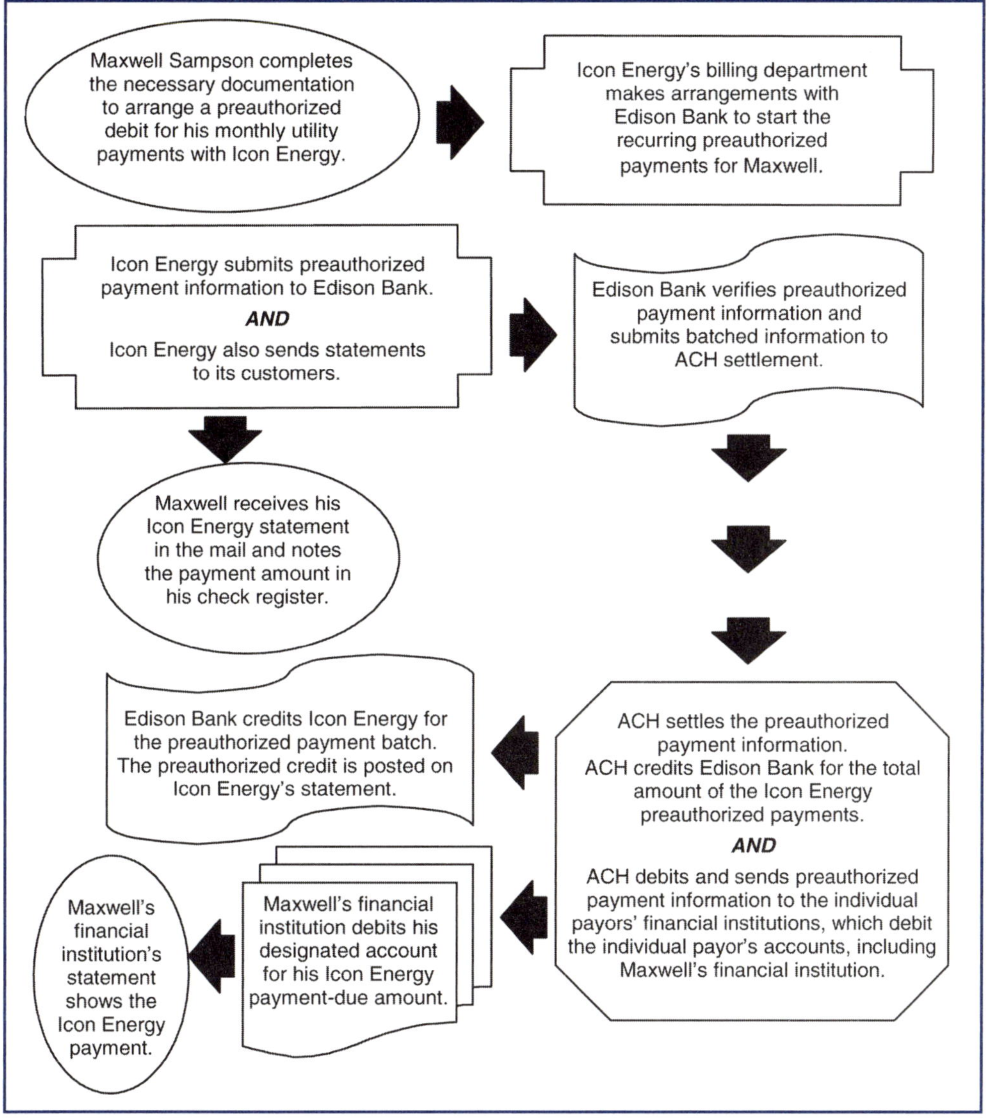

Securities brokers and dealers do not use Fedwire directly; they have accounts at depository institutions that are Fedwire participants.

CHIPS

CHIPS stands for the Clearing House Interbank Payments System. It is a bank-owned system for clearing mostly large-value payments. It is the focal point for payments in the international dollar market, serving 51 of the largest banks in the U.S. and 20 other countries around the world (see exhibit 5.2, next page). In 2013, more than 103 million international interbank dollar transfers were made, totaling nearly $380 trillion, through CHIPS. Payments coming from outside the United States often enter the Fedwire Funds Service and the ACH network through CHIPS, which handles 95 percent of U.S. dollar cross-border payments. Payments processed through CHIPS include large and small payment transactions, U.S. dollar foreign exchange settlements, and other financial settlements, such as loan and interest payments and commercial and off-shore payments.

Situation

Hattie's Pizza Haven has a POS terminal that captures information on a paper check for electronic transmission. Ann presents her check for payment to Hattie, who then swipes it through the check-reader POS terminal. At that point, the payment information is sent to the processor and ACH system. When payment approval is sent back to Hattie's check reader, an authorization slip is printed. Hattie gives Ann the original check, now stamped VOID, and a copy of the authorization slip. All of Hattie's Pizza Haven electronic transactions are stored in the POS terminal. At the end of the day, Hattie presses a button to batch, close, and print all approved transactions. This information is then sent to the processing center, which bundles the various bank payment notifications and transmits them through the ACH payment system. On receiving notification, Ann's bank debits her account for her transaction, and Hattie's bank credits her Pizza Haven account.

U.S. Bank Members of CHIPS

- Bank Leumi USA
- Bank of America, N.A.
- Branch Banking and Trust Company
- Brown Brothers Harriman & Co.
- Citibank, N.A.
- Deutsche Bank Trust Co. Americas
- Fifth Third Bank
- Habib American Bank
- HSBC Bank USA
- Israel Discount Bank of New York
- JPMorgan Chase Bank, N.A.
- Manufacturers and Traders Trust Company
- The Northern Trust Company
- State Street Bank and Trust Company
- The Bank of New York Mellon
- Union Bank, N.A.
- Wells Fargo NY Intl. fka Wachovia
- Wells Fargo Bank, San Francisco

Source: CHIPS

Exhibit 5.2: CHIPS Members' Countries

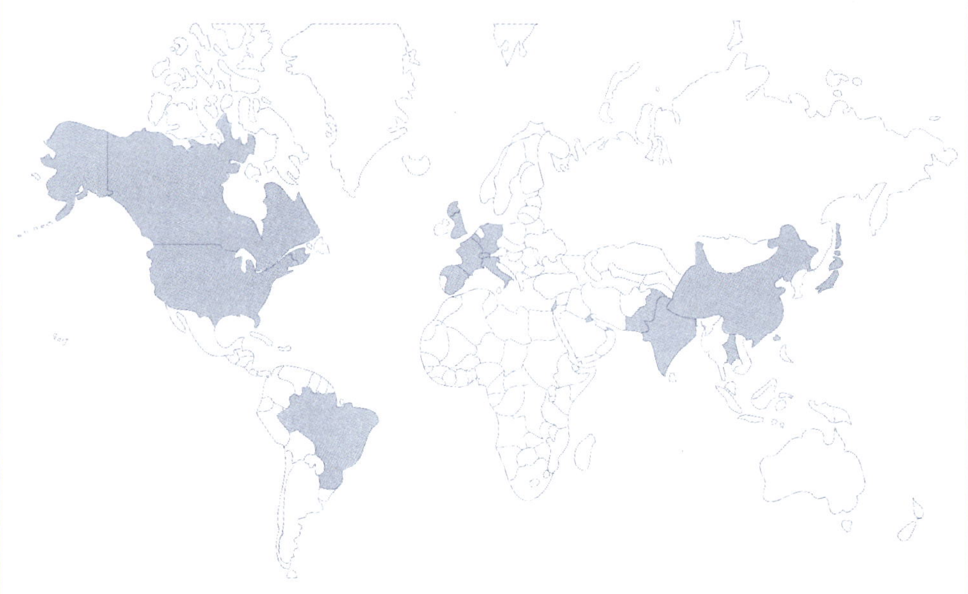

SWIFT

The Society for Worldwide Interbank Financial Telecommunication (SWIFT) runs a worldwide network by which messages concerning financial transactions, such as letters of credit, payments, and securities transactions, are exchanged among banks and other financial institutions. The traffic in messages exceeded 20 million per day in 2012. SWIFT serves more than 10,000 financial institutions in 212 countries. Members include banks, broker-dealers, and investment managers. SWIFT also encompasses corporate and market support systems for payments, securities, and trades.

Other Federal Reserve Services

The U.S. payments system is the largest in the world. Most of the payments underlying those transactions flow between depository institutions, a large number of which maintain accounts with Federal Reserve Banks. The Federal Reserve, therefore, is a crucial intermediary for the clearing and settling of interbank payments.

National Settlement Service

The National Settlement Service, owned and operated by the Federal Reserve Banks, is offered to depository institutions that settle for participants in clearing houses, financial exchanges, and other clearing and settlement groups. Settlement agents acting on behalf of those institutions electronically submit **settlement** files to a Federal Reserve Bank, which then processes them and automatically posts the entries to the Federal Reserve Bank accounts of the depository institutions. Once posted, entries are final and irrevocable. The service improves operational efficiency and controls settlement risk for participants.

settlement—The conclusion of a transaction, including completing all necessary documentation and making the necessary payments; the point at which claims and obligations are satisfied.

Federal Reserve Intraday Credit

In the course of a day, so much electronic money flows in and out of the nation's large banks so quickly that banks sometimes inadvertently pay more than they have on deposit. This usually occurs when there is a mismatch in timing between the settlement of payments owed and the settlement of payments due. These **daylight overdrafts** typically last for only a few minutes, but in a fast-paced technological environment, that is still a considerable risk.

The Federal Reserve Banks extend intraday credit, also known as daylight or daylight overdraft credit, to facilitate settlements and ensure the smooth functioning of the U.S. payments system, subject to a series of rules. The Federal Reserve uses an automated system to measure an institution's intraday account activity and calculate the fee it charges for the intraday credit.

daylight overdraft—(1) A negative balance created in an account when payments made during business hours exceed incoming funds actually received; (2) an overdraft in a bank's reserve account at a Federal Reserve Bank during business hours.

direct deposit—A process by which funds are deposited electronically to bank accounts. Commonly used for payroll and Social Security payments.

ELECTRONIC BANKING AND CONSUMERS

Banking at traditional brick-and-mortar branches no longer is the first choice of banking customers. According to a 2013 survey conducted by the American Bankers Association, when consumers were asked how they preferred to do their banking, almost 40 percent chose the Internet, either using a laptop or PC (see exhibit 5.3). Another 8 percent preferred using a mobile device to access banking services.

For many customers, electronic banking may consist solely of the **direct deposit** of wages, dividends, or benefit payments to their bank accounts and occasionally checking their account balances. There are many other electronic banking services, however, that are becoming more visible and accepted. The main avenue for delivering these services is through bank websites.

Exhibit 5.3: Consumer Banking Preferences

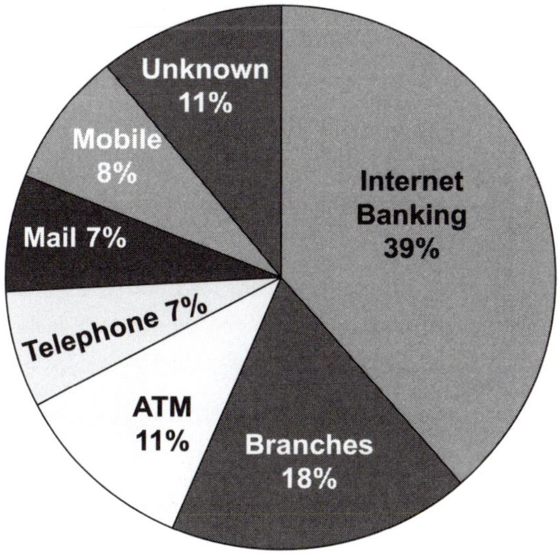

Source: American Bankers Association

Bank Websites

Banks use the Internet to provide all forms of credit, payment, and deposit services to consumers and businesses and to communicate with different audiences for a multitude of purposes. Today, the main portal for accessing electronic banking services is a bank website.

A few bank websites are informational only, used to provide details about branch locations and hours of operation, and perhaps to promote deposit or loan products. Most banks have websites that allow consumers to transact business—for example, to apply for loans, open deposit accounts, check account balances, or transfer funds between accounts. Banks are also using their websites to bundle information and services in useful ways, making their websites into electronic resource centers and virtual malls, with links to other services and vendors from whom they generate referral fees and commissions. A bank's website also may provide virtual personal assistants that can help with shopping for such items as automobiles, travel services, and other consumer needs.

Internet Banking Services

Banking on a personal computer (PC banking), the precursor to Internet banking, allows customers to execute transactions from a personal computer using the bank's proprietary financial software. Customers log into the bank's system and download data, such as account balances and statements. Many banks also allow bill payment and account transfers.

With Internet banking, customers interact with the bank using browser software residing on the bank's Internet server rather than on their personal computer or mobile device. Consumers have access to the same services commonly offered with PC banking—opening accounts, submitting loan applications, viewing check images, and making investments—plus protections that use account authentication and encryption. Exhibit 5.4 lists many of the banking services that are now accessible through the Internet.

Internet Banking Account Management

Internet banking sites allow customers to order checks, view their deposit history, make transfers between accounts, and pay bills. Customers can also view up-to-the-minute account balance information, interim statements that show current activity, and previously issued statements. Some banks offer an electronic statement that customers may download; others allow customers to view electronic copies of the front and back images of paid checks.

To facilitate account reconciliation, account activity statements include deposits made, checks paid, and transfers posted. Items that do not match to the customer's monthly statement, such as those not cleared, are entered manually. Then a debit and credit summary is posted and the customer is given a final balance.

Using Internet banking, customers can access and make transfers between accounts and instruct their bank to make recurring transactions automatically. Usually, banks provide a confirmation number when a funds transfer is completed.

Exhibit 5.4: Banking Services Commonly Available Online

Internet and Mobile Banking Services for Consumers and Businesses

Deposit accounts
- Deposit wages, dividends, and benefit payments
- View account balances
- Transfer funds to and from accounts
- Schedule transfers for future dates
- Set up repeating transfers
- Transfer funds internationally
- View and search account history
- Search check and debit transactions by number, amount, or date
- Receive bank text messages of important account activities
- Receive text messages when account statements are ready
- View check images online
- Reorder checks
- Order foreign currency

Bill payment
- Merchant bills
- Tax bills
- Bank loans

Loan application
- Business
- Personal
- Auto and RV
- Home equity
- Mortgages

Credit cards
- View credit card transactions
- Pay credit card bills
- View current credit card transaction information
- Print credit card account statements
- Access credit card account balances and credit information
- Receive email alerts when credit card payments are due

Mortgages
- Make mortgage payments
- View current loan information
- View escrow analysis or year-end mortgage interest statement
- Request copies of loan documents or coupon books
- Receive email alerts when mortgage payments are due
- View loan amortization schedule and payoff information

Investment services
- Perform online trading
- Research company information
- Receive real-time quotes for stocks, bonds, and mutual funds

Employee benefits
- View account balances and current allocations
- View fund values and rates
- View contribution, transfer, and withdrawal histories
- Transfer funds and reallocate balances among funds

Trust assets
- View current transaction statements
- View current trust asset statements

Other
- Locate bank branches and ATMs
- Get directions to bank branches and ATMs
- Communicate with bank staff via email

Internet Bill Payment

Internet bill payment, the financial service that allows customers to pay recurring bills over their computer or mobile device, uses ACH network capabilities. Generally, customers create a list of payees—companies or persons they regularly pay—and then instruct their bank to make the payments. The information provided usually includes the payor's name (company or person), the account receiving the funds for deposit, the receiving depository's name, the account from which funds are to be drawn, the payment amount and date, the payee's name, the transaction type, and the origination date.

In the Internet bill payment process, the ODFI receives the customer's Internet instructions for payment, consolidates all payments going to particular payees (such as utility companies), and provides the payees with a list of the amounts and payors included in the consolidated payment. Payments are sent through ACH to the RDFI or, if necessary, checks are printed and mailed to the payees. The transaction is listed on the originating customer's statement.

Situation

Carl just received an invoice from his doctor's accounting office saying he was 30 days late in making the payment for his annual check-up. Knowing he had paid the bill the day he received it, Carl logged onto his account using his bank's Internet banking service. There he found his previous statement listing the payment and an image of the cancelled check, both front and back. He printed a copy of the check and the next day called the doctor's accounting office. When Carl gave the details, the accountant was able to locate the posting for the payment, which had been made to another patient's account by mistake. The next week, Carl received a corrected statement from the doctor's office.

Banks that offer Internet bill payment as an account service have found that it helps retain customers. Once all the payees are established and the convenience of the service is experienced, customers are less likely to close their accounts and change banks.

Internet Loans

Banks—and many of the financial companies with which they compete—are making it easier for customers to apply for loans on their websites. Web-based mortgage services, for instance, include financial calculators, home shopping information, and a range of rates and loan applications based on the customer's answers to a few basic questions. Some bank websites combine electronic and personal service. For example, standard loan applications for both personal and mortgage loans are often provided. After an application is processed, a customer service representative then follows up by calling the customer.

Internet Investments

Online investing is growing phenomenally. Many banks now offer customers the ability to trade in stocks, bonds, and mutual funds. Once an investment account is set up, customers can use their computers or mobile devices to manage their investments on a 24/7 basis. Online services offer customers the ability to:

- Research investment options by accessing real-time price quotes, market news, educational material, financial calculators, and other tools
- Purchase and sell investments by transferring funds between checking and investment accounts
- View account balances, holdings, asset allocation, and losses and gains
- Receive electronic versions of documents, including trade confirmations and tax documents
- Download account information to financial and tax preparation software

Types of investment accounts that may be offered online include individual and joint accounts, corporate accounts, trust accounts, and retirement accounts.

Online investing is a service for which banks face considerable competition. For example, Federal Reserve Banks offer investment opportunities because they manage the U.S. Treasury Department's TreasuryDirect system. This is a convenient way for individuals to hold U.S. Treasury securities directly rather than through a depository institution such as a bank. Customers can buy directly from the U.S. Treasury when the securities are issued, or they may instruct brokers to deposit securities in their TreasuryDirect account. The U.S. Treasury uses the ACH to directly deposit interest or principal payments to customer accounts at their depository institution.

Card Access to Funds

Using an access card, consumer and business customers may withdraw cash, use credit, make a payment, or transfer funds between accounts.

ATM Cards

An ATM card—a plastic access card—is commonplace for getting quick cash or making a deposit. For years, consumers have used ATM cards at retail POS terminals to pay for purchases by electronically debiting their accounts. At many ATMs, customers can buy stamps or cash checks. Some of the larger banks have linked their ATMs to the Internet so customers may, for example, pay utility bills and buy concert tickets.

Did You Know ...

In 1939, Luther George Simjian sought a patent for his not-very-successful "Bankmatic," an early version of the ATM. About 30 years later, Don Wetzel, then vice president of product planning at Docutel, along with Tom Barnes, chief mechanical engineer, and George Chastain, electrical engineer, patented and introduced a working prototype of the Docutel networked ATM machine.

Debit Cards

The debit card, also called a check card, is quickly replacing the ATM card. Like checks, debit cards allow customers to pay for purchases or services directly from their checking account. Debit cards usually are embossed with either the VISA or MasterCard logo and use the credit card association's payment system to effect transactions at the customer's bank. Like credit cards, debit cards may be used at POS terminals, for personal identification number (PIN) payments, for signature-receipt payments, and for transactions over the telephone or Internet. Exhibit 5.5, next page, illustrates the processing of a debit card transaction.

Credit Cards

Traditional credit cards allow customers to access funds in their credit card account at a bank. Like debit cards, they can be used at ATMs to get cash advances or in retail establishments to make purchases. The difference is that credit card accounts are assessed an immediate finance charge for cash advances, although many credit card issuers do not assess finance charges for credit card purchases when the account holder pays the statement balance in full each month. Many customers use credit cards rather than debit cards and then pay off their balances from interest-earning transaction accounts in order to earn reward points, such as free airline miles.

Stored-Value Cards

Unlike ATM, debit, or credit cards, stored-value cards (also known as prepaid cards) are access cards with an encoded amount of cash. Although these cards once were issued primarily by transportation systems and retailers, banks now offer stored-value (gift) cards through their affiliation with VISA, MasterCard, or American Express. Government agencies also issue access cards for **electronic benefit transfers** (EBTs) to people who do not have bank accounts into which benefit funds can be deposited directly. Private industry also has adopted EBTs, issuing payroll cards to employees so they may access their wages through bank ATMs.

electronic benefit transfer (EBT)—A system for electronic payment of government-sponsored benefit programs using plastic cards and point-of-sale (POS) technology.

Some stored-value cards, such as gift or telephone cards, have a one-time encoded value. Once that value is depleted, the card is obsolete. Other cards can be reloaded with additional funds, usually through the POS system used by the issuer. For example, the same machine on buses that accepts payment in cash or by stored-value card also allows customers to add value to their cards using cash or a credit or debit card.

> ## *Situation*
>
> Juanita is an avid coffee drinker. She buys her café espresso at the coffee shop across the street from her job. One day she received a thank-you card and a $25 stored-value gift card for her favorite coffee shop from her supervisor, who likes to give gift cards to her team members in appreciation for their good efforts during the year. For the next week, Juanita used the gift card to pay for her morning café espresso. With each use, the card's value was reduced. Juanita liked the gift card and decided to buy some for her friends and family members for the holidays.

Exhibit 5.5: Debit Card Point-of-Sale Transactions

Unlike using credit cards, the customer is not billed at the end of the month in a POS debit card transaction. The purchase amount is electronically deducted directly from the customer's bank account at the time of sale. The customer authorizes this transaction by providing a debit card and a personal identification number (PIN) or a signature.

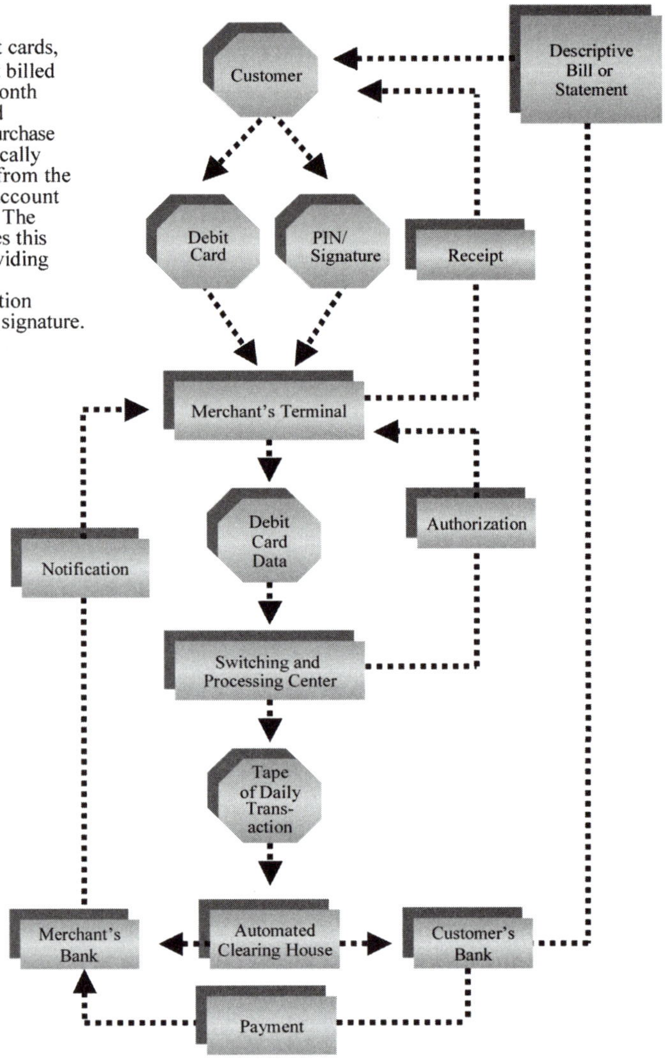

Contactless Payment Cards

With traditional debit and credit cards, information is transferred to a card reader through a series of contact points on the card. Now, contactless cards that use **radio frequency identification** (RFID) technology to transmit information to the card reader are being used by more businesses. This technology allows customers to wave the card in front of the device, eliminating the need to hand over the card, sign a receipt, or input a personal identification number. These cards also have a standard magnetic strip so they can be used in traditional contact (swipe) machines.

radio frequency identification (RFID)—An automatic identification method that relies on storing and remotely retrieving data using devices that can be attached to, or incorporated into, products such as tags or transponders.

Because of their convenience, contactless cards are often used for small-ticket items such as fast food, parking meter fees, or convenience store purchases. VISA and MasterCard are introducing RFID technology for debit as well as credit cards. Contactless payments through enabled mobile phones are also gaining traction and could eventually replace contactless payment cards.

ELECTRONIC BANKING AND BUSINESSES

The electronic banking benefits enjoyed by individual consumers are also available to businesses. In addition, businesses are the principal customers of several other electronic banking services, from wire transfers and direct deposits to online account reconciliation and, more recently, remote deposit capture.

Direct deposit is probably the most widely known and promoted business service. Even small companies, especially those using an outside payroll vendor, often arrange to have wages sent directly to employees' bank accounts. Vendor payroll companies and banks compete for this account service. When a bank manages a direct deposit program, the business provides a list of its payroll employees. The bank then debits the business's account and sends the funds to the banks where individual employees have their accounts. The federal government does the same with benefit checks such as Social Security payments.

Most cash management services now are supported by Internet banking technology, giving company finance managers online access to their business's accounts and flexible tools with which to review, direct, and authorize company deposits, withdrawals, transfers, payments, and investments. Letters of credit, which have supported merchant transactions for centuries, are now processed electronically. Many of the services offered to businesses are supported by bank-owned electronic systems or organizations of which banks are members or customers.

Did You Know ...

Prepaid cards remain the most used alternative financial service: 15 percent of consumers used a general-purpose prepaid card in 2013, 8 percent used a government-provided card, and 3 percent used a payroll card. Of the general-purpose cards in use, 38 percent of users had cards that were reloadable with additional funds.

Source: Federal Reserve Board, *Consumers and Mobile Financial Services*, March 2014

Electronic Bill Presentment and Payment (EBPP)

One Internet bill paying service that focuses on business needs is electronic bill presentment and payment (EBPP). This service allows major companies to send their bills to customers online and for customers to pay online. The two systems currently marketed are biller direct and bill consolidator. Each system reduces the cost of billing and accelerates vendor receipt of payments.

Biller Direct

The biller direct service allows a company to post its consumers' bills on its website. Consumers access the site and pay their bill through an ACH transfer, credit card, debit card, or prepaid card.

Bill Consolidator

A bill consolidator is a third-party presenter that collects bills from a number of companies and makes them available to consumers on its own website. Consumers access the site and pay their bills through the site by ACH transfer, credit card, debit card, or prepaid card. Banks may operate as consolidators.

Imaging and Remote Deposit Capture

Although the number of paper checks processed each year continues to decline, banks still process billions of them annually. Today, developments in technology and the law allow a paper check to be scanned to create an electronic image that is then transferred as an electronic file for collection, reducing operator error and check payment risks.

Retail merchants scan checks into a check reader that converts the data to an electronic transaction. The merchant then returns the check to the customer, and the electronic check is processed for payment.

Other business customers and banks also are using check imaging. Many small businesses now scan checks and send the images to the bank for deposit, a process known as **remote deposit capture** (RDC) or check truncation. Some scanners capture both sides of the check. For businesses and banks, check imaging reduces the cost of processing checks and records and facilitates the transmission and storage of financial data. For small businesses, RDC also offers the convenience of depositing checks without having to visit the local bank branch.

remote deposit capture (RDC)—A service that allows consumers or businesses to scan checks and transmit the scanned images or automated clearing house data in an encrypted form to a bank for posting and clearing.

electronic check—An electronic version of a paper check that includes the date, payee name, payment amount, and signature. Checks bear a digital signature security code proving payment was authorized by the account holder.

Check imaging makes it possible for businesses with outlets in several states to consolidate their accounts at a single bank, thereby reducing the need to deposit checks in a local bank at each locality. The technology also enables community banks to extend their geographical market area by offering check imaging and related services to more businesses of various sizes and structures in other localities.

E-Checks

The next step in the evolution of check imaging and Internet banking is the **electronic check** (e-check), a computer file that is processed and exchanged electronically. Using e-checks, businesses can issue, receive, and process payments electronically, either singly or in batches. Computer software is used to generate and process e-checks.

E-checks must be properly signed and endorsed using a digital signature that is encrypted to protect against forgeries. Digital signatures make it possible to verify transaction information each step of the way—a major advantage over paper checks. Encryption also prevents e-checks from being modified without invalidating the signatures, providing another protection against forgery.

LAWS AND REGULATIONS

Electronic banking received official recognition in the Electronic Fund Transfer Act, a federal law enacted in 1978 that defines the rights and responsibilities of users

Customer Tips: Electronic Checks

Before you agree to electronic check conversion, you should first ask yourself:
- Do I understand that the information from my check will be used to make an electronic payment from my account?
- Do I have enough money in my account to cover the payment?

Before you leave the store, you should ask yourself:
- Did I receive a receipt?
- Does the amount on the receipt match the amount of my purchase?

When you receive your statement from your financial institution, you should:
- Make sure that the charges on your statement match your records.
- Contact your financial institution right away if you notice a problem.

Source: Federal Reserve Board, *When is Your Check Not a Check? Electronic Check Conversion* consumer brochure and providers of consumer EFT services. Other banking laws, such as those discussed in the following paragraphs, also affect electronic banking activities. The bank regulators implement the laws through their regulatory and enforcement powers. Regulations that apply to traditional methods of banking also apply to electronic banking, as do federal privacy laws. Banks, the government, and the public all have vested interests in ensuring that electronic banking services are functional, fair, and secure.

Electronic Fund Transfers

The Electronic Fund Transfer Act, implemented by Regulation E, establishes the rights, liabilities, and responsibilities of participants in EFT systems when they initiate or receive transactions, such as ATM transfers, telephone bill payment services, retail POS terminal transfers, and preauthorized transfers from or to consumers' accounts, such as direct deposits of wages or Social Security payments.

Regulation E's rules, which are now written and enforced by the Consumer Financial Protection Bureau (CFPB), cover all transactions initiated through an electronic terminal, telephone, computer, or magnetic tape that instruct a financial institution to either credit or debit a consumer's asset account. For example, Regulation E limits the customer's liability for unauthorized use of an access device, such as a debit card, to $50 if the customer informs the financial institution promptly that the card has been lost or stolen.

The CFPB amended Regulation E so that it now also governs remittance transfers, which are funds wired electronically by someone in the United States to a person or business in a foreign country. Banks that provide a specified number of remittance transfers must abide by notice, disclosure, and transfer cancellation requirements.

Funds Availability

Federal Reserve Regulation CC implements the Expedited Funds Availability Act (EFAA). Enforced by the Federal Reserve Board, Regulation CC requires banks to make funds deposited in transaction accounts available to their customers within specified timeframes, to pay interest on interest-bearing transaction accounts no later than the day the bank receives credit, and to disclose their funds availability policies to customers.

Funds deposited by check must be made available to the customer for withdrawal by the second business day. Certain types of checks, such as U.S. Treasury checks and state or local government checks that are deposited into an account, are required to have next-day availability under most circumstances. Regulation CC also requires banks to make payments received by wire transfer and ACH transfers available to customers by the next business day.

Check Collection and Funds Transfers

Federal Reserve Regulation J, the Collection of Checks and Funds Transfers, applies to checks and other transactions moving through Federal Reserve Banks and funds transfers through Fedwire. Together with Regulation CC, Regulation J

Banker Profile

Carole Chang came to banking after working as an Internet website designer for a major California advertising firm. Having earned her master's degree in fine arts at a top West Coast arts school, Carole also garnered many awards for her graphic design skills and innovations in website design. An established community bank in California first came to know Carole through her work as a contractor on a pilot information website. The marketing and IT department managers were both impressed. They convinced the bank president to hire her to completely redesign the bank's website and develop a strategic plan for Internet banking delivery opportunities. Carole took the challenge and, at the same time, earned her ABA Bank Marketing diploma and Supervisor certificate. The bank president was equally impressed, particularly when a survey confirmed high customer satisfaction with the website. Carole was quickly promoted from marketing manager to vice president and manager of Internet services, a new department reflecting the bank's growth strategy.

sets the rules under which depository institutions such as banks can return unpaid checks, including check images, through the system.

Check Conversion

Check 21—the Check Clearing for the 21st Century Act—made the substitute check possible by designating it as the legal equivalent of the original check for all purposes, provided the substitute check contains an image of the front and back, has the MICR line and physical characteristics of a check, accurately represents all the information on the original check, states that it is a legal copy of the check, includes all endorsements, and identifies the party creating it. If a bank does not exchange checks electronically, or if a customer wants a copy of the check, the legal status of a properly rendered substitute check makes it possible for the electronic file to be converted back to a paper item.

Electronic Signatures

The Electronic Signatures in Global and National Commerce Act (E-Sign Act) 2000 gives e-contracts and e-signatures the same status as paper records. Both parties must agree to the electronic contract. Thus, prior to obtaining agreement, a bank must inform customers of:

- Their ability to have their records in paper form and the procedures for obtaining a paper copy of an electronic record
- Their ability to withdraw their consent, the consequences for doing so (such as an end to the agreement), and the procedures for withdrawing consent
- Their need for certain hardware and software to access and retain their electronic records

Banks must abide by the rules of the E-Sign Act and the related Uniform Electronic Transactions Act (UETA), which is a uniform law adopted by many states to further e-contracts and electronic commerce for certain Internet-related banking activities, such as providing electronic disclosures to consumers for loan or deposit transactions.

SUMMARY

- Electronic banking is becoming an increasingly important delivery channel for customer services. Although electronic banking has been around for decades, Internet banking has become the most popular delivery channel for banking services, far surpassing banking at traditional brick-and-mortar branches.
- For many years, MICR symbols on the front of checks provided identifying information for automated processing. Automated processing now is being replaced with check imaging, a technology that enables banks and other commercial establishments to capture an electronic image of a check that can be transferred for paperless processing. Electronic banking has evolved to the point that some banks do not have brick-and-mortar branches, instead providing services only

through the Internet. These virtual banks may not be as convenient for customers to use, but they often offer competitive yields and lower fees. Whether virtual or traditional, banks are expanding the bank services they offer via a mobile wireless device such as a smart phone or tablet. Customers are even accessing banking services via text messaging. Another development is virtual currency, such as bitcoins, which are now used for some transactions.

- Banks use EFT systems to borrow funds from each other, invest daily surplus funds, settle clearing balances, and provide services to customers. Banks, corporations, and governments use batch-processing ACH services to make recurring payments, such as payroll deposits. Customers use ACH when they authorize automatic payments of insurance premiums, mortgages, loans, and other bills. Fedwire is used for interbank, government, and customer transfers, and CHIPS is used for transfers in the international market. Federal Reserve Banks also operate the National Settlement Service, which allows financial institutions that participate in clearing houses to do so efficiently and with reduced risk. SWIFT is an industry-owned cooperative that supplies secure messaging services and interface software to large financial institutions worldwide.

- A primary portal for accessing electronic banking services is a bank's website. Banks use their websites to market services, and most now bundle information and services to make their websites into electronic resource centers for their customers. Banks can also generate fees when they link to other services and vendors. Some banks offer travel and shopping services.

- Direct deposit is the most familiar electronic banking service for most consumer and business customers. Electronic banking also allows customers to access funds, make purchases, and in some cases, make deposits and transfers using ATM, debit, credit, and stored-value cards. Contactless payment devices using RFID technology are becoming popular. Other electronic services include account management, bill payment, loan application and servicing, and investment services.

- Electronic banking services commonly used by businesses include electronic bill presentment and payment (EBPP) and imaging and remote deposit capture (RDC). EBPP allows business customers to send and receive payment for bills online. With RDC capabilities, businesses scan customer checks and send the images to their bank for deposit. RDC differs from electronic checks, which allows payments to be processed without the need for paper at any point. Electronic checks are signed and endorsed using digital signatures.

- The main laws and regulations that relate directly to electronic banking are the Electronic Fund Transfer Act, implemented by Regulation E, which covers EFT transactions; the Expedited Funds Availability Act (EFAA), implemented by Regulation CC; and Regulation J, which covers check collection and funds transfers through Fedwire. The E-Sign Act is important for the electronic delivery of disclosures and contracts to consumers, such as those supporting the delivery of bank services through the Internet.

Learning Check

SELF-CHECK AND REVIEW

1. How do virtual banks operate?
2. How are electronic fund transfers (EFTs) and Automated Clearing House (ACH) services related?
3. What are Fedwire, CHIPS, and SWIFT?
4. How do contactless payment cards work?
5. How is check imaging used, and what are the benefits to a business?
6. What federal regulations apply directly to electronic banking?

Lending

6

Learning Objectives

After studying this chapter, you should be able to

- Explain the importance of the lending function
- Describe lending products and services for bank customers
- Describe the steps in the lending process
- Explain how the bank board of directors governs loan policy
- Describe laws and regulations relating to lending

Introduction

The practice of borrowing and lending dates back to the earliest civilizations. In the ruins of ancient Babylon, archeologists discovered written evidence of a loan made to a farmer, who promised to pay it back with interest after he sold his crops. In the Middle Ages, goldsmiths, who held precious metals and other valuables belonging to their customers for safekeeping, often made loans against the value of those assets. In the 1700s, two Continental Congresses financed the American Revolution in part through loan certificates. The federal government has since borrowed to finance every war involving the United States.

Banks offer a wide variety of loans to consumers, businesses, and governments. To maintain the quality of a bank loan portfolio, bankers must adhere to the bank's loan policy and carefully complete the lending process. Taking the application, matching financial need to the appropriate product, establishing customer credit-worthiness, properly documenting the loan, and carefully rendering a credit decision are all vital aspects of the loan process. Following the legal and regulatory requirements ensures that the bank is balancing its operating objectives for liquidity, safety, and income.

Did You Know ...

One of the earliest records of lending are found in tablets written by Hammurabi, an ancient ruler of Babylon in 1750 BC. The tablets contain Hammurabi's pronouncements on lending between parties, and also standardized how loans should be repaid and what kind of recourse a lender would have if a borrower were unable to repay a loan.

THE LENDING FUNCTION

Lending is one of the cornerstone functions of banking, along with the deposit and payment functions. It is usually the most significant source of income for banks and often the foundation of a bank's relationship with its customers. Under the Community Reinvestment Act (CRA), banks are evaluated and assigned a public rating based on their record of helping to meet the credit needs of their communities, such as making loans to individuals for home mortgages, small businesses, and small farms, including loans to low- to moderate-income customers. The quality of its loan portfolio often is critical to a bank's survival, and lending is essential for a healthy economy.

Sources of Credit

Credit is available from many sources. Consumers can apply for credit from a commercial bank, savings bank, credit union, or finance company. They can borrow from an insurance company against their life insurance policies or from a brokerage firm against the value of their securities. There are also specialized lenders; consumers can buy merchandise on credit from a retailer and obtain a home mortgage or home equity loan from a mortgage broker.

Commercial enterprises also can choose among many sources of credit. Although commercial banks traditionally have been the primary source of **business loans**, in recent decades competitors have emerged. **Savings banks** offer business

business loan—A loan to a business to meet short-term or long-term needs. Also known as a commercial loan.

savings bank—An institution that primarily accepts interest-bearing time and checkable deposits for investment in mortgages and high-grade securities. A savings bank may also make loans to businesses and consumers.

loans. One business may extend credit to another by releasing merchandise in advance of payment—similar to a consumer buying merchandise on credit. Insurance companies often make large **long-term loans** for constructing shopping centers, office buildings, and factories. Many large corporations offer consumer and business loans through **captive finance companies**, such as General Electric through GE Capital. Commercial financing firms are another source of credit. Businesses may go to these nonbank lenders to obtain **asset-based financing** to meet operating needs, such as building inventories, consolidating debt, or increasing cash reserves. Also, instead of borrowing from financial institutions, many large corporations with excellent credit ratings borrow in the money markets by issuing unsecured, short-term notes known as **commercial paper**.

Federal, state, and local governments use a wide variety of short- and long-term borrowing techniques to raise funds. Banks themselves often borrow by using, for example, the facilities of the Federal Reserve to obtain short-term credit.

long-term loan—A loan of a fixed amount that is repaid according to a specific schedule over a period of several years, typically one to 30 years.

captive finance company—A finance company owned by a manufacturer to finance dealer inventory and/or to make loans to consumers for the purchase of its products.

asset-based financing—A financing method usually focused on the cash flow of a particular asset or asset group for return on an investment or loan.

commercial paper—Negotiable, short-term, unsecured promissory notes in bearer form issued by major corporations with unquestioned credit standing as a means of borrowing.

Banks as Lenders

Although there are many sources of credit, banks are a very important lending source and are the largest provider of commercial (business) loans. Banks can offer attractive rates because their cost of funds is relatively low.

Consumers, small and large businesses, and governments take advantage of the variety of personal and commercial loan products that banks offer. A bank loan term may be as short as 30 days or as long as 30 years. Although most loans are secured by collateral, some are unsecured. With unsecured loans, the bank relies only on the customer's written promise to repay.

LOAN CATEGORIES

Banks divide their loans into categories for reporting to government agencies and for internal monitoring and planning. The major categories are:

- Consumer loans
- Real estate loans
- Commercial loans
- Government and government-sponsored loans

Within these major categories are a wide variety of loan products. All are important assets for banks, but some more so than others, as shown in exhibit 6.1, next page. The exhibit lists the total amount of different types of loans held by all FDIC-insured depository institutions during a recent quarter.

Different operations centers in a bank may manage different types of loans. Home equity loans and lines of credit often are managed by the consumer loan department, for example. Many banks classify business loans by industry to monitor how much of their portfolio is committed to certain sectors of the economy, such as housing, retail, or agriculture. If problems arise in an industry, an astute banker will be aware of the number and size of loans that may be affected and will act to limit the bank's exposure.

Did You Know ...

As of February 2014, commercial banks had made over $1.65 trillion in loans to businesses of all sizes.

Source: Federal Reserve Bank of St. Louis

Types of Consumer Loans

- Personal
- Automobile (direct and indirect)
- Automobile leases
- Mobile home
- Recreational vehicle
- Marine (boat)
- Home improvement
- Home equity or second mortgage
- Home equity line of credit
- Bank card credit
- Non-card revolving credit
- Education
- Unsecured line of credit

Exhibit 6.1: Largest Sources of Bank Loans

	Amounts in $ Millions
1- to 4-family residential mortgages	1,841,445
Commercial & industrial loans	1,571,822
Nonfarm nonresidential	1,092,487
Credit cards	677,074
Home equity lines	517,749
Auto loans	346,503
Multifamily residential real estate	252,342
Construction and development	206,145
Loans to depository institutions	120,209
Loans to U.S. states & political subdivisions	109,713
Lease financing receivables	107,207
Farmland	76,662
Farm loans	67,996

Source: Federal Deposit Insurance Corporation, 3rd quarter 2013

Consumer Loans

consumer loan—A loan extended to consumers, either individually or jointly, primarily for the purpose of buying goods and services for personal use.

secured loan—A loan for which the customer has pledged some form of collateral to protect the lender in case of default.

Consumer loans make up a large part of most bank loan portfolios, and banks direct much of their attention to serving this profitable market. Consumer loans are attractive to banks for several reasons:

- Interest income contributes to bank profits.
- Most consumer loans are repaid as agreed.
- Consumer loans are part of full-service banking.
- Other bank services, such as deposit products, can be cross-sold to build long-term customer relationships.

To meet the diverse needs of this segment, banks offer a wide range of consumer loan products. These loans generally fall into two broad categories: open-end (revolving) credit and closed-end (installment) loans.

Open-End Credit

In an open-end line of credit, a borrower may draw on funds up to a credit limit preapproved by the bank. Two examples are a home equity line of credit and a credit card.

With a home equity line of credit, the borrower's residence is pledged as collateral. Because it is **secured**, the interest rate is usually lower than for open-end unsecured credit, and the interest paid may be tax-deductible. The customer may borrow money at any time before the stated maturity date and can elect to repay any amount above a specified minimum amount. Funds may be used for any purpose, including home remodeling, paying off high-interest-rate loans, taking a vacation, or purchasing a new car.

Credit cards are another flexible source of credit. Unlike a home equity line of credit, credit card debt is **unsecured**. The cardholder can control how and when to use credit. Instead of receiving a single amount, as in a personal closed-end loan, the cardholder can draw on the credit line as needed to travel, entertain, or purchase merchandise and services.

Because they are flexible and easy to use, credit cards are popular with consumers. The customer receives a monthly statement from the bank listing purchases made that month and has the option, each month, of paying the entire balance, a minimum payment, or an amount in between. Generally, there is no finance charge if the entire outstanding balance is paid before the payment due date (**grace period**).

Credit cards carry a high degree of risk for the bank, primarily from fraudulent charges to stolen cards, but also because the debt is generally unsecured and default rates are higher than with other types of loans. For these reasons, the interest rate charged on credit card debt is typically higher than for other types of credit.

unsecured loan—A loan for which the borrower has not pledged some form of property as collateral in the event the loan is not repaid in full.

grace period—The period of time before the payment due date during which a credit card account holder is allowed to pay off the monthly bill without having to pay additional interest.

amortization—The periodic reduction of the principal amount due on a mortgage or other term loan. When the full amount is repaid, the loan is fully amortized. An amortization schedule is a table listing how much of each loan payment is applied to the principal and how much is applied to the interest.

promissory note—A written document with the customer's (maker's) promise to pay a certain sum of money to the bank (the payee), with or without interest, on demand or on a fixed or determinable future date.

Closed-End Credit

Closed-end loans are for a specified amount and have a maturity date. They may be single payment loans, or they may **amortize** over the course of the loan term, with payments on the principal and interest made in installments on specific dates. The customer receives a lump sum up front. For payment, the bank may automatically debit the customer's deposit account or provide coupons to accompany payments. When coupons are used, the customer sends the coupon and payment to the bank, which then credits the loan account. With an automatic preauthorized debit, the bank charges the customer's deposit account for the loan payment and transfers it to its own accounts, if it is the creditor, or sends it to another creditor electronically. The payment is then listed on the customer's deposit account statement.

Closed-end loans may be secured or unsecured. An automobile loan may be secured by the car that was purchased with the loan funds. When an auto loan is secured, the bank holds title to the vehicle until the loan is paid in full. In making such loans, banks rely on the customer's ability to repay as agreed in a signed **promissory note**.

A home equity loan is a secured closed-end loan. Like a home equity line of credit, it is secured by the customer's residence. The interest paid may be tax-deductible. Whereas a home equity line of credit may be used whenever the customer needs funds, a home equity loan is for a one-time borrowing need such as a new deck or a kitchen remodel. Both home equity loans and home equity lines of credit may offer a fixed or a variable interest rate.

Real Estate Loans

Real estate loans can be for consumer or business purposes. Banks are primarily involved in two areas of real estate financing: short-term construction loans and longer-term mortgage loans.

Construction Loans

Real estate developers use construction loans to demolish and clear property and erect a new structure, such as a shopping mall, an office park, or a residential complex.

Situation

John and Nancy are shopping for a home equity line of credit. They have some credit card bills to pay off and also want money to remodel their basement. John and Nancy have checking, savings, and retirement accounts at several banks. They are considering consolidating their accounts with one bank if they can find a bank that meets all their needs.

adjustable-rate mortgage (ARM)—A mortgage on which the rate is subject to periodic adjustment. The rate usually is tied to a widely published market index or rate of interest.

foreclosure—A procedure to obtain legal title to property, typically for the purpose of selling the property to recover loan amounts.

Consumers use construction loans when they are building a home. Businesses may use a construction loan to build a new plant or add warehouse space. A bank may write a construction loan to accommodate either a developer or a consumer.

Construction loans are relatively short-term, with maturities consistent with the construction period. The customer makes periodic interest payments on the loan and, at the end of the term, the bank may convert it to a mortgage loan. Often, one bank provides the construction loan and, upon completion of the project, another bank or a combination of banks provides the mortgage loan.

Mortgage Loans

Mortgage loans are closed-end, long-term credit with terms extending to 30 years or longer. To secure the loan, the customer pledges property as collateral. Banks extend mortgage loans on homes, office buildings, apartment houses, and shopping centers. Payments on the loan are generally made monthly. Because they are closed-end loans, the payments cover both interest and principal. The portion of the payment that is applied to interest and the portion that is applied to principal are determined by an amortization schedule and are usually not equal. Instead, over time the interest portion of the loan payment decreases as the loan balance decreases, and the amount applied to principal increases so that the loan is paid off by the specified loan term.

Interest rates on mortgage loan can be fixed or adjustable. The interest rate for fixed-rate mortgage loans remains constant over the life of the loan—it is not tied to some other factor. The **adjustable-rate**, or variable-rate, loan has made the mortgage lending market attractive to both customers and lenders. With such loans, the interest rate on the mortgage is periodically adjusted according to the terms of the loan documents.

Interest rates for adjustable-rate loans are based on an index, such as the prime rate, plus a percentage. Many banks use a national prime rate, such as the Wall Street Journal (WSJ) Prime Rate, as an index for adjustable-rate mortgages (ARMs). They do this because, under federal mortgage regulations, banks must use an index for ARM loans that is not subject to the bank's control. If interest rates decline, the borrower pays a lower interest rate, and the payment owed either decreases or the portion applied to loan principal increases. If interest rates rise, the borrower pays a higher interest rate, and the payment owed either increases or the portion applied to loan principal declines.

Terms for most ARMs are between 5 and 15 years; the mortgages must be paid off or refinanced at the end of the term. Other pricing methods for consumer and real estate loans are defined in exhibit 6.2.

The pricing and availability of home mortgage loans are based on the customer's income and creditworthiness and the appraised value of the property. Because mortgage loans are secured by the property, if the customer is unable to make the payments, the lender may proceed with **foreclosure** and sell the property at auction to recover the unpaid balance on the loan.

Reverse Mortgages

Reverse mortgages are so-named because the homeowner cashes in some of the equity in the home. As a result, the homeowner's equity diminishes over time,

Exhibit 6.2: Consumer Loan Pricing Methods

Simple interest
Interest is computed by applying a daily periodic interest rate to the principal amount outstanding. Thus, if the customer pays additional amounts on principal, the loan's total interest amount is reduced.

Discount method
Interest payment is deducted up front from the requested loan amount so that the borrower receives less principal than requested.

Add-on method
Total interest due on the loan is calculated as principal loan amount times the interest rate. This amount is then added to the principal, and the total is paid in equal installments over the life of the loan, resulting in more interest being paid by the borrower because the total interest is calculated on the initial principal amount.

Compensating balance
The interest rate that is applied may be adjusted up or down from a market rate based upon compensating balances maintained in deposit accounts by the customer.

rather than increases as is normally the case with mortgages. With a reverse mortgage, the lender provides the homeowner with loan proceeds, which can be taken as a lump sum, an open line of credit, or as monthly payments. The principal and accrued interest on the borrowed money is repaid after the homeowner dies or moves out—usually with the sale of the house.

Home equity conversion mortgages (HECMs) are a type of reverse mortgage insured by the federal government. HECMs are available only through a lender approved by the Federal Housing Administration (FHA). When first introduced in 1989, only 157 HECMs were made. In subsequent years, HECMs grew rapidly in popularity, exceeding 100,000 annually by 2007, according to the Department of Housing and Urban Development.

The financial crisis that began in 2008 diminished housing values nationwide, lowering the number of HECMs that were originated to around 54,000 by 2012. Nonetheless, more than 800,000 HECMs have been made, and the expectation is that their number is likely to increase further as a consequence of an elderly population that has built up substantial equity after long years of home ownership. Another factor is longer life expectancies, which has resulted in some elderly homeowners taking out reverse mortgages as a way to help meet their retirement expense needs.

Did You Know ...

Reverse mortgages are the one loan product specifically attractive to the elderly customer. The average age of a Home Equity Conversion Mortgage borrower in 2012 was 72.

Source: Department of Housing and Urban Development

Business Loans

Business loans are one of the largest components of most bank loan portfolios. Banks offer a wide variety of business loan products because businesses have diverse financing needs. A nursery, for example, may need a seasonal line of credit to finance purchases of plants and gardening equipment each spring; an airplane manufacturer may need a term loan to expand a manufacturing facility. Secured or unsecured, business loans typically are categorized by type and by maturity—that is, as either short-term or long-term.

Short-Term Versus Long-Term Loans

Short-Term Loan
Repayable in one year or less. For businesses, used to finance current assets, such as inventory or accounts receivable

Long-Term Loan
Repayable in more than one year. For businesses, used to finance fixed assets, such as equipment and real estate

Situation

ABC Manufacturing Company received an unusually large order from a new customer. ABC typically has enough funds to buy the raw materials it needs to fill orders, but it does not have enough cash available for this order. The new customer plans to place large orders several times a year. ABC wonders if a working capital line of credit could be a solution for its periodic financing needs.

fixed assets—Assets used by a business for its long-term conduct of its enterprise, such as building, machinery, and furniture.

The following discussion briefly explains some of the most common types of business loans.

Working Capital Loans

A working capital loan is a short-term loan (typically 30 to 90 days) used to finance a variety of operating needs. It is not used to finance long-term assets. A working capital loan might, for example, be used to finance a retailer's additional inventory during the holiday season or to provide additional capital for hiring personnel to fulfill a contract.

Working Capital Lines of Credit

A working capital line of credit provides funds for a business to access for recurring financing needs throughout the year. Banks often require borrowers to fully repay the credit line for a designated period of time during the business's annual operating cycle. Rates typically are variable and are based on an index selected by the bank, such as LIBOR (London Interbank Offered Rate) or prime rate.

Term Loans

A term loan has a maturity of one to five years and is used to purchase **fixed assets** other than real estate. Generally, the payment schedule is tied to the useful life of the asset. Plant equipment, for example, is financed over a longer period than personal computers.

Participation Loans

A participation loan is made to a single customer by two or more banks acting together. Common in business lending, these loans usually are made when the amount exceeds one bank's loan policy limits or legal lending limit. Also known as syndicated loans, participation loans allow the lending banks to share the risk of extending considerable credit.

Indirect or Third-Party Loans

An indirect or third-party loan is made to customers of dealerships, such as automobile or appliance dealers, to purchase big-ticket items. The dealers work directly with their customers to complete consumer loan applications, which are then forwarded to a bank for approval and funding. Indirect loans are a source of new consumer business for banks.

Floor Plan Loans

Floor plan loans finance consumer goods displayed or sold by a dealer, enabling a business to have a large and varied inventory of goods on display. The consumer goods, such as automobiles or appliances, are collateral for the loan.

Letters of Credit

A letter of credit is an instrument issued by a bank that substitutes the bank's credit for the credit of the buyer of goods. This allows a buyer to pay after goods have been received and thus be able to conduct more transactions. Letters of credit are used most often by buyers and sellers who want to do business together but need a bank to add strength and neutrality to the transaction.

Lease Financing

In a lease financing arrangement, the bank owns the collateral and leases it to a customer for his or her use for a specified period and monthly payments. Depending on the terms, ownership may transfer to the customer when the lease ends. Businesses may use lease financing to purchase manufacturing equipment like specialized machinery.

Asset-Based Loans

Asset-based loans are short-term loans secured by salable business assets, such as inventory (raw material and finished goods) or accounts receivable. These loans allow a business to obtain operating funds more quickly, without waiting for inventory to sell or customers to pay for goods purchased.

Leveraged-Buyout Loans

Leveraged-buyout (LBO) loans finance mergers and acquisitions. An LBO loan is often used to help finance the purchase of a company by a group of investors who plan to return value to the business after reorganization. Investors may include some senior managers from the merged or acquired companies.

Agricultural Loans

Banks also lend to agricultural enterprises, such as farms, ranches, and fish, poultry, and other livestock operations. For example, agricultural loans support the financial needs of farmers, ranging from the purchase of farmland and equipment to crop planting and livestock care and feeding. These loans have varying terms, depending on the need. Short-term loans are used to finance operating expenses, such as the purchase of seed and fertilizer for growing crops and grain for feeding livestock. Intermediate-term loans finance farm machinery, and long-term credit is used for financing buildings and land.

Loans to Financial Institutions

Other financial institutions are also customers for commercial bank loans. Banks lend to other banks, insurance companies, finance companies, and brokerages.

Business Loan Pricing

Business loans may be priced like consumer loans. Often, however, business loans require more complex analysis and structuring, and therefore, more complex pricing. Two common methods are cost-plus pricing and relationship profitability pricing.

Cost-plus pricing

The interest rate is determined by setting it at a fixed amount or percentage above the costs to make the loan. Costs include such items as the cost to the bank to raise funds for the loan amount (such as interest on deposits), an amount for default risk (loan loss), and a profit margin.

Relationship profitability pricing

The customer's total banking relationship is considered: all the revenues less all the costs associated with the relationship divided by the requested loan amount. The result determines the net return to the bank for the relationship and the loan.

Applying the Cost-Plus Pricing Method

By The Numbers

Business customer requests a $3 million loan.

Negotiable certificates of deposit are sold at 3% to raise funds	3%	Cost of funds
Operating costs for loan maintenance	1%	of loan amount
Default risk amount	2%	of loan amount
Profit margin	1%	of loan amount
Recommended interest rate	*7%*	

One of the most common bank-to-bank lending methods is associated with the Federal Reserve's bank reserve requirements. Banks lend their excess reserve amounts to other banks that need the funds through arrangements known as federal funds (or "fed funds") loans. These are typically overnight transactions.

Government as Borrower and Loan Supporter

Like consumers and businesses, state and local governments borrow from banks when, for example, tax revenues are insufficient to finance road repair equipment or police cars or to meet working capital needs. Consequently, a government entity will seek approval from its board or elected oversight body to obtain a bank loan for a specific purpose. Governments often seek financing with terms similar to business loans. Banks may also provide short-term loans based on anticipated tax revenues to pay off the loan.

Government-sponsored loan programs are another way for banks to lend. Through legislative mandates, government-sponsored bank loan programs promote social and economic objectives, such as affordable housing, access to higher education, and small business development.

Did You Know ...

By mid-2010, total student loan debt, at over $830 billion, surpassed credit card debt for the first time in U.S. history. By July 2013, student loan debt had grown to over $1.2 trillion, of which $1 trillion represented student loans held or guaranteed by the federal government. The balance was private student loan debt.

Source: Federal Reserve Board, Consumer Financial Protection Bureau

Affordable Housing

Through loan subsidies and guarantees, federal agencies such as the Veterans Benefits Administration (VBA) and the FHA make mortgages available to people who are otherwise unable to afford them. States may subsidize mortgage loans for low-income or first-time homebuyers.

Access to Higher Education

Student loans are available from private lenders, such as banks, to meet the education-related financial needs of students and their families. The federal government, however, also provides student loans. Federal student loan programs offer low-interest or fully subsidized-interest loans, with repayment deferred until after the student graduates. Federal loans for students include Direct subsidized and Direct unsubsidized loans (Stafford loans) and Perkins loans. PLUS (an acronym for Parent Loan for Undergraduate Student) loans help parents pay for the cost of their children's higher education. Direct PLUS loans are for graduate and professional students or parents.

Small Business Development

The Small Business Administration (SBA) guarantees loans made to qualified small businesses, thus transferring some of the risk from the lender to the SBA.

Other Government-Sponsored Lending

Government-sponsored enterprises, such as the Federal National Mortgage Association (Fannie Mae) and the Federal Home Loan Mortgage Corporation (Freddie Mac), play an important role in the mortgage lending market. Through the **secondary mortgage market**, Fannie Mae and Freddie Mac buy loans granted by mortgage lenders and issue mortgage-backed securities (MBS) for sale to investors.

secondary mortgage market—Transactions involving selling and purchasing mortgages. Mortgage loans originate in the primary mortgage market. Bundles of those mortgage loans may then be sold to investors in the secondary market.

Fannie Mae and Freddie Mac became insolvent in 2008 as a result of the subprime mortgage crisis and required government support. Both organizations are in the process of resolution and are expected to emerge as government-sponsored enterprises with a more limited role in the secondary mortgage market.

The Government National Mortgage Association (GNMA or Ginnie Mae), a corporation within the U.S. Department of Housing and Urban Development (HUD), guarantees the principal and interest of pools of residential loans insured by the FHA or guaranteed by the Department of Veterans Affairs (VA). GNMA-approved lenders with a pool of loans having similar rates and maturities can issue MBS in the amount of the loan pool. Other eligible guarantors or issuers of loans are the Department of Agriculture's (USDA) Rural Housing Service and HUD's Office of Public and Indian Housing.

The Federal Agricultural Mortgage Corporation (Farmer Mac), which was federally chartered by Congress in 1988 and is stockholder-owned, fosters a secondary market program for agricultural real estate and rural housing loans. Among other services, Farmer Mac purchases eligible mortgage loans from lenders and sells them as MBS in the secondary market. In addition, USDA Rural Development provides both direct and guaranteed loans for rural businesses and cooperatives, housing and community facilities, and rural utilities.

THE LENDING PROCESS

Although banks differ in their credit standards and policies, all follow a general lending process that includes the loan application and interview, investigation, documentation, and credit administration.

Each step has a cost and a risk to the bank. Larger loans require more detailed investigation, documentation, management, and monitoring than smaller loans. Lenders assess each request in terms of its risk, cost, and profitability, and then apply that assessment to the steps in the lending process.

Regardless of the type or size of credit, a rigorous lending process helps protect the bank against loss. There is, however, always some risk in lending. No formula or system positively guarantees full and timely repayment of loan principal and interest. Exhibit 6.3, next page, illustrates the lending process.

Did You Know ...

Small businesses are generally defined by the federal government as independent businesses with fewer than 500 employees. Small businesses make up 99.7 percent of U.S. employer firms.

Source: Small Business Administration

The Application and Interview

The lending process begins with the application and the loan interview. The goal of this step for banks is to understand the customer's needs, gather supporting documentation, and help the customer, if eligible, to choose the most appropriate loan product.

To gather preliminary information, most banks have the customer complete a loan application. The information may be elicited beforehand on a form or during

Situation

Cindy and George both have stable jobs that give them a comfortable income. Three years ago they finished paying off loans for their children's education. Except for a home mortgage, on which they have paid monthly for 20 years, they are debt-free. When Cindy and George applied to a bank for a home improvement loan, they were surprised to have their request rejected on the basis of a negative credit report from a credit reporting agency. They contacted the credit reporting agency and discovered that the college loans they had paid were incorrectly listed as being delinquent. After their credit report was corrected, their loan request was approved.

Types and Sources of Credit Information

Types of credit information
- Credit history
- Income
- Employment
- Residence
- Collateral value

Sources of credit information
- Application
- Internal bank files
- Directly from other financial institution
- Credit reporting agencies
- Public records

Exhibit 6.3: The Lending Process

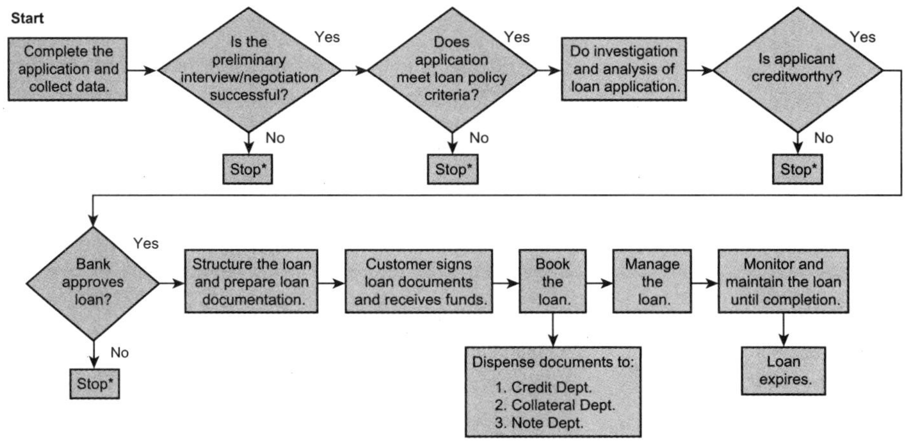

*Unless application has been withdrawn, send the customer a written Notice of Adverse Action. Oral notification may be sufficient in the case of some commercial loans.

the loan interview, which may take place in person, over the phone, over the Internet, or through a third party.

The nature and details of the loan requested determine the scope of the interview process. For example, a loan officer may meet several times with a business owner who is seeking a complicated business loan so as to understand the company's financial situation. In other situations, a loan officer may not work directly with a loan applicant and instead relies on a third party. For example, a car dealer may interview a customer applying for a consumer automobile loan. Exhibit 6.4 lists some questions typically asked of an applicant during a loan interview.

After the application and interview are completed, the bank decides whether to continue with or deny the loan request, ask for additional information, or direct the customer to other financing sources. Loan officers must be aware of bank policy

Exhibit 6.4: Sample Loan Interview Questions

How much money do you need?

How did you arrive at your loan request?

How will you use the loan proceeds?

What financing needs are you projecting?

What terms are you requesting?

How did you decide what terms are best for you?

What is your repayment source?

What is your income?

Will personal assets be pledged as security for the loan?

Who owns the collateral?

Where is the collateral located?

How is the collateral valued?

Are there guarantors? If so, who are they, what is their relationship to you, and what is their financial strength?

What banks do you currently use?

Have you approached other banks with the loan request?

Do you have loans outstanding with other creditors?

What is the nature and extent of these loans?

and the relevant law throughout the lending process. If the loan request is inconsistent with bank lending policy, it should be rejected. Consumer protection laws, such as the Equal Credit Opportunity Act and the Truth in Lending Act, impose specific requirements on lenders, beginning with loan solicitation and application.

Lending Over the Internet

The Internet has advanced the delivery of loan products. Through interactive websites, banks offer both consumer and business loans to prospective customers, sometimes all across the country. Today, the entire lending process—from application to approval—can be conducted online. Most bank websites offer tools for customers to determine the type of loan they need, compare different terms and interest rates, calculate payments, and determine whether they qualify for a loan. Then the customer can submit an online application and receive a decision on the loan request online shortly thereafter. Customers can also make loan payments online or direct the bank to periodically withdraw payments from a deposit account.

The Investigation

A credit investigation is conducted to evaluate a customer's ability to repay the loan. When making credit decisions, banks evaluate information on the loan application and balance it against the potential cost and risk of making the loan. An incomplete credit investigation can increase the bank's risk of a loss.

Consumer Credit Investigations

Credit investigations usually consist of verifying the applicant's employment, income, credit history, and current debt. A first step in credit investigation is to check records held by the bank and other lenders.

Banks also rely on credit reporting agencies for information. The three major credit reporting agencies are Equifax, Experian, and TransUnion. Credit reporting agencies keep detailed records on consumer credit histories and activities. These agencies can give a bank daily input on new loan applications, repayments, rejected requests for credit, and delinquencies. Information the applicant provides is cross-checked with credit reporting agency reports to determine its accuracy.

Credit scoring is also used with electronic underwriting. The electronically generated score determines whether the applicant profile falls within the bank's acceptable range. This cost-effective procedure allows the bank to process a large number of loan applications. Only loan applications that fall into a defined gray area are referred to a loan officer for further evaluation.

If a bank declines a consumer loan request on the basis of unfavorable credit information (called taking an adverse action), it must disclose the source and nature of the negative information to the consumer within 30 days of the application. The bank is required to inform the consumer that a credit report was used to make the decision. Consumers have the right to contact the credit reporting agency to see their credit report and to have any erroneous information corrected.

Banker Profile

Marta Gleason started working at the bank soon after she graduated from high school. She worked in the proof department full-time in the evenings, including Friday nights. This job paid her bills, but when a position opened up in the loan servicing department that had normal daytime hours, she jumped at the chance. Being quick and dependable, and continuing with her professional development, Marta advanced to assistant supervisor and then department supervisor. While earning her ABA Mortgage Lending Diploma and several certificates, Marta continued to advance her career, becoming a mortgage underwriter and then a mortgage originator and manager. Today, Marta is a senior vice president in charge of the bank's mortgage lending department.

Credit File Contents

Credit files contain:

- Copies of loan documents
- Financial information
- Credit inquiries and reports
- Collateral information
- Correspondence and memos
- Information like business annual reports

Loan documentation for a home equity line of credit includes:

- Promissory note with disclosure of credit terms
- Mortgage agreement (deed of trust)
- Insurance binder
- Title search
- Appraisal
- Flood determination (flood plain check)
- Rescission notice

Did You Know ...

Most credit reporting agencies provide credit scores, offer fraud detection, identify Social Security number discrepancies, and disclose legal notices, such as liens, lawsuits, and encumbrances. Consumers are permitted by law to obtain one free credit report each year from the three major credit reporting agencies.

Business Credit Investigations

Compared to consumer loans, commercial loan requests are generally for larger amounts and involve many more uncertainties. For example, one of the main considerations in evaluating a consumer loan request is the applicant's income, which is easily ascertained and generally stable and predictable. In the case of a commercial loan, business income is far less predictable; it is affected by factors such as current and long-term economic conditions, supplier relationships, accounts receivable aging, and so forth. In the case of a small business loan, an added factor is the business owner's credit, which can play a part in judging the creditworthiness of the loan request.

Thus, the investigative process is more detailed for business loans than for consumer loans. Many sources of information are used.

Loan Analysis (Credit) Department	Credit files on business accounts provide a history of the bank's relationship with a customer. They contain reports of interviews, copies of correspondence, financial statements supplied by the customer, internal memos, previous credit analyses, average balances, previous loans, overdrafts, and loan approval documentation.
Credit Agencies	Agencies like Dun & Bradstreet publish regular business reports that provide current financial information on larger companies. Reports cover the firm's history, management structure, products, scope of operations, and payment history with suppliers.
Suppliers	Because most merchandise is sold with credit terms, the bank must know a company's history of paying suppliers. Information can be found in credit agency reports or through direct contact with the borrower's suppliers.
Internet	Many companies have their own websites where banks can access annual reports and information about a company's products, services, and history.
Tax Returns and Financial Statements	Accountant-prepared financial statements and tax returns provide information about a company's growth and earnings, industry trends, and repayment sources.

Loan Documentation

Loan documentation begins at the time of application and ends with completion of all forms necessary to secure the lender's interest and comply with federal and state requirements.

The purpose of loan documentation is to have a written, legally enforceable understanding of the obligations of both borrower and lender. Failure to properly document the loan could make the loan agreement unenforceable. Proper loan documentation is an important responsibility for the lender because it helps to:

- Protect the bank's investment
- Ensure that the customer understands the loan terms
- Prevent litigation against the bank
- Prevent losses on the loan for the bank
- Avoid penalties for failure to comply with regulations

Loan documentation is a detailed process and must abide by federal and state requirements. The loan officer or loan assistant ensures that all sections are complete; all calculations and the collateral description are correct; signatures and dates are obtained and, if necessary, witnessed; and any alterations are understood, accepted, and initialed by all parties.

Lenders also use documentation to meet their obligation to inform customers about the major components of the loan. Federal law, notably the Truth in Lending Act, requires that consumers be informed of the repayment program, **annual percentage rate** (APR), total cost of the loan, consequences of not paying on time, and information about collateral. Lenders use disclosure forms and the contract to provide the necessary detail at this stage.

Different types of loans require different types of documentation; the requirements also vary from bank to bank and from state to state.

Collateral

The documentation of collateral is governed by many federal and state statutes because a variety of assets can be pledged as security for a loan. Government obligations such as U.S. Treasury bills, securities, savings or certificate of deposit account balances, residential or commercial property, and vehicles are among the assets that can be pledged as collateral.

While banks may be able to take physical possession of and hold some types of collateral, it is often difficult to do. In many other cases, the size or nature of the collateral, such as a vehicle or a house, makes it unreasonable or impossible to hold the collateral. Therefore, the bank's right to the collateral must be documented. A security agreement is the standard document for establishing this right; it creates a **security interest** in the collateral. Article 9 of the Uniform Commercial Code (UCC) dictates how the security agreement must be registered to **perfect** the security interest. UCC Article 9 has been adopted as law in every state.

Although it should never be the sole reason for approving a loan, collateral may strengthen a borrowing position. However, it is not profitable for a bank to be in the practice of foreclosing, repossessing, or seizing real estate, automobiles, or factories. Usually, the bank incurs additional costs if it must do so, sometimes resulting in a loss. Also, there is the risk that the collateral might be incorrectly valued or will lose value over time. For this reason, it is important that a lender correctly value collateral

annual percentage rate (APR)—The cost of credit on a yearly basis. Expressed as a percentage, APR results from an equation that considers three specifically defined factors: the amount financed, the finance charge, and the term of the loan. The APR is usually expressed in terms of the effective annual simple interest rate.

security interest—The right a lender has to obtain possession of the collateral, sell it, and retain the proceeds (up to the amount of the remaining debt) if the customer is unable to repay the loan.

perfection—The process by which a secured party protects its security interest from third parties by taking possession, holding certificate of title, controlling, or filing or recording documentation of the security interest in local or state public records.

Early Signs of Credit Problems

- Paying only the minimum amount month after month
- Being out of cash constantly
- Being late in making important payments, such as rent or mortgage
- Taking longer and longer to pay off balances
- Borrowing from one lender to pay another

payment protection— Products that are sold in conjunction with loans so that the loan can be paid if the customer dies, is injured or disabled, or loses a source of income.

during the loan process to protect the bank against losses in the event of foreclosure or repossession.

Loan Decision

In deciding whether to approve an application for credit, a bank evaluates all the information collected, from credit reports to financial statement analyses. If at any time during the lending process it becomes clear that the purpose, amount, or terms of the loan do not meet the bank's lending standards, the loan request should be rejected, although the bank may want to offer an alternative credit arrangement or direct the applicant to another lender.

If the decision is made to reject a consumer loan (and some commercial loans), the Equal Credit Opportunity Act and Regulation B require the bank to provide the applicant with a written adverse action notice explaining why the request was denied.

Payment Protection

The lender may offer the consumer a payment protection plan that will ensure repayment of the loan during difficult times. **Payment protection** may be an insurance or a fee-based product.

Credit insurance is issued by an insurance company and may cover life, disability (accident and health insurance), or loss of income. The insurance premium is added to the loan amount, and the premiums are paid with the loan payments.

Bank fee-based products include debt cancellation agreements (DCAs) and debt suspension agreements (DSA). These services are purchased separately from the loan and paid for when the loan is consummated. DCAs pay part or the entire debt in case of certain events, such as the customer's death. DSAs suspend payments for a time, such as while a customer is unemployed or disabled.

Loan Administration

The loan is finalized when all documents are complete, forms are signed, funds are disbursed, and documentation is filed. At this point, the loan moves into the administration phase. Loan administration tasks include:

- Transmitting or mailing regular statements
- Receiving and posting payments
- Keeping address information current
- Ensuring that the bank's security interest is recorded, filed, and returned to the bank
- Answering customer inquiries
- Reporting the loan to credit reporting agencies
- Maintaining documentation for examination by internal and external auditors and regulatory agencies
- Closing the loan and taking if off the books when the final payment is received
- Releasing any security interests in collateral

After it has been approved and placed in the bank's loan portfolio, the bank monitors the loan to ensure it does not become a problem loan—one in which the customer is not adhering to the terms of the agreement. For business loans, the loan officer monitors the company's financial performance and usually keeps in contact with the company to stay informed about developments that could affect loan repayment. Consumer loans are also monitored for failure to adhere to repayment terms or other signs that the loan may become a problem.

> **Situation**
>
> Rick Dunlap is a senior vice president at Dunkirk Bank, N.A. Last year, the bank ran a home equity loan campaign advertising a loan-to-value ratio of 100 percent for qualified borrowers. The bank also allowed for lower credit scores than normally required. It was a campaign to win back lost business from larger regional banks, and at the time, real estate values were robust.
>
> Now the real estate market has bottomed-out, home values have dipped as much as 35 percent, and home sales have slowed. After a recent examination, Dunkirk's federal regulator classified 30 percent of its home equity loans as substandard, 20 percent as doubtful, and 10 percent as loss loans.
>
> Regulators required Dunkirk to revise the bank's loan and marketing policies and procedures and evaluate all such loans for default and collateral risk. Rick also must report back to Dunkirk's board of directors and to the regulators and obtain approval of both the new loan policies and a strategy to handle the problem loans.

Loan Review and Asset Recovery

Because interest income on loans is a major source of bank revenue and loan portfolio quality is vital to overall bank asset quality, loan losses and underperforming loans are of serious concern to stockholders, directors, and regulators. **Loan review** gives management and directors assurance that:

- Lending officers are staying within their authority
- Lending policies, procedures, laws, and regulations are being followed
- Investigation and analysis are adequate
- All necessary documentation on each loan has been obtained and filed

If the size of the portfolio warrants, the review may cover unsecured and secured loans, loans made previously, and new loans.

Inevitably, some loans become problem loans. In such cases, asset recovery departments help prevent losses by taking timely action to collect late payments and, if necessary, by restructuring the terms of a loan for the benefit of both bank and customer. Asset recovery officers watch for any indications of poorly performing loans. They examine loans that have late payments, identify existing or potential problems, and recommend corrective action, perhaps including an increase in the bank's loan loss reserve.

Regulators examine bank loan portfolios for soundness, and banks are rated on the quality of their assets. Loans found to be an immediate risk are labeled **substandard, doubtful**, or **loss loans** and are assigned a weighted numeric value that is then compared with bank loan loss reserves and capital to determine a bank's safety and soundness. If it is determined unsafe, the regulators may require changes in bank policy and practice or higher loan loss reserves or capital levels.

loan review—The function of examining loan documents to ensure they are accurate, complete, and conform to laws and regulations and the bank's loan policies and procedures.

substandard loan—A loan whose risk is high given the collateral and the loan's structure.

doubtful loan—A loan that probably will not be collected in its entirety and poses default risk.

loss loan—An uncollectible loan or a loan that is not an appropriate asset for the bank.

LOAN POLICY

As the governing body of the bank, the board of directors, along with the bank's chief credit officer, set bank loan policy and oversee the lending function. A loan policy contains all the information necessary to guide the bank's lending practices. As the reference document for all bank employees, it covers areas such as:

Collection and Recovery Objectives
- Keep delinquencies and losses within set limits
- Generate loss recovery at desired levels
- Counsel customers who have difficulty managing debt
- Ensure adherence to bank objectives and legal requirements
- Manage collection and recovery efficiently

- Organization of the lending function
- Lending objectives
- Loan criteria and standards
- Loan risk rating standards
- Levels of loan authority
- Review and charge-off procedures
- Policy on loans to bank officers and directors

The board of directors reviews and approves the loan policy at least annually. Directors, usually working through a loan committee, are actively involved in the following activities:

- Determining the types of loans the bank will consider or refuse to make
- Tightening credit standards when conditions warrant
- Establishing and monitoring both legal lending limits and minimum loan amounts
- Determining policies that define loan collateral and maturities, outline maximum lending to certain business sectors, and set standards for down payments on automobiles or residences
- Assigning lending authority to bank loan officers so that they know the maximum amount they can approve individually and the combinations of higher authority needed for larger loan approvals
- Authorizing loans above a stipulated amount, that is, loans that exceed the authority of any combination of officers' lending authority
- Reviewing outstanding loans to ensure that the bank is meeting the credit needs of its customers and the community, in compliance with the Community Reinvestment Act
- Conducting periodic reviews (audits) of the loan portfolio to ensure that proper procedures are followed and no undue risks are being incurred

LAWS AND REGULATIONS

State banking departments and federal agencies ensure that loans comply with regulations and periodically monitor the quality of bank and savings institution loan portfolios.

Lending is subject to stringent regulation to ensure that depositors' funds are lent wisely, customers are given appropriate credit information, and loan terms are fair, applicants are not improperly discriminated against, enough loans are made within the community, and loans to bank insiders are restricted.

Because lending is essential to the economic prosperity of communities and the nation, bank regulators periodically issue guidance on adjusting lending practice in response to unusual economic conditions. For example, at the local or regional level, the agencies often encourage banks to work with borrowers experiencing financial difficulties beyond their control as a result of natural disasters, such as hurricanes, fires, flooding, or severe winter weather. On a national level, the agencies sometimes issue statements designed to stimulate lending and assist consumers and businesses that have loans.

For example, the great recession that began in 2008 caused high unemployment and a collapse in housing prices, both of which triggered home foreclosures nationwide. To help homeowners recover, federal regulators issued rules encouraging mortgage lenders to make loan modifications for homeowners at risk of losing their homes and allowing mortgage lenders to change loan terms without affecting how the loans are weighted for the purpose of holding regulatory capital. Then, in 2010, Congress enacted the Dodd-Frank Wall Street Reform and Consumer Protection Act (more commonly known as the Dodd-Frank Act).

The purpose of the Dodd-Frank Act was to prevent a recurrence of events that led to the financial crisis that began two years earlier. The Dodd-Frank Act made pervasive changes in how financial institutions are regulated and the activities in which they may engage.

Dodd-Frank and Consumer Lending

The Dodd-Frank Act has affected consumer lending in many ways. One section of the act, Title X, created the Consumer Financial Protection Bureau (CFPB), which has broad powers to write regulations governing consumer financial products and services. Besides its authority to write rules, the CFPB also has regulatory enforcement authority over the consumer activities of large banking institutions and nonbank financial service providers, while the bank regulators continue to enforce the consumer protection laws and regulations for small and mid-size banks.

The CFPB's authority is wide-ranging, and the agency is continually monitoring potential areas of abuse and issuing rules and guidance affecting many areas of the consumer borrower-lender relationship. For example, the CFPB has issued rules and guidance regarding student loans, lending to military service members, and disclosures at automated teller machines (ATMs).

The CFPB has been especially active in issuing regulations to reform mortgage lending practices, as mandated by Title XIV of the Dodd-Frank Act. The reforms include rules that:

- Require lenders to make a reasonable, good faith determination that prospective borrowers have the ability to repay the mortgage being offered
- Protect borrowers from risky lending practices, such as underwriting loans based on low introductory "teaser" interest rates
- Require consumers to receive counseling before obtaining high-cost mortgages, and require **mortgage servicers** to provide periodic account statements and rate adjustment notices to mortgage borrowers, as well as engage in early intervention when borrowers become delinquent
- Require lenders to provide a new, integrated disclosure form for closed-end consumer loans secured by real estate, combining the disclosure requirements under the Real Estate Settlement Procedures Act and the

mortgage servicer—A company that collects mortgage payments from the borrower and performs other services, such as paying insurance and taxes from the borrower's escrow account.

Truth in Lending Act to help consumers better understand the transaction, both when applying for, and closing on, such loans

- Require appraisals for mortgages classified as higher-risk mortgages—that is, mortgages offered at an APR that exceeds by a specified percentage the average prime offer rate
- Impose new requirements on mortgage loan originators, including registration and licensing, minimum qualifications, and compensation limits

As these examples show, many laws and regulations that govern bank lending are regularly revised by legislators and regulators. A discussion of other important lending-related laws that have been enacted over the years follows.

Equal Credit Opportunity Act

The Equal Credit Opportunity Act (ECOA) of 1974 and Regulation B, which implements the act's provisions, prohibit lenders from denying a loan or increasing the cost of a loan based on personal characteristics or conduct unrelated to creditworthiness. Specifically, lenders are prohibited from discriminating against applicants on the basis of age, race, color, religion, national origin, sex, marital status, or receipt of income from public assistance programs. Lenders are also prohibited from discriminating against a person who has exercised his or her rights under the Consumer Credit Protection Act (which includes ECOA and the Truth in Lending Act). Regulation B requires lenders to give consumer applicants written reasons when a loan application is rejected or a statement that they may request the reasons.

Truth in Lending Act

The Truth in Lending Act (TILA), implemented by Regulation Z, applies to loans primarily for personal, family, or household purposes. TILA does not apply to business loans. There are times, however, when a loan made to a business customer could be considered a personal loan and subject to the regulation.

Regulation Z prescribes uniform methods for calculating the cost of credit and providing an early disclosure of credit terms. Required early disclosures for certain types of loans, which must be made within three business days after a written loan application is received, include:

- APR
- Finance charge
- Amount financed
- Total of payments
- Payment schedule
- Itemization of amount financed

Under the Mortgage Disclosure Improvement Act of 2008, disclosures, once limited to loans secured by a consumer's "principal dwelling," are now required for loans secured by any dwelling of a consumer and, therefore, cover refinancing and home equity loans as well. A lender must also wait until at least seven business days after delivery of the early disclosures before consummating a mortgage loan. A lender cannot charge a consumer any fee, except to obtain a credit report, until after the disclosures have been provided. A consumer can also expedite the closing of a mortgage loan subject to the early disclosure provisions to address a personal financial emergency, such as foreclosure. A consumer who applies for a home equity line of credit, which is considered open-end credit, is also entitled to receive an early disclosure of account terms at the time of application.

Beginning in August 2015, for consumer mortgage loans, lenders will be required to incorporate the TILA disclosures into a new Loan Estimate form, which must be given to consumers no later than three business days after receiving an application, and a Closing Disclosure form, which must be given to consumers no later three business days before closing.

By The Numbers

Calculating APR—Sample Actuarial Method

Example: Monthly Payments (regular first period)
Amount advanced (A) = $5,000
Payment (P) = $230
Number of payments (n) = 24
Unit-period = 1 month
Unit periods per year (w) = 12
Advance, 1-10-20XX
First payment, 2-10-20XX

From 1-10-20XX through 2-10-20XX = 1 unit period
(t = 1, f = 0)
APR (I) = wi = .0969 = 9.69%

This is an example of an actuarial method. It is a single advance transaction, illustrating monthly payments with a regular first period.

When this actuarial method is used, it is expected that calculators or computers will be programmed to carry all available decimals throughout the calculation and that enough iterations will be performed to make certain that the APR obtained, when rounded to 2 decimals, is correct. The example here used a 10-digit programmable calculator.

Source: Regulation Z, Appendix J to Part 226—Annual Percentage Rate Computations for Closed-End Credit Transactions

Regulation Z also gives consumers the right to rescind certain types of credit transactions (like home equity loans) that are secured by the borrower's primary residence, and prescribes fair credit billing rights for open-end credit.

Credit CARD Act

TILA was amended in 2009 when Congress enacted a law to provide additional protections for consumers who have credit card accounts. The Credit Card Accountability, Responsibility and Disclosure Act, more commonly known as the Credit CARD Act, subjects card issuers to many new requirements with respect to credit card interest rates, fees, and practices. For example, credit card companies must provide 45 days of notice before increasing card interest rates. Late fees, over-limit fees, and other penalty fees are limited and can only be levied under certain conditions. Card issuers must also evaluate a consumer's ability to pay before opening a new credit card account or increasing a credit limit. The CFPB has responsibility for administering the act.

Community Reinvestment Act

CRA, enacted in 1977, and its implementing Regulation BB, address what Congress perceived to be unfair treatment of prospective customers by financial institutions on the basis of arbitrary considerations, such as geographic location—a practice known as **redlining**.

redlining—Excluding potential loan customers because they wish to finance real estate located in a certain geographic area, regardless of whether they are depositors or meet all other criteria of creditworthiness.

CRA affirms that every financial institution has an obligation, consistent with safe and sound practices, to help meet the needs of its entire community, including individuals and businesses in low- and moderate-income neighborhoods. Although CRA is often thought of as a consumer-related law, small business loans are also taken into account when assessing a bank's compliance with the law.

CRA gives regulators the authority to assess a bank's record of meeting the needs of its community in three categories—lending, investments, and service—and to take that record into account in evaluating the bank's applications for mergers, acquisitions, and branches.

Loans to Bank Insiders

Regulation O implements the insider transaction restrictions of the Federal Reserve Act and the Financial Institutions Regulatory and Interest Rate Control Act of 1978. Regulation O places tight restrictions on Federal Reserve member banks in extending credit to their executive officers, directors, and principal shareholders. The Federal Deposit Insurance Corporation (FDIC) implements Regulation O for depository institutions that are not members of the Federal Reserve.

Home Mortgage Disclosure Act

Regulation C implements the Home Mortgage Disclosure Act (HMDA). HMDA requires many banks to keep records of purchase and refinanced mortgage and home improvement mortgage lending by geographical area. Smaller banks and banks that do not have a home or branch office in a metropolitan statistical area (MSA) are exempt from reporting. HMDA's purpose is to allow the public to determine whether banks are serving the housing credit needs of neighborhoods and communities where they are located.

Real Estate Settlement Procedures Act

The Real Estate Settlement Procedures Act (RESPA) and its implementing Regulation X (now the responsibility of the CFPB) require mortgage lenders to give customers information about the costs of residential real estate transactions. The purpose is to enhance the ability of borrowers to shop for mortgage loans by comparing settlement costs and loan terms from competing lenders.

Under RESPA, a Good Faith Estimate (GFE) of closing costs is required at the time of loan application, and a HUD-1 Settlement Statement of disclosures is generally required at closing. Separately, TILA requires additional disclosures at application and closing. However, for consumer mortgage transactions, these forms will be replaced in August 2015 with forms that combine the disclosures required by RESPA and TILA. Under an integrated mortgage rule issued by the CFPB, the GFE and related TILA disclosures will be replaced by a single Loan Estimate form that must be given to consumers no later than three business days after application. The HUD-1 Settlement Statement and related TILA disclosures will be replaced by a single Closing Disclosure form that must be given to consumers no later three business days before closing.

RESPA also contains prohibitions against kickbacks and unearned fees. For example, a bank cannot pay a fee for a referral of business in connection with a mortgage loan. A bank may pay fair value fees for settlement services actually provided.

Fair Credit Reporting Act

The Fair Credit Reporting Act (FCRA), passed in 1970, ensures fair and accurate credit reporting and protects consumers' rights to privacy concerning their credit reports. The law was amended in 2006 by the Fair and Accurate Credit Transactions Act (FACT Act) with the objective, among others, of making credit reports more accurate. Customers are entitled to one free credit report a year from each credit reporting agency and may have access to credit scores for a reasonable fee. Also, any bank submitting negative information to a national credit reporting agency must give consumers a written notice that it has done so or may do so.

Banks cannot report information they know or believe is inaccurate, and they must investigate claims that the information they furnished was inaccurate.

The FACT Act also added to the FCRA provisions regarding medical information. Creditors cannot obtain or use a consumer's **medical information** in making a credit decision unless permitted by certain regulatory exemptions. Consumer reporting agencies are restricted in disclosing or sharing medical and related information with creditors.

medical information— Under the FACT Act, which amended the FCRA, information, oral or recorded in any form, created by or derived from a health care provider or a consumer that relates to the past, present, or future physical, mental, or behavioral health or condition of an individual, the provision of health care, or payment for the provision of health care.

Flood Disaster Protection Act

Enacted in 1968, the Flood Disaster Protection Act mandates that banks require borrowers to purchase flood insurance for loans secured by a house, mobile home, or other property located in Special Flood Hazard Areas. Flood insurance reforms were recently adopted under the Biggert-Waters Flood Insurance Reform Act of 2012.

Bank Lending Limits

Lending limits are set to prevent banks from placing too much capital in loans to any one customer. The limits safeguard depositor funds by spreading bank loan risk over more borrowers. In 1982, the Garn-St Germain Depository Institutions Act increased banks' lending limits. The Office of the Comptroller of the Currency (OCC) issues regulations to implement the lending limits applicable to national banks and federal savings associations. States have similar laws that impose lending limits on state-chartered banks.

SUMMARY

- Because lending contributes a significant portion of a bank's income, the profitability of any bank depends to a large extent on the quality of its loan portfolio. Bank loans also serve a valuable economic need; they are an essential source of financing for individuals, businesses, and governments.

- Most banks divide loan operations into categories that reflect their primary customer bases: consumer, real estate, business, and government. To meet the diverse credit needs of these customers, banks offer an assortment of loan products. Consumer loans are either open-end (revolving) credit or closed-end (installment) loans. These loans may be unsecured, such as credit cards, or secured, such as home mortgages. Real estate loans include construction and mortgage loans. Reverse mortgage loans have become more popular among the elderly, who are able to access accrued equity in their houses.

- Business loans, which may make up a large proportion of a bank's total loan portfolio, are lines of credit and short- and long-term loans and may be secured and unsecured. Purposes include working capital, inventory, letters of credit, lease financing, or leveraged buyouts. Two business loan pricing methods are cost-plus and relationship profitability pricing.

- State and local governments borrow from banks to meet working capital needs that tax revenues cannot immediately finance. Banks also offer a variety of loan products in conjunction with government-sponsored or supported programs.

- The loan process begins with the loan application and interview. The bank then decides whether to continue with the loan request. A decision to decline a loan may be made at any time during the loan process, in which case the customer must be given a written adverse action notice. If the bank continues with the loan request, the next step is to conduct a credit investigation, which includes obtaining a credit report for consumer loans and extended inquiries and analysis for business loans. Loan documentation begins at the time of application and includes all the forms necessary to secure the lender's interest and comply with federal and state requirements.

- After the loan is properly documented and closed, it moves into the loan administration phase. Loan administration includes such activities as posting payments and maintaining files and documentation. Loans are periodically reviewed to ensure the quality of the portfolio. Asset recovery specialists monitor loans for potential problems and take action as needed to prevent losses. Regulators rate banks on the quality of their assets, including loans. Loans at immediate risk may be labeled as substandard, doubtful, or loss loans.

- The board of directors and bank executive management establish bank loan policy and oversee the lending functions. The directors' responsibilities include reviewing the loan portfolio, assigning lending authority, and adjusting credit standards.

- Lending is highly regulated. Some of the laws or regulations that apply are the Dodd-Frank Wall Street Reform and Consumer Protection Act (Dodd-Frank Act), Equal Credit Opportunity Act (Regulation B), Truth in Lending Act (Regulation Z), Credit Card Accountability, Responsibility and Disclosure Act (Credit CARD Act), Community Reinvestment Act (Regulation BB), Home Mortgage Disclosure Act (Regulation C), Real Estate Settlement Procedures Act (CFPB Regulation X), Fair Credit Reporting Act, Flood Disaster Protection Act, and regulations on bank lending limits. Banking regulators also periodically issue guidance on adjusting lending policies and practices in response to unusual economic conditions that occur, for example, during natural disasters or economic recessions.

SELF-CHECK AND REVIEW

Learning Check

1. Why is the lending function so important to banks?
2. What is the difference between open-end and closed-end credit? Give some examples of each type of consumer loan.
3. Why are home equity loans and home equity lines of credit popular?
4. If a business wants to purchase a piece of equipment, what loan type is appropriate—working capital or term loan? Why?
5. Why do applications for business credit typically require a more thorough investigation than applications for consumer credit? What sources of information can be tapped to provide this more thorough level of investigation?
6. What kinds of payment protection are available to consumers?
7. What are some activities involved in loan administration?
8. What is the function of loan review?
9. What roles does the bank board of directors play in the lending function?
10. What are some laws with which a loan officer must comply when making a mortgage loan?

Personal Financial Planning

7

Learning Objectives

After studying this chapter, you should be able to

- Explain the need for financial planning services
- Describe the financial planning tools and process
- Identify the insurance and investment products banks offer
- Identify retirement planning considerations and products
- Describe trust services banks offer
- Discuss laws, regulations, and expectations for banks and bankers engaged in providing investment, insurance, and trust services

Introduction

Andrew Carnegie, the great American industrialist and philanthropist, advised others to "Concentrate your energies, your thoughts, and your capital. The wise man puts all his eggs in one basket and watches the basket."

Few have attained the wealth Carnegie had in his day, but everyone wants to improve their financial situation in life and enjoy the stability and security that comes with that.

Most bank customers, whatever their financial status, want guidance on how to manage their finances, their "basket of eggs." Some want to set money aside for major expenses such as a down payment on a home or to pay for their children's college education. Others want to save for their retirement, realizing that life expectancies today exceed those of any previous generation. Banks can help people meet these goals, adding to the assets their customers have through investment products and protecting what their customers have with insurance products.

Many banks also offer their customers trust services, which until recently were primarily intended for wealthier customers. However, full-service banking is now available on a much broader scale; banks everywhere have expanded their business lines and are offering more trust, financial planning, wealth management, and investment products and services relevant to almost every customer's financial needs.

FINANCIAL HEALTH EQUALS PERSONAL WEALTH

The Great Recession of 2008–2009 cast a harsh spotlight on the tenuous financial condition of the typical American household. In a relatively short amount of time—in the approximately two years from the beginning of the recession to its end—U.S. households lost a combined $12 trillion in wealth, falling to a combined $57 trillion. Much of this loss was attributable to a collapse in the U.S. economy that caused home prices in many areas of the country to fall by 20 percent or more, and stock values to drop even more sharply.

However, the dire financial condition that many Americans found themselves in could not all be blamed on a poor U.S. economy. A lot of the problem was self-inflicted. In almost every year during the 1960s and 1970s, the personal savings rate of Americans averaged 10 percent or greater. However, beginning in the early 1980s, the savings rate began a slow decline that continued for more than two decades, finally bottoming out at 2 to 3 percent between 2005 and 2008 (see exhibit 7.1). Savings only began to rebound in 2009 after the public grew worried in the midst of the recession and began once again to set money aside.

Time-Honored Principles for Financial Health

- Budget to save
- Save and invest
- Control debt
- Protect accumulated wealth

Source: Federal Reserve Bank of Dallas

Exhibit 7.1: Personal Savings Rate in the United States

Source: Federal Reserve Bank of St. Louis

Increased savings, along with a turnaround in house and securities values, means that Americans are finally regaining the wealth they lost during the Great Recession. In fact, by the third quarter of 2013, the Federal Reserve reported that U.S. household wealth had reached a record high of $77.3 trillion.

Nonetheless, these gains have not been realized by all Americans, particularly those who do not own homes or stocks. Many Americans still hold too much consumer debt, especially in the form of credit card debt and student loans. In some markets, housing prices have yet to fully rebound, with homeowners still owing more on their mortgages than their houses are worth.

Further, many Americans approaching retirement age are also in poor financial shape. According to a recent survey by the Employee Benefit Research Institute, only 66 percent of U.S. workers have saved any money for their retirement, and 57 percent have less than $25,000 in total savings. Those workers who have not saved for retirement have little other savings. Sixty percent have less than $1,000 in savings and investments, and 18 percent have between $1,000 and $9,999. The inability of many Americans to save for retirement has serious long-term implications on both a personal and national level.

To address this national problem of excessive debt and inadequate savings, government, industry leaders, educators, and consumer interest groups have joined forces to educate Americans of all ages on the value of, and the methods for obtaining, maintaining, and restoring, financial health.

The word "wealth" conjures different images, from opulent splendor and the ability to purchase almost anything to simple peace-of-mind and the ability to pay bills on time and meet basic food, shelter, and clothing needs. Regardless, most would agree that personal financial wealth consists of assets accumulated free and clear of any obligations.

No matter what their income level, Americans face challenges budgeting for their ongoing financial obligations and managing their accumulated wealth. By

"Annual income twenty pounds, annual expenditure nineteen six, result happiness. Annual income twenty pounds, annual expenditure twenty pounds ought and six, result misery."

— Wilkins Micawber in *David Copperfield by* Charles Dickens serving as trusted advisors and managers of wealth, banks are helping Americans meet this challenge.

Banks and Financial Planning

The personal wealth management services that banks offer range from the most basic financial planning information to complex high-end trust and investment services. By providing these services, banks fulfill their role as trustworthy guardians of money. Banks serve as investment advisors and financial planners for consumers, corporations, pension plans, endowments, and public agencies.

Financial Planning Goals

Financial planning is the drafting and implementation of a personal program to achieve specified financial objectives. The goal is to maximize income and minimize expenses to attain short-term objectives, such as an automobile purchase, and long-term objectives, such as saving funds for higher education or a comfortable retirement.

Banks offer financial planning for a number of reasons, from meeting customer requests for such services to developing long-term customer relationships. Customers who buy investment and trust products use more bank services, contributing to their bank's fee income. Furthermore, by providing quality financial planning services, banks improve their position in the community as dependable and knowledgeable advisors.

Time Value of Money

"Remember that time is money," counseled Benjamin Franklin. Indeed, when building personal wealth, money and time are related in many ways. The values of assets, liabilities, and earnings are affected by time.

For example, inflation can undermine the value of an asset, while a growing scarcity of an asset can increase its value. Similarly, interest can have both a negative and positive effect. On one hand, interest earned on assets such as savings accounts and bonds adds to income and, ultimately, to the value of the assets. On the other hand, interest paid on loans, such as real estate mortgages, adds to the cost of the asset and increases the owner's liability. Most homeowners count on their home to appreciate in value to offset and eventually reward them for the debt incurred when they purchase such a significant asset.

Financial planning, therefore, takes into account the interplay of time and value. To reach wealth management goals, financial plans should ensure that earnings on assets offset and surpass inflation's eroding effect on the value of money and, thus, on the assets' values as measured in terms of money. Simply put, earnings on assets should exceed the inflation rate.

Risk Management Considerations

An important aspect of financial planning is managing the **risk/return trade-off** by choosing investments and assets that are appropriate for the customer's goals and life stage. The general assumption is that younger people are willing to take more risks in the hope of greater return, but as people approach retirement, they

Did You Know ...

People whose income is below a certain level can open an individual development account (IDA) in some communities. IDAs are opened at local banks as part of a money management program suggested by a nonprofit group. Deposits are matched with funds provided by a combination of federal grants and nonfederal contributions from state and local governments, financial institutions, and the philanthropic community. IDAs are used to meet an eligible person's savings goals, such as purchasing a home, paying for education or job training, or starting a business.

IDAs can be a good opportunity for banks as well. Opening a checking or savings account is the first step toward becoming a customer of other bank products and services, such as credit products, investments, and insurance.

risk/return trade-off—The relationship between an investment's risk and its potential return; the lower the investment's risk, the lower the return, and vice versa.

look for safer investments because they have less time to recover from market changes that may result in losses. In addition to age, other personal considerations, such as a customer's risk tolerance level, will determine how risk is managed in his or her financial plan. A financially conservative investor, for example, may be more concerned with safety than return.

Financial advisors often think in terms of a risk pyramid for investments (see exhibit 7.2). Like the broad base of a pyramid, most people have more assets invested in cash, cash equivalents, and other liquid investments.

> **By The Numbers**
>
> ***Determining Future Value***
>
> The calculation for determining the future value of an investment increasing per period is
>
> $$FV = P(1+i)^{EB}\left[\frac{(1+i)^n-(1+g)^n}{i-g}\right]$$
>
> P = present value
> 1 = initial investment
> i = interest rate
> g = increase in the investment
> EB = exponent, 0 is the end of the period and 1 is the beginning of the period
>
> An employee invests his annual bonus of $10,000—which will increase by 7 percent annually—for five years in a deferred compensation plan that pays 10 percent annually. If $10,000, increasing at 7 percent each year, is invested at 10 percent annually for five years the accumulated value will be $76,251.37.
>
> $$\$76{,}251.37 = \$10{,}000(1+.10)\left[\frac{(1+.10)^5-(1+.07)^5}{.10-.07}\right]$$

The Role of the Financial Planner

A financial planner is an advisor who helps customers develop a plan to realize their financial objectives. An effective plan takes into account such objectives as:

- Short-term safety net
- Debt reduction
- Housing options
- Investment options
- Asset protection (such as insurance)

Exhibit 7.2: The Risk Pyramid

> **The Values of Money**
>
> - **Time value of money**—The idea that a dollar today is worth more than a dollar in the future because the dollar received today can earn interest until the time the future dollar is received.
> - **Present value**—The amount in today's currency that future income or outlay would be worth if received or paid today.
> - **Future value**—What money or assets currently in hand will be worth at a specified time if left to grow at a given rate.
> - **Net present value**—The difference between the cost of an investment and the discounted present value of that investment's future earnings.
> - **Net future value**—The difference at a specific future date between the sum of the future values of all earnings and the sum of the future values of all costs resulting from a current investment.

- Education plans (personal and for **dependents**)
- Planning for such emergencies as disability
- Retirement strategies
- Estate planning

The planner's job is to help the customer set priorities and make appropriate financial decisions. To do this, the plan must help the customer stay ahead of inflation, minimize costs, manage unexpected expenses, and fulfill short-term and long-term needs and objectives at each life stage.

Ethical Standards

As in every other aspect of banking, bankers providing financial planning services must be professional and ethical. The first duty to the customer is to provide objective information, without considering which financial product brings more income for the bank. To avoid any potential conflict of interest, a banker must fully disclose all costs and requirements, such as fees, commissions, and penalties that are associated with a recommended product.

The financial planner is a generalist who helps the customer coordinate the work of specialists such as accountants, brokers, lawyers, and insurance agents. When offering financial planning services, bankers must be careful not to stray into areas beyond their professional expertise and licensed qualifications, such as giving specific legal advice that is more appropriate for a lawyer to give or tax advice that is more appropriate for a certified public accountant to give. Although the planner can provide information on the elements of a will and affordable investments that would achieve the plan's objectives, the choice should remain with the customer.

Minimizing Tax Liability

Although bankers must be careful to avoid the unauthorized practice of law, they can inform customers about the tax benefits of products customers are considering for their financial plans. In addition to contributions to deferred compensation plans, such as 401(k) plans, customers may open individual retirement accounts (IRAs) or buy annuities to be drawn on after they reach retirement age and are typically in a lower tax bracket. They may choose to invest in municipal bonds, which provide income that is traditionally exempt from federal taxes. They may donate to charitable organizations, or they may set up **trusts** into which they put assets for the benefit of others and thus avoid estate taxes on those assets when they die. For the same reason, customers may buy life insurance. Minimizing costs or liabilities, including taxes, should be factored into a customer's financial plan.

FINANCIAL PLANNING PROCESS

The financial planning process begins with an analysis of a customer's current position, including net worth, and a discussion with the customer about his or her financial needs and goals. Using this information, cash flow and investment strategies are designed and incorporated into a plan, which is then implemented by the customer

dependent—A person, such as a child, who depends on another person, such as a parent, for care and financial support.

trust—A fiduciary relationship in which one party (a person or a corporation) holds title to property for another party based on a legal agreement and the fiduciary principles of law.

Factors in Risk Level Choices
- Financial goals over time
- How long money can be invested
- Ability to take on more financial risk
- Inflation risk

Did You Know ...

Many Americans lack the necessary knowledge to improve their financial condition (commonly referred to as "financial literacy"):

- Fifty-six percent do not have a budget.
- One-third do not pay all of their bills on time.
- Thirty-nine percent carry credit card debt over from month to month.
- Forty percent are saving less than they were one year ago.

Source: National Foundation for Credit Counseling

and qualified experts. Financial plans should be reviewed, usually annually, to identify any needed modifications related to changes in the customer's life and goals.

Customer Life Stages

Although everyone needs a financial plan, a customer's life stage will affect the services and products a bank may recommend. Knowing the customer's situation and life stage helps the financial planner build a relationship, understand the customer's financial position, and make meaningful contributions to his or her plan.

Young Adults

Adults in their early twenties are fairly new to the job market. They are still getting their bearings as they handle an independent life and take on adult responsibilities. Most need a savings account to build liquidity in case of an emergency. Many have experience using checking accounts, debit cards, and credit cards, but it is a good idea to inquire whether they are managing these bank services well. They probably will want to buy a vehicle and eventually a home, and they typically will need loans for these purchases. Young adults usually do not need much life insurance and might benefit more from disability insurance. Even if they receive disability insurance from their employer, they may need more coverage depending on their life style and working situation. When they are ready to invest, depending on their risk tolerance level, young adults usually begin at the middle of the risk pyramid, buying stocks that have potential for **appreciation**.

Adults with Children

Adults with children need comprehensive financial planning. They probably should aim for long-term growth without high risk because they need to build assets as well as meet current needs such as housing and education. Adults with children may elect to invest in stocks and a growth mutual fund, with perhaps a conservative municipal bond fund, such as those at the lower and middle levels of the risk pyramid, in addition to their more liquid savings accounts. Adults in this segment should take advantage of any 401(k) benefits or contribute to IRAs and invest in long-term certificates of deposit.

Adults with children should also consider educational savings accounts. In addition, both spouses need life insurance; they should also make sure that their mortgaged property is properly insured for replacement cost and that they have other property and liability coverage. Given their responsibilities, adults should be encouraged to make wills, specifically naming guardians for any minor children. If they have sufficient assets, adults with children should also seriously consider **estate** planning, especially trusts.

Empty Nesters

Older adults who no longer have to worry about raising and educating children can live with less asset growth and more stability. Although older adults may no longer have the costs of providing for dependents, other costs, such as health care expenses, may increase, so there is an ongoing need to generate some income from investments

Financial Planning Steps

- Determine customer's needs
- Prepare a net worth statement
- Identify short-, medium-, and long-term goals
- Decide how to bring the present position into balance
- Prepare a cash flow strategy
- Draw up a full plan
- Put the plan into action
- Reassess the plan regularly

appreciation—The increase in the value or usefulness of an asset.

estate—The assets (property) a person owns such as real estate, cash, stocks, bonds, and all other personal property, and the person's liabilities (debts) and other legal obligations. Often used to describe the property of a decedent.

to supplement prospective Social Security and private pension income. For investments, empty nesters may put half or more of their money in a mix of short- and long-term municipal bond funds, some in money market funds, and perhaps a small percentage in an aggressive growth fund. They will not need much life insurance once the children are independent, but they should certainly consider long-term care insurance. Empty nesters definitely should consider estate planning if they have not done so already.

Variations on Standard Life Stages

Although these descriptions and possibilities apply in most situations, financial planners undoubtedly will encounter variations. Some young adults have been working since their teen years and already have good liquidity positions in their savings accounts. Some customers may never marry, or they may have inherited a small fortune and have no experience handling large sums. Other customers never will enjoy an empty nest because of the need to care for a parent or a child with special needs. In all situations, there will be bank products—from savings to insurance to investments and trust-related services—that meet the unique needs of customers.

> **Situation**
>
> Phyllis is working on her financial plan. Her bank provided her with a worksheet to help determine her net worth. After adding up all her assets, including a car she received from her parents and an inheritance from her grandmother, and then deducting her student loans, she determines she has a net worth of $30,000. That is quite good for a young professional not long out of college, so she thanks her mom and dad for teaching her good savings habits. Now Phyllis is ready to meet with her banker and the bank's financial planner to discuss strategies to build her personal wealth.

Financial Planning Goals

After listening carefully and gathering all the necessary background information, financial planners then discuss with customers the specific areas that need to be addressed when building their plan. Goals need to be set to:

- Cope with current demands, such as food, housing, and transportation
- Protect against personal risks, such as physical incapacity and property loss
- Set aside funds for emergencies, education, and investments
- Prepare for retirement
- Minimize taxes
- Provide for **heirs**

heir—A person who inherits property.

Some financial advisors think in terms of "buckets" for different purposes, one for immediate needs and others for a variety of future needs. A good financial plan will cover how assets will be managed and by whom. Investments in a mutual fund, for example, require less customer attention than managing individual stocks.

Among other considerations, financial plans must ensure that funds are available when they are needed; liquidity is important for stability.

Financial Products

Banks have the authority to provide brokerage services, including investment management services, through subsidiaries or affiliates. Trust departments also provide these services, usually once a trust is established. By providing a mix of savings, insurance, and investment products, banks help customers achieve their investment goals such as maintaining liquidity, preserving capital, minimizing risk, or generating income. Financial products can be categorized by the risk of loss.

Conservative-Growth Assets (Lower Risk)

Traditional bank products such as savings accounts, money market accounts, and certificates of deposit are conservative assets that focus on protecting principal and generating some income. They are typically used to meet everyday expenses and often provide a small investment return. Many of these products are liquid and insured by the Federal Deposit Insurance Corporation (FDIC). (See bottom level of the risk pyramid in exhibit 7.2.)

Moderate-Growth Assets (Moderate Risk)

These assets have the potential to increase both principal and income but at moderate rates. Some examples of these types of investment products are municipal bonds and stock in larger companies (commonly referred to as **mid-cap stock** or **large-cap stock**), as measured by the market value of their shares of stock. However, these investments are not FDIC-insured. (See middle level of the risk pyramid in exhibit 7.2.)

Aggressive-Growth Assets (Highest Risk)

Investments in the aggressive asset growth category are characterized by increased risk, but they offer the possibility of higher returns than conservative and moderate growth products. Examples include investments in the stock of small companies (**small-cap stock**) or new companies and those in emerging markets. Real estate, commodities, and high-yield bonds are also considered high-risk investments. Only knowledgeable investors with ample income and liquidity usually consider these investments. Because the risks are great, these investment products usually are part of a diversified portfolio. They should not be the main investment vehicle. (See top level of the risk pyramid in exhibit 7.2.)

large-cap stock—Generally, stock of companies whose market value is greater than $10 billion.

mid-cap stock—Generally, stock of companies whose market value is between $2 billion and $10 billion.

small-cap stock—Generally, stock of companies whose total market value is less than $2 billion.

net worth—The difference between total assets and total liabilities as calculated for an individual or business.

depreciation—The decrease in the value or usefulness of an asset.

Net Worth Statement

All financial accounts can be expressed in numbers. After gathering information about needs and goals, the details of a customer's financial position must be analyzed to assess his or her current net worth. Exhibit 7.3, next page, is a simple worksheet that both the financial planner and customer may use as a starting point. The **net worth**—or a person's personal wealth—is determined by subtracting total liabilities from total assets.

Assets (owned) – Liabilities (owed) = Net worth

Assets that are accumulated for personal wealth should be separated from assets that are used for current needs, which are not subject to appreciation. For example, an automobile may be an expensive asset for a young adult, but it does not generally appreciate after it is purchased and used. Instead, it **depreciates** in value. Thus, a car is not an asset that generally increases in value and accumulates personal wealth. Rather, it is an asset that is used to satisfy current needs.

Often customers have not thought about the elements of their financial situation that go into a net worth analysis. The net worth analysis helps clarify where current allocations are out of balance. Is the customer spending too large a percentage of his or her income on housing or to pay down debt, for example? Questions like this are part of the value of financial planning because they help a person evaluate what money is available, where current spending goes, and where the gaps are between the current financial picture and the one the customer envisions for the future.

Exhibit 7.3: Net Worth Worksheet

Assets		**Liabilities**	
Cash on hand	$_____	Accounts payable	$_____
Checking accounts	$_____	Credit cards	$_____
			$_____
			$_____
Savings accounts	$_____	Health care bills	$_____
	$_____		$_____
	$_____		$_____
Stocks, bonds, other securities	$_____	Other	$_____
Cash value of life insurance	$_____	Notes payable	$_____
Amounts owed by others		Vehicle notes	$_____
Cash	$_____	Installment purchases	$_____
Promissory notes	$_____	Bank loans	$_____
		Life insurance loans	$_____
Real estate		Taxes due	
Home	$_____	Federal	$_____
Vacation home	$_____	Property	$_____
Income-producing real estate	$_____	State and local	$_____
		Other	$_____
Vested pension (present value)	$_____	Mortgages	
	$_____	Home	$_____
	$_____	Other	$_____
401(k) or other company plan	$_____	Informal loans from others	$_____
Annuities	$_____	Other	$_____
Investments in a business	$_____		
	$_____		
	$_____		
Other assets			
Home furnishings (discount 15% a year since purchase, or estimate 5% of the home's value)	$_____		
Sports equipment	$_____		
Art, antiques, and other collectibles	$_____		
Cars, boats, and RVs (Blue Book values)	$_____		
Other			
Total assets	**$_____**	**Total liabilities**	**$_____**
Minus total liabilities	($_____)		
Net worth	**$_____**		

Cash Flow Strategy

Every financial goal has an allocation of resources. The net worth analysis helps refine and prioritize goals, identify them as long- or short-term, and draw up a cash flow strategy. For most customers, this information will be used to generate a monthly budget, calculate monthly income and expenses, and make adjustments to their overall financial plan. Exhibit 7.4 illustrates a monthly cash flow plan for a young bank customer. By adjusting income and expenses, a person can generate additional funds to save, invest, or contribute to a retirement plan.

In combination, the net worth analysis and cash flow strategy help the financial planner and customer objectively consider how the plan can accommodate life's unexpected financial crises—high inflation, job loss, a natural disaster, home damage, or a debilitating illness, for example. Recognizing such possibilities while they still seem remote is the foundation of a good financial plan. The plan will ensure that, in addition to cash for day-to-day needs, other liquid assets will be available for emergencies and insurance will be purchased to protect against specific crises.

Average Annual Household Expenditures in 2012:

- Food $6,599
  - At home $3,921
  - Away from home $2,678
- Housing $16,887
- Apparel and services $1,736
- Transportation $8,998
- Health care $3,556
- Entertainment $2,605
- Cash contributions $1,913
- Personal insurance and pensions $5,591
- All other expenditures $3,557

TOTAL $51,442

Source: Bureau of Labor Statistics, 2013

Exhibit 7.4: Monthly Cash Flow Plan for a Single Working Person

	Income		
	Current	Change	Adjustment
Salary	$2,350		$2,350
Commissions	250	250	500
Interest on savings	500		500
Other income			
Total income	**$3,100**	**$250**	**$3,350**

	Expenses		
	Current	Changes	Adjustment
Rent	$950		$950
Renter's insurance	30		30
Electricity	20		20
Transportation	50		50
Water	25		25
Telephone	50		50
Internet service	45		45
Insurance	50		50
Charitable donations	0		0
Credit card interest	25		25
Groceries	250		250
Clothing	200	-50	150
Student loan payments	100		100
Gym fees	80		80
Entertainment	200	-50	150
Miscellaneous	100		100
Total expenses	**$2,175**	**$-100**	**$2,075**
Monthly net	$925		$1,275
Available to save, invest, or contribute	**$925**		**$1,275**

INSURANCE PROTECTION

Insurance, an established way to preserve assets, is vital to risk management and thus to a financial plan. Most states require property and liability insurance for motor vehicles, for example, and banks require insurance for homes on which they hold the mortgage.

When the Gramm-Leach-Bliley Act (GLBA) was enacted, banks were permitted to offer a full range of insurance products. Banks may act as brokers by offering product lines from different insurance companies. Financial holding companies may underwrite insurance and annuities, either directly or through a nonbank affiliate. Insurance products tied to investments, such as whole and variable life insurance policies and annuities, are considered **nondeposit investment products** and are not FDIC-insured. Noncredit-related insurance products offered by banks include life, health and disability, long-term care, property, and liability insurance.

nondeposit investment product—Any financial product with an investment component that is not a deposit product and thus not insured by the Federal Deposit Insurance Corporation (FDIC). Stocks, bonds, insurance products, and government and municipal securities are examples.

premium—(1) The payment for insurance coverage in either a lump sum or installments; (2) the amount or percentage above face value at which securities are bought or sold.

Life Insurance

Life insurance replaces the income the policyholder was contributing to the family when he or she died. Single people with no dependents usually need only enough life insurance to cover funeral expenses and unpaid debts. Adults with dependents need more life insurance to ensure that their dependents' future living expenses, including care giving, are covered. Life insurance generally is categorized as term or whole life.

Term Life Insurance

For term life insurance, the purchaser pays a specified amount of money for a specified amount of life insurance for a period (term) of one to 30 years. At the end of the term, no excess **premium** remains and the contract ends. Premiums for term life insurance may start low, but rise dramatically as the insured ages because the risk of dying increases with age.

Whole Life Insurance

Whole life insurance is both an insurance product and an investment vehicle. So long as the premiums are paid, the policy remains in force for the life of the insured. The policyholder pays a fixed premium to the insurance company, which invests it in stocks, bonds, money market instruments, or other assets, depending on the product features. In addition to paying a stated amount in the event of the insured's death, a whole life insurance policy accumulates a cash value that the policyholder can redeem or borrow against. The policy may pay a fixed or variable return, and income taxes on the gain do not have to be paid until the policy is cashed. Premiums for whole life insurance tend to be higher in the early years than the cost of term insurance because they are used to build the policy's cash value. Whole life premiums then level off or lessen as the insured ages, reflecting the increase in cash value.

Term Life Versus Whole Life

- **Term life**—Short-term insurance with no savings element.

- **Whole life**—Long-term insurance with a savings element.

Other Types of Life Insurance

Other types of life insurance products include variable life insurance and universal life insurance, both of which separate the insurance protection from the savings part of the policy. This means the buyer assumes more risk on the savings end in the hope of a better return. Both are interest-sensitive. In contrast, traditional whole life is not interest-sensitive. This means that whole life insurance is inherently safer, but because it is safer, the return is lower and the cash value builds more slowly.

Life insurance may not be the best way for all customers to build cash for later years. If life insurance is not needed to take care of a spouse or dependents, customers might benefit more by putting their money into alternative investments such as certificates of deposit, U.S. Treasury securities, mutual funds, or bonds.

Credit life insurance is similar to term insurance in that there is no savings feature. Instead, it is purchased to pay an amount equal to that owed on a loan. Banks sell credit life insurance policies in conjunction with bank loans. If the insured dies when the loan is still outstanding, the loan is paid off rather than having the debt passed on to the deceased's estate.

Health, Disability, and Long-Term Care Insurance

Rising health care costs make being injured or sick expensive. For this reason, health insurance should be an important part of any financial plan. Group health insurance premiums paid through an employer, or a professional association, generally are lower than premiums for individual policies because the risk is spread over a large group of insured. Shared risk is also the principle underlying the creation of health insurance marketplaces by the Patient Protection and Affordable Care Act (also known as the ACA or "Obamacare"). The ACA requires all individuals to have health insurance, either through their employer or through individual policies purchased from federal or state marketplaces.

Most basic health insurance policies set time and dollar limits on benefits for hospital room and board and may pay only a percentage of medical and surgical costs. Because basic policies may not fully cover health costs, customers may want to buy supplemental medical insurance for additional protection against the high cost of serious and continuing illnesses or injuries. Insurance policies are also available that cover vision, dental care, prescription drugs, and nursing home care.

Disability insurance is as important as life insurance because, statistically, a person is more likely to be disabled—temporarily or permanently—before retirement age than to die. Because the chances of becoming disabled increase with age, coverage is especially important for older workers. Disability insurance pays a weekly or monthly income benefit if the policyholder is partially or totally disabled due to a covered injury or illness. Employers often offer group disability income coverage to their employees, but individual policies are also available.

Long-term care insurance is becoming a necessity as life expectancy increases. A healthy retirement fund or savings plan can be depleted quickly by the cost of nursing home care. A long-term care policy supports an individual who is chronically ill or functionally handicapped, which is commonly defined as being unable to walk, bathe, dress, or perform other basic daily living activities. Services covered may include home health care, care in assisted living facilities and nursing homes, respite care, and hospice care. Long-term care policies typically are issued to individuals between ages 30 and 85. As the U.S. population ages, the percentage of people

Situation

George Morgan is concerned that his family does not have enough money on hand in case of an emergency. After talking to his banker, he sets up a separate savings account and arranges to have $300 transferred into it every month from his checking account. He makes sure this account is not accessible by ATM. The banker assures him that, once he reaches a certain minimum balance, he will begin earning a higher interest rate. Then his banker shares with George a brochure about the bank's insurance products and explains the features and benefits of life insurance. George thanks the banker, takes his business card, and makes an appointment to purchase some insurance.

needing long-term care is increasing. Consequently, long-term care policies have become a popular form of insurance.

Property, Title, and Vehicle Insurance

Property insurance protects the value of things a consumer owns—homes, boats, jewelry, silverware, money, and so forth—that can be lost to fire, theft, lawsuits, natural disasters, or other events. Home replacement cost coverage, which normally covers the cost to rebuild a structure using modern materials according to current building standards, is recommended.

Title insurance protects homebuyers from financial loss due to questions about property ownership. It differs from property insurance in that it protects the title of the property rather than the property itself. If someone came forward with a valid claim on property that, for example, had been surveyed incorrectly, title insurance would reimburse the owner for the loss.

Vehicle insurance typically includes coverage for both personal liability and collision arising from the ownership, maintenance, or use of automobiles, motorcycles, snowmobiles, and other motorized vehicles. Vehicle liability insurance covers the bodily injury or death of people caused by the insured. Claims for bodily injury may include medical bills, loss of income, or pain and suffering. Liability coverage also extends to damage caused to property of others. Collision coverage applies to losses arising from physical damage to a covered vehicle or other object. Vehicle insurance usually is required by state law.

Liability Insurance

Liability or casualty insurance protects an individual or business against losses resulting from bodily injury or property damage suffered by other persons. These policies normally cover legal expenses, medical expenses, and funeral expenses incurred by persons who are injured or killed, and the cost of repairing or replacing damaged property. Professional liability insurance protects the insured against claims arising out of the practice of professional services.

INVESTMENT SERVICES

Banks or financial holding companies may offer investment and brokerage services through a third-party arrangement, a joint venture, or an in-house brokerage, as follows:

- **Third-party arrangement.** Banks arrange for a licensed brokerage firm to operate on their premises, for which they are paid a fee. Earnings are lower this way than when a bank offers the services itself, but it has fewer responsibilities. This arrangement simply makes the services available to the bank's customers.
- **Joint venture.** Banks arrange with broker-dealers to sell securities, with employees working directly for either the bank or the broker-dealer. Those working for the broker-dealer generally are licensed and registered representatives who have taken qualifying exams. The licensed broker-dealer must supervise any brokerage functions performed by bank employees.

- **In-house brokerage.** Banks sell brokerage products through their own discount or full-service brokerages, formed either as bank subsidiaries or through affiliates in a financial holding company. Discount brokerages sell investment products and services but do not offer investment advice. Therefore, they are typically less expensive than a full-service brokerage. Full-service brokerages sell securities and offer investment advisory services. They may perform the same services as large nonaffiliated brokerage houses, including underwriting and dealing in equity securities.

By The Numbers

The Power of Compound Interest

Compound interest is interest paid on previously earned interest as well as on the original deposit or investment.

$$P = C(1+r/n)^{nt}$$

P = deposit or investment value at maturity
C = initial investment
r = interest rate (expressed as a decimal: for example, 6 percent = 0.06)
n = number of times per year interest is compounded
t = number or years invested

If **C** is $10,000, **r** is 6 percent, **n** is 1 (annually), and **t** is 1, what would **P** be at maturity?

Answer: $10,600.00

Now, what is the future value when interest is compounded more frequently (only n changes)?

n	P
2 (semi-annually)	$10,609.00
4 (quarterly)	$10,613.64
12 (monthly)	$10,616.78

Because investment products, such as stocks, bonds, annuities, and mutual funds, are not bank deposits, they are not FDIC-insured. Banks must make sure that customers understand this important difference before selling them a nondeposit investment product.

Investment Strategies

The three basic investment strategies are conservative, moderate, and aggressive. Determining the appropriate strategy will depend on the customer's risk tolerance and return objectives. Factors that influence the decision are life stage, personal circumstances, and financial plan goals. Common motivations are to safeguard or increase principal, produce income, or pursue high returns.

The investment choices shown in the risk pyramid in exhibit 7.2 correspond to investment strategies. Conservative investors looking to safeguard principal probably will have a **portfolio** heavily weighted toward cash equivalents, such as certificates of deposit and money market funds, as well as lower-risk investments such as highly-rated bonds. Moderate investors will often seek to maintain a balance of principal maintenance and growth, and are likely to have a mix of stocks and bonds. Aggressive investors seek capital growth and usually carry a portfolio that is heavily weighted in equity investments, including some stock in small cap, international, and emerging market companies.

For all three strategies, **diversification** of the portfolio is usually a standard recommendation.

portfolio—The assets owned by one organization or person and managed as a collective whole to reach specific investment goals.

diversification—A method of decreasing the total risk of investments by investing funds in different kinds of assets.

Stocks

A share of stock represents a share of ownership interest in a company. For the issuing company, stocks provide capital. For investors, stocks often provide a share of the company's earnings in the form of **dividends** (although dividends are not guaranteed) and an increase in the stock's price resulting from appreciation. Because a stock can lose value, it is a higher-risk investment than an insured bank product, such as a certificate of deposit. Historically, however, the return on stocks has outpaced that of many other investment types, making them a good investment choice for the long term.

dividend—Payments made by a corporation to its stockholders. The payments are based on a percentage of the corporation's after-tax earnings and are usually made quarterly.

closed-end fund—An investment fund that allows only an original prescribed number of shares to be distributed. It raises substantially all of its funds at the time the fund is established. The fund is traded like a stock on an exchange. Compare to open-end fund.

open-end fund—A mutual fund that sells new shares directly to new investors and redeems shares at the market price when investors wish to sell. Assets in the fund increase or decrease as investors move money into or out of the fund.

annuity—An insurance product that provides a systematic payment for a specified period, usually a number of years. Payments typically are made monthly but can be made quarterly, semiannually, or annually.

annuitant—The beneficiary of an annuity; the person insured under an annuity plan and on whose life expectancy annuity payments are based.

Bonds

Investors who buy bonds are, in effect, lending money to the issuing corporation or government authority. Corporations issue bonds to improve their businesses. Federal, state, and local government authorities issue bonds for specific purposes, such as building sewer systems or schools. Interest usually is paid at specified times until the bond's maturity date, at which time the face value is returned to the investor. Income from most municipal bonds usually is exempt from federal, state, and local income taxes.

Municipal or corporate bonds carry varying degrees of risk, depending on the issuer's fiscal soundness, fluctuations in interest rates, and the nature of the funded project. Like stocks, bonds can lose or gain value. This happens when a bond's interest rate is less than or more than the prevailing interest rates for similar bonds.

Mutual Funds

A mutual fund is a fund operated by an investment organization, such as a mutual fund company, that pools money from many investors to purchase large amounts of assets. The assets may include stock in companies, bonds, or commodities such as gold. Mutual funds make it possible for individual investors to diversify their assets by owning a small percentage of a large pool of assets. Furthermore, mutual funds are managed by investment professionals who know more about the assets than the average investor. The initial investment often is low, and risk is spread over all the securities in the fund's portfolio.

Mutual funds may specialize narrowly, perhaps investing only in health care stocks, "green companies," companies operating internationally, or municipal bonds. Funds may invest for aggressive growth, income, or security. Index funds buy the stocks featured in a specific market index, such as the Dow Jones Industrials. Funds may also be either closed-end or open-end. **Closed-end funds** sell a limited number of shares, after which the fund is closed to new investors. **Open-end funds** issue shares continuously to investors.

Annuities

The primary benefit of **annuities** is to pay financial benefits during the lifetime of the **annuitant**, who usually is the investor. In effect, investors are paying the insurance company that sold the annuity to help them manage their money.

The two basic types of annuities are deferred (pay-in), for which the investor makes regular contributions over time and defers payments until later, and immediate (payout), in which the investor puts up the money first and then has disbursements at regular intervals during a set period or the annuitant's lifetime.

Annuities may cover more than one person ("joint and survivor"), and the rates of return may be fixed or variable. Fixed-rate annuities promise the same payout amount throughout the annuitant's lifetime. Variable annuities come in several forms, depending on how the insurer invests the funds. The payout amount and the interest rate of variable annuities are not guaranteed.

Portfolio Management

Successful investors not only buy stocks and hold them for long periods, they also regularly monitor how their investments are doing. At least once a year, they review everything they own to make sure it is still making the expected contribution toward their financial goals. Securities held by the mutual funds in which they are invested are reviewed to make sure the funds are providing the required diversity. Any major change, such as a divorce or the birth of a child, should trigger a review of the customer's financial plan and investments so that the portfolio may be rebalanced accordingly.

Most banks do more than just sell investment products. Through holding company affiliates or nonaffiliated broker-dealers, banks provide investment management services and advice to both individuals and corporations.

Asset Management Accounts

Asset management accounts provide a convenient way for customers to consolidate investments, which then can be accessed via check or debit card. Typically, a minimum initial investment is required and a fee is charged, although the fee may be waived if a required minimum balance is maintained. In return, customers are provided up-to-date account information online or in monthly statements, an annual summary statement that recaps all account activity, a daily sweep of credit balances, direct deposit services, and dividend reinvestment services.

Trading Accounts

Trading accounts allow customers to research and place trades either online or through a bank-affiliated financial consultant. Access to proprietary research, such as third-party stock research and mutual fund profiles, is typically offered. Customers may trade in a wide array of investments, including stocks, bonds, and mutual funds. Trades are subject to commissions and fees, which may be waived for active traders and customers who maintain high balances in bank-affiliated investment or deposit accounts. Customers usually have online access to trade confirmations, account histories, balances, and positions.

Banker Profile

Shelly Klein once worked as an investment banker at a Wall Street firm. Her job paid well, but required long hours, and the commute to her New Rochelle home was long. Shelly was under pressure to produce increasingly higher levels of sales to bolster the firm's commissions and fees. This life was not what she planned for in college. Helping people improve their financial position from bad-to-good and good-to-even-better was one of the personal rewards she sought. She left investment banking and joined a bank's wealth management department. Now, Shelly Klein, CTFA, is happy with her life. Although she still needs to book business, she has more time to build relationships with customers, volunteer through the bank's civic outreach programs, and enjoy the fruits of her good work.

RETIREMENT PLANNING

As life expectancies continue to increase, financial assets are stretched over more years. Therefore, retirement planning is more important than ever to ensure an adequate lifestyle after retirement. However, while income needs are greater than ever, the

Did You Know ...

A 20-year-old investing $3,000 per year in an IRA at an 8 percent return can expect the IRA's value to be more than $1,200,000 by age 65. To demonstrate that it is never too late to improve future income, a 40-year-old investing $3,000 for 25 years can expect the investment to be worth more than $200,000 by age 65.

sources of that income are growing more uncertain. Social Security only partially meets the financial needs of most retirees, and fewer companies offer pension plans that provide a defined benefit payment that can be relied upon each month. In short, most Americans have a greater responsibility than ever to fund their own retirement needs.

As noted earlier, Americans are, as a group, falling short in retirement savings, even though the federal government has made it attractive to save for retirement via tax-deferred IRAs and 401(k) plans. As with other aspects of the financial planning process, banks also have an important role to play in the effort to prepare customers for life after retirement. However, before a customer's retirement needs can be assessed, his or her current financial position must be known. Retirement planning necessitates answers to questions such as these:

- What are the customer's current expenses?
- What major expenses, such as those for a chronic medical condition, are likely to continue?
- What major expenses, such as college tuition or medical care, are likely to occur? When will they begin and end?
- Does the customer have life, health, and property insurance? How will insurance needs change over time?
- When does the customer or the spouse plan to retire?
- Where does the customer plan to retire—in the same area and home or elsewhere?
- What does the customer plan to do in retirement? If plans include work, what income can be expected?
- What health problems might prevent the customer from working?
- What assets does the customer already have for retirement?
- How much, therefore, will the customer need for retirement?

Answers to these questions will help customers identify a retirement income goal. Customers will be able to estimate what they will need and begin to think about how to reach their goal. Doing so may mean acquiring skills to do a new kind of work or putting more money aside now so it can grow for retirement. Exhibit 7.5 contains a worksheet that bankers can use to help customers estimate their retirement income needs.

Social Security and Pensions

Most Americans contribute to Social Security throughout their working lives and become eligible for full benefits in their mid-60s. However, the age of eligibility is edging upward. For example, people born between 1943 and 1954 receive full benefits when they are 66. Those born in 1960 or later will start receiving full benefits at 67. Social Security benefits can be received as early as age 62, but the benefit amount is reduced by a defined percentage for every year the benefit is taken before

Exhibit 7.5: Retirement Saving Worksheet

Using a simple worksheet like this one can help customers understand where they are today, where they'd like to be tomorrow, and what must be done to get there.

Before starting, customers need to decide how much income they will need annually. A common rule of thumb is 75 percent of current income. Customers also must decide how long they will need that much annual income. For people retiring at age 65, 20 years is reasonable. Customers then might plan to take 5 percent a year out of principal accounts, such as an IRA.

The Social Security Administration sends annual statements of the monthly benefit a taxpayer might expect to receive on retirement. This amount should be multiplied by 12 to calculate the annual income.

Income Source	*Principal*	*Annual Income*
Social Security	NA	$
Pension	NA	$
401(k) or equivalent		$
IRAs		$
Savings		$
Other assets		$
1.		$
2.		$
3.		$
4.		$
5.		$
Total available annual retirement income		$
Annual income needed		$
Annual income surplus or shortfall (+/-)		$

full retirement age. The benefit reduction is approximately 30 percent when taken at age 62. Likewise, those who wait until after their full retirement age to take Social Security receive a correspondingly larger benefit when they retire. The benefit increase is 8 percent annually between full retirement age and age 70, after which time the amount of benefit no longer increases.

As more Americans age and retire, the ability of Social Security to provide the current level of benefits has been debated. Consequently, when planning for their retirement needs, adults of all ages should consider that Social Security benefits could be reduced in the future.

Although there are still some people who belong to **defined benefit pension plans**, the number is shrinking. More companies are turning to **defined contribution pension plans**, such as 401(k) plans (see exhibit 7.6, next page). Defined contribution plans put more of the responsibility on employees to contribute to the plan (although employers usually match employee contributions up to a certain percentage) and to manage the investments. Annual contributions up to a certain legal limit and earnings on those contributions are tax-deferred until they are withdrawn from the plan. Those who are self-employed can set up Keogh accounts that are similar to 401(k)s or IRAs for the self-employed called Simplified Employee Pension (SEP) IRAs.

defined benefit pension plan—A pension plan that guarantees the payment of a specified benefit at retirement.

defined contribution pension plan—A retirement plan fund that takes in employee contributions, which may be matched by employer contributions, and then invests the contributions into one or more investment alternatives determined by the employee.

Exhibit 7.6: Amounts Held in Private Pension Plans in the United States

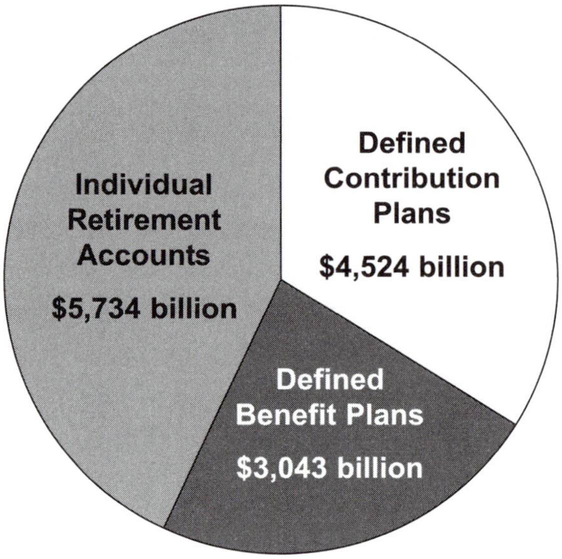

Source: Federal Reserve, Financial Accounts of the United States, Third Quarter 2013, Tables L.118b, c, and L.225i

Individual Retirement Accounts

Most banks and many financial institutions offer IRAs that provide tax advantages for retirement savings. Investment choices vary, depending on the bank. For many banks, IRAs are invested in time deposits, which often mirror a certificate of deposit. If a bank offers brokerage services or has a trust department, customers may have the option of investing in other types of assets, such as mutual funds or securities.

Contribution limits and eligibility requirements for IRAs are sometimes changed by federal legislators. The best source for confirming IRA limits and requirements is the IRS website where IRA contribution and deduction limits are posted for the current year. For example, in 2014, the maximum contribution limits for traditional and Roth IRAs combined is $5,500 for individuals less than age 50 and $6,500 for those age 50 or older.

IRA products are the traditional IRA, Roth IRA, SEP IRA, and spousal IRA.

Traditional IRA

The traditional IRA accumulates funds for use during retirement by investing in savings accounts, certificates of deposit, mutual funds, or securities. Taxes due on both annual account contributions (up to a limit) and account earnings are deferred until withdrawn. Penalty-free distributions (withdrawals) may begin at age 59½ but must begin by age 70½.

Roth IRA

Contributions to Roth IRA accounts are not deducted from taxable income, but there is no tax on account earnings. Certain distributions to the account holder or beneficiaries may be made without tax penalty at any time. Unlike traditional IRA accounts, there is no requirement to begin distributions at any age. Exhibit 7.7 compares the traditional IRA to the Roth IRA.

SEP Plan

The SEP IRA is designed for the self-employed or small business owner. Employees do not pay taxes on SEP IRA contributions until they are withdrawn. Employers receive a business deduction for contributions made to SEP IRAs on behalf of employees. Employees set up the IRA to accept the SEP contributions. The contribution limits and eligibility requirements for SEP IRAs are different from those for traditional or Roth IRAs. For example, the maximum contribution limit, which is based on adjusted earned income, can be much higher than for traditional or Roth IRAs.

Spousal IRA

IRAs cannot be opened as joint accounts. Spouses who have little or no earned income can open a spousal IRA. A spousal IRA is subject to the same rules and limitations that apply to traditional and Roth IRAs.

Estate Planning

Estate planning—planning for the disposition of assets both before and after a customer's death—should be part of a comprehensive financial plan. Some states

Exhibit 7.7: Traditional IRA Versus Roth IRA

	Traditional IRA	Roth IRA
Contributions	Tax deductible Must cease at age 70½	Not tax deductible May continue for lifetime
Earnings	Not taxed until distribution	Not taxed
Distributions	Penalty free after age 59½ Mandatory at age 70½ Taxable as income	No specific age
Withdrawal penalties	Ten percent penalty for distributions before age 59½	No penalty for withdrawals if requirements are met
Eligibility	Fully or partially deductible subject to income limitations that phase out at $70,000 (single) and $116,000 (joint) in 2014, with income limits annually adjusted	Fully or partially deductible subject to income limitations that phase out at $129,000 (single) and $191,000 (joint) in 2014, with income limits annually adjusted
FDIC-insured	Yes for bank-deposited IRAs	Yes for bank-deposited Roth IRAs

probate—A judicial procedure whereby the validity of a will is proved and a decedent's estate, in accordance with a will if it exists, is administered.

require decedent's assets of $10,000 or more to go through **probate**, whether or not the decedent had a will. Certain assets may avoid probate, however, including:

- Assets owned jointly with a right of survivorship
- Life insurance, annuities, retirement accounts, and brokerage and bank accounts for which a beneficiary is named
- Assets in revocable living trusts

Situation

Louise has been putting $1,000 annually into a UTMA account for her grandson Sebastian, who is now in school. He plans to keep the money in the account until he finishes both college and flight school at the commercial pilot academy, at which time he will be 21 years old. Her grandson then plans to draw on the account to invest in a small local commercial airline company and establish himself in the business.

Objectives of estate planning include disposing of the estate's assets as the customer wishes, minimizing estate taxes and other taxes for both the customer and the customer's beneficiaries, ensuring security for the customer's family, and arranging for continuity of the customer's business, if applicable.

One savings product that is available to most customers is the result of the Uniform Transfers to Minors Act (UTMA), which replaced and continued the custodial account arrangement under the Uniform Gifts to Minors Act in 1983. Basically, a UTMA account may be used to make an untaxed transfer of assets to a minor, thus reducing federal income taxes on earnings from the assets. Legally, the account transfers to the child the responsibility of paying income tax, which would be taxed at the minor's tax rate. The account is managed by a designated adult (the custodian) until the minor is of age (typically 18 or 21 years old).

Trusts are another way to manage estate assets. Trusts may be used to:

- Build assets for a specific purpose or person through the accumulation of interest or dividends until the beneficiary reaches a specified age
- Receive the proceeds of an insurance policy for the benefit of minor children
- Give money to charity, either by providing a steady income or by arranging for income to go to another beneficiary, with the principal going to the charity after the designated individual dies
- Prevent irresponsible beneficiaries from squandering capital by allowing the trustee to distribute only interest, not principal

Estate planning requires expert advice, which bank trust departments can provide to customers who have specific needs regarding the management and distribution of assets.

TRUST SERVICES

Trust services complement other banking services and facilitate a total financial relationship with individual and business customers. To offer trust services, the bank's federal or state charter must accord it trust powers. Many banks in recent years have applied for and received trust powers so they can serve the growing wealth management market.

The trust structure has four components:

- **Trust**—The property (cash, stocks, bonds, real estate, or any other item of value) with which the trust is created
- **Trustor**—The person creating the trust
- **Trustee**—The person or entity that takes control of the trust property and administers the trust
- **Beneficiary**—The person for whose benefit the trust was established

"Put not your trust in money, but put your money in trust."
— Oliver Wendell Holmes

When banks provide trust services, they act in a fiduciary capacity which, by law, requires adherence to fiduciary principles, such as acting in the sole interest of the beneficiaries, avoiding conflicts of interests, and carrying out duties with prudence, loyalty, and care. Banks, in their role as trustee, must observe the following fiduciary principles:

- **Prudent investor principle**—Banks are required to act with caution, skill, diligence, and a sense of responsibility. The standard is applied to the total portfolio, not to isolated investments, and to the overall investment strategy. The bank has a duty to diversify investments unless it is not prudent to do so. The bank must be loyal and impartial in how it delegates authority and selects supervising agents. The costs the bank incurs must be reasonable in amount and appropriate for the services provided.
- **Segregation of trust assets**—Assets of each trust must be kept separate from those of other trusts and from the bank's own assets. Trust departments usually are segregated from the rest of the bank, with their own vaults, data processing equipment, and other facilities. Many banks use outside investment advisors to manage trust accounts.
- **Prevention of conflicts of interest**—Banks should have no interest whatsoever in the investments bought or sold for trust funds. The bank should not purchase or benefit in any way from property or other assets held in trust.

Depending on market needs and business volume, banks may offer personal trust services such as estate settlement, trust administration, guardianships, and personal agency services.

Estate Settlement

When a customer with a trust dies, a trust officer will help settle the decedent's estate. Outstanding debts or taxes may need to be paid, and the estate assets distributed to the decedent's heirs.

A trust department's estate planner advises customers to have a valid will that describes the property owned and its location. The will should designate the beneficiaries to whom the property will be left and the person or entity (such as the bank) that will carry out the terms. That person or entity is referred to as the **executor**

executor—A party, often a bank, trust company, attorney, or even an heir, who is appointed in a will to carry out the terms of the will.

or, in some states, the personal representative. The executor may be a relative, friend, beneficiary, bank, lawyer, or some combination of these.

If the decedent did not leave a will, or if the will is not valid, the decedent is said to have died **intestate**, and the estate is distributed in accordance with the laws of the state. The probate court appoints an administrator to carry out the terms of the will if the executor cannot or will not serve and the will is valid. Basically, the duties of executors and administrators are the same. They include:

intestate—Derived from the Latin word *intestatus*, meaning one who dies without having made or left a valid will.

- Taking inventory to determine the exact value of the estate, and itemizing and showing a dollar value for each of the decedent's assets
- If necessary, taking control of some or all of the assets
- Filing notice in a newspaper or other medium of public circulation requesting submission of any claims against the estate
- Filing federal and state tax returns and paying all taxes on the basis of the estate's value
- Settling all debts and claims against the estate
- Preparing a final accounting of the estate for the court
- Distributing the remaining assets, either according to the terms of the will or as directed by state law

When a bank acts as administrator or executor, by law, it must keep detailed records and is accountable to the court and beneficiaries for its actions.

Situation

Adam, a retired businessman, wants to revise his will. Ten years earlier he had named his son as executor. Since that time, however, his assets have grown considerably, and he has acquired works of art and real estate. Although he still wants his son involved in the settlement of his estate, he feels his son would benefit from the services of a professional as well. He solves this problem by naming his son and his bank's trust department as co-executors in his will.

Trust Administration

Trust administration services are for bank customers who seek professional management of their assets to ensure financial objectives are met, beneficiaries are provided for, and trust assets are distributed to heirs. The most common types of trust funds administered by banks are testamentary trusts, living trusts, and charitable and institutional trusts.

- **Testamentary trust**—A trust established under the terms of a decedent's will. As trustee, the bank is responsible for managing assets turned over to it by the executor or administrator and for making payouts to the beneficiaries as specified in the will.
- **Living trust**—A trust created by living individuals who execute a trust agreement and transfer property to the trust. Individuals often want to avoid the details of probate or keep the transfer private. Sometimes individuals no longer wish to manage their affairs because of illness, extensive traveling, or lack of financial expertise. The trustee then manages the trust's assets.
- **Charitable and institutional trust**—A trust set up by an individual to benefit a university, hospital, or other charitable organization. Sometimes the beneficiary may make the actual arrangements for the trust on behalf of the individual. The trustee then manages the trust's investments.

Guardianships

A guardianship (sometimes called a conservatorship) is established by court order for the benefit of a minor or incapacitated person, known as the ward. A bank trust department often is appointed to manage the property for the minor or incompetent person. To prove that all the proceeds are being used for the person's benefit, the trust department periodically provides an accounting to the court.

Did You Know ...

Sixty-one percent of Americans do not have a will, leaving them at risk of dying intestate and leaving it up to a probate court to determine how their estate will be distributed. In addition, 70 percent of Americans with children under 18 in the household have no will, putting their children's future at risk.

Source: Harris Interactive, April 2013 poll

Personal Agency Services

Bank trust departments may offer agency services, which by law, differ from trust services. Whereas trustees assume legal title to property turned over to them, agents do not. Instead, an individual who retains legal title to the asset gives specific authority to the agent. However, as with a trustee relationship, a bank functioning as an investment advisor or agent must act in accordance with fiduciary standards. Safekeeping, custody, investment advice, and investment management are the most common agency services banks provide to individuals.

- **Safekeeping**—The bank accepts, holds, and on request, returns stocks, bonds, or other assets to the customer.
- **Custody**—The bank holds assets in safekeeping and collects income. Custodians buy and sell securities when specifically instructed to do so by the customer or an appointed agent. Banks provide custody services for individuals, correspondent banks, and government agencies.
- **Investment advisor**—The bank performs the duties of a custodian plus other responsibilities granted to it by the individual. When handling securities, the bank may review investments and suggest the retention, sale, exchange, conversion, or purchase of new securities. As investment advisors, banks may handle real estate. The bank may act in an agency capacity to collect rental income, pay property taxes, arrange for property upkeep and maintenance, and disburse any net income as directed by the owner.
- **Investment manager**—The bank, acting as investment manager, also may make financial decisions on the customer's behalf, based on previously established investment criteria.

LAWS AND REGULATIONS

The banking industry is authorized to offer a full range of financial services as a result of the enactment of the Gramm-Leach-Bliley Act (GLBA) in 1999. The law was designed to modernize the nation's financial system and put banks on a more competitive footing with other types of financial service providers. The primary vehicle for reform is the financial holding company, which can engage in any activity that is "financial in nature," including underwriting and selling insurance and dealing in securities. Banks may also petition for the authority to engage through a nonbank affiliate in any financial activity that is not specified in the GLBA.

The GLBA established a **functional regulation system** that applies to all traditional and nontraditional products and services offered by banks, including insurance, investments, IRAs, and trusts.

functional regulation system—A regulatory principle incorporated in the Gramm-Leach-Bliley Act that requires certain authorized banking activities to fall under the authority of federal and state regulators other than the principal federal bank regulators (this was somewhat modified by the Dodd-Frank Wall Street Reform and Consumer Protection Act of 2010).

> **Situation**
>
> Monica creates a living trust in which she places $300,000 worth of stock. The dividends are to benefit her oldest son, who is disabled. The trustee is a long-time friend of the family. In her will, she also creates a testamentary trust into which all her assets will go at the time of her death. Income from the trust property will be used to support her husband. At his death, the trust will be terminated and the assets divided among all her children. The trustee for this trust is the family bank.

The following are examples of laws and regulations applicable to trust and investment services.

Retail Sales of Nondeposit Investment Products

As discussed earlier, investments such as stocks, bonds, annuities, and mutual funds are not bank deposits and, therefore, are not FDIC-insured. Bank regulators recognized the need to protect bank customers who were purchasing these products. In 1994, the regulators issued an Interagency Statement on Retail Sales of Nondeposit Investment Products, which emphasizes that banks must disclose to customers that these products are not FDIC-insured. Banks selling investment products must take several precautions, including:

- Marketing nondeposit investments in a manner that does not mislead or confuse customers about the products or the risks, such as by separating retail deposit-taking and retail nondeposit sales functions within the bank
- Prohibiting bank employees, such as tellers, from offering investment advice
- Refraining from offering uninsured retail investment products with a product name identical to the bank's name
- Conspicuously disclosing that investment products are not FDIC-insured, are not obligations of or guaranteed by the bank, and carry investment risk and possible loss of principal

Consumer Protection in Sales of Insurance

In 2001, the federal banking regulators issued regulations under GLBA that apply sales disclosure and practice rules to retail sales of insurance products sold for personal, family, or household purposes. The requirements are similar to those established in the interagency statement on nondeposit investment products. Basically, customers must be made aware that insurance products are not FDIC-insured. The disclosures must be given both orally and in writing, and consumers must acknowledge their receipt in writing.

Uniform Trust Laws

Historically, laws governing the creation and administration of trusts have been implemented at the state level. However, in 2000 the Uniform Law Commission (then known as the National Conference of Commissioners on Uniform State Laws) moved to address the differences among states by creating and offering a uniform set of rules, known as the Uniform Trust Code (UTC), that states could use as a model for their trust laws. By offering a set of basic rules that govern voluntary trusts, the Uniform Law Commission helped create some uniformity in how trusts are governed. To date, more than one-half of the states have substantively adopted the UTC, and several more state legislatures have introduced it for enactment.

Other uniform rules apply to trusts as well, although differences among states remain. Examples include:

- **Uniform Probate Code**—Pertains to the succession of property at the time of an owner's death, as controlled by the will, intestacy statute, and the probate process
- **Uniform Prudent Investor Act**—Provides rules for investing trust assets by requiring trustees to apply modern portfolio theory to investment decisions and to invest as a prudent investor would; namely, taking into account the purposes, terms, distribution requirements, and other circumstances of the trust and using reasonable skill and care
- **Uniform Principal and Income Act**—Sets forth rules for allocating a trust's principal and income, apportionment of income, the right to payment, and the trustee's powers to adjust principal and income with regard to prudent investor obligations and other duties

SUMMARY

- The financial status of U.S. households today is a matter of concern. The recession of 2008-2009 lowered the personal net worth and delayed the retirement plans of millions of Americans. Since then, savings rates have rebounded but still have not returned to what they were in past decades. In response, government, industry leaders, educators, and consumer interest groups have joined forces at the grassroots and national levels to educate Americans of all ages on the value of and methods for obtaining, maintaining, and restoring financial health. Banks play an important role in this effort by providing personal wealth management services from the most basic financial planning information to more complex high-end trust and investment services. In doing so, they fulfill their fiduciary role as trustworthy financial resources.

- Financial planning is the development and implementation of a plan to achieve a person's overall financial goals, including maximizing income and minimizing expenses to achieve both short- and long-term objectives. The financial planner advises customers with regard to their financial decisions and helps customers coordinate the work of specialists such as accountants, brokers, lawyers, and insurance agents. Because financial planners are generalists and not specialists, they must be careful to avoid the unauthorized practice of law. Financial planners, however, can inform customers about the tax-deferral and other features of products they are considering for their financial plan.

- Financial planning should be tailored to the age of the client. For example, the financial needs and goals of young adults differ from those of adults with children or empty nesters. Financial planning thus begins with an appreciation of the customer's life stage and present financial situation and then continues with an analysis of such factors as inflation, the time value of money, and the risk-reward factor for each asset and investment choice. Net worth is calculated and a cash flow strategy drawn up. The customer and the necessary experts put the plan into action and then reassess the plan, usually annually, for needed modifications.

- Many banks now offer noncredit-related insurance products, including life, health and disability, long-term care, property, and liability insurance. Two general life insurance categories are term and whole life. Banks also offer credit life insurance to pay off an insured's loan in the event of death. Property insurance protects the value of anything consumers own that might be lost due to fire, theft, lawsuits, or other events. Title insurance protects homebuyers from losses due to questions about the ownership of the property. Vehicle insurance policies provide liability coverage and optional collision coverage.
- Bank subsidiaries or holding company affiliates may offer investment and brokerage services through third parties and joint ventures or as an in-house function. Banks must fully disclose that these products are not FDIC-insured. Whatever the investment strategy—conservative, moderate, or aggressive—diversification usually is recommended.
- Stocks, bonds, mutual funds, and annuities are the most common investments used in financial plans. Whatever types of investments a customer chooses, the portfolio should be evaluated regularly to ensure that the results meet the goals set out in the financial plan, including diversification. Banks also offer portfolio management services such as asset management and trading accounts.
- Retirement planning must take into account increased life expectancies. Many people will receive Social Security benefits, some will receive pensions from defined benefit plans, and many will receive income from defined contribution plans, such as 401(k) and Keogh plans. Most banks today offer traditional, Roth, and SEP IRAs.
- An estate plan prepares for the disposition of assets both before and after the customer's death. The objectives of estate planning include ensuring that the right people receive the right assets and that taxes are minimized for both the customer and the customer's beneficiaries. One savings product that is available to most customers is a Uniform Transfer to Minors Act account that can be used to make an untaxed asset transfer to a minor, thereby reducing federal income taxes on the asset's earnings.
- Trust services complement other banking services and facilitate a total financial relationship with individual and business customers. The trust structure has four requirements: the trust, the trustor, the trustee, and the beneficiary. As trust services providers, banks act as fiduciaries and must abide by the prudent investor principle, segregate trust assets from bank assets, and ensure against conflicts of interest. Trust services provided by banks to individuals include estate settlement and the administration of testamentary trusts, living trusts, and charitable and institutional trusts. Trust departments also provide guardianship and personal agency services, including safekeeping, custody, investor advice, and investment management services.
- While the GLBA allows the banking community to offer products that were previously off limits, such as insurance and investment services, banking laws and those pertaining to other specialized areas still apply certain limitations and requirements. Examples include the sale of retail nondeposit investment products and consumer protections regarding the sale of insurance. The uniform trust laws also impose principles and requirements on bank trust services in the states where the laws have been adopted.

SELF-CHECK AND REVIEW

Learning Check

1. Why do many Americans have reason to be concerned about their financial affairs?
2. What are a bank financial planner's ethical responsibilities?
3. What factors and effects must be taken into account in financial planning?
4. What are the preliminary steps in financial planning?
5. What is the purpose of life insurance, and who needs it?
6. What are the three basic investment strategies and motivations that influence investment choices?
7. What are the two basic types of personal trusts?
8. How are banks structured to deliver investment and brokerage products? Through what channels are these products delivered?
9. What are the requirements for the sale of retail nondeposit investment products?
10. List some bank deposit, insurance, investment, and trust products that can help meet customers' basic retirement needs.
11. What law and bank organizational structure allows banks to be full-service centers for retirement planning? What regulatory principle operates to ensure that the nondeposit functions in banks are regulated and examined for compliance?

Business and International Banking Services

8

Learning Objectives

After studying this chapter, you should be able to

- Identify cash management services for businesses
- Identify insurance products banks offer to businesses
- Describe capital market products and services
- Explain bank trust services available to businesses
- Discuss international banking services that foster foreign trade
- Describe some laws and regulations that pertain to business and international banking services

Introduction

Banks have traditionally provided their customers with checking, savings, and loan accounts. Today, they seek full customer relationships that serve all of their customers' financial needs. The Gramm-Leach-Bliley Act (GLBA) and technological advances in payment and information systems have helped banks become full service providers to a greater extent than ever before.

For business customers, full service means providing payment, investment, cash management, and loan services, along with financial expertise appropriate to the nature, size, and scope of the business. Business products and services include trusts, investments, insurance, capital market services, and international banking. Banks offer business products and services in different combinations, sometimes directly and sometimes in partnership with other service providers or through subsidiaries or affiliates.

BUSINESS BANKING SERVICES

The most basic deposit and credit services for businesses were discussed earlier in this textbook. Closely aligned with deposit accounts are a wide variety of cash management services.

Cash Management

Banks offer cash management services to both businesses and consumers. Cash management services help businesses collect incoming payments quickly, manage and reconcile outgoing payments efficiently, keep surplus funds invested, and obtain timely and complete information on their bank accounts.

Cash management services are attractive to corporations and small businesses that have significant billings and payments or that need to put their money to work instead of leaving balances in noninterest-bearing demand deposit accounts.

Account Management

accounts receivable—An amount owed to and not yet delivered or accepted by a company.

With account management services, the bank essentially handles bookkeeping and accounting functions for the business. The bank pays incoming invoices for the business, manages **accounts receivable** for payments coming into the company, handles payroll and employee benefit accounting, disburses dividend payments, balances accounts, and performs many other accounting tasks required for the business's working operations.

Cash Vault Services

Cash vault services help businesses safely deposit funds while maximizing their availability. Deposits are delivered directly from the business to the bank's cash vault. To ensure the safety of deposits in transit, banks offer such safeguards as tamper-evident deposit bags, video surveillance, and dual custody processing. Because company employees do not carry cash to the bank, they are not put at risk. The bank provides expedited processing so that deposits received by the deadlines are given same-day credit.

Account Reconciliation

With account reconciliation, banks provide detailed reports on payments made and outstanding (and the amount of each), balance the accounts, and keep the records. Various specialized reports can be generated to allow company managers to monitor operations and gather more detailed information on account activity. In addition to check truncation and electronic payment services (covered in chapter 5), most banks offer online access to current, real-time account reports. Thus, for a fee, businesses realize efficiencies in operations and gain cash management opportunities.

Positive Pay

A related cash management tool that is also an anti-fraud tool is positive pay. Businesses electronically send banks lists of issued checks with account numbers, check numbers, and dollar amounts. Banks then match checks presented for payment against the lists of checks. Those that do not match are rejected as exception items and reported to the customer. A check image may be sent as well. The customer then notifies the bank whether the exception check should be paid.

Did You Know ...

Sixty-one percent of organizations experienced attempted or actual payment fraud in 2012. Of these, 87 percent experienced check fraud, 27 percent ACH debit fraud, 16 percent consumer credit card fraud, 11 percent wire transfer fraud, 8 percent ACH credit fraud, and 7 percent corporate card fraud. Among organizations that suffered a fraud loss, the average loss was $20,300.

Source: 2013 AFP Payments Fraud and Control Survey, Association for Financial Professionals

Lockbox Services

Lockbox services help companies access their incoming payments faster. Before the advent of lockbox services, a customer would mail a payment, for example, directly to a business, a government unit, correspondent bank, university, or hospital accounts payable office. These payments were subject to delays at every point—transit, processing, deposit, and collection.

With lockbox services, payments are sent directly to a special post office box managed by the bank. The bank retrieves payments from the lockbox, deposits them immediately, and sends the business a record of payments made and by whom. Delays in collection and deposit processing are reduced.

Traditional lockbox services were enhanced by Check 21 and continue to be improved with advances in electronic banking. Many banks offer image-based services where everything sent to the business's lockbox is scanned so that it can be viewed online, thereby giving the business almost immediate access to images of check payments, remittance documents, and any other items received at the lockbox. For businesses, the fees for lockbox service are offset by improved funds availability and lower staff requirements, so the net cost is lower.

Remote Deposit Capture

With advances in check imaging, the advantages of account reconciliation and lockbox services have been greatly enhanced. Remote deposit capture, also referred

to by one of the check conversion variants— accounts receivable conversion (ARC), point of purchase (POP), and back office conversion (BOC)— allows businesses to scan checks and convert the data into automated clearing house (ACH) debits that they send to their banks for credit to their accounts. Automated clearing house (ACH) industry regulations and Regulation E, Electronic Fund Transfers, require (if the customer is a consumer) that customers be notified of the intent to convert an eligible check for payment.

POP conversion takes place at the point of sale—for example, at a retail or grocery store where a check is presented for payment. ARC and BOC check conversion can be done by the company's own accounting office, by its bank (as with paper-based check processing), or by a third-party processor.

Banks also benefit from remote deposit capture services, such as when their business customers use BOC. For example, the cost of processing paper checks is reduced. Also, the service allows banks of all asset sizes to strengthen current customer relationships and expand their geographic boundaries to attract more customers without incurring the costs of maintaining a branch location.

Remote Deposit Capture Benefits to Businesses

- Reduced payment processing costs
- Reduced transportation costs
- Low item costs
- Accelerated clearing
- More centralization of back office functions
- Easier account reconciliation
- Reduced return item risk
- Expedited returns

Direct Deposit

Direct deposit transactions processed electronically through an ACH enable businesses to deposit employee pay, reimbursements, commissions, retirement plan payments, pension benefits, dividends, and other payments into the checking or savings accounts of the intended recipients. For businesses, direct deposit services eliminate the cost of creating and distributing paper checks and reduce exposure to check fraud. For recipients, direct deposit expedites their access to funds and offers the convenience and security of having payments posted electronically to bank accounts, thus avoiding trips to the bank to deposit paper checks.

With electronic benefit transfers (EBT) and payroll cards, employees do not need to maintain a separate bank account. Instead, a company arranges with a bank to provide payroll cards, which are similar to ATM debit cards or stored-value cards, to their employees. Each payday, the employer credits the employee's account or a subaccount of a company account for the employee's compensation. The employee then uses the payroll card to withdraw the funds at an ATM and to make purchases at merchant point-of-sale terminals. Payroll card products can substitute for traditional consumer transaction accounts at a financial institution.

Did You Know ...

Thirteen percent of checks written were converted to electronic payments, either by merchants at the point of sale or by billers that received bill payments by check.

Source: *The 2013 Federal Reserve Payments Study*

Controlled Disbursement

Controlled disbursement provides same-day notification of the dollar value of checks that will clear against the company's disbursement account, so that payments can be funded immediately from the company's concentration account or line of credit. The company must fund the disbursement account that day to prevent an overdraft when the full value of the checks that are scheduled to clear posts against the disbursement account.

Cash Concentration Accounts

With cash concentration accounts, businesses collect balances from various deposit accounts into one account. To collect funds, the business initiates ACH debits to the various deposit accounts and credits the concentration account. Cash concentration and controlled disbursement allow companies to take advantage of overnight investment opportunities because surplus funds are consolidated in the concentration account. Exhibit 8.1 illustrates the relationship between the cash concentration account and various deposit accounts.

Exhibit 8.1: Cash Concentration

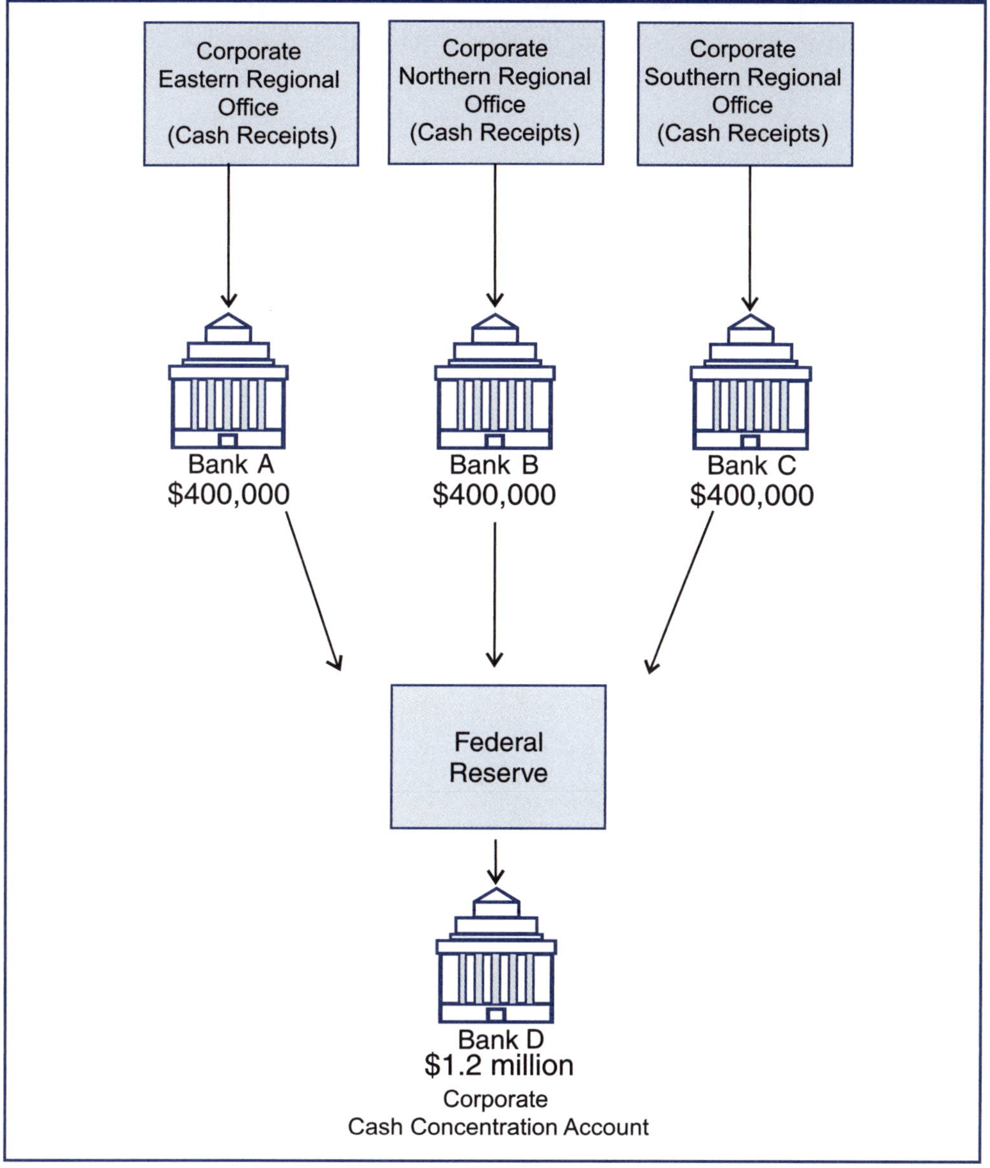

Zero-Balance Accounts

A zero-balance account is a demand deposit account that maintains a zero balance because it is linked to a concentration account or a line of credit. As checks are presented for payment, the bank automatically transfers funds from the concentration account or line of credit to pay the checks and to keep the account balance at zero.

A positive balance in the account is transferred to the concentration account to earn interest or for investment, or to the line of credit to pay the balance.

Wire Transfer Services

This electronic funds transfer service facilitates a customer's cash management. At the direction of the customer, funds are wired to another bank to fulfill a business transaction. Banks also offer wire collection services.

Merchant Card Services

Banks make it possible for merchants to accept customer payments by credit or debit card or electronic check. The market for merchant card services includes retailers, online businesses, and telephone and mail-order companies. Banks that offer merchant card services supply businesses with the equipment to process transactions, including card terminals and receipt printers. The business has an account with the merchant bank card processor, which provides settlement services for a fee, usually a percentage of each customer transaction. Merchant card services provide immediate approval of transactions, reduce the risk of returned payments, reduce labor costs associated with check handling, and make funds available quickly.

Sweep Accounts

In this business account service, banks transfer (sweep) excess funds from the customer's business account every night to aggregate with the surplus funds of other customers. The aggregated funds are then invested, usually in overnight government securities and **repurchase agreements**, on behalf of participating customers. The interest each customer earns is based on the amount invested.

Insurance

In providing full service to businesses, banks go beyond deposit- and accounting-related services. Many banks also assist businesses of all sizes with their insurance needs. Through insurance affiliates or partnering companies, banks can provide businesses with insurance products for employees, such as health insurance, key person insurance, and directors and officers (D&O) liability insurance.

Health Insurance

Companies are the biggest purchasers of health insurance, purchasing group policies to cover the cost of physician and hospital care for their employees. The health insurance business is flourishing, and typical policies also cover vision, dental care, and prescription drugs. If employer-provided health insurance is not available, employees of business customers may buy an individual policy personally. Retirees buy health insurance to supplement their Medicare hospital and medical care coverage.

The Patient Protection and Affordable Care Act (ACA), the full implementation of which began in 2014, extensively revised the health insurance marketplace. The reform law includes employer shared responsibility provisions that, starting in 2015 and 2016, will require businesses with 50 or more employees to provide their workers with affordable health insurance that offers at least minimum essential coverage or face a penalty. Small businesses are also encouraged to offer health

Situation

David Toombs is a cash manager for S&S Services, a firm that specializes in security operations and hiring. The firm has grown from a regional company to a nationwide company. David attributes some of the company's success to the business services offered by RJY Bank, N.A. Advised by the bank, David was able to set up cash management services that allow the company to reduce operating staff and costs and increase sales staff and locations. Lockbox, controlled disbursement, and cash concentration accounts allow David to collect receivables quickly, use the bank's branch offices across the country, and take advantage of overnight investment opportunities. It's a win-win relationship.

repurchase agreement—A sale of securities with a simultaneous agreement to buy back the same securities at a stated price on a stated date. It is the most common form of overnight investment for corporate funds, supported by securities (usually U.S. Treasury bills) from the bank's (or broker's) inventory.

insurance to their employees with premium tax credits and a special online marketplace where they can compare policies and costs. Banks and their insurance partners are making far-reaching changes in their health insurance business models to comply with the ACA.

Key Person Insurance

Key person insurance is purchased by a company to cover the loss by death or disability of employees whose absence would hurt the company financially. Executives and other employees with specific managerial or technical expertise are usually insured. Small businesses, which are more vulnerable than larger ones to the loss of a key employee, often buy key person policies.

Proceeds from a key person policy can be used to recruit and train a successor and help replace profits the company might have earned had the employee been working. Such policies also help reassure creditors and suppliers about the continuity of the business.

Directors and Officers Liability Insurance

This type of coverage also provides insurance protection for key business employees—namely, the directors and senior managers (officers) of a company. Almost every large corporation has D&O liability insurance, and in increasingly litigious times, the insurance has become popular with smaller businesses as well.

D&O policies protect directors and officers from liability arising from actions connected to their corporate positions. In the event of a claim made against a director or officer for a wrongful act, such as a shareholder suit charging mismanagement of company assets or an employee lawsuit alleging discrimination or wrongful termination, a D&O insurance policy pays for the damages and reimburses the director or officer. Companies may also purchase D&O policies to provide coverage for their costs, such as when a corporation **indemnifies** directors and officers who incurred defense costs or paid claims made against them.

Capital Markets

Banks offer a variety of services to help companies raise money for their business operations by accessing public and private equity and debt markets. For many years, capital market services could only be offered by investment banks, as mandated by the Glass-Steagall Act, which was passed in the midst of the Great Depression. The GLBA largely removed this barrier between commercial and investment banks in 1999. Commercial banks may now offer many capital market services through an affiliated broker-dealer. The capital market services provided to corporate customers range from specialized lending and asset management to advisory services. Among them are:

- Pooling, structuring, and distributing debt securities supported by assets (asset-backed **securitization**)
- Underwriting and distributing corporate equity, debt, and preferred shares
- Structuring and syndicating loans

Did You Know ...

Over one-half (55 percent) of American workers received health insurance coverage through their employer in 2011. Over one-third (34.7 percent) of Americans who did not work also received employment-based health insurance, usually from a former employer or another person's employer.

Source: U.S. Census Bureau

indemnification—An action taken to compensate or reimburse someone for losses or damages incurred.

securitization—The pooling of debt, such as mortgage loans, and selling the consolidated debt as securities to investors. In the case of loans, the loans are then no longer assets of the lending bank, although the bank may continue to service them.

investment banking—The marketing of new security issues, usually through an investment banker or underwriter.

secondary market—A market for the resale of securities (such as the dealer market, a stock exchange, or the mortgage-backed securities market) where ownership is transferred from one owner to another. The first sale of any security is in the primary market; all subsequent sales are in the secondary market.

primary market—The market in which an issuer sells new securities to investors. Among middlemen who aid in the sale of a company's securities are investment bank underwriters, brokers, and dealers.

underwrite—To assume a risk for a fee, such as for insurance or investments. Insurance underwriting guarantees cash payment if there is a loss or casualty. Investment underwriting guarantees the purchase of new offerings of corporate stock or debt securities of a corporation or government entity by purchasing the entire offering and then selling it in the market.

indenture—A contract underlying a bond issue, signed by the issuing corporation and the trustee, who acts for the bondholders. It sets forth the rights and responsibilities of the corporation, trustee, and bondholders and the terms of the issue.

- Providing assistance on structuring and negotiating the sale or purchase of business assets in mergers and acquisitions
- Structuring and distributing private placements
- Underwriting and distributing the debt securities of state governments, municipalities, and other public institutions
- Providing financing to specialized businesses, such as real estate developers

Investment Banking

Nonbank affiliates of financial holding companies can offer a wide variety of **investment banking** services, among them direct investment by a financial holding company in nonfinancial companies. The financial holding company is an actual investor and may assume an active role in the company in which it has invested, including having a representative serve on the board. In addition to providing capital, investment banking may extend to corporate lending, leveraged finance, financial consulting, and other corporate services to help businesses grow.

Rather than investing their own capital, investment bankers operate on behalf of clients, helping them raise capital in the form of debt (bonds) or equity (stocks). Stocks and bonds offered to the public for the first time—new issues—are not listed on the trading exchanges, which constitute the **secondary market**. Rather, the investment banker creates a **primary market**.

The first sale of company stock to the public is known as an initial public offering (IPO). If the issue is too large or carries too much risk, an **underwriting** syndicate consisting of more than one investment bank will make the sale.

With bond issues, the investing public wants assurance that periodic earnings will be distributed, and at maturity, the principal investment will be redeemed. An investment bank does not provide these services, but a bank trust department does.

BUSINESS TRUST SERVICES

In the early years of U.S. banking, trust services were offered only by trust companies. In time, trust companies assumed commercial bank functions: they accepted deposits, extended credit, and obtained state banking charters to become bank and trust companies. With the Federal Reserve Act of 1913, national banks were allowed to offer trust services as separate operations.

A bank may serve as a trustee for the issuance of corporate or municipal bonds. As a corporate trustee, the bank monitors compliance with the **indenture** agreement between bond issuer and bondholders, often handles interest payments to bondholders, and protects the interests of bondholders if the issuer defaults. Exhibit 8.2 illustrates a corporate trust chain of events.

Trust services complement other business banking services and facilitate a total financial relationship between the bank, the business, and its owners. If a bank is to offer trust services, its federal or state charter must accord it trust powers. Many banks have applied for trust powers so that they may offer wealth management counseling to their business customers. Two main lines of trust business serving the business community are corporate agency services and employee benefit services.

Exhibit 8.2: Corporate Trust Chain of Events for a Bond Offering

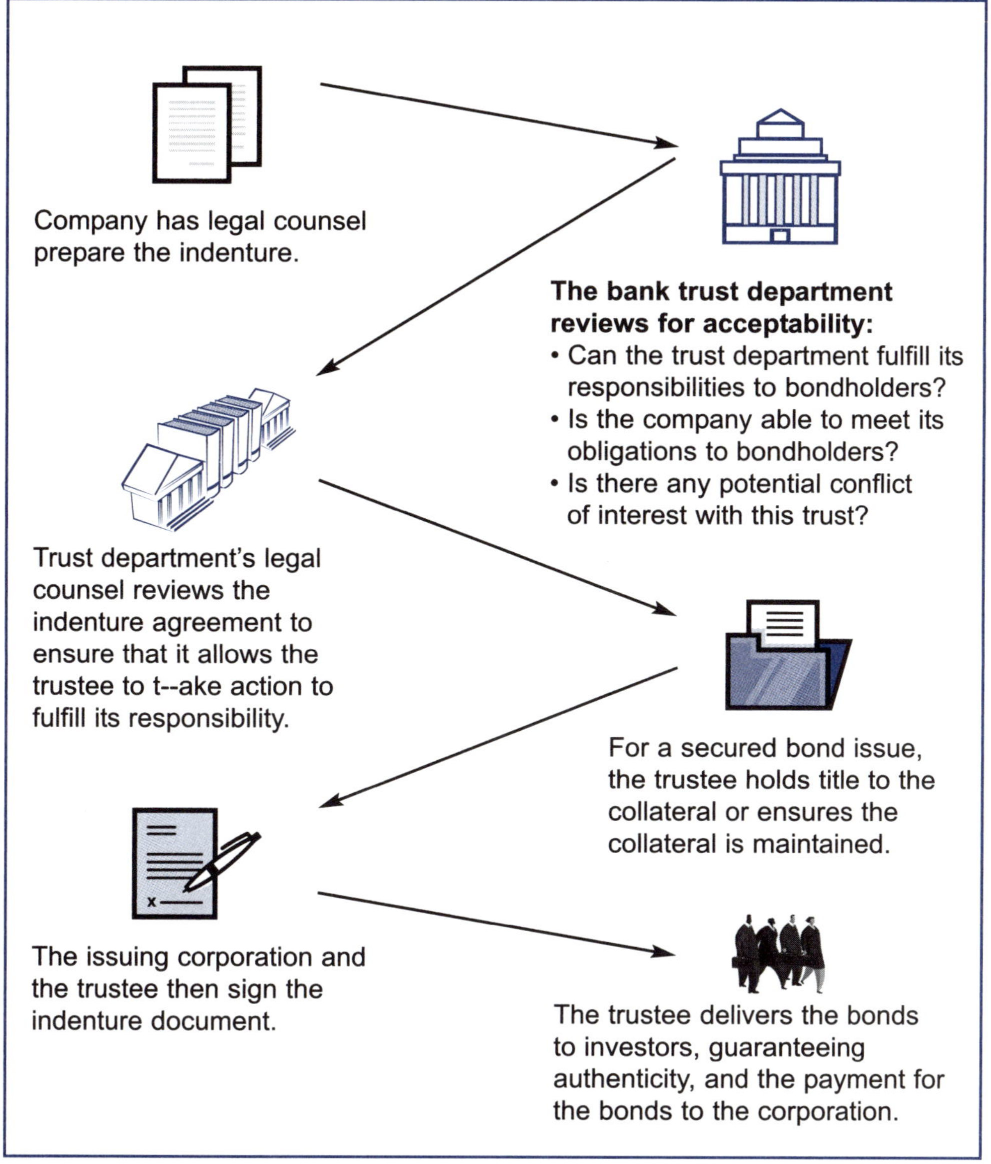

Corporate Agency Services

The financial needs of companies are similar to those of individuals, and thus, the legal relationship of the trust department to the business customer is the same as **agent** and principal. For corporations and government agencies, bank trust departments provide paying agent, registrar, and transfer agent services.

Paying Agent

Stocks and bonds are used by corporations and government entities to raise capital for operational purposes. In return, the purchasers of stocks and bonds may receive interest and/or dividend payments on those instruments. As paying agent, the bank ensures that holders of stocks and bonds receive their interest and dividend payments. The paying agent also redeems bonds as they mature.

Did You Know ...

Merchant banking can be traced back to the Middle Ages when Italian merchant houses began financing trading journeys that usually consisted of lengthy sea voyages to distant foreign lands. The merchant houses received a share of the profits from trading, but they were also exposed to the risk of investment loss from bad weather, war, piracy, and other dangers.

Source: "Merchant Banking: Past and Present," *FDIC Banking Review*

Requirements of a Trust Relationship

Trust—A legal structure created to hold property or other assets

Trustor—Person who creates the trust

Trustee—Person who administers the trust

Beneficiary—Person who benefits from the trust

agent—A person or company that acts for another person or company (the principal) by the latter's authority.

Trustee's Fiduciary Responsibilities

- Act solely for beneficiaries
- Avoid conflicts of interest
- Be a prudent investor
- Delegate authority to other experts as needed
- Select agents as needed
- Segregate trust assets

book entry—A method for electronically registering and keeping a record of securities ownership without issuing physical certificates to owners. Securities are not in printed form but exist on the books of the issuer's agent. Transfer is by electronic debit and credit.

call—The right of a corporation to repurchase a bond obligation or stock.

proxy statement—A document intended to give shareholders the information they need to vote knowledgeably on matters brought up at shareholder meetings.

employee benefit program—A program established or maintained by an employer, employee organization, or both to provide employees with a certain benefit or set of benefits, such as pensions, profit-sharing, stock bonuses, and life, health, accident, and disability insurance.

Registrar

Corporations and government entities establish the maximum number of bonds and shares of stock they wish to issue. Banks assist in that task by providing registrar services. Registrar services include keeping records of stock and purchases and sales, ensuring that the issuance maximum is not exceeded, and maintaining records of cancellations and reissuances.

Transfer Agent

As transfer agent, the bank is responsible for changing ownership title on the corporation's shares of stock, as is required when shares change hands. Old shares are canceled and new shares issued in the name of the new shareholder. Bank trust departments facilitate securities transfers using **book entry**. Most securities today are held in electronic form and settled via an electronic settlement system managed by the Depository Trust and Clearing Corporation. Electronic settlement has largely replaced physical settlement involving the exchange of paper securities certificates.

Other Agency Services

Additional bond and stock agency services include:

- Paying principal when a bond matures or is cancelled or **called**
- Processing defaults on bonds
- Safekeeping collateral for a secured bond issue or not-yet-issued stock certificates
- Replacing and record keeping of lost stock certificates
- Responding to stockholder inquiries
- Reporting shareholder demographic information to the corporation
- Sending corporate information to shareholders, including annual reports, shareholder meeting notices, and **proxy statements**
- Tendering stock during a company acquisition by either paying company owners for their stock in cash or converting the stock to the acquiring company's stock
- Handling stock conversions in mergers
- Managing stock subscriptions, buybacks, warrants, options, and rights

Employee Benefit Services

Managing trust funds for paying pensions and other benefits to employees of corporations, large nonprofit organizations (such as trade associations), and state and local governments is one of the fastest growing and most competitive trust areas. **Employee benefit programs** are generally either employee benefit welfare programs or employee benefit pension programs.

Employee benefit welfare programs are established by an employer or employee organization to provide a particular benefit (such as health insurance, sick leave, vacation, disability pay, or job training) to participants or their beneficiaries.

Employee benefit pension programs are **deferred compensation** programs established to provide income for employees upon retirement. Employee benefit pension programs usually take the form of either defined benefit plans or defined contribution plans.

Defined Benefit Plans

A defined benefit plan is a pension plan in which an employee receives a predetermined monthly benefit upon retirement. The retirement benefit, which is usually based on employee salary and years of service, may be adjusted periodically to include a cost-of-living increase. The employer is responsible for funding the plan and assumes the investment risk. Consequently, if investment earnings exceed or fall short of earnings necessary to fund benefits, the employer's contributions are adjusted accordingly. Annual contributions are determined on an **actuarial** basis. Benefits are made as an annuity distribution. Plans are either qualified or nonqualified.

Qualified retirement plans. A qualified retirement plan must meet requirements of Section 401(a) of the Internal Revenue Code (IRC) and the Employee Retirement Income Security Act (ERISA). If these requirements are met, the plan is eligible for favorable tax treatment. For example, employers can deduct annual allowable contributions for participants; contributions and earnings on those contributions are tax-deferred until withdrawn by participants; and some of the taxes can be deferred longer when funds are transferred into a different type of retirement plan. Exhibit 8.3, next page, defines some of the requirements that qualified retirement plans must meet.

Nonqualified retirement plans. A nonqualified retirement plan (also called a supplemental executive retirement plan (SERP) or salary compensation plan) does not meet IRC and ERISA requirements for favorable tax treatment. Nonqualified plans are more flexible than qualified plans, but they do not have the tax benefits. The greater flexibility of a nonqualified plan makes it attractive to highly compensated key employees, such as company executives. For example, there is no legal cap for contributions to nonqualified plans, but the contributions are taxable to the employer. Depending on the plan's structure, the earnings before distribution may be taxed to employees, and the assets may be subject to claims by the company's creditors.

Defined Contribution Plans

Unlike a defined benefit plan, a defined contribution plan does not guarantee a predetermined benefit at retirement. Instead, an employer promises to contribute a defined amount to the employee's plan. The ultimate amount of the benefit at retirement will vary, depending on such factors as annual contributions to the plan, its gains or losses, and its expenses. The benefit ceases when plan assets are exhausted. The basic defined contribution plan types are money-purchase, profit-sharing, 401(k), 403(b), and employee stock ownership plans (ESOPs).

Money-purchase plans. With a money-purchase plan, the employer makes a fixed contribution to the plan on behalf of each employee, thus controlling how much

deferred compensation—The contractual postponement of payment for services rendered until a future date; commonly used with respect to retirement benefits (qualified or nonqualified) to be paid in the future.

actuarial calculation—The mathematical determination of rates and premiums for life insurance, disability insurance, and pension benefits based on tables detailing the frequencies of mortality (death) and morbidity (disability).

Did You Know ...

United States Trust Company of New York, founded in 1853, was the first trust company in the United States. The company was created to provide executor and trustee services for corporate clients and wealthy individuals such as Marshall Field, founder of the famed department store. U.S. Trust Company merged with Bank of America in 2007.

Exhibit 8.3: Qualified Plan Requirements

Plan exclusiveness	The plan must be exclusively for the benefit of employees who are participants; no other groups may participate.
Formal construction	The plan must be adopted formally by the employer and governed by a plan document.
Nondiscrimination	The plan cannot discriminate against any class of employee in the organization that otherwise qualifies to participate. Restrictions on participation must be fair and generally based on criteria such as legal age, time of service, citizenship, full-time employment, and whether the employee is a member of an employee association subject to good faith bargaining and a separate defined benefit plan.
Contribution limits	The plan must maintain annual compensation limits, annual contribution limits, and limits on the payable benefit.
Active funding	Contributions must be made annually according to the plan formula.
Plan disclosure	The plan regularly discloses to employees in an understandable way features such as the summary plan description, individual participant benefit statements, and summary of any amendments to the plan.
Plan performance	The plan should be designed and maintained to be permanent. There should not be a termination date.
Investment prudence	The plan's trustee, investment manager, and administrator must take a prudent approach to the investment and management of plan funds.
Vesting	Participants should have a nonforfeitable vested interest in the plan at some point. It may allow vesting immediately, 100 percent after so many years of service, or graduated percentages over time.
Established retirement age	The plan must have provisions for normal retirement age and for early and late retirement.
Calculation of benefits at retirement	Plans may vary. Most allow for full benefits at the established retirement age, such as 65; a reduced benefit for early retirement, such as at age 55; and an increased benefit for employees who leave after the full retirement age.
Constructive receipt	Contributions and earnings to the retirement plan are tax deferred for the employee. However, when the money is paid and available to the employee (constructive receipt), it is taxable.
Plan integration	Employers may offer more than one plan. Within allowable parameters, they may integrate the plans to determine the employee's pension benefit.
Pension Benefit Guaranty Corporation (PBGC)	A government-owned corporation, PBGC administers an insurance program that guarantees defined benefit plan participants the basic or vested retirement benefit payments if the plan is terminated or lacks funds to make payment. The employer pays an annual premium for this protection.

it contributes. Generally, this is a percentage of the employee's annual compensation, weighted for years of employment and investment performance.

Profit-sharing plans. A profit-sharing plan provides an employee with a share of the net profits of the business. The shares may be distributed periodically, often annually, as cash bonuses, or they may be accumulated for the employee in a deferred retirement plan and paid if a specified event (retirement, death, termination or layoff, or disability) occurs. The employer is not committed to making contributions, but if it does, contributions can be made according to a formula or at the discretion of the company's board of directors.

401(k) plans. A 401(k) plan is a type of salary reduction plan—that is, employees reduce their salaries by contributing a portion to the plan. In so doing, the compensation (salary) that would have been taxed is not taxed when it is earned. Contributions to a 401(k) plan are tax-deferred—that is, taxable only when funds are withdrawn, usually at retirement. Additional, but taxable, contributions may be made to a 401(k) plan. Tax on earnings is also deferred until withdrawals are made. Employers may, but do not have to, make matching contributions up to a certain percentage. Contributions may be made in different forms, including employer stock. Plan participants are given investment options, but they cannot hold the employer or the plan's trustee responsible for the performance of the investments they choose.

403(b) plans. A 403(b) plan is available to educators, health care workers, and employees of religious institutions and nonprofit organizations. Often referred to as tax-sheltered annuities, 403(b) plans were once restricted to investments in annuity contracts.

ESOPs. Usually taking the form of a supplemental retirement plan, an ESOP allows employees to invest in the securities of the employer, obtaining an ownership share in the company. Some companies are entirely employee-owned under an ESOP.

Plan Trust Services

Accounting, legal, insurance, actuarial, and banking experts can advise employers about establishing retirement plans. Bank trust departments help employers determine what plan to use, whether employee contributions should be a plan feature, what the plan qualifications should be, and how the plan should be administered. Unless benefit plans are for insurance only, the law requires that plan assets be held in a trust.

As plan trustee, a bank may directly bear, or delegate to others, the responsibility to receive regular contributions from the employer and the participants, invest the contributions, keep detailed records to show the accrued value for each employee, make disbursements, provide details of transactions, and file tax reports. Trust departments may provide services directly or contract with professional experts, such as investment managers, actuaries, plan administrators, accountants, or legal counsel, to provide the required services.

Other IRS Qualified Plan Requirements

- Begin paying benefits no later than April 1 of the year after participant reaches age 70½
- Protect plan assets if there is a merger
- Designate the type of qualified plan
- Allow for option to roll over lump-sum distributions

Other Employee Benefits

- Stock options
- Physical exams
- Vision care
- Sick days
- Severance pay
- Bonus/incentive compensation
- Dependent care
- Life insurance
- Travel and entertainment
- Parking and commuting reimbursement
- Tuition reimbursement

INTERNATIONAL BANKING

For a country's economy to flourish, it must engage in international commerce. As Adam Smith, the eighteenth century pioneer of modern economic thinking, observed in his classic work, *The Wealth of Nations*: "When the produce of any particular branch of industry exceeds what the demand of the country requires, the surplus must be sent abroad and exchanged for something for which there is a demand at home. Without such exportation, a part of the productive labor of the country must cease, and the value of its annual produce diminish."

International commerce includes the export and import of goods and services and the exchange of foreign currency. International banking services meet the needs of businesses operating in a world where countries are increasingly dependent on trade with one another, and money flows unhampered across geographic boundaries. Each day, billions of dollars are transferred electronically among international money centers such as Hong Kong, London, Tokyo, Paris, Frankfurt, and New York. Bank products and services facilitate all these activities.

Trade Categories

- Trade in goods
  - — Raw materials
  - — Crops
  - — Manufactured goods
- Trade in services
  - — Engineering
  - — Scientific
  - — Personal
  - — Processing
- Capital exchange
  - — Long-term plant investment
  - — Short-term financing
  - — Stock ownership

International Banking Structures

To conduct an international business, banks may establish a number of different structures. These include international departments, Edge corporations, foreign and shell branches, international banking facilities, foreign representative offices, and foreign subsidiaries and joint ventures. Banks that do not have their own international structure often work through domestic correspondent banks that do.

Edge Corporations

Established under the Edge Act (a 1919 amendment to the Federal Reserve Act of 1913), these corporations are U.S. bank subsidiaries for either foreign trade-related banking or foreign investment. Through such corporations, banks can open domestic offices outside their home state to transact international business only and thus offer services to international customers and correspondent banks. Most are located in New York City.

Foreign Branches

These are full-service branches operating in a foreign country. To open a foreign branch, banks obtain the permission of the host government and approval of the Federal Reserve Board. Once established, the foreign branch must comply with local banking rules, exchange controls, and regulations. Its activities are subject to examination by both the host country and U.S. banking authorities. Usually, capital of a foreign branch is segregated from the capital of its domestic parent.

Shell Branches

A shell branch is a special-purpose overseas branch that has no physical location and does not conduct transactions in the local economy. Instead, it serves a particular banking or investment purpose, such as taking **Eurodollar** deposits or "warehousing" loans originated in a foreign country.

Eurodollars—Deposits denominated in U.S. dollars at banks and other financial institutions outside the United States. Although the name originated because large amounts of such deposits were held at banks in western Europe, similar deposits in other parts of the world also are called Eurodollars.

International Banking Facilities

International banking facilities (IBFs) are established by banks to participate in the Eurodollar market without the expense of an overseas branch. IBFs enable domestic banks to accept deposits and offer loans to foreign customers and businesses. The accounts are separated from those of the bank's domestic offices.

Foreign Representative Offices

A foreign representative office is a U.S. bank office, usually located in another nation's capital, that does not provide the extensive services of a foreign branch. The representative office builds business for the bank and calls on customers, but it cannot take deposits or make loans. Instead, banking services are provided by the U.S. bank or one of its foreign branches.

Foreign Subsidiaries

A U.S. bank may establish a foreign subsidiary in a country where foreign branches are not permitted. A foreign subsidiary can perform functions that the host country prohibits for branches, such as securities and investment activities. The U.S. bank holds a majority interest in the subsidiary or has some other form of control.

Foreign Joint Ventures

In a foreign joint venture, a U.S. bank shares ownership and management interest in a foreign company with other banks. Operating under its own name, the joint venture functions as an independent bank.

International Payments

Businesses active in the international market need a safe and efficient payments system. Commercial banks often provide this service. Although domestic payments are made using the services of central banks, such as the Federal Reserve in the United States, international banking uses a system of links between correspondent banks.

To facilitate the exchange of funds, correspondent banks set up due-to accounts and due-from accounts. Foreign banks set up due-to accounts in U.S. correspondent banks to facilitate payments in U.S. funds. U.S. banks set up due-from accounts in foreign correspondent banks to facilitate transactions in the currency of that country. Agreements are made for payment in various forms such as cash, sight and time **drafts**, banker's acceptances, letters of credit, and electronic fund transfers.

Foreign Drafts

A foreign draft is a negotiable instrument drawn by a bank on a foreign correspondent bank. It is issued in any currency and is used when payment accompanies documents, such as an order for goods, an invoice paid in foreign currency, or a **bill of lading**. Most common are **sight drafts** and **time drafts**.

Banker's Acceptances

A banker's acceptance is a draft drawn by a company on a bank and "accepted" by the bank. It contains instructions to pay a designated party a certain sum of money

Situation

Waldo Manufacturing needs to purchase pistons from Pittman Piston Company in Scotland, U.K. Waldo provides a letter of credit drawn on its bank in the United States to Pittman to guarantee payment if the pistons are received. Pittman ships the pistons to Waldo, but they can only be claimed with a bill of lading. The documents to claim the pistons are sent in a draft to Waldo's bank. The bank checks the documents, confirms they are in order, and pays the amount of the letter of credit. Waldo is then able to use the documents to claim the pistons.

draft—A signed order by one party (the drawer) addressed to another (the drawee) directing the drawee to pay, at sight or at a definable time in the future, a specified sum of money to the order of a third person, the payee.

bill of lading—A document given by the shipper of goods to the recipient acknowledging receipt of shipment and the terms of delivery.

sight draft—A draft payable on demand when presented to the drawee.

time draft—A draft payable at a fixed or determinable future time.

at a specified time. The bank that accepts the draft assumes the obligation of making payment when the acceptance matures, usually within 30 to 180 days.

Letters of Credit

A letter of credit issued by a bank substitutes the credit standing of the bank for the credit standing of an importer (buyer) of goods, thus providing a guarantee that the exporter (seller) will be paid if all the terms of the contract are met. It also protects the buyer by assuring that no payment will be made until the contract has been fulfilled. A letter of credit is underwritten and analyzed like a loan, and the customer signs an agreement with the bank.

Revocable letters of credit are rare today; most are **irrevocable**. Standby letters of credit are paid when something does not happen during the course of the transaction, such as when a contractor does not complete a project on time. They have a maturity or renewal period and simply reinforce a customer's credit standing.

revocable letter of credit— A letter of credit that may be withdrawn by the issuer at any time without prior notice to the beneficiary.

irrevocable letter of credit— A letter of credit that, once issued, cannot be cancelled and can be modified only with the consent of all parties to the credit, including the beneficiary (often an exporter).

foreign exchange—The trading in or exchange of foreign currencies for other foreign currencies.

International Electronic Fund Transfers

When international transactions require the transfer of large amounts of funds electronically, global clearing house systems are often used, similar to such domestic clearing house systems as the Automated Clearing House (ACH) network or the Fedwire system. Examples are the Clearing House Interbank Payments System (CHIPS) in New York and the Society for Worldwide Interbank Financial Telecommunication (SWIFT). These were discussed in more detail in chapter 5.

Foreign Exchange Services

Foreign exchange is another service large banks make available to corporations operating around the world. International commerce cannot occur unless money can be exchanged easily from one currency to another. U.S. banks that offer foreign exchange send and receive payments in all major currencies worldwide.

International banking departments offer corporate customers the ability to send and receive payments in dozens of currencies. Payment can be made by wire,

international ACH, draft, traveler's checks, and foreign currency banknotes (cash), or through other channels using other financial instruments. A key function of international banking departments is to monitor the exchange rates of the world's currencies to keep current with what the U.S. dollar is worth in euros, yen, or other currencies. Exchange rates then can be calculated immediately for international transactions.

By The Numbers

Currency Conversion for U.S. Dollars

Foreign Currency x Foreign Currency Exchange Rate (in U.S. dollars) = U.S. Dollars

Your company is importing auto parts from Germany, which uses euros as its currency. Each part costs 150 euros. The currency exchange rate at the present time is 1 euro = 1.35 U.S. dollars. How much does each part cost in U.S. dollars?

150 euros x 1.35 = 249.75 U.S. dollars

LAWS AND REGULATIONS

Business transactions may be subject to an array of state, federal, and international laws and regulations. Many bank charters include trust powers that require banks to comply with state and federal common law fiduciary principles. The Uniform Law Commission, previously known as the National Conference of Commissioners on Uniform State Laws (NCCUSL), drafted a Uniform Trust Code that has been adopted by more than half of the states. Trustees are subject to all state laws that are not preempted by federal law.

The International Chamber of Commerce (ICC) establishes uniform rules that govern international trade, such as the Uniform Customs and Practices for Documentary Credits (UCP 500) and the Uniform Rules for Collection. These international trade rules support and supplement the Uniform Commercial Code (UCC) Article 5 rules for letters of credit, with which U.S. banks must comply.

Other laws and regulations of note include Regulation 9, the GLBA, UCC Article 5, and Regulation K.

Fiduciary Activities of National Banks, Regulation 9

Title 12, Chapter 1, Part 9, of the Code of Federal Regulations (Regulation 9) governs the fiduciary activities of national banks. It sets out specific rules on trust administration and custody of assets, among other topics. Regulation 9 applies to national banks acting in a fiduciary capacity under the trust powers granted in their charters. It covers such fiduciary activities as collective investment funds established by a bank or an affiliate for the investment and reinvestment of money the bank manages as a trustee, executor, administrator, guardian, or custodian under the Uniform Transfer to Minors Act, or as the fiduciary for retirement, pension, profit-sharing, stock bonus, or other trust funds exempted from federal income tax.

Gramm-Leach-Bliley Act

Before the GLBA was enacted in 1999, banks that engaged in securities underwriting and dealing had to do so through "Section 20" firms. Section 20 of the Banking Act of 1933, also known as the Glass-Steagall Act, legally separated most aspects of commercial and investment banking.

Did You Know ...

Selected Currencies of the World

dollar: United States, Australia, Canada, Hong Kong, New Zealand, Singapore, Taiwan

yuan: China

rupee: India

yen: Japan

peso: Mexico

won: South Korea

pound: United Kingdom

euro: European Economic and Monetary Union member countries

dinar: Algeria, Bahrain, Iraq, Jordan, Kuwait, Libya, Macedonia, Serbia, Tunisia

ruble: Russia

As a result of Glass-Steagall, banks were no longer allowed to affiliate with firms engaged principally in underwriting and dealing in securities (such as purchasing stock for themselves or others). Banks wishing to offer investment banking services had to form subsidiaries called Section 20 broker-dealer firms that could engage in securities activities, although there was a limit on the amount of revenue they could earn. The GLBA repealed the Glass-Steagall Act to allow banks to once again engage in certain securities activities on a par with other financial service providers.

Specifically, Congress incorporated underwriting, dealing in, and making a market in securities in the list of permissible "financial-in-nature" activities. This GLBA provision allowed banks to underwrite and deal in commercial paper, asset-backed securities, and corporate debt and equity. Banks also can deal in mutual funds and make a market in securities, unrestricted by percentage limits.

The GLBA requires banks to conduct securities activities through a nonbank entity. The GLBA also created a new way of supervising financial institutions by their business activities. Under this system—known as functional regulation—subsidiaries or affiliates engaged in securities activities are regulated by the Securities and Exchange Commission (SEC). However, the GLBA recognizes that banks engaged in securities activities that are associated with traditional bank products and services should not have to register as broker-dealers and be subject to SEC oversight. Such permissible securities activities include investments that banks traditionally have made in U.S. government and agency securities.

The Dodd-Frank Wall Street Reform and Consumer Protection Act reintroduced some aspects of the Glass-Steagall Act's separation of commercial and investment banking. Known as the "Volker Rule," this financial reform provision limits banks' ownership and investment in hedge funds or private equity funds and prohibits speculative investments using the bank's own funds.

Uniform Commercial Code Article 5

UCC Article 5 governs letters of credit and the rights and responsibilities of the parties involved in such transactions. Another source of rules for letters of credit in international banking is the ICC's UCP 500. The requirements for letters of credit, as stipulated by Article 5, include the following:

- *Agreement by the parties.* Unlike a negotiable instrument, there is no particular form required for a letter of credit, but it must be on record and authenticated by signatures or in another manner agreed to by the parties.
- *Enforceability.* A letter of credit is irrevocable unless it states otherwise. It becomes enforceable against the issuer when the issuer sends or electronically transmits it to the advisor or to the beneficiary.
- *Payment responsibility.* When the required documents are received from the beneficiary, the issuer must examine them to ensure that they comply with the letter of credit, but the issuer does not need to determine if the

Banker Profile

Anton Martens, a native of the Netherlands, has a bachelor's degree in finance from the London School of Economics. When he graduated five years ago, he was recruited by the London branch of a management consultant firm because his academic performance was excellent and because he speaks French, German, Dutch, and English. When his firm advised a U.S. money center bank about restructuring its international division, Anton was recruited to join the division as a corporate banking officer for the European market. He did so and moved to New York, where in addition to his duties for the bank, he is pursuing his studies through the Institute of Certified Bankers to become a Certified Lender Business Banker (CLBB).

contract terms have been explicitly met. For documentary drafts, the issuer may take up to the end of the seventh business day after receipt of documents to make a payment decision. If there is a discrepancy, it must dishonor the draft and either return the documents or notify the presenter that they are being held for further instruction.

- *Wrongful dishonor.* The issuer's responsibility to the beneficiary if a court decides it has wrongfully dishonored a letter of credit payment is the amount of the dishonored draft and any damages, interest, reasonable attorney's fees, and other litigation expenses that may have been incurred.

Federal Reserve Regulation K (International Operations of U.S. Banking Organizations)

Regulation K, issued and enforced by the Federal Reserve Board, governs the international operations of U.S. banking organizations and the operations of foreign banks in the United States. The regulation defines permissible activities and investments of foreign branches of U.S. banks and permissible activities of Edge corporations. Lending limits and capital requirements are specified in the regulation, as well as supervision and reporting standards.

SUMMARY

- In addition to basic banking products such as checking and savings accounts and loans, banks offer businesses an array of specialized services, such as cash management, insurance, capital markets products, trust services, and international banking.
- Cash management services help businesses collect income and payments quickly, manage and reconcile outgoing payments efficiently, obtain timely and complete information on their bank accounts, and invest surplus funds for additional income. Banks help businesses achieve these objectives through cash vault, account reconciliation, positive pay, and lockbox services; remote deposit capture; direct deposit systems; controlled disbursement services that use cash concentration and disbursement accounts; zero-balance accounts; wire transfer, merchant card services, and sweep accounts.
- Through insurance affiliates or by partnering with third parties, banks can offer their customers insurance products. For businesses, banks sell and manage health insurance, key person insurance, and directors and officers liability insurance.
- By accessing public and private equity and debt markets, large banks offer a variety of services to help companies raise money for their operations. Capital market services for corporate customers include specialized lending; structuring, distributing, and underwriting debt; merchant banking; and facilitating sales of assets in mergers and acquisitions.
- Banks offer companies trust and agency services. Corporate agency services include safekeeping of stocks and transfer, registrar, and paying agent services. Bank trust departments also manage employee benefit programs such as those that support

employees' welfare (insurance and payments for sick leave, vacation, disability, and training) and pension needs (defined benefit and defined contribution plans). Retirement plans can be qualified or nonqualified, depending on whether they meet requirements of the Internal Revenue Code and the Employee Retirement Income Security Act. Qualified retirement plans are eligible for favorable tax treatment, but they do not offer the same flexibility as nonqualified plans.

- More than ever, banking and commerce are global enterprises. To stay competitive, banks offer services to customers that transact international business through a variety of structures, among them Edge corporations, foreign branches, shell branches, international banking facilities, foreign representative offices, foreign subsidiaries, and foreign joint ventures. Correspondent banking relationships provide access to international banking for banks that do not have their own international banking departments. Payment services, such as banker's acceptances, letters of credit, and foreign exchange services, protect the interests of both buyers and sellers in the international marketplace.
- Among laws and regulations pertaining to business and international banking are Regulation 9, Fiduciary Activities of National Banks, which provides rules on trust administration, custody of assets, and other trust-related issues; the Gramm-Leach-Bliley Act, which allows banks to underwrite and deal in commercial paper, asset-backed securities, and corporate debt and equity; and Uniform Commercial Code Article 5, supplemented by the International Chamber of Commerce's Uniform Customs and Practices for Documentary Credits (UCP 500), which provides rules governing letter of credit transactions. Regulation K (International Operations of U.S. Banking Organizations) governs Edge corporations and foreign branches of U.S. banks.

Learning Check

SELF-CHECK AND REVIEW

1. What types of cash management services help a corporate customer optimize the interest earned by deposits or reduce the interest expense of loans?
2. What check imaging advance is rapidly gaining acceptance in the business community and changing the way banks deliver cash management services?
3. How does key person insurance differ from directors and officers liability insurance?
4. What types of customers need capital market services? What are some examples of capital market services that banks provide?
5. What corporate trust services do banks typically provide?
6. What organizational structures can banks use to facilitate delivery of international banking services?
7. How does a letter of credit protect the interests of both the buyer and the seller of goods?

8. Your Japanese company is importing semiconductor parts from the United States. Each part costs 30 U.S. dollars. The currency exchange rate at the present time is 104 yen = 1 U.S. dollar. How much does each semiconductor part cost in yen?

9. What does UCC Article 5 govern? What are some sample rules? Is there an international law similar to UCC Article 5?

Building Relationships: Marketing, Sales, and Customer Service

9

Learning Objectives

After studying this chapter, you should be able to

- Discuss how marketing, sales, and service help build customer relationships
- Explain the components of a market-driven strategy
- Identify what customers expect from bankers
- Discuss the nature and importance of cross-selling and referrals
- Explain how a customer makes a purchase decision
- Identify the components of effective product development
- Describe the laws governing marketing by phone, fax, email, the Internet, and mobile devices

Did You Know ...

The majority of bank marketing expenditures is allocated to ads (over 50 percent of every marketing dollar), followed by public relations (28 percent), sales promotions (16 percent), and staff training and market research (about 1 percent each).

Source: 2012 ABA Marketing Survey Report

Introduction

Like other businesses, to be successful banks need to build relationships with customers, provide excellent customer service, and create and sell products that meet customer needs and expectations. In providing those products and services, banks must honor their legal and ethical responsibilities to customers and shareholders. Every day, banks must demonstrate that the money entrusted to them is safe, well managed, and accessible, and that serving the needs of customers is paramount.

Marketing, sales, and customer service are important in today's financial services environment, and building long-term relationships with customers is vital to a bank's success. Every bank employee has a role in relationship building. Customers have specific expectations for service, and all employees can help to meet these expectations. In creating and selling products and services, banks incorporate their understanding of customer needs and expectations and how customers make purchase decisions.

MARKETING AND SELLING TODAY

A customer in a long-term relationship with a bank may regard the bank as the primary, even lifelong, source of financial services. To create good, sustainable customer relationships, all banks need to practice a customer-centered philosophy. The customer experience may involve interaction with a bank employee, or as is growing increasingly common, it may involve digital interactivity—that is, via a computer or mobile device such as a smart phone or tablet.

Marketing and Sales

Many banks have a marketing department or officer responsible for promoting products and services and projecting an image of the bank that differentiates it in a positive way from its competitors, thereby creating a strategic advantage. Some smaller banks outsource the marketing function.

Marketing is fundamental to building relationships. By advertising through a variety of channels, the marketing department ensures that both current and prospective customers are aware of bank products and services that will help them meet their personal financial goals. Banks advertise through a variety of channels, the most common being newspapers, radio, direct mail, email, the Internet, television, magazines, and ads included with other bank communications, such as deposit account statements, delivered either by mail or electronically. The target audience should be considered when choosing the marketing channels for each message or promotion.

Many banks handle all of their own marketing and sales efforts, particularly tasks such as ad placements, public relations, and sales promotions. Smaller banks may outsource these tasks, and it is very common for banks to hire outside firms to handle the creative aspect of marketing, such as conceiving and producing television ads. Market research is another function that is often outsourced.

Since banking has become a commodity, many banks differentiate themselves by focusing on building relationships. Marketing must develop and articulate a genuine Unique Selling Proposition (USP) to capture new business. Determining how the bank is unique is only part of the equation. The USP message should then be communicated in a way that resonates with the target audience through integrated marketing channels and results in profitable new business.

Apart from the marketing department, bankers of all levels and departments have sales and business development responsibilities. The bank president often has a prominent role in selling products and services to community leaders. Members of the board may bring in new customers through their ties to the business community. Although larger banks often employ business development officers whose job is specifically to find a place for the bank's financial services in the marketplace, most banks require all their officers to seek such opportunities. Officers in lending, trust, commercial services, and retail banking employ sales strategies to ensure the bank captures and retains **market share**.

Another important aspect of marketing and sales is public relations. Employees engaged in the marketing function usually have public relations responsibilities as well, such as promoting a bank's charitable work and sponsorship activities. The extent of public relations activities varies among banks; for example, some banks encourage all employees to participate in volunteer work regardless of their job title. Public relations initiatives also include making donations to community and charitable organizations, sponsoring special events, conducting media outreach, sending press releases, and supporting education programs.

Banks are increasingly using social media in their public relations programs. Social media provides a platform for leveraging media coverage, highlighting employee volunteerism, and promoting local events, educational programs, and grand openings to a broad audience.

Did You Know ...

Since the ABA Education Foundation's Teach Children to Save program started in 1997, some 130,000 bankers have taught savings skills to over 6 million students.

Source: American Bankers Association

market share—One seller's portion of the total sales of a product, usually measured as a percentage. In the financial services industry, market share is typically expressed as a percentage of deposits.

Customer Service

If a customer's everyday banking experience is unsatisfactory, the bank's marketing and sales efforts are placed in jeopardy. Whenever interacting with customers, bank employees must keep in mind their responsibility to help the bank build long-term relationships with its customers. Customers consider every transaction to be important. Care, accuracy, and professionalism in processing transactions ensure that the customer will want to return to the bank and refer other customers. Smiling, remembering the customer's name, taking time to understand and answer a question, and expressing genuine appreciation for the customer's business may seem like small gestures, but they are powerful incentives for customers to continue their relationship with the bank. Recommending a product that makes a customer's life easier or satisfies a current need can make a customer for life.

To be a successful salesperson:

- Know your customer.
- Know your bank's products and services.
- Match your bank's products and services to your customer's needs.
- Demonstrate the benefits.
- Anticipate questions and be prepared to answer.
- Ask for the business.

Even employees whose jobs do not involve face-to-face contact with customers are important in the relationship-building process. For example, a bank will have difficulty convincing customers that it cares about their business if it regularly makes errors in posting transactions. A loan approval that takes too long may result in a potential borrower finding another source of credit.

Marketing, the Internet, and Electronic Devices

In today's financial services environment, many customer experiences are not personal. The rapid development of the Internet and mobile devices has reinvented how bank products and services are marketed and sold.

When investigating financial products and services, many consumers turn to their personal computers and mobile devices to access individual bank websites or financial sites that provide comparative shopping information. Bank websites have become an important venue for displaying ads that promote products and services. In addition to ads, bank websites are enhancing the total shopping experience with other features such as product reviews; financial assistance tools; connections with the bank and other customers via Facebook, Twitter, Flickr, or other social networking services; and opportunities to chat with customer service representatives.

Marketing and sales opportunities arise every time bank customers access their computers, smart phones, or tablets to perform banking tasks, such as reviewing account balances or making deposits. By employing these various marketing and sales tools, banks can interact with customers and bring a level of personal service to the less-than-personal digital environment.

THE MARKET-DRIVEN STRATEGY

A market-driven strategy is broader than the advertising and promotional activities most often associated with the marketing function. It holds that a business can best reach its objectives by first identifying customer needs and wants and fulfilling them through an efficient total company- and management-supported effort. The famous business writer and consultant, Peter Drucker, captured well the essence of a market-driven strategy when he said, "The aim of marketing is to know and understand the customer so well the product or service fits him and sells itself."

The four pillars of the market-driven strategy are total company effort, customer satisfaction, profitability, and social responsibility.

Total Company Effort

To customers, bank employees are the bank. Every time a customer interacts with an employee, the bank sells itself. If a call center employee is rude to a customer, then as far as the customer is concerned, the bank is rude. If a teller makes a mistake in processing a transaction, then as far as the customer is concerned, the bank is careless and untrustworthy. No matter what an employee's job, marketing is an inherent part of it and an integrated function across all areas of the bank. By doing the job well, the employee is selling the bank and its products, services, and customer service standards.

In an organization with a market-driven strategy, every department sees itself as serving customers in some way. Employees understand that, if they are not serving the customer directly, they are serving someone in the bank who is serving the customer. For that reason, employees regard other employees as their internal customers. They treat each other like professionals, all working toward the same goal of serving customers with care and distinction.

Customer Satisfaction

A market-driven strategy requires bankers to recognize that satisfying customers is the core business of banking. If customers are not satisfied, the bank will not only lose them, it will be incapable of building strong relationships with the customers who remain. Moreover, word-of-mouth criticism by disgruntled customers can have devastating, long-term consequences, an effect that is even more pronounced when customer dissatisfaction is expressed through social media. Customer retention and relationship building depend on customers perceiving that the bank values their business.

Customer satisfaction is therefore good business. Retaining customers costs less than attracting new ones. Marketing to the general public via newspapers, television, radio, or the Internet is more expensive and less likely to produce results than marketing to current customers who are satisfied with the service they are currently receiving. Thus, the very best and least costly way to promote the bank is to provide excellent customer service, thereby generating satisfied customers, creating positive word-of-mouth promotion, and differentiating the bank from its competitors.

Customer satisfaction is achievable only when the bank organizes its processes to best serve the interests and convenience of its customers. Although certain forms, disclosures, and account opening procedures are required by law, how they are processed and how the customer is treated during the transaction make an important difference. Banks that strive for high customer satisfaction attempt to always put the customer, not the paperwork, at the center of each transaction.

One example is the universal account agreement in which previously acquired information about the customer is retained. Later, a customer who decides to open another account has less paperwork to complete. To make banking more convenient, many banks have extended their hours and offered new ways for customers to interact with bank employees. For example, lobby and drive-up service hours may be expanded to include weekends and evenings, or advanced automated teller machines (ATMs) may be installed to allow videoconferencing with off-site tellers during nonbusiness hours.

Mobile banking services, including Internet banking via the computer and mobile devices, offer the ultimate in customer convenience. They allow customers to handle bank transactions from nearly everywhere and at any time of the day.

Profitability

Profitability is an important part of the market-driven strategy. Without profits, the bank will not have the capital and resources to retain and grow its business.

Profitability and customer satisfaction are not mutually exclusive. Indeed, the market-driven strategy holds that profit objectives are best met by keeping customers satisfied.

Customer satisfaction has a direct bearing on pricing for services. Satisfied customers are less price-sensitive than unhappy ones. This is important because banks must charge fees that reflect the true cost of services. A satisfied customer accepts a reasonable fee for high-quality, attentive service. A displeased customer, on the other hand, is likely to shop around for competitive pricing on products and services.

value—The worth of a product or service that is expressed in money (price) or a quantity of another product or service. It is also the quality that makes something desirable or important.

Consistent with customer needs, a successful organization seeks ways to use resources efficiently. It prices products and services to both provide **value** to customers and earn a profit for the bank. For example, banks set loan interest rates that are attractive to borrowers and contribute to earnings while covering costs and risks. Banks that build value into products and services attract more customers at higher prices than competitors who charge less but also offer less value. Value leads to customer satisfaction, which in turn improves bank earnings by enlarging the customer base, increasing deposit balances, and raising interest and fee income. Furthermore, understanding how the bank makes money and how decisions affect the "bottom line" are important to the progression of any career path in banking.

Situation

Newlyweds Jim and Carlene open both a checking and savings account at the bank. They are pleased with the service and the friendly bank employees, but especially Susan, who Jim sees every other Friday when he deposits his paycheck at the drive-in window. Because of this excellent service, when Jim and Carlene decide to buy a second car they consider the bank first for an automobile loan. A few years later, Jim and Carlene have their first child. One Friday, when Jim is depositing his paycheck, Susan tells him about her bank's college savings accounts. Jim is very interested, so Susan sets up a meeting with Tom, the bank's financial planning advisor.

Social Responsibility

Although they are private or shareholder owned businesses, banks are expected—and, in fact, required—to contribute to the well-being of their communities, including low- to moderate-income customers. One banking law in particular, the Community Reinvestment Act, requires the regulators to rate banks in three areas that are considered measures of social responsibility:

- Record of lending in the community (specifically, home mortgages, small business loans, small farm loans, community development lending, and consumer loans)
- Record of meeting community credit needs through qualified investments, excluding lending
- Record of delivering retail banking and community development services

Thus, by assuming a prominent role in their community's economy—providing financial resources so that individuals, families, and businesses may prosper—banks also fulfill a legal and regulatory requirement.

Banks also serve the nation. They act as fiscal agents of the federal government; collecting tax deposits from businesses. They work with the government to help implement the nation's monetary policies and keep the economy strong. They also help the government fight financial crimes by reporting suspicious activities that may indicate fraud, money laundering, or terrorist financing.

Bankers also serve the public by becoming involved in their community. Many banks give employees time off to engage in public service, such as charitable events and disaster relief. Through their community relations programs, banks support the arts, philanthropic causes, scholastic achievement, school programs, and amateur sports.

Even more pertinent, banks have an important role in advocating for public financial education. For example, one way bankers have served this educational responsibility is by participating in the ABA Education Foundation's Teach Children to Save program, which conveys to young people the importance of managing their personal finances.

Providing financial education to all Americans is wise business practice as well. There are over 40 million unbanked and **underbanked** people in the United States who do not use banks or credit unions for their financial service needs. Many of these Americans are not **financially literate**, and consequently pay far more than they should for basic banking services, such as cashing a check or taking out a loan for a car, than they would if they operated in the financial mainstream. Banks that offer financial services for this market segment and provide financial education for the next generation of savers and borrowers generate customers while helping Americans avoid costly alternative financial services so they can build and protect their wealth.

underbanked—An individual who may have a checking or savings account but relies heavily on alternative financial services, such as payday loan providers, rent-to-own businesses, or pawn shops.

financially literate—Having a basic understanding of financial matters, especially as it pertains to personal finances, such as making wise savings and borrowing decisions.

MEETING CUSTOMER EXPECTATIONS

In building customer relationships, bankers must be mindful of customer expectations. These are the standards to which bankers are held in their financial service and sales interactions with customers. Asked what they want most in a bank, customers usually respond with the following:

- Responsive service
- Competent staff
- A customer perspective
- Courteous treatment
- Reliable service
- Viable products and services
- Professional appearance
- Access to funds and staff
- Financial privacy

Responsive Service and Problem Resolution

Customers want their bankers to be ready to serve them. Responsive service demonstrates that the bank values the customer's business. Responsiveness involves:

- Acknowledging customers as they approach
- Being ready to help customers
- Listening carefully to understand customer needs
- Taking responsibility for resolving the problems customers present
- Functioning as a team member with other bank employees to solve problems and serve customers
- Solving problems promptly and accurately
- Being friendly and caring when problems are particularly complicated

Did You Know ...

Bilingual advertising, flexible underwriting standards, financial education seminars, and community partnerships are among the strategies banks are using effectively to reach out to the many customers who do not speak English.

Did You Know ...

Banks spent the most marketing their deposit services (33.8 percent of marketing expenditures), followed by mortgage services (23.3 percent), credit services (18 percent), debit cards (5.4 percent), and trust/private banking/ wealth management services (4.6 percent).

Source: 2012 ABA Marketing Survey Report

Competent Staff

Customers expect employees to have the skills and knowledge necessary to explain bank products and services and answer questions clearly. They expect to be directed to the products and services that will be most useful to them. Demonstrated competence reassures customers that their money is in good hands.

Customer Perspective

In all interactions with customers, it is important to understand their perspective. Both written and spoken communication should be clear, concise, and recognize the customer's point of view. Although the statement "Preauthorized automatic transfers are available with this account" may be operationally correct, the customer will better understand if a bank employee rephrases it to say, "You may arrange to have funds automatically transferred from your checking account to your money market savings account, making regular saving easier for you."

Similarly, bank employees should avoid bank jargon when helping customers. Terms such as "truncation," "demand deposit," "foreign bank," and "amortization" may be familiar to bank employees, but they are not familiar to the average bank customer. Acronyms such as PMI, APY, and even CD may draw puzzled looks. Unless using them is necessary to comply with regulations, technical terms and acronyms should be avoided when a simple explanation will suffice. When technical terms are required, they should be explained in language the customer can understand.

Courteous Treatment

Customers want to be treated in a friendly, thoughtful, efficient, and respectful manner. When customers believe they have been treated discourteously, they conclude that they and their business are not important to the bank. They may feel uncomfortable interacting with bank employees and ultimately take their business elsewhere. In contrast, satisfied customers feel valued and believe the bank wants their business. Courteous behavior is conveyed by:

- **Making eye contact.** Looking customers in the eye as they approach lets them know the employee is interested in their business.
- **Being present.** Focusing on the customer being served and not being distracted by other functions or people demonstrates the value the employee holds for the customer.
- **Smiling.** A smile communicates warmth. When employees smile, they convey to customers that the bank is happy to serve them.
- **Acknowledging and greeting the customer.** Customers expect to be acknowledged and greeted promptly when they approach. Bankers should stand, shake hands, and initiate introductions. Doing so makes customers feel comfortable stating their business.
- **Using the customer's name.** Calling customers by name makes them feel at home. It raises the interaction to a more personable level.
- **Using expressions of courtesy.** "Please," "thank you," and "excuse me" should be used often in all customer contacts.

- **Having a positive attitude.** Employees should always be helpful, cheerful, and interested when they respond to customers. Even when customers are upset or angry, bank employees should show that they are willing to listen calmly.

Reliable Service

Customers understandably expect excellent service from banks. They expect statements to arrive on time and to be accurate; they expect to receive renewal notices for certificates of deposit; they expect mobile banking services to be available when needed; and they expect problems to be resolved quickly. Reliable service does not mean just meeting customer expectations; it means exceeding customer expectations.

Reliable service also entails timely and consistent follow-up to a customer request for information or to a customer complaint. By responding as soon as possible or moving quickly to resolve a concern or complaint, and then contacting the customer to explain the response or resolution, a bank employee is able to show customers that the bank can be relied on to understand needs and solve problems.

Appropriate Products and Services

Customers expect banks to have a variety of banking products, and they expect each to have specific benefits that address different financial needs. The following are examples of appropriate bank products and services to address four basic financial needs.

Financial Need	*Product or Service*
Save money	Savings account, money market deposit account, certificate of deposit, investment advisory services
Borrow money	Auto loan, mortgage, home equity loan, home equity line of credit, personal loan, credit card
Move money	Checking account, automatic transfer, direct deposit, Internet banking, telephone banking, ATM, wire transfer, bill payment
Protect assets	Trust services, insurance services, deposit insurance

Situation

Elva, the widow of a small business owner, comes to her community bank to apply for a loan. She has had little experience in banking transactions. It is a very busy day, and the banker, Anthony, has a number of loan applications that need review before sending them on to credit investigation. Anthony notices the woman is struggling to complete her loan application. Instead of hurrying her along, he first assists Elva before returning to his paperwork.

Professional Appearance

Customers expect the place where they bank to look like a safe place to put their money. Customer attitudes are shaped in part by the appearance of the bank facility and its employees. Uninviting or disorganized facilities and employee dress that is too casual can erode confidence.

Banks have traditionally designed their facilities to project the image of trust and strength. Today, many bank lobbies are designed to also convey a retail-oriented atmosphere.

When employees dress professionally, customers feel more confident about the bank. Banks require employees who interact with the public to dress professionally. However, as clothing trends have become more casual, many banks have adopted a business casual dress code for most employees, including retail customer-contact employees. All bank employees are required to maintain a professional appearance in terms of grooming and clothing style, but a bank may decide that its customers are more comfortable dealing with employees who are dressed more like the customers they serve. Many banks also issue policy expectations to employees about other aspects of personal appearance, as long as the guidelines do not discriminate against a protected group of employees. Professional appearance conveys the impression that employees respect themselves and their customers; and in turn, they deserve respect from their customers.

Access to Funds and Staff

Customers expect services and employees to be available when and where they need them. Internet banking, ATMs, and mobile banking are examples of how banks use technology to deliver bank products and services to customers at any hour of the day, giving them access to their funds whenever they need them.

Banks may have extended branch banking hours to meet customer needs for services that require direct employee interaction. This "customer first" attitude is expressed by employees who are accessible and willing to help, and it should be demonstrated by all employees, not just those with customer-contact responsibilities.

Financial Privacy

Bank customers expect their accounts to be handled in complete privacy. As the amount of personal information stored and transmitted electronically grows, so does consumer anxiety about confidentiality. Because banks have in their databases more confidential information about their customers than most other businesses, their employees must honor the bank's privacy policies and never discuss accounts or transactions with friends or neighbors. Simply telling others that someone has an account with your bank is also unacceptable and a privacy violation.

Banking laws, such as the Gramm-Leach-Bliley Act (GLBA), require financial institutions to protect the privacy of personal customer information. The GLBA requires banks to tell customers whether they share customer information with third parties and to refrain from doing so if the customer objects. Banks have always made protecting customer account information a priority, but the GLBA privacy provisions offer additional assurance that the banking industry is committed to protecting private financial information.

cross-selling—A sales practice whereby a customer is invited to purchase additional products and services that are related to the product or service acquired.

referral—Directing a potential customer from one area of the bank, such as consumer lending, to another area, such as insurance, to help the customer obtain information about or purchase another product or service.

CROSS-SELLING AND REFERRALS

On average, the more products and services a customer uses, the more likely the customer will remain loyal to the bank—and the more profitable the customer relationship will be. The best way for bank employees to extend the relationship with customers is through **cross-selling** and **referrals**.

Cross-selling is an important objective for all banks. In today's competitive environment, it has become essential for all bank employees—not just those in sales and marketing—to recognize a customer's financial needs and recommend bank products and services that will simplify or enhance fulfillment of those needs. Many customers still go to an insurance company for insurance, a brokerage company for investments, and a bank for a checking account, not realizing that they may be able to access all these services at a bank. Cross-selling should not, however, be thought of as only beneficial to the bank—it is also good customer service. Everyone is interested in improving their financial position, and customers appreciate bank employees who take the time to offer solutions for doing so.

A good banker, therefore, listens and encourages a customer to talk about their financial situation and pulls clues from that conversation that may help to cross-sell additional products or services. For instance, a customer who wants or has a mortgage may also benefit from a:

- Safe deposit box to store mortgage papers
- Checking account with automatic payment to ensure the mortgage is paid on time
- Homeowner's policy through the insurance subsidiary
- Personal line of credit to help cover the incidental expenses of new home ownership

Cross-selling opportunities often occur when customers express an interest in one bank product or service when, in fact, another product or service would better fulfill their needs. To cross-sell effectively requires that bank employees recognize both their customers' needs and have a thorough knowledge of the bank's products and services so they can be matched when an opportunity arises.

When a bank employee does not have the expertise or authority to sell a product or service, or the product or service is offered by another department or a bank affiliate, the customer is best served by a referral to someone who can be of assistance. The customer is directed to speak to another employee in the bank or bank affiliate who can explain a product or service that would be appropriate. In both cases, listening to customers to recognize their needs is the crucial first step.

A bank that effectively cross-sells additional products and refers business to other departments or affiliates expands its customer relationships, helps customers meet their financial goals, and sells more products, both immediately and in the long term. Furthermore, when employees cross-sell and make referrals, customers feel appreciated and realize that their bank values their business and has their financial interests in mind.

To cross-sell and make referrals, bankers must be aware of marketing and sales opportunities. For example:

- A teller who notices that a customer has a large balance in a savings account suggests a money market account or a certificate of deposit (cross-sell) or the bank's investment services (referral).

Did You Know ...

Approximately 50 percent of all banks have a company-wide cross-selling plan.

Source: 2012 ABA Marketing Survey Report

- A loan officer who helps a customer finance a new car suggests opening a checking account to facilitate automatic loan payments (cross-sell) and an insurance review with the bank's insurance subsidiary (referral).
- A call center employee who fields a customer inquiry about an account statement or transaction history suggests Internet banking or mobile banking (cross-sell).
- A commercial loan officer who works with a small business owner who has an established credit relationship with the bank recommends cash management services for the business (cross-sell) and private banking services (referral) for the owner.
- A teller who notices that a business customer makes deposits every day suggests remote deposit capture (cross-sell) or refers the customer to the cash management department (referral).

THE PURCHASING PROCESS

Essential to building customer relationships is understanding what is involved when a customer decides to make a purchase. The customer purchasing process is influenced by every transaction, communication, and experience with the bank. Knowing the steps in the process (see exhibit 9.1) helps bankers facilitate customer decisions to obtain a product or service. The purchasing process usually happens in four phases: needs identification, prepurchase searching, the purchase decision, and postpurchase assessment.

Needs Identification

The starting point for any purchase is an unsatisfied need. There are two basic types of needs: recognized needs and unrecognized needs.

Customers are aware of recognized needs. For example, a young college graduate who has found a job recognizes the need to establish credit. A regular savings account customer realizes that more interest can be earned by investing in a certificate of deposit.

Customers are unaware of unrecognized needs. The college graduate turned professional may not know all the credit options and financial planning services that are available. The savings account customer may not realize that savings can grow faster over the long term if invested in the equities market or may be used more effectively for purchasing an annuity.

Exhibit 9.1: The Purchasing Process

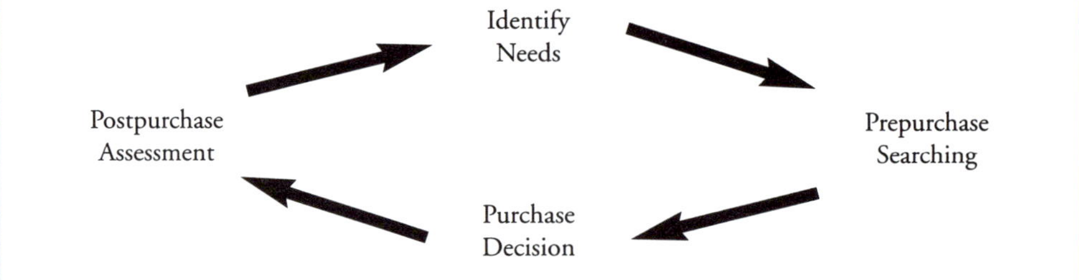

Bank employees can be very helpful in identifying needs. Most customers welcome advice on how their bank can serve them better. For employees to offer advice, they must both know their customers and thoroughly understand their bank's products and services. In short, bank employees should be alert for opportunities to recommend a product to a customer.

Did You Know ...

Psychologist Abraham Maslow identified five levels of need that motivate human behavior: physiological need, the need for a sense of security, the need to belong, the need for a sense of self-esteem, and the need for self-actualization.

Prepurchase Searching

Once a need is identified, the customer begins to search for the best way to satisfy it. How much effort is expended in this search depends on such factors as the cost, return, or complexity of the product or service being sought. The customer contemplating the purchase of a savings product may simply look at newspaper ads or visit websites to compare the rates offered by competing financial institutions. The customer shopping for a mortgage loan or a home equity line of credit may search longer and more carefully because mortgage products are complicated and require an understanding of a variety of conditions that can be attached to such products.

Although prepurchase searching often includes talking to other people, reading pamphlets, requesting a loan application, or researching on the Internet, the most important source of information is a bank's employees. Often a prospective customer will call the bank or approach an employee in person to solicit information, offering an opportunity to sell a bank product or service. An employee who shows interest in the customer's needs, conveys enthusiasm about the bank's products, and demonstrates knowledge and capability is more effective in selling than any promotional material.

Features and Benefits

Much of the customer's prepurchase activity consists of gathering information about **features** and **benefits** of possible product solutions. Features are characteristics of the product or service such as interest rate or term. Product benefits address the four basic financial needs: save money, borrow money, move money (including making payments), and protect assets.

Two examples of bank products and their corresponding features and benefits.

feature—A characteristic of the product or service, such as the interest rate or the term.

benefit—The value the product's or service's features gives to customers to meet their needs, such as earn money, save money, save time, provide convenience, or provide security.

Product	*Features*	*Benefits*
Home equity line of credit	Revolving credit line	Customers can use funds as needed, pay interest only on the outstanding balance, save time and money, and perhaps qualify for a tax benefit
Money market account	A higher yield than statement savings accounts, no fixed maturity date, limited transactions	Customers earn more money with this deposit account than with statement savings accounts and can move money more freely than with time deposits

In discussing products with a customer, bankers translate product features into benefits the customer will appreciate. For example, "With Internet banking you can pay bills online. For you, this means time saved writing checks and money saved in postage. You are also assured the bill will be paid on time."

Purchase Decision

In deciding to make a purchase, the customer uses information gathered in the previous phase to weigh the advantages and disadvantages of the product or service, compare the relative merits of alternatives, and choose particular features. In financial decisions, this may mean choosing the most appropriate type of individual retirement account or applying for a fixed-rate rather than an adjustable-rate mortgage.

purchase decision—In the buying process, the culmination of prepurchase activity, in which a customer first assesses information gathered to reduce the risk associated with a decision about a product and then makes the purchase.

The **purchase decision** is often the result of an informed choice; the choice becomes more complex as the product or service becomes more complex. Bankers play an important sales and service role by answering any questions the customer may have and either moving to close a sale, if possible, or referring the customer to other bank personnel who are more familiar with, or qualified to sell, the product or service.

Postpurchase Assessment

After customers make a purchase, they often reassess their decision. Customers want assurance that they made the right choice. Many customers experience anxiety, especially if the purchase decision was difficult or attractive alternatives were also available and rejected. Was the decision the right one? Were the chosen features the best ones? Most customers ask themselves questions like this as they reevaluate products or services they have just bought.

Bankers, aware of this stage in the purchasing process, take steps to ease customer anxieties and offer evidence that the decision was good. They know that a customer generally needs continuing support after a purchase. In the banking world, reassuring new customers may entail:

- Sending them letters reaffirming the benefits of their decisions
- Calling to thank them for their business and offer further assistance
- Answering questions after they deposit their money or sign loan papers

PRODUCT DEVELOPMENT

Banks not only market and sell current products, they also research and introduce new ones. The GLBA financial modernization reforms expanded the types of products and services banks may offer, and today many customers demand more products to meet their financial goals.

Developing new products is a multiphase process (see exhibit 9.2): conducting market research, profiling the market, soliciting new product ideas, testing the concept, and conducting a business analysis. The product is then test-marketed before it is rolled out to the entire market. Finally, the product is evaluated to see if it is meeting the bank's objectives.

Exhibit 9.2: New Product Development

Conduct Market Research
Obtain current information on customers, market, and competitors.

↓

Profile Customers, Market, and Competitors
Aggregate data for meaningful analysis.

↓

Getting New Product Ideas
What is the need in the marketplace?

↓

Screening New Products
What is the initial reaction against the bank's objectives, other products, and company resources?
Are there regulatory constraints?

↓

Testing the Concept
What do the small focus groups say?

↓

Business Analysis
Is there sufficient demand for the product?
Does it fit with the bank's goals and objectives?

↓

Developing the Product
What will the features be?
How will the bank promote, distribute, and price the new product?

↓

Test Marketing the Product
What target markets will the bank test the product in?
How will the bank promote the product in those markets?

↓

Introducing the Product
How will the bank introduce the product?
What impact will this product have on the existing product line?

↓

Evaluating the Product
How does the progress of the new product meet the company's goals?
What adjustments are necessary?

In most banks, product development is a joint effort of the marketing officer, department managers, and senior managers. Compliance or risk management officers are often part of the team because many new products have regulatory or risk implications.

Product development includes many of the following activities:

- **Conducting market research.** Up-to-date information about customers, the market, and competitors is drawn from internal records, such as the **marketing customer information file** (MCIF); local contacts, such as the

marketing customer information file (MCIF)—A software program that can sort and analyze customer information and serves as a customer information database.

chamber of commerce; regulatory agency reports; the Internet, such as other bank websites; surveys, such as those about customer preferences; and secondary sources, such as lists of new housing developments.

profile—In marketing, identifying relevant characteristics of customers to gain insight about the need for a product in the marketplace.

- **Profiling customers, the market, and competitors.** The bank **profile** of its customers may include information about age distribution, occupation, educational level, income, and geographic location. A market profile may describe the number and value of housing units, population data, and other demographic information about the area. A competitive profile may include information on competitors' market shares and the types and prices of services they offer.
- **Soliciting new ideas.** Ideas for new products—such as health savings accounts, insurance, and investments—come from many sources: market research, management or employees, or authorization by laws and the regulators.
- **Screening the product.** New product ideas are screened against the bank's objectives, policies, resources, and the probable effect on current products. The bank then decides whether to continue developing the product or start over.
- **Testing the concept.** A promising product idea is tested in the marketplace through customer focus groups or customer surveys.
- **Performing a business analysis.** Market and business analysis techniques determine market share, product demand, and compatibility with bank goals, including whether the product presents an acceptable financial and regulatory risk. Then, product objectives, target market, and strategy are defined.
- **Developing the product.** The product is defined in terms of features and benefits, pricing, processes, the procedures necessary to support the product, and distribution and promotion strategies.
- **Testing and marketing the product.** The product is tested in one or more of the bank's geographic markets, using different features, distribution methods, and promotion strategies.
- **Introducing the product.** Rolling out a new banking product requires a substantial investment in advertising, sales promotions, and employee training. Customer-contact employees in particular must understand product features and customer benefits.
- **Evaluating the product.** Evaluating product performance helps identify any adjustments needed, the effect on other product lines, and other product development opportunities.

Situation

To reach new customers, Mesquite Valley Bank launches a marketing campaign targeting the Hispanic population in its area. The bank begins advertising in Spanish in local media, including transit advertising, billboards, and the Internet. All of its branches now have at least one Spanish-speaking person, and its call center, ATMs, and website are bilingual as well.

Having researched the financial needs of potential customers, the bank decides to lower the cost of attractive services such as international transfers of money and check-cashing services, which it promotes through culturally relevant brochures. The bank also develops relationships with groups that serve the needs of the local Hispanic community, including local churches, community centers, and nonprofit organizations. These collaborations result in the bank sponsoring bilingual seminars on such topics as money management and purchasing a new home.

LAWS AND REGULATIONS

Like other commercial enterprises, banks must abide by laws and regulations that protect other businesses and consumers. Because **advertising** and **sales promotions** may mislead customers or invade their privacy, both federal and state governments supervise bank marketing practices. For marketing activities, banks must abide by the consumer financial protection rules written and enforced by the Consumer Financial Protection Bureau as well as other rules issued by the banking regulators and various other federal and state regulators.

advertising—Any form of communication paid for by a sponsor for the purpose of informing and persuading consumers to buy goods, ideas, or services.

sales promotion—Any activity, other than advertising, publicity, and personal selling, that provides incentive to the consumer to purchase goods or services; for example, offering premiums and having in-branch displays.

official advertising statement—Mandated by FDIC regulation, a statement that must be included in all advertisements (unless specifically exempted) that the bank is a member of the FDIC. Specific requirements apply as to the wording, size, and placement of the statement.

Some of the marketing laws and regulations are targeted to specific bank products—for example, the Truth in Lending Act and the Truth in Savings Act govern how loan and deposit products can be advertised in all marketing forums, whether through print or broadcast media, websites, lobby posters, social media, or statement stuffers.

As new bank products have been introduced or existing bank products have grown more complex, advertising rules and regulations have been amended to further aid consumer understanding of the features and conditions of the products being advertised. For example, granting banks the authority to offer nondeposit investment products necessitated new advertising requirements, including the mandatory disclosure "Not FDIC Insured, No Bank Guarantee, May Lose Value" whenever nondeposit investment products are advertised. Similarly, the Truth in Lending Act was later amended to add new requirements for marketing credit cards, which had grown increasingly complex in their features, such as multiple interest rates.

Marketing laws and regulations that apply to specific bank products and services are covered in the chapters of this book that deal with those products and services. A discussion of the laws and regulations that apply to bank marketing in general follows.

FDIC Insurance Notification

Federal Deposit Insurance Corporation (FDIC) regulations require that, when a bank advertises deposit accounts or products (which are insured by the FDIC) or the bank itself, the public must be made aware of FDIC insurance protection by including an **official advertising statement**. The advertising statement consists of the words "Member of the Federal Deposit Insurance Corporation," "Member of FDIC," or "Member FDIC." FDIC regulations provide some exceptions to this requirement, such as when radio or television advertisements do not exceed 30 seconds in length.

Unfair, Deceptive, or Abusive Acts or Practices

Virtually all states have laws regulating deceptive trade practices, but the principal federal statute governing business marketing practices in the United States is the Federal Trade Commission (FTC) Act. Enacted in 1914 to regulate industrial policy and commercial trade practices, the law created the Federal Trade Commission, whose first enforcement efforts were directed to price-fixing, monopolies, and unfair practices in commercial competition. The FTC has since taken on consumer protection as well.

Although the FTC has authority strictly over nonbank businesses, the federal banking regulators and the CFPB have the authority to enforce the FTC Act, Section 5, which details the unfair, deceptive, and abusive practices that are forbidden in the financial industry.

Marketing departments should develop productive working relationships with the bank's compliance department. A strong, respectful relationship between these two departments can assist marketing with proper disclosures and help ensure that messages are delivered in customer-friendly language.

Deceptive acts or practices are those that are likely to mislead the reasonable consumer and constitute a material practice, defined as follows:

- **Likely to mislead.** A representation, omission, act, or practice can mislead. Examples are false oral or written representations, misleading claims about costs, **bait-and-switch** tactics, and failure to provide the service or product.
- **Reasonable customer.** The act or practice would be deceptive to a person of average intelligence exercising an average amount of judgment. Omitting material information from an otherwise truthful advertisement could mislead a reasonable customer and thus be deceptive.
- **Material practice.** The misrepresentation, omission, act, or practice affects the customer's choice or conduct, as when misleading information about costs leads the customer to decide to buy the product.

bait-and-switch—Advertising a product or service at an attractive price (bait) and then informing a consumer who is ready to purchase that the product or service is not available or is of lesser quality and encouraging the consumer to purchase (switch) to a higher-priced product or service.

The FTC Act, Section 5, defines the elements of unfair acts or practices as those causing substantial injury or injuries that are not outweighed by the benefits and could not be reasonably avoided, defined as follows:

- **Substantial injury.** This occurs when a customer suffers, for example, monetary harm, such as paying an unnecessary fee or interest charge due to an unfair practice. The injury may be small but affect many people or be significant for a single customer. An example would be claiming there are no fees in the promotion and mentioning the fees only in the small print.
- **Benefit less than the injury.** For this element, the net effect of the practice is analyzed to see if the overall benefits are not greater than the harm caused by incomplete or misleading communications.
- **Not a reasonably avoidable injury.** The consumer could not avoid the injury. This can occur when information is withheld or distorted to impede the customer's reasonable choice.

The Dodd-Frank Wall Street Reform and Consumer Protection Act added "abusive" acts or practices to the scope of the FTC Act. An abusive act or practice is one that would meet one of these tests:

- Materially interferes with a consumer's ability to understand the terms or conditions of a financial product or service
- Takes unreasonable advantage of the consumer's lack of understanding of the material risks or costs of the product or service
- Takes unreasonable advantage of the consumer's inability to protect his or her own interests when selecting or using a financial product or service

Do Not Call, Do Not Fax

Telemarketing involves using telephone lines (phone or fax) to promote products and services. Because customers are contacted in their own homes or offices, telemarketing raises questions about privacy, full disclosure, and whether there are places that marketers should be off-limits.

In 2007, the Federal Financial Institutions Examination Council (FFIEC) approved updated interagency examination procedures for consumer compliance with the Telephone Consumer Protection Act of 1991 and the Junk Fax Prevention Act of 1994. Banks are subject to the Federal Communications Commission (FCC) regulations implementing the two acts.

The FCC regulations give consumers options to avoid unwanted telephone solicitations. For example:

- No seller, or entity telemarketing on behalf of a seller, may initiate a telephone solicitation to residential telephone subscribers who have registered their number on the National Do Not Call Registry.
- Calls (other than pre-recorded calls) are permitted, however, to those with whom the seller has an **established business relationship**.
- Banks must maintain bank-specific do-not-call lists with the names of people with whom they have a business relationship who have asked to be excluded from telemarketing.
- Telemarketing calls may be made between 8:00 a.m. and 9:00 p.m. only.
- Telemarketers must comply with limits on **abandoned calls**.
- Consumer-friendly practices must be used when calls are made with automated telephone-dialing equipment.
- Prerecorded messages must identify the name and telephone number of the entity responsible for the call.
- Telemarketers must transmit caller ID information, when available, and refrain from blocking such transmissions to the consumer.
- The advertiser must first obtain the written permission and signature of the intended recipient before sending unsolicited advertising fax transmissions unless there is an established business relationship and the recipient has provided a fax number for such communications.

Examples of Bait-and-Switch

A car dealer runs a newspaper ad offering an amazingly low price on a popular car make and model without disclosing that there is only one car available at that price. An interested buyer is told that the car was sold "right before" she came into the dealership, but she should check out the bigger, nicer, or more sporty models available.

A furniture store advertises a type of sofa at a bargain price. When shoppers come into the store to try to buy the sofa, the sales personnel explain that the particular type of sofa is poorly made and that they really should buy a different, much better, and much higher-priced sofa.

established business relationship—A commercial relationship in which the consumer has purchased, rented, or leased the seller's goods or services or conducted a financial transaction with the seller within the 18 months immediately preceding a telemarketing call; or has inquired about, or applied for, a product or service offered by the seller within three months immediately preceding the call.

abandoned call—A telemarketing call that is not connected to a sales person within two seconds after the recipient answers the telephone and completes a greeting.

> **Situation**
>
> James opened a savings account on February 15, 2013, and closed it on January 3, 2014. It is his only account with the bank. Based on this transaction, James has an established business relationship with the bank from February 15, 2013, to August 15, 2014 (18 months after opening the savings account). Because of the established business relationship, the bank can call James until August 15, 2014, to solicit other business even if his phone number is registered on the FTC National Do Not Call Registry. However, if James asks the bank to put his phone number on its internal do-not-call list (per FCC rules), the bank cannot call him about other product or service opportunities.

PRESCREENING

To make the best use of marketing expenditures, banks sometimes prescreen prospective customers. When undertaking a mass marketing effort, such as a direct mail campaign to offer credit cards, a bank may match its credit criteria against credit reporting agency data to create a list of prospective new accounts. Individuals whose credit scores meet or exceed the bank's credit criteria are included in the mailing campaign.

When banks prescreen customers for marketing purposes, the Fair Credit Reporting Act (FCRA) contains several rules with which banks must comply. Banks that prescreen consumers must offer to extend credit to anyone who applies for it. If a consumer responds to a prescreened offer, the bank normally does a more in-depth credit analysis. Recipients of the advertising must be informed that they received the solicitation based on information in their credit reports and that they satisfied the bank's criteria. Consumers must also be told that they may prohibit the use of information in their credit file in connection with future prescreened offers.

The FCRA also defines when banks can share third-party information (such as credit reports or transaction or experience information) with affiliates for marketing purposes. The requirements of the FCRA with regard to information sharing were subsequently amended and then changed again by the Fair and Accurate Credit Transactions Act. As it now stands, before a bank can use certain information about a consumer received from an affiliate to solicit the consumer for marketing purposes, the customer must be given an opportunity to opt out.

Fair lending laws prohibit creditors from prescreening credit applicants on a prohibited basis—that is, based on the applicant's race, sex, national origin, or other prohibited personal characteristic.

E-COMMERCE AND SOCIAL MEDIA GUIDANCE

Marketing laws and regulations have had to keep pace with the ever-changing ways that bank products are sold. In particular, the rise of e-commerce has created a vast new area of marketing mandates.

The FTC addressed the issue of online marketing as far back as 2000 when it published the *.com Disclosures* guide. The guidance said that the FTC's consumer protection rules and regulations regarding unfair and deceptive advertising in traditional media (such as print media, radio, and television) apply to online advertising as well. For example, material information presented to consumers on websites cannot mislead, as discussed earlier in this section.

In 2013, the FTC updated its *.com Disclosures* guide to reflect the new digital technologies and practices that have been adopted since 2000. The FTC said that all advertisers must ensure that their ads comply with the agency's broad principles, whether those ads appear on websites, social networks, mobile devices, tablets, or whatever devices might be invented in the future. Reflecting the unique nature of online advertising, the FTC's guidance contains recommendations pertaining to hyperlinks, scrolling, click-through pages, and other attributes that do not apply to traditional media. Complying with the FTC's marketing disclosure requirements is made especially difficult considering that the devices on which the disclosures must be made can be small, as is the case with smart phone screens.

Bank regulators, under the auspices of the FFIEC, also issued guidance that pertains to e-commerce and social media use by banks. The FFIEC's guidance addresses the risks of social media use by banks to conduct their business, the purpose often being to market and sell to consumers. Social media refers to any online communication in which the bank interacts with the public, such as Facebook or Twitter. It also includes online forums, blogs, customer review websites, bulletin boards like Yelp, photos and video sites such as YouTube, and professional networking sites such as LinkedIn. The FFIEC notes that the consumer protection laws apply to all forms of consumer and customer communications, regardless of the medium.

CAN-SPAM Act

In addition to this recent guidance from the FTC and FFIEC, specific laws and regulations have been imposed to curtail opportunities for abusive marketing and sales practices through electronic channels. One of the most notable is the Controlling the Assault of Non-Solicited Pornography and Marketing Act of 2003, better known as the CAN-SPAM Act. The CAN-SPAM Act sets rules for commercial use of electronic mail.

Email solicitations are inexpensive, immediate, direct (reaching the recipient's computer inbox in a matter of seconds), and actionable (inviting a reply with just a click of the mouse). Those benefits also invite abuse, which prompted passage of the CAN-SPAM Act. The law protects recipients who do not wish to be subject of multiple emails or children who should not be the target of marketing efforts in the first place.

The CAN-SPAM Act covers email that has as its primary purpose the advertising or promotion of a commercial product or service. It does not cover emails facilitating a transaction or providing information to a customer with whom there is an established business relationship. Both the FTC and the Department of Justice enforce the CAN-SPAM Act. The act prohibits, for example, false or misleading header information and deceptive subject lines, and requires senders to give recipients an **opt-out** method, respond to opt-out requests, and identify commercial email as advertising. The CAN-SPAM Act focuses on:

- **False or misleading header information.** The email address must be accurate and identify the person who initiated the email.
- **Deceptive subject lines.** The subject line may not mislead the recipient about the message's contents.
- **Opt-out methods.** The message must contain a return email address or other Internet-based response mechanism allowing recipients to opt out of future email messages.
- **Response to opt-out requests.** Senders must process opt-out requests for at least 30 days after the original commercial email. Upon receipt of an opt-out request, the sender has 10 business days to stop sending the emails.

opt out—Explicitly choosing not to do something, such as to not receive bank product literature. As opposed to opt in, which is explicitly choosing to do something.

Banker Profile

Winona Provencher started out as a teller at a community bank in Nebraska. She was already well-known in the community because she had had a stellar career as a high school track athlete. Her bank trained all staff thoroughly in the importance of customer service and sales. Winona has a naturally winning personality, so she regularly led the suburban branch team in cross-selling competitions. Meanwhile, she took courses at a nearby community college that offered ABA classes and earned her ABA Personal Banking Diploma. Promotions ensued and today Winona is manager of the bank's main office downtown.

- **Identifying commercial email as advertising.** The email must clearly state that the message is an advertisement or solicitation and that the recipient can opt out of future emails. A valid postal address is required.

One of the purposes of the CAN-SPAM Act is to deter phishing, which is the illegal transmission of email masquerading as coming from a legitimate sender. Phishing and other targeted scams are discussed in detail in chapter 10. Because the purpose of phishing is to obtain sensitive personal and financial information such as bank account numbers and Social Security numbers, the fraudulent email is often in the guise of a marketing solicitation that appears to be from a bank.

SUMMARY

- The most successful banks build long-term relationships with their customers. To form and sustain good customer relationships, the entire bank—systems, procedures, and people—must adopt a customer-centered philosophy for doing business. Every employee, including those who do not have daily contact with customers, can build customer relationships. The Internet and electronic devices such as computers and smart phones have also enhanced the customer marketing and sales experience.
- A market-driven sales strategy is fundamental to building customer relationships. The broad concept of a market-driven sales strategy holds that the objectives of a business are best reached by identifying the needs and wants of its customers and meeting them through an integrated, efficient, organization-wide effort supported by management. The pillars of the market-driven sales strategy are total company effort, customer satisfaction, profitability, and social responsibility. In fulfilling the social responsibility pillar, banks help fulfill their Community Reinvestment Act obligations and can serve the needs of the unbanked and underbanked, thus creating more bank customers.
- To succeed in today's sales-oriented banking environment, employees must have the necessary personal and professional skills. Customers have a right to expect responsive service, competence, courteous treatment, reliable service, professional demeanor and appearance, and privacy in their interactions with employees. They have a right to expect the employee to understand their perspective and identify products and services that will meet their needs.
- The best prospects for new sales are current customers. This is the underlying principle behind cross-selling—getting users of one or more services to buy additional services. To cross-sell, bankers must constantly be aware of sales opportunities and provide the best service at all times so that customers want to buy other products. Referrals involve listening for customer needs and then arranging for the customer to talk to another knowledgeable staff member or employee of a bank affiliate for more information about a particular product or service.

- In keeping with a customer-oriented philosophy, bank employees should understand the four stages a customer goes through in purchasing a product: needs identification, prepurchase searching, the purchase decision, and postpurchase assessment. As they interact with customers during these stages, bank employees have opportunities to build customer relationships.
- Banks must not only successfully market and sell current products, they also must introduce new ones. Developing a new product begins with conducting market research and drawing up a market profile. New product ideas can come from many sources, including employees. Product ideas are screened and tested. If a business analysis indicates that consumer acceptance is likely, the product is refined and test-marketed before being introduced to the entire market.
- Advertising should accurately portray product features to the public. In the case of bank products, this is especially important because of the potential for financial loss. For this reason, banks are required to identify in their advertising what products are and are not insured by the FDIC. Federal and state government regulators also supervise bank marketing practices to ensure that advertising does not mislead customers or invade their privacy. For marketing activities, banks must answer to their federal and state regulators and to the Federal Communications Commission (FCC). They must abide by their bank regulators' directives that implement Federal Trade Commission (FTC) and Department of Justice rules. FDIC insurance notification, the FTC's unfair, deceptive, or abusive acts or practices principles, the Fair Credit Reporting Act, laws and guidance covering telemarketing and e-commerce, and the CAN-SPAM Act all apply to bank marketing activities. Phishing and improper prescreening are among the practices these laws are designed to halt.

SELF-CHECK AND REVIEW

Learning Check

1. Do employees who rarely interact with bank customers have a role in building customer relationships? Why or why not?
2. What are some of the ways a bank employee can demonstrate responsiveness to customer needs?
3. How does marketing fulfill a social responsibility? Why is this good business practice as well?
4. What are the benefits of cross-selling and referrals?
5. What are some of the things customers do in anticipation of making a purchase?
6. What is the difference between a product feature and a product benefit?
7. What steps are involved in bringing a new product to market?

8. A bank advertisement for a home equity loan promoting the special interest rate of 3.25% catches Patty's eye because home equity loans offered by other lenders are around 4%. The ad says the loan is subject to a credit check and house appraisal. Patty applies for the loan and is approved. At closing, the loan papers state that the interest rate is 3.75%. When Patty points this out, the loan officer tells her that to receive the 3.25% rate she must open a deposit account with the bank so that the amount due on the loan each month can be automatically withdrawn. What is Patty the victim of? Explain. Why does the bank's ad fit the FTC's definition of a deceptive act?

Safeguarding Customers and the Bank

10

Learning Objectives

After studying this chapter, you should be able to

- Describe methods by which banks secure customer information
- Describe how banks identify customers
- Explain the types of fraud perpetrated against bank customers and how fraud can be prevented
- Describe the responsibilities of bank personnel in safeguarding bank assets and preventing crime
- Explain the important role of banks as stewards and protectors of the nation's financial system
- Discuss some of the laws and regulations that pertain to safeguarding customer information and protecting bank assets

Introduction

Banks are considered safe repositories for people's money. Just as important, banks must be safe repositories for customers' financial and personal information, which in this electronic age can be more valuable than money and, if misused, can cause customers great harm.

Bank employees have an obligation to safeguard customers' information and ensure that customers are not victimized by financial fraud resulting from information security breaches. Banks, recognizing that customers trust them to protect their financial and personal information, have implemented security programs to safeguard customers' information.

At the same time, bank shareholders and the public expect that banks will protect their financial assets so that loan and investment funds will be available to keep local economies strong. Because banks occupy a unique position in the nation's economic life, managing risk in banking is very important, and banking regulators work to ensure that banks manage risk well.

With all these critical roles to fulfill, banks have a special duty to safeguard customer and bank assets, deter financial crimes, and help protect the nation's financial system against misuse, corruption, and disruption. That is why banking has been called a "public trust," and bank employees have a responsibility to protect that trust.

PROTECTING CUSTOMER INFORMATION

Protecting customers' financial and personal information is at the forefront of banking concerns today. The increased use of technology and the passage of such legislation as the Gramm-Leach-Bliley Act (GLBA) have raised the bar even higher. Banks not only must have a reliable **information security program** in place, they must communicate clearly the protective steps they are taking so customers know their information is secure. Banks must also demonstrate to regulators that they have assessed the risks to customer information and have controls in place to manage those risks.

information security program—A plan for ensuring that data and technology systems are not accessed by unauthorized users.

Banks, unlike many other industries, have a strict regulatory system designed to prevent data breaches and to notify customers if a breach occurs that could put their identity at risk. By protecting customers' information and privacy, banks provide peace of mind. This becomes ever more important each time banks undertake a new Internet or mobile banking initiative. Even when banks outsource information technology services, they cannot outsource the liability. For the banking industry, an information security program is a business priority.

Data Security

Every bank employs multiple layers of physical and electronic security to safeguard customer information. There are many points of access into a bank's information system. For example, many bank employees regularly use computer terminals and company-issued personal computers and mobile devices to connect to the bank's computer network. When a customer logs on to the bank's website via a home computer or mobile device, the bank's information systems are also accessed.

Some of the security measures banks employ to prevent unauthorized access of customer information include:

- **Automatic session expiration.** This security feature closes an online banking session after a certain period of inactivity, typically 5 or 10 minutes. This protects the data when the authorized user steps away from a computer or fails to sign out properly, leaving account information displayed on a monitor.
- **Automatic account lockout.** This security measure registers failed login attempts and, after a certain number of failures, shuts down further attempts. Activity considered suspicious is relayed to appropriate bank personnel to alert them to potential problems.
- **Direct deposit.** When salary, government, and other benefit payments are directly deposited into customers' deposit accounts, criminals cannot steal the payments and customer information, as is the case through the mail.
- **E-alerts.** These short messages, sent via email or text message, confirm activity, such as electronic debits, credits, and loan payments. This service, usually requiring customers to opt-in, keeps customers instantly apprised of account transactions, including any that are unauthorized.
- **Masking sensitive information.** Sensitive customer information such as account numbers, Social Security numbers, and credit card numbers, are partially masked with a series of asterisks or another type of symbol. Masking presents enough characters and/or numbers to allow confirmation of identity without presenting the full information that could be stolen and used in fraud.
- **Online bill payment and online statements.** This service allows customers to manage monthly bills and regularly scheduled payments from a single device. Customers no longer need to deal with utility, credit card, or other paper statements that contain confidential personal information. This protects customers from having the information stolen from mailboxes or the postal delivery services. Online statements are another way to avoid theft of confidential personal information.
- **Personal identification numbers (PINs) and passwords.** PINs and passwords are used to access online statements and other bank services. They may be bank-issued or chosen by the customer.

Password Versus Passphrase

Password—An arbitrary string of 6 to 10 characters chosen by or assigned to a user to authenticate the user attempting to logon to a computer system. An example is "treebumper."

Passphrase—An arbitrary string of up to 100 characters similar to, and used like, a password but that provides more security. An example is "*bumping!trees963$$."

CUSTOMER IDENTIFICATION

Identity verification is not always easy because the United States does not have a single standard form of identification. A driver's license is the most common means of verifying identity, but it can be altered. Businesses with fiduciary responsibilities may incorporate document verification systems that analyze various security features, such as holograms and state seals. These systems can detect subtle ink shifts and slight color changes that are not visible to the naked eye.

Because there are many acceptable forms of customer identification, some more reliable than others, banks have a challenging job ensuring that those they serve are properly identified during all banking services—from opening accounts to accessing accounts online, in person, or over the telephone.

Account Identification Requirements

The Uniting and Strengthening America by Providing Appropriate Tools Required to Intercept and Obstruct Terrorism Act (better known as the USA PATRIOT Act) requires banks to implement a customer identification program (CIP) for new relationships. Although the intent was to stop terrorists from using the U.S. financial system to launder money and finance crimes, the CIP program provides another layer of security for customers' financial and personal information. A bank's written CIP incorporates reasonable procedures to:

- Collect identifying information about an individual opening an account, such as name, date of birth, street address, and Social Security or taxpayer identification number
- Verify the customer's identification
- Determine if the customer appears on any government list of known or suspected terrorists
- Maintain records of the information used to verify the customer's identity

authentication—(1) Determination that a message comes from a source authorized to originate the message; (2) a measure designed to protect against a fraudulent transmission by establishing the validity of a transmission, message, station, or person.

security token—A physical device that communicates with a computer, either by direct attachment or wireless communication, to confirm a person's identity for the purpose of performing authorized transactions.

Account Access Identification Methods

Whether serving customers in person, over the telephone, or online, bankers follow procedures to confirm the identity of the person with whom they are communicating. That is why a customer using a drive-through banking window may be asked to present a valid ID, and a customer accessing bank accounts by telephone, such as through a bank call center, may be asked to enter a PIN or respond to a predetermined question, such as "What is your grandmother's maiden name?" In each case, the request seeks to ensure that the customer's privacy is preserved.

Banks engaged in Internet banking are required to have sufficient security measures in place to verify, or authenticate, customer identity. There are three types of **authentication**:

- Something the user knows—such as a password or PIN
- Something the user has—such as an ATM card, smart card, or **security token**
- Something the user is—a unique physical identifying characteristic such as a fingerprint or voice scan

Multifactor Authentication

Most banking transactions require **multifactor authentication**—that is, a minimum of two of the three types of authentication. An automated teller machine (ATM) transaction that requires, to complete it, both a PIN (something the customer knows) and an ATM card (something the customer has) is an example of multifactor authentication.

multifactor authentication—Authentication by two or more of the following: something the customer knows, has, or is.

biometrics—Automated methods of identifying a person based on a physiological or behavioral characteristic, such as a voice, fingerprint, or typing pattern.

Biometric Identification

Biometric authentication is becoming a considerably more reliable security measure than passwords or PINs because biometrics link authentication to a specific person. Unlike a password or PIN, a biometric identifier cannot be lost, stolen, or used without a person's consent. Not only are biometric security methods convenient and more accurate, they also provide an audit trail.

A variety of biometric options are now available, and more are being tested. The public is gradually becoming more comfortable using common biometric methods, including voice identification, keystroke dynamics, digital finger printing, three-dimensional (3-D) facial recognition, and hand scanning.

- **Voice identification.** Voice identification stores a voice print, called a voice reference template, of a customer speaking a specific phrase. The template is built from dozens of measurements that record pitch, dynamics, and wave forms for physiological and behavioral distinctions. The result is a unique digital representation of the customer's voice. The voice print security system compares the spoken phrase with the template to authenticate the customer before allowing account access.
- **Keystroke dynamics.** Keystroke dynamics identifies customers by the way they type, measuring dwell time—the amount of time a particular key is held down—and flight time—the amount of time a person takes to move from key to key. Keyboard dynamics requires a reference template that is created from customers typing the same characters several times. This is a behavioral rather than a physiological measurement that works best with customers who can touch-type.
- **Digital fingerprinting.** The most popular and successful biometric device in recent years is fingerprint imaging. Credit card companies have started using this method to identify cardholders at the point of purchase. Some computers and mobile devices also include a fingerprint reader and related software to authenticate users. The technology captures unique fingertip line patterns, such as the loop, whorl, and arch patterns in the skin ridges.
- **3-D facial recognition.** 3-D facial recognition is primarily used to authenticate a computer user via an external camera (webcam) integrated into the computer's hardware. To effectively deploy this method of authentication, the user must first undergo a digital face scan. As the technology advances, 3-D facial recognition may become more prevalent in the banking industry.

Situation

Carla is a bank card call center employee. She handles hundreds of calls each week from customers around the world. Many customers want information about their account statements, while others might want to sign up for new or additional credit cards for family members. Before Carla conducts business with a customer, she obtains proper identification, including special passwords and other personal identification information. Her bank has instituted such security procedures to ensure that its customers' identities and financial privacy are protected.

- **Hand scanning.** Some banks have adopted hand-scanning technology for safe deposit box vault entry, replacing the master key system that bank employees typically use to admit box holders. The customer's hand is scanned and a record is made of identifying traits. To enter the vault, the customer enters a PIN that calls up the appropriate handprint, places his or her hand over a reader, and if it matches the record, the vault door opens automatically. The customer still needs a key to remove and open his or her assigned safe deposit box.

Identity Theft

A main purpose of customer identification is to prevent identity theft. Identity theft—the theft of a person's personal or financial information—is a serious offense and allows the criminal to commit many types of financial fraud. Identity theft has a detrimental effect on a bank and a devastating effect on bank customers who are victimized. The consequences range from the misuse of a person's information to the general takeover of the victim's identity wherein the thief gains access to bank accounts and applies for loans and credit cards in the victim's name.

Personal information commonly stolen and used to commit identity theft includes:

- Name and address
- Date of birth
- Mother's maiden name
- Social Security number
- Financial account numbers and bank names
- Place of employment
- Children's names
- Driver's license number

Criminals use both low- and high-tech methods to obtain confidential information in order to exploit a person's assets and credit. These methods include:

- Dumpster diving—rummaging through trash looking for receipts, bills, personal records, or other papers containing personal and financial information
- Skimming—stealing credit/debit card numbers by using a special storage device when processing a bank card
- Phishing—pretending to be a bank or company and sending **spam** or pop-up messages to trick the victim into revealing personal information
- Changing an address—diverting billing statements to another location by completing a change of address form
- Theft—stealing a wallet or purse; stealing mail, including bank and credit card statements, preapproved credit offers, and new checks or tax information. Theft also includes stealing personnel records or bribing employees who have access to such records.

spam—Unsolicited junk emails sent to a large number of people to promote products or services or to spread computer viruses.

- Intercepting—hacking into personal records or otherwise obtaining information transmitted electronically. Even when banks employ stringent security measures, hackers can still obtain access to sensitive customer information, such as customer names, credit card numbers, expiration dates, and PINs, when they breach a retailer's or other third party's computer systems or networks.

As trusted advisors, bankers must be prepared to inform customers about how to avoid identity theft and help them recover if they are victimized. The best deterrents against identity theft are vigilant bank employees and informed customers.

Identity Theft Prevention

All employees have a role to play in curbing identity theft, especially front-line tellers and customer service representatives who receive or are asked to provide account information or who accept applications. Bank employees also can remind customers how to safeguard their information.

By law, every bank is required to have comprehensive security procedures that specify appropriate employee conduct for handling customer information. Banks also have strict guidelines about how to communicate with customers seeking information about their account or with a third party, such as another bank, seeking to verify the authenticity of a customer's account. Employees should never provide information to someone claiming to be a customer without the caller first providing a PIN, passphrase, or another identifier known only to that customer. For example, this security information could be answers to questions such as: "What is the name of your first pet?" or "Where were you born?" Such secure identifiers are often established when an account is opened.

When another financial institution or merchant calls seeking information, banks often use caller-ID, verify the phone number, and then call back the institution or merchant to verify the caller's identity before releasing information. Banks may prohibit releasing some customer information over the telephone under any circumstances.

FRAUD SCHEMES

Bank customers can fall victim to many types of financial crimes. When these crimes occur, banks often reimburse the victims and thus are directly affected financially. A less apparent but sometimes far greater cost is the potential damage to a bank's reputation.

Properly identifying customers and securing their financial and personal information are part of an ongoing battle against criminals who defraud consumers. The list of fraud schemes, many aimed at perpetrating identity theft, continues to grow. Many federal agency websites, including those of the bank regulatory agencies, Federal Trade Commission, Secret Service, United States Postal Inspection Service, and Federal Bureau of Investigation (FBI) post scam alerts to keep banks, consumers, and businesses current on the latest schemes. Some of the more common schemes follow.

Did You Know ...

In December of 2013, a breach of Target Corporation's computer systems resulted in hackers gaining access to as many as 110 million consumer credit and debit card records issued by financial institutions.

Credit Reports

One of the best ways for bank customers to combat identity theft is to regularly request and review copies of their credit reports from the major credit reporting agencies (Equifax, Experian, and TransUnion). All consumers are entitled to one free annual credit report from all credit reporting agencies. Customers should look for debts they did not incur, inquiries from companies they did not contact, and accounts they did not open. To protect their credit rating, customers should immediately query unusual actions, such as an unexpected credit denial. To order these reports for free, the federal government sponsors a website at annualcreditreport.com.

Did You Know ...

Identity theft has been the number one consumer complaint for 13 consecutive years. In 2012, over 369,000 identity theft complaints were filed with the Federal Trade Commission.

Source: Federal Trade Commission

Bank Card Fraud

Criminals who commit bank card fraud steal a credit or debit card or number and then fraudulently purchase goods or services. The potential for loss is high because criminals often make purchases before victims know their card is being misused. Criminals obtain bank card information in a number of ways, such as:

- Taking a card from a stolen wallet or handbag
- Stealing a card or statement from a mailbox or the postal delivery service
- Copying information from a card presented for a legitimate transaction, usually by a salesperson or server
- Paying dishonest employees of card issuers who seek to sell account information
- Stealing statements from files or trash cans
- Accessing online account information
- Security breaches of merchant card payment information

Many tools are used to counter unauthorized bank card transactions. Most bank cards now feature holograms and embossed lettering and numbers that are difficult to replicate. To thwart mailbox theft, customers can be requested to call a toll-free number to confirm they are the legitimate cardholder and not a thief in possession of the card. For transaction approval, a customer's card must have a current expiration date, account number, and special digital code. Card companies also use sophisticated software to monitor accounts for unusual increases in activity, uncharacteristically high spending volume, increases in mail orders, or use in parts of the country or world where the customer is not likely to travel, all of which can trigger a warning on the account. These suspicious transactions will often result in credit card companies calling consumers to review the uncharacteristic activity.

Situation

When looking over her monthly bank card statement, Chris notices several charges for purchases at a store called Midtown Liquor Mart. Chris does not recognize the store, so she calls her bank card company. After an investigation, the bank card company discovers that Chris is a victim of bank card fraud. Her bank card account is closed, and she is not charged for the unauthorized purchases.

Telephone Fraud

Although technology has helped reduce the incidence of telephone-originated fraud, it is still a prevalent means for fraud artists to trick people, including bank customers and employees, into divulging confidential information. Telephone fraud includes caller-ID manipulation and spoofing, pretext calling, and telecommunications relay service scams.

Caller-ID Manipulation and Spoofing

Many consumers and businesses invest in caller-ID capability to screen calls. The technology can be manipulated, however, to make the identification number or name of an incoming call appear as if it is coming from a reliable party, such as a bank. This practice is known as caller-ID manipulation or spoofing.

Spoofing also can be perpetrated through emails. The "from" line is modified to appear as if it is from a known or legitimate sender or from an agency's or corporation's internal address.

Pretext Calling

In a scam known as **pretext calling**, bank employees are conned by criminals posing as bank customers. By offering a phony excuse, such as that account information was misplaced or lost, these bogus customers trick trusting bank employees into divulging information.

pretext calling—Attempts to use the phone to gain access to another's account information by pretending to be the account holder or an authorized signer on the account.

Telecommunications Relay Service Scams

Some scammers make fraudulent use of telecommunications relay services, typically used by the deaf and hearing- or speech-impaired for making telephone calls. These systems use a text telephone (TTY) or an Internet connection to relay a conversation through an operator to a hearing person—for example, a bank employee. When the hearing person responds, the operator relays a typewritten response back to the caller. The relay operator is required to keep all calls confidential and may not otherwise intervene in a call. This privacy rule may inadvertently allow a dishonest call originator to hide his or her identity. Such scams have been used to defraud businesses and to steal credit card numbers, bank account numbers, and other payment information.

Advance Fee Fraud

Advance fee fraud victimizes banks and their customers. The scam often begins with the intended victim receiving an unsolicited letter, fax, or email allegedly from a foreign national who claims to be a high-level civil servant. The "official" requests assistance in depositing millions of dollars that his or her government allegedly overpaid on a contract. Other fraudulent requests may involve disbursements from wills, proceeds from real estate sales, conversion of hard currency, or sales of crude oil at below-market prices.

In return for assisting with the funds transfer, the recipient of the correspondence (the fraud victim) is promised a large commission. Inevitably, something arises to threaten the deal, such as an unforeseen tax or fee that must be paid, which the victim is asked to advance, with reimbursement promised when the funds are remitted. Meanwhile, the victim has provided the perpetrator with sensitive bank account information but, of course, never receives the promised funds.

Did You Know ...

One of the most common versions of advance fee fraud is Nigerian advance fee fraud or 419 fraud. 419 refers to the section of the Nigerian penal code that deals with this type of fraud. It is so-named because this scam gained notoriety in the mid-1980s when Nigerian students began targeting businesses with fraudulent letters and faxes. As email became more prevalent, Nigerian advance fee fraud spawned imitators around the world, principally in Africa, Asia, and Eastern Europe.

Source: U.S. State Department

Letter of Credit Fraud

As discussed in chapter 8, banks issue letters of credit to facilitate transactions between buyers and sellers of goods, especially in international transactions involving the shipment of goods. Banks can fall victim to letter of credit fraud when they accept false documentation showing that goods were shipped when, in fact, no goods or inferior goods were shipped.

Prime Bank Note Fraud

With prime bank note fraud, criminals take advantage of the strong financial reputation that banks enjoy. In this scheme, fraudsters offer investments with exceptional returns that can be bought at a discount and allegedly come with "bank guarantees."

Banker Profile

Jim Weatherbee is only 23 but already has an undergraduate degree in systems engineering and is working on a master's degree. After thorough background checks and testing, a regional bank hired him while he was in college to work in the information technology department part-time during the school year and full-time during the summers. One of his tasks is to help procure software to protect the bank's servers. The bank regularly sends him to intensive workshops on information security, sometimes sponsored by banking associations and sometimes by hardware and software manufacturers. Jim has a clear job path with the bank and wants to pursue a career in bank systems management and security.

To make the investments even more attractive, these fraudsters often refer to the "guarantees" as being issued by the world's "prime banks," thus the term "prime bank guarantees." Official sounding terms such as "prime bank notes" and "prime bank debentures" may be used, and phony legal documents are often associated with the scam. For example, the victim may be requested to sign nondisclosure or noncircumvention agreements designed to prevent the victim from independently verifying information about the fraudulent investment.

Cashier's Check Scams

Cashier's checks are direct obligations of banks. Bank customers may receive them in the course of conducting business, whether in person or over the Internet. Among the fraudulent cashier's check schemes now in practice are:

- **Unexpected windfall.** Customers are told they have won a lottery or are beneficiaries of an estate, and the proceeds will be sent to them when taxes or fees are paid. Fraudulent cashier's checks are provided to cover the charges, and customers are asked to deposit the checks and then wire the funds when the checks clear.
- **Purchase price differential.** As part of a sales transaction on the Internet, customers receive cashier's checks for amounts greater than the purchase price. Buyers tell sellers to deposit the fraudulent checks and wire the excess amounts when the checks clear.
- **Money transfer agent.** Customers are solicited to act as money transfer agents and are told that they will receive cashier's checks to deposit into their accounts. They are told to wire sums to other persons or accounts in other countries.

With current printing and copying methods and software, fraudulent checks are difficult to detect. Checks can be made to look genuine by, for example, altering genuine checks. An altered check may list the name of one bank, but use the routing number of another bank; or parts of the check may be illegible so that manual processing is necessary. When the check is returned, the bank reverses the deposit and withdraws the funds from the customer's account.

Phishing

Phishing (pronounced fishing) involves sending customers seemingly legitimate email requests that direct them to a phony website where they are asked to provide personal and financial information. This type of fraud commonly incorporates a bank's name, logo, graphics, and other proprietary information on the emails to trick victims into providing their account numbers, Social Security numbers, or passwords. The illegally obtained confidential information is then used in identity theft and credit card and Internet-based frauds. When phishing is perpetrated by a telephone call—that is, the victim is provided with a telephone number to call, allegedly to update or renew account information—it is known as "vishing," short for voice phishing.

Pharming

Pharming fools consumers into entering sensitive data, such as a passwords or credit card numbers, on a website that impersonates a legitimate website. Unlike phishing, the thief does not have to rely on the victim performing an action, such as clicking a link in an email. Even if the consumer enters a correct URL (web address) in the browser's address bar, pharming redirects the victim to a different website. Sometimes this is accomplished by changing a file on the victim's computer; more often it is done by exploiting a vulnerability in the domain name system (DNS) software. DNS servers are computers responsible for translating Internet names into their real addresses.

Text Message Fraud

Online fraud has made its way to mobile devices. An example is text message fraud. It begins with the victim receiving a cell phone text message purportedly from a legitimate financial institution. The message claims that a banking service has expired and the recipient of the message should either call a telephone number or click on an Internet link to renew the service. The victim is then asked to provide personal or financial information.

Elder Financial Abuse

Many of the aforementioned types of fraud especially target the elderly. As the baby boomer generation ages and life spans lengthen, the incidence of elder financial abuse will likely increase in the future. Legislatures, law enforcement agencies, social service agencies, and businesses with fiduciary responsibilities, such as banks, have added elder financial abuse to their watch lists and established related policies, procedures, and employee training programs.

Senior citizens can be victimized by family members, caregivers, neighbors, and strangers who "befriend" them. Financial abuse includes depleting joint checking accounts, misusing ATM cards and powers of attorney, and neglecting fiduciary obligations in trust relationships.

Senior citizens are targeted for many reasons. For example, seniors are less likely to report the abuse because they might not realize it is happening, they might be embarrassed and ashamed, or they might be afraid they will not be believed.

Banks are taking a more proactive role to prevent or stop elder financial abuse. Among the signs banks watch for are:

- Unusual recent withdrawals or changes in elderly customers' accounts
- New persons added to elderly customers' accounts
- New persons coming to the bank with senior citizen account holders
- Use of an ATM by an elderly customer who has not previously used ATMs
- Elderly customers who appear confused, unkempt, or afraid

Because banks have regular contact with most older customers, they are in a good position to notice changes or suspicious circumstances. Taking steps to protect elderly customers promotes goodwill; in some states it is mandated by law.

Preventing Online Fraud

Banks combat online fraud in many ways, including:

- Providing notices on websites and printed materials reminding customers that the bank never uses emails to request confidential information and asking them to report any such requests to the bank
- Restricting electronic customer communications to an email system available through the bank's secure Internet banking application
- Using authentication methods
- Explaining how customers can verify the authenticity of the bank's webpages
- Introducing methods by which customers can be sure they actually are on the bank's website by, for example, displaying an illustration or a phrase customers have chosen after they login
- Assigning dedicated staff to monitor online transactions for fraud

SAFEGUARDING BANK ASSETS

One responsibility of banks is to safeguard their customers' assets; another is to ensure their own safety and soundness. A bank may be a profitable business enterprise, with income exceeding expenses, a growing market share, and satisfied customers, and still have its future undermined by employee or vendor misconduct; bank robberies, counterfeiting, computer attacks, or other crimes perpetuated by outsiders; and even so-called acts of nature such as pandemics or weather events.

Corporate Governance and Ethical Behavior

Banks are occasionally victimized from within. An inattentive board of directors or audit committee, senior managers who reward harmful employee practices, an employee who embezzles, or a dishonest vendor all pose a threat to a bank's safety and soundness. The best responses to these kinds of behavior are high standards of corporate governance, a strong code of ethics, vigilant oversight of hiring and contracting procedures, and consistent monitoring.

Corporate governance is the manner in which a company is managed and its assets are accounted for and reported to the public. Bank regulators expect a bank's board of directors and senior managers to take the lead in setting and abiding by standards of ethical behavior—often referred to as "tone at the top"—and that those standards will be followed by all employees.

After lax or dishonest corporate governance practices caused the failure of several major corporations in the late 1990s and early 2000s, Congress enacted the Sarbanes-Oxley Act (SOX) in 2002 to strengthen corporate governance. The act imposed significant new responsibilities on boards of directors, corporate executives, audit committees, and internal and external auditors of public companies. SOX applies only to publicly owned corporations, but all banks, whether publicly owned or privately held, are subject to corporate governance and financial reporting requirements that are very similar.

Board of Directors and Management Responsibilities

All bank employees must observe the highest ethical standards and be committed to doing the right thing when a choice presents itself. The conduct and practices of several parties, however, are especially important to good corporate governance. These include the following:

- **Board of directors.** The board of directors sets policies and directives and ensures that management carries them out. The board is primarily responsible for establishing and maintaining policies and procedures for managing risks, and is ultimately responsible for ensuring that depositor funds are protected and public confidence in the bank remains high.
- **Audit committee.** The board's audit committee monitors management and staff compliance with board policies and with all laws and regulations. This committee also elects internal and external auditors, oversees the internal audit function, receives audit reports and reviews the conclusions with management, and ensures that management takes necessary corrective actions.

Did You Know ...

Banks are now required to report elder financial exploitation to the Financial Crimes Enforcement Network. In 2012, reports of elder exploitation increased almost 400 percent from the previous year.

Source: Financial Crimes Enforcement Network

Situation

Bob is a senior citizen who uses Internet banking because it is more convenient. One day Bob receives a telephone call from someone claiming to be an auditor from the bank. The caller tells Bob there has been a security breach and that everyone who has an online bank account should change their password. The caller asks Bob for his password to make the change. Bob remembers the advice in a bank brochure about identity theft that recommended never giving personal or account information over the phone. He declines the caller's request and immediately reports the incident to the bank.

- **Senior management.** By their words, attitudes, and actions, senior managers define and reinforce ethical behavior among all employees. They must avoid policies and practices that encourage inappropriate behavior, such as undue emphasis on and rewarding short-term performance; inadequate oversight and segregation of duties, which can invite misuse of resources or conceal poor performance; and insignificant penalties for improper behavior.

Auditor Responsibilities

Internal auditors evaluate a bank's internal control and risk management systems; ensure the safeguarding and proper recording of bank assets; and verify compliance with laws, regulations, and established bank policies and practices. **External auditors** typically focus on financial reporting and associated processes and matters that relate to a bank's financial statements.

internal auditor—An auditor who is employed by the bank, regularly working with all levels of management.

external auditor—An auditor who is independent of the bank, usually reporting directly to the internal auditor or the board of directors or audit committee.

Employee Responsibilities

The bank's expectations for employee conduct, both professionally and personally, are communicated in a code of conduct or code of ethics. The code helps employees decide what is in the best interests of the bank rather than their own personal interests. Employees should review the bank's code of conduct periodically. Exhibit 10.1 lists some of the areas typically covered in a bank code of conduct.

Exhibit 10.1: Contents of a Typical Bank Code of Conduct

- Corporate creed or letter from the senior executive
- Organization principles and values
- General statement of compliance with laws and regulations
- Equal Employment Opportunity Statement
- Fair Lending and Community Reinvestment Statement
- Environmental laws
- Conflict of interest
- Criminal activity
- Confidential information
- Insider trading
- Purchasing defaulted property
- Relationship with the investment community
- Financial accountability and internal controls
- Integrity of accounting and financial information
- Money laundering and transaction structuring
- Embezzlement, theft, and misapplication of funds
- Use of corporate name and letterhead
- Relationship with the media
- Things offered to employees
- Things offered by employees
- Estate matters
- Outside activities
- Sound personal finances
- Employment of relatives or persons having close relationships
- Safety
- Disclosure and recordkeeping
- Acknowledgment
- Code of conduct violations

whistleblower—An employee who reports fraud or other wrongdoing within a company.

civil money penalty (CMP)—A fine imposed by a civil court on an individual, business, or organization that has profited from illegal or unethical activity or has violated a law or regulation. Also known as civil monetary penalty.

fraud—An intentional misrepresentation made by one person to another who, believing the misrepresentation, takes some action and suffers a loss of property or a right to the first person. The elements of common law fraud are: (1) a false representation, (2) with respect to a material fact, (3) made with knowledge of its falsity, (4) with intent to deceive, and (5) with action taken in reliance on that representation.

Bank employees also have a responsibility to report ethical violations and misconduct. Bank regulation provides protections for corporate **whistleblowers** and mandates a confidential process for reporting alleged misconduct. More specifically, the Federal Deposit Insurance Act mandates that banks may not discharge or otherwise retaliate against an employee who provides information regarding a possible legal or regulatory violation, gross mismanagement, gross waste of funds, abuse of authority, or a substantial and specific danger to public health or safety. By the nature of their job responsibilities, employees play a key role in detecting financial fraud, which is why it is especially critical for banks to have whistleblower policies and procedures that encourage the reporting of violations.

SOX and the Dodd-Frank Wall Street Reform and Consumer Protection Act also encourage whistleblowers to report financial fraud and other corporate misconduct, offering whistleblowers anti-retaliation protections and financial rewards in some circumstances.

Employee Hiring and Vendor Management

Recognizing such risks as insider theft, identity theft, data breaches, and even terrorism, more banks, with the encouragement of the regulators, are focusing on pre-employment screening and vendor management to protect bank assets and fulfill their fiduciary responsibilities.

Pre-employment Screening

Screening job candidates before they are hired helps reduce turnover costs because potential employees' skills, certification, license, or degrees can be verified. At a minimum, pre-employment screening checks references, experience, education, professional qualifications, and the applicant's identity. Additional screening depends on the risks of a given job. Similar screening may be continuous or scheduled periodically for all employees.

Banks also check for any criminal record an applicant may have. Most banks have applicants fingerprinted and send the prints to the FBI to be checked against FBI records. The Federal Deposit Insurance Corporation (FDIC) also recommends that banks check applicants' names against each federal banking agency's list of individuals who have been assessed **civil money penalties** (CMPs) or have been prohibited from being employed by or associated with a bank. The Federal Deposit Insurance Act prohibits a person convicted of a criminal offense involving dishonesty, breach of trust, or money laundering from working at a bank unless the FDIC gives prior approval.

The bank pre-employment screening process covers information about the prospect's credit, character, general reputation, mode of living, and personal characteristics. Under the Fair Credit Reporting Act, the bank must have the applicant's written consent before obtaining a credit report for employment purposes. If the applicant is denied employment because of negative credit report information, the bank must provide contact information for the credit reporting agency and any third-party screening company used. Applicants have the right to correct credit report information and to review their credit report file.

Crimes Against Banks

- Larceny
- Robbery
- Forgery
- Embezzlement
- Mail fraud
- Wire fraud
- Bankruptcy fraud
- Bribery
- Insider trading
- Money laundering
- Identity theft
- Cyber theft

Recognizing the important role banks play with regard to national security, the USA PATRIOT Act gives banks additional latitude to share employment information of *suspected* criminal activity. A bank can disclose, in written employment references provided to another insured depository institution at its request, information about a current or former employee's suspected involvement in unlawful activity. The disclosures in the employment references cannot be knowingly false or made with malice or reckless disregard for the truth.

Bank employees who are considered mortgage loan originators (MLOs) under the Secure and Fair Enforcement for Mortgage Licensing Act (SAFE Act) are required to register with the Nationwide Mortgage Licensing System and Registry, which maintains fingerprints and identifying information for registered MLOs. Regulated institutions must not permit employees who are not properly registered to act as MLOs.

Vendor Management

Banks often outsource a variety of functions, including human resources, marketing, and technology. Outsourcing helps banks manage costs, obtain necessary expertise, expand customer product offerings, and improve services. However, it also introduces risks that banks and bank regulators are concerned about managing.

As is true of pre-employment screening, managing outsourced relationships is important to safeguarding bank assets. For example, banks commonly outsource technology services associated with offering bill paying, fund transfers, and Internet communications. These services have their own inherent risks, even if the bank handles them directly. Having them outsourced to a third-party provider adds another level of risk, particularly in today's business environment where technology has grown increasingly complex and may be handled by companies operating overseas. Besides performing due diligence before executing contracts, banks must continuously monitor vendor performance, including service providers':

- Financial condition and operations
- Quality of service and support
- Contract compliance and any emerging need to update or revise the contract
- Business continuity, business contingency, or emergency preparedness plans

Exhibit 10.2, next page, outlines some guidelines for managing vendor relationships. Just as banks apply strict standards to their own operations in fulfillment of their fiduciary and legal compliance duties, they must also hold their vendors to high standards of performance and integrity.

Crimes Against Banks

Criminal threats against banks can occur both from within and outside the organization. Banks must remain vigilant to **fraud** committed by insiders—bank management or employees—and to bank robbery, currency counterfeiting, and computer attacks committed by outsiders.

Situation

Southwest Bank has a contract with B&V Management Systems Company to have its item processing operations managed in B&V's facilities. The contract is for a five-year term with a renewal option. B&V provides this service to many banks, some of which are Southwest's competitors. Southwest has a vendor management program to protect itself. B&V was selected after rigorous due diligence and its security program was scrutinized. The bank's lawyers worked with management to negotiate a contract with the protective provisions Southwest needed. B&V is audited regularly, both on-site and off-site. The vendor management process gives senior management, directors, and regulators greater assurance that the bank's data and customer information are secure.

Exhibit 10.2: Outsourcing Services—Vendor Management

Policies and procedures	Boards of directors and management establish policies for monitoring service providers.
Risk assessment	Vendor relationships carry risks, such as strategic, transaction, compliance, market, reputation, and country risk. Banks assess the risks and those managing the relationship help determine specific risks, such as the sensitivity of data or the transaction volume.
Due diligence	A "pre-employment screening" for the vendor covers its financial condition, reliability, security, growth capacity, and its third-party service providers. All references are checked, as well as the vendor's expertise, reliability, and capabilities.
Contract points	Contracts define rights and responsibilities of bank and vendor, service-level agreements, disaster recovery and business continuity plans, detailed pricing terms, data ownership, compliance with regulations, audit reports, the dispute resolution process, allowed subcontracting relationships, and termination and continuation conditions.
Monitoring the relationship	Management reviews compliance with service-level agreements, the financial condition of the provider, audit reports, and business continuity plans, especially with regard to changes in regulation or the economy.
Providers in foreign countries	Management assesses the risk of the relationship with regard to the bank's strategy. It ensures the choice-of-law and jurisdiction monitoring procedures are reviewed before any contracts are finalized. It assesses the country-risk factor in the relationship, such as the potential for changes in government, the economy, or social environment. The vendors must be in compliance with U.S. laws, and their operations may be examined by a U.S. bank regulator.

Source: FFIEC IT Handbook, "Outsourcing Technology Services"

embezzlement—A crime involving the fraudulent use or keeping of money or other property that has been entrusted to one's care. Also known in banking as misappropriation of funds.

insider fraud—Fraud perpetrated by someone who works inside an organization.

Insider Fraud

Employee theft, **embezzlement**, and other types of **insider fraud** cause far more losses than bank robberies. Banks are particularly vulnerable to insider fraud because so many of their employees work with large sums of money, securities, and other financial assets. Insider fraud can cause significant financial losses as well as loss of confidential information. If it goes undetected for a prolonged period, insider fraud can threaten the bank's safety and soundness.

The most common type of employee fraud is asset misappropriation, such as embezzling money or stealing blank cashier's or treasurer's checks. Employees also may overcome information security controls to steal the personal and financial information of bank customers. The information can be used or sold to third parties to illegally access accounts and move money electronically.

Banks try to minimize insider fraud by carefully screening prospective employees. They also have systems and procedures in place to prevent or identify insider fraud, including dual custody, transaction balancing, and reconciliation procedures; internal audits; and insider hotlines to report illegal activity. The best defense against insider fraud, however, is a corporate culture in which high standards of ethical behavior are expected and reinforced by a clearly articulated and enforced employee code of conduct.

Bank Robbery

Although banks as a whole suffer more losses from fraud schemes, bank robbery is the most worrisome because of its potential for personal trauma, injury, and loss of life. According to FBI statistics, around 5,000 bank robberies occur in the United States each year. In almost half of them, tellers or other bank employees are threatened or physically attacked.

Although banks have a basic responsibility to protect depositor funds, their primary objective during a robbery is to ensure the safety of employees, customers, and law enforcement officers. Limiting losses and helping to identify and prosecute offenders are secondary objectives.

During a holdup, tellers and other bank employees should not resist because resisting places not only their own safety, but also the safety of others, at risk. FBI statistics show that, in about one-quarter of robberies, a firearm (usually a handgun) was used.

While all bank robberies may not be preventable, their number can be reduced. Banks equip their premises with surveillance cameras and alarm systems. Those in high-crime areas limit access to the lobby and put bullet-resistant glass in front of teller stations.

During robberies, banks employ a variety of measures to help catch or identify robbers. By using an alert button or device in the cash drawer, tellers can activate silent alarms. Tellers may also give the robber decoy or marked money. Some banks prepare special bundles of money that contain an exploding device filled with dye or tear gas. The best security measure is still attentive employees who know and follow bank procedures. Exhibit 10.3, next page, offers some bank robbery response tips.

Currency Counterfeiting

Banks must also be on the alert for counterfeit money. High-resolution scanners and printers are used to forge paper currency as well as counterfeit checks. To combat the use of digital imaging technology to counterfeit currency, the U.S. government has implemented dozens of counterfeit-resistant features in the most commonly used U.S. currency, beginning in 2003 with the $20 note and proceeding in subsequent years with the $50, $10, $5, and most recently, the $100 notes. These features help tellers authenticate notes and make it difficult for criminals to produce counterfeits.

Hand examination, which most tellers do, is the most effective way to detect counterfeit notes. The new currency contains security features that can help bank employees quickly determine whether a note is real or fake. All bank employees should be familiar with these characteristics, which can be found at the federal government's website, NewMoney.gov. The redesigned notes contain such security features as watermarks, security threads, and microprinting. The new $100 bill contains the most advanced security features, including:

Situation

Ed, a former director, president, chief executive officer, and chairman of the bank's loan committee extended loans totaling more than $5 million to one borrower in violation of the bank's internal lending limit. He exceeded the lending limit by dividing the loans among various relatives of the borrower; however, proceeds of the multiple loans were funneled to one deposit account. Ed did not disclose to the board that the loans were for the benefit of a single borrower or that the source of repayment for all loans was the same. Ed substituted loan customer names on bank records so that it appeared the bank was complying with its lending limit. He also falsified loan documents and failed to inform the board of the true purpose of the credits. As a result of poor internal controls, Ed was able to fund loans in excess of his authorized lending authority without prior board approval. Although Ed did not personally benefit, the bank suffered a loss of $1.4 million on the loans.

—from an actual case investigated by the FDIC

Exhibit 10.3: Bank Robbery Response Tips

During a Robbery

Remain calm.
Assume that the robber has a weapon and that it is real.
Do exactly as the robber instructs.
Follow the bank's robbery procedures.
Do not try to overpower or out-think the robber.
Be observant.
Form a good mental picture of the robber's appearance.
Carefully observe the robber's speech or mannerisms.
Retain evidence such as a note.

After a Robbery

Remain as calm as possible.
Activate the alarm and dial 911.
Look for victims and check for injuries.
Lock cash drawers and other valuables.
Try to observe the robber's direction of escape, color or ethnicity, and make of the get-away vehicle, license tag, and other details.
Do not chase the robber or leave the bank for any reason.
Write down names of customers who were served immediately before, during, and after the crime.
Lock exterior doors if advisable.
Stop people in the lobby and other witnesses from leaving if possible.
Record the name and address of anyone who insists on leaving.
Preserve evidence by cordoning off areas touched by the robber.
Do not touch evidence, such as a note.
Refrain from discussing the incident with the media.

Did You Know ...

In 2008, the French bank Societe Generale lost $7.1 billion in a case of insider fraud. The crime, perpetrated by a single employee who orchestrated a series of bogus transactions, destabilized one of the world's largest banks and created upheaval in international financial markets.

- 3-D security ribbon that is woven into the note, not printed on it. As the note is tilted, the bells on the ribbon change into "100s."
- Color-shifting bell in a copper inkwell. As the note is tilted, the bell changes from green to copper, making it seem to disappear.

Another form of counterfeit currency is altered or "raised" currency. One or two ends or the corners of a smaller denomination bill, such as a $1 or a $5, are replaced with the ends or corners of a larger bill, such as a $10, $20, or $50. The bill is redeemed for the value of the raised currency (see exhibit 10.4).

Did You Know ...

In 2011, more bank robberies occurred on Friday between the hours of 9 and 11 a.m. than during any other day or time. Male bank robbers outnumber female bank robbers by more than 10 to 1.

Source: Federal Bureau of Investigation

Computer Attacks

Because banks store sensitive customer financial information on computers, illegal attempts to gain access to private accounts are a special concern for banks' data systems specialists. Computer attacks can come from inside the bank, perpetrated by disgruntled employees who are knowledgeable about the bank's computer security systems, or outside the bank, perpetrated by hackers using malicious software,

Exhibit 10.4: Know Your Money—Raised Bank Note

Compare the denomination numerals on each corner with the denomination written out at the bottom of the note (front and back) and through the Treasury seal.

Compare the suspect note to a genuine note of the same denomination and series year. Pay particular attention to the portrait, vignette, and denomination numerals.

Source: U.S. Secret Service

commonly known as **malware**. Computer attacks threaten banks as well as their customers. Critical customer information is compromised as a result of these types of attacks, and banks incur the cost of restoring data.

For example, one of the major threats to businesses comes from distributed denial of service (DDoS) attacks. DDoS attacks often target sites or services that have many users, and for this reason banks and other financial institutions are often the victims. DDoS attacks involve flooding the target system with external communication requests, overwhelming the system to the point where it cannot respond to requests from legitimate users. Past DDoS attacks have successfully disrupted the websites of major U.S. banks, resulting in customers being unable to access online or mobile banking services. DDoS attacks are sometimes launched in conjunction with other computer attacks intended to perpetrate fraud or steal customer information from the affected system.

The best way to prevent computer attacks is for bank employees, and data security systems employees in particular, to be well informed about the latest technology developments and fraud schemes. Most banks have central virus protection software and install security software on employees' work computers and mobile devices. As directed by the bank, employees maintain backup files, practice safe Internet and email usage habits, and otherwise follow bank policy regarding the secure use of computers. The stakes are high, so all bank employees are trained on safe computer usage, not just for their computers at work but also at home.

Malware falls into three categories: viruses, worms, and Trojan Horses.

Viruses

Viruses attach themselves to a program or file, spreading from one computer to another, infecting each one as it goes; or to email messages, sending duplicates across the Internet using the infected computer's address book.

Most **viruses** are created to cause destruction. The virus waits for a trigger event and then opens a small program that performs a disruptive task or even destroys information maintained on computer devices.

Did You Know ...

Under contract to the ABA, Union Pacific Railroad, and Great Northern Express Company, the Pinkerton National Detective Agency identified and hunted down the "Wild Bunch" gang. By September 1902, the Pinkerton Agency believed that only three members of the gang remained alive: George Parker, alias "Butch Cassidy"; Harry Longbaugh, alias the "Sundance Kid"; and William Cruzans.

Source: American Bankers Association

malware—Derived from a combination of the words "malicious" and "software," it broadly applies to viruses, Trojan Horses, worms, and any other software programs designed to damage computers and computer systems.

virus—A software program capable of reproducing itself that usually causes great harm to files or other programs on the same computer.

Situation

John, a former director and executive vice president, embezzled funds by issuing cashier's checks and making offsetting entries to a general ledger receivables account. John then deposited the cashier's checks into his personal accounts at another bank. This process was repeated numerous times. John concealed the growing receivables account by manipulating bank records before the end of a calendar quarter, at month-end, and before a regulatory examination. During these periods, John would clear out the receivables account with offsetting false entries to both legitimate and fictitious loan accounts. John was able to conceal the fraud activity due to the bank's internal control deficiencies and his management position. The bank suffered a loss of $1.6 million.

—from an actual case investigated by the FDIC

spyware—Computer software that collects personal information about users without their informed consent. (Anti-spyware is computer software that blocks and prevents the use of spyware to invade a personal computer, computer server, or data processing system.)

keystroke tracking—The practice of monitoring the keys struck on a computer keyboard, often done covertly to obtain passwords and other protected information.

Worms

Worms are maliciously written software code that is transmitted from computer to computer, usually as an attachment to an email. Worms are very destructive—they can reproduce quickly, consuming all available system resources, overwhelming Internet servers, and halting Internet access for millions in a matter of hours. Further, worms can unleash embedded viruses designed to modify or eliminate existing files, address books, and directories. They can also attach themselves to electronic address books and direct the transmission of corrupted email messages throughout a bank, its customer base, or vendor listings.

Trojan Horses

A Trojan Horse is a seemingly benign computer program that is often forwarded from a legitimate source. When installed by the end user, it turns destructive. Unlike viruses and worms, Trojan Horses do not replicate themselves. Some Trojan Horses are more annoying than malicious. However, others can cause serious damage by deleting files and destroying information on a computer or network system. The most destructive Trojan Horses allow identity thieves to install malicious viruses as well as **spyware** and **keystroke tracking** programs designed to collect critical access and password data. Using network scanning equipment, these criminals routinely sweep the Internet searching for computers infected with their previously transmitted Trojan Horse programs.

Mobile Device Theft

To gain access to sensitive bank information, criminals do not necessarily have to resort to malware. Sometimes it is as easy as stealing a piece of hardware that the information resides on—specifically a laptop or other mobile computer device. In a case that attracted much media attention, a laptop belonging to the service provider to a major U.S. bank was stolen. It contained unencrypted data on users of the bank's prepaid debit cards.

The risk of mobile device theft has grown with the number of mobile devices in use. The damage caused by a stolen device can far exceed the replacement cost and is especially problematic for banks because it can open the door to identity theft and unauthorized account access. Consequently, vigilance from the many employees who use laptops and other mobile devices in their work is an important element in a bank's overall information security program. Many banks do not have good procedures for securing mobile computing and communication equipment. Often, the reason given is the lack of good options for "locking up" transportable computers. However, security measures such as biometrics, encryption, remote wiping, and smart chips can help protect data in the event a laptop is stolen.

Wireless Hacking

The growing use of wireless devices has opened a new door for identity thieves to enter and steal financial information from banks and bank customers. In one case of wireless hacking, identity thieves sitting in a parking lot outside a local branch office were able to gain access to the branch's computer network and then hack into accounts and download information from numerous credit card transactions.

Bank computer networks are not the only targets of hackers. With today's proliferation of laptop computers equipped with **Wi-Fi** and the number of **Wi-Fi hot spots** increasing exponentially at places like hotels, airports, and Internet cafes, customers who access their online banking and investment accounts on wireless devices are ripe targets for hackers. Once a computer is hacked, a criminal can record everything an unsuspecting bank customer does on the Internet, such as inputting credit card numbers, user names, and passwords. With access to the victim's online banking user name and password, identity thieves can even access the bank's network and steal sensitive financial data.

Wi-Fi—Short for wireless fidelity. Wireless fidelity is a radio frequency standard that is used to connect devices, such as computers, together using a wireless connection.

Wi-Fi hot spot—An area that allows computers equipped with wireless fidelity (Wi-Fi) to receive Internet connection.

The best defenses against wireless hacking are bank employee and customer awareness and adherence to information security safeguards, including changing bank network passwords frequently, using data encryption whenever possible, disabling networks when not in use, and erecting firewalls to block incoming transmissions at the network level.

SAFEGUARDING THE ECONOMY AND THE NATION

Occasionally events remind everyone of the critical importance of banks to the economic vitality of the United States. The terrorist attacks of September 11, 2001, on the World Trade Center in New York City was one such event. New York City is home to the New York Stock Exchange and many of the largest and most influential banks, securities firms, clearing and settlement organizations, and payment system operators in the country. Despite the terrible loss of life and the enormity of the damage on September 11, the nation's financial markets and payment systems continued to function without major disruption.

Little more than ten years later, the same area of the country was devastated by Hurricane Sandy, whose floodwaters displaced hundreds of thousands of residents and businesses and seriously damaged the regional infrastructure. Again, financial institutions were able to quickly resume critical functions.

More often, the threats are localized, such as a bomb threat received by a specific bank or a snowstorm that prevents bank employees from going to work. Most banks today are prepared for every disruptive event that could occur.

Emergency Preparedness

A critical obligation of banks is to plan for emergencies. Banks, like all businesses, have a moral responsibility to protect employees while at work. Emergency preparedness can also improve a bank's capacity to return to business, thereby continuing to serve its customers' financial needs, maintaining and preserving customer relationships, and minimizing financial loss. Emergency preparedness can also help mitigate the damage to buildings, equipment, and other physical assets. Consequently, all

business contingency plan—A plan for maintaining or resuming business operations should unexpected events occur. Also known as business continuity plan.

pandemic—A disease spread over a large geographical region and affecting a large proportion of the population.

banks have disaster recovery programs and **business contingency plans** for resuming critical functions. These plans are reviewed continually by bankers and regulators.

The importance of disaster recovery programs and business contingency plans was emphasized following Hurricane Katrina in 2005, one of the greatest natural disasters in recent history. Hurricane Katrina severely tested the ability of banks in the Gulf Coast region to remain functioning after the infrastructure of the affected area was damaged or destroyed.

In the aftermath of Hurricane Katrina, the federal and state governments and the banking industry revaluated their emergency preparedness and response efforts. The Federal Financial Institutions Examination Council (FFIEC), its member regulatory agencies, and the Conference of State Bank Supervisors analyzed bank experiences during and after the storm and found:

- Communications outages made it difficult to locate missing personnel.
- Access to, and reliable transportation into, restricted areas were not always available.
- Lack of electrical power or fuel for generators rendered computer systems inoperable.
- Many facilities were destroyed outright or sustained significant damage.
- Some branches and ATMs were underwater for weeks.
- Mail service in some areas was interrupted for months.

In response, the banking industry and the government formulated planning tools and guidelines to help banks better prepare for and respond to emergencies. Recommendations included restoring communications, partnering with local agencies, distributing financial assistance, anticipating emergencies and the needed response, mitigating the economic impact, and preparing for unique emergencies, such as a **pandemic**.

Terrorism

The events of September 11, 2001, gave terrorism a new meaning for all Americans. Terrorism kills and destroys innocent lives. It has a wider purpose, however—to spread fear and disrupt economic and financial activity. Because banks play a central and very visible role in the U.S. economy, they are targets for terrorist groups, domestic or foreign. Terrorist activity often requires vast sums of money. These funds

Disaster Assistance Card

In the event of a natural disaster, financial aid can be provided directly to disaster victims by providing them with Red Cross Client Assistance Cards (CACs) or Federal Emergency Management Agency (FEMA) debit cards. Funds can be loaded and reloaded with specific dollar amounts.

can be gained from supporters, but more commonly arise from illicit activity. Banks are, therefore, on the front line in combating the financing of terrorist organizations.

Tactics used to cause terror are wide-ranging and unpredictable. Bomb threats, often used in bank robberies, are also among the most common form of terrorist threats employed against banks.

Fully aware of the consequences, banks take terrorist threats very seriously. Maintaining adequate security systems is a high priority. Keeping employees apprised of the risk of terrorist acts and how to respond is an important part of contingency planning. Employees need to know how to protect themselves, their coworkers, and their customers (see exhibit 10.5).

Exhibit 10.5: Suspicious Package Poster

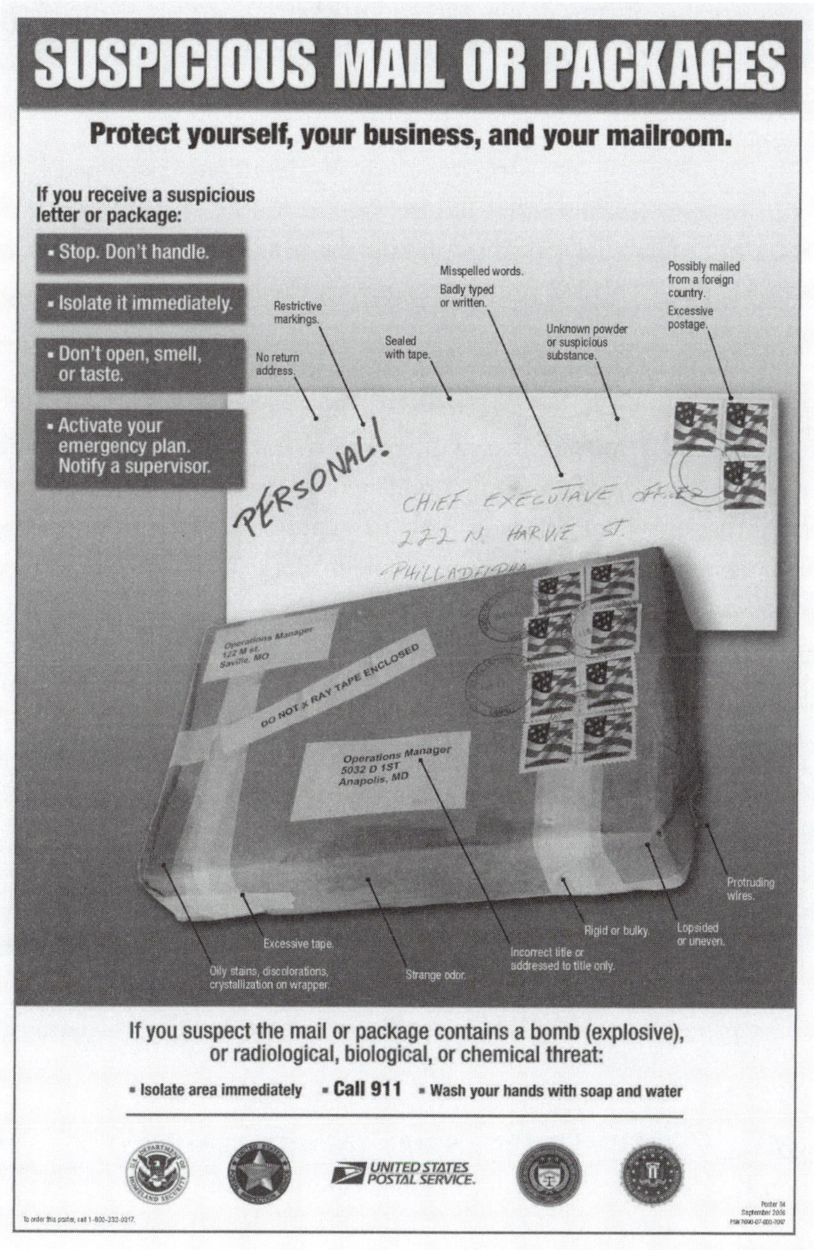

money laundering—Moving large amounts of illegally obtained cash through many bank accounts or to other legal investments or assets in order to hide the source of the money.

incident response program (IRP)—A comprehensive plan for reacting to threats to the security of a bank's data, systems, employees, or facilities.

Money Laundering

Money laundering is associated with many crimes, from racketeering and drug dealing to terrorism. Banks are the first line of defense in the battle against the illegal flow of money. They are required to report suspicious financial transactions that may be associated with criminal fundraising and funds transfers. Banks are obligated to exercise due diligence to know who their customers are and judge whether transactions are legitimate. Banks also assist the federal government by freezing the assets of organizations or individuals suspected of terrorist activities. Two laws in particular, the Bank Secrecy Act and USA PATRIOT Act, require banks to play an active role in combating money laundering.

Freezing Assets

As part of foreign policy, the federal government uses economic sanctions against individuals, terrorist organizations, and countries hostile to the United States. The Office of Foreign Assets Control (OFAC) in the Department of the Treasury posts a list on its website of nations, individuals, and entities subject to sanctions, which may include blocking accounts and freezing assets.

Banks must regularly check their records to identify assets owned by nations, individuals, or organizations that appear on the OFAC list. When a match is found, the bank must take action to prevent the funds being withdrawn and used for illegal activities. Specified procedures govern the handling of frozen assets and blocked accounts.

Security Breaches

To protect customer information and other bank data, federal regulators and sound business practices require banks to be prepared to respond to any security breach. Recognizing that every bank is susceptible to improperly configured systems and to software vulnerabilities, regulators have adopted rules requiring financial institutions to put in place **incident response programs (IRPs)** that follow certain standard procedures. Moreover, laws in most states mandate that individuals be notified if there is a breach in the security of electronically held customer information.

LAWS AND REGULATIONS

The Truth in Lending Act, the Fair Credit Reporting Act, the Fair Debt Collection Practices Act, the Equal Credit Opportunity Act, the Electronic Fund Transfer Act, and the unfair, deceptive, or abusive acts or practices provisions of the Dodd-Frank Wall Street Reform and Consumer Protection Act all safeguard consumer information. Several other laws, however, are more directly related to customers' financial privacy and identity protection. Still other laws pertain to safeguarding the bank itself and the nation as a whole.

Privacy of Consumer Financial Information

Regulation P, Privacy of Consumer Financial Information, implements the GLBA financial privacy provisions. Through the GLBA, Congress restricted the ability of banks to disclose customer information to third parties. The law and regulation also require banks to provide customers with a notice of their privacy policy when a banking relationship is established and annually thereafter. Customers can opt out of certain disclosures of personal financial information.

Interagency Guidelines on Information Security

Banks regularly collect personal information from their customers, such as their names, addresses, and phone numbers; bank and credit card account numbers; income and credit histories; and Social Security numbers. Section 501 of the GLBA requires financial institutions to ensure "the security and confidentiality of customer records and information, protect against any anticipated threats or hazards to the security or integrity of such records, and protect against unauthorized access to or use of such records or information that would result in substantial harm or inconvenience to any customer."

To assist banks in implementing the requirements of Section 501, bank regulators issued the Interagency Guidelines Establishing Standards for Safeguarding Customer Information, commonly known as the Safeguards Rule. The Safeguards Rule requires banks to have a comprehensive written information security program that:

- Ensures the security and confidentiality of customer information
- Protects against any anticipated threats or hazards to the security or integrity of customer information
- Protects against unauthorized access to or use of customer information that could result in substantial harm or inconvenience to the customer

In addition, banks must have standards for the proper disposal of customer information, which is also a requirement of the Fair and Accurate Credit Transactions Act (FACT Act).

Interagency Guidance on Internet Authentication

In 2001, federal banking regulators issued guidance on methods for verifying the identity of customers using electronic banking services. Titled "Authentication in an Internet Banking Environment," the guidance provides direction for evaluating and implementing authentication systems and practices. Although the guidance, updated in 2005 and again in 2011, focuses on Internet banking delivery channels, it also applies to all types of electronic banking. The guidance's purposes are to safeguard customer information, prevent money laundering and terrorist financing, reduce fraud, inhibit identity theft, and promote the enforceability of electronic agreements and transactions.

Protecting Children Online

In 1998, Congress enacted the Children's Online Privacy Protection Act to prohibit unfair or deceptive acts or practices in the collection, use, or disclosure of personal information from and about children on the Internet. The act protects the privacy of children and requires operators of websites directed toward children to obtain consent from parents before collecting data about their children.

Right to Financial Privacy

One of the older privacy laws, the Right to Financial Privacy Act, was passed in 1978 to protect the financial records of individuals from unwarranted access by the federal government. The act establishes criteria under which federal government agencies may obtain financial records and imposes a duty on financial institutions to screen requests for information to ensure they meet the requirements of the law before releasing the requested records.

State Requirements Protecting Social Security Numbers

Most states have laws restricting the use or dissemination of Social Security numbers (SSNs). These restrictions are often included in state information privacy and security laws. Because bankers handle SSNs for a variety of purposes, it is important for them to know the requirements of their respective state laws. In general, these state laws prohibit:

- Publicly displaying, intentionally communicating, or otherwise making an SSN available to the general public
- Intentionally printing an SSN on a card required to access goods or services or to enter a location (such as an employee identification card)
- Requiring a customer to transmit an SSN over the Internet unless the connection is secure or the SSN is encrypted
- Requiring a customer to use an SSN to access a website unless a password, a unique PIN, or other authentication is also required
- Printing an SSN on any materials that are mailed to a customer unless required by law

Most state laws do, however, have exceptions for using SSNs for internal verification needs, fraud investigations, or administrative purposes associated with legitimate banking functions.

Red Flag Rules

One of the requirements of the FACT Act directs banks to develop and implement written identity theft prevention programs. Bank identity theft prevention programs must include policies and procedures for identifying and detecting warning signs—or "red flags"—of identity theft. These requirements are more commonly known as the Red Flag Rules. An identity theft program must also spell out appropriate actions the bank will take when red flags are detected, and it must be periodically updated to reflect new risks.

Bank Security Systems

Banks are required by law to have security systems and equipment that discourage crime and physical damage to bank structures. Under the Bank Protection Act, enacted in 1968, banks must select, test, operate, and maintain security devices, including:

- Vaults to protect cash or other liquid assets
- Lighting systems to make areas such as the vault visible from within and outside the building
- An alarm or similar system to notify the nearest law enforcement officers of an attempted robbery or burglary
- Tamper-resistant locks on exterior doors and windows that could be opened

Bank Secrecy Act

The Bank Secrecy Act (BSA) requires banks to record and report certain financial transactions as a way of curbing illicit activities. Banks must file currency transaction reports (CTRs) on all deposits, withdrawals, and exchanges of currency that exceed $10,000.

Since its passage more than 30 years ago, BSA has been amended often to expand its scope. For example, in 1986 Congress made money laundering a federal crime, allowed laundered funds to be seized and forfeited, and required banks to have a formal BSA compliance program. In 1990, Congress created the Financial Crimes Enforcement Network (FinCEN) to detect financial crimes, and in 1994 FinCEN took over responsibility for BSA. In the late 1990s, regulatory agencies shifted their emphasis from the technicalities of reporting large currency transactions to monitoring and reporting suspicious activities. Banks are required to file suspicious activity reports (SARs) whenever they detect suspicious activity.

USA PATRIOT Act

After the September 11 terrorist attacks, detecting and reporting suspicious activities became a national imperative, especially because of the close link between money laundering and the funding of terrorist activities. In 2001, Congress enacted the USA PATRIOT Act. Its anti-money laundering provisions include a requirement for financial institutions to establish anti-money laundering compliance programs that include training, a designated compliance officer, policies, procedures, and internal controls, and an independent review. New customer identification program requirements imposed significant mandatory procedures for identifying both loan and deposit customers.

SUMMARY

- Banks protect customer transactions in a variety of ways, including automatic session expiration, automatic account lockout, direct deposit, e-alerts, unique numbers and passphrases, and online statement access and bill payment. Although banks do their best to prevent attacks on customer data, they also are aware that they must be ready in case an attack does occur. Federal regulators have mandated that banks and other financial institutions implement incident response programs that follow certain standard procedures. Taking decisive action to contain damage from a security breach protects customers and preserves the bank's assets and reputation.

- The USA PATRIOT Act requires banks to have and follow a customer identification program (CIP) during the account opening process. When banks communicate with customers in person, over the telephone, and online, they need ways to authenticate the identity of those with whom they are dealing. There are three types of authentication: something the customer knows, something the customer has, and something the customer is. Multifactor authentication is the combination of two or more of these categories. Biometrics is an emerging authentication method. Some common biometric methods are voice identification, keystroke dynamics, digital fingerprinting, 3-D facial recognition, and hand scanning.
- The main purpose of customer identification is to prevent identity theft. Identity theft can occur through low-tech thievery such as stealing purses and wallets, as well as high-tech methods such as intercepting electronic transmissions. Bank regulators have issued guidelines calling on banks to institute safeguards against identity theft. The best deterrents are vigilant bank employees and informed customers. Employees must stay alert to avoid compromising customer financial information by following bank policies and procedures at all times.
- Authenticating a customer's identity is not enough, however. Banks must also address an ever-expanding list of frauds against their customers. Common fraud schemes are bank card fraud, telephone fraud, advance fee fraud, letter of credit fraud, prime bank note fraud, cashier's check scams, phishing, pharming, and text message fraud. The elderly are especially vulnerable to many of these types of fraud.
- A bank must safeguard itself as a corporate entity. Occasionally banks are victimized from within—unethical or irresponsible behavior can occur anywhere in a bank. An inattentive board or audit committee, senior managers who reward bad employee practices, an employee who embezzles, or a dishonest vendor each poses a threat to bank safety and soundness. The best antidotes to these kinds of behavior are high standards of corporate governance, a strong code of ethics, quality hiring and contracting procedures, and vigilant oversight. Criminal threats to banks and their assets are insider fraud, robbery, and currency counterfeiting. Banks are also vulnerable to computer attacks, both from disgruntled employees and from hackers. In recent years, distributed denial of service (DDoS) attacks have become especially worrisome for banks. Critical bank information can be damaged or destroyed by malware—viruses, worms, and Trojan Horses. Mobile device theft and wireless hacking are two other means by which criminals can gain access to sensitive bank information.
- Banks are essential to safeguarding the economy and the nation. They help federal and state law enforcement agencies fight criminal activity, especially terrorism and money laundering. By filing currency transaction reports (CTRs) and suspicious activity reports (SARs), and by freezing the assets of suspected terrorist individuals, organizations, and states subject to sanctions, banks help protect the United States against terrorism, money laundering, and other financial crimes. Banks also draw up business contingency plans so they can readily resume critical functions if a disaster, terrorist act, or other business interruption occurs. Being prepared for emergencies allows banks to respond to special needs of their customers, their communities, and the nation's financial system.

- Most consumer protection laws and regulations have some provisions for safe-guarding consumer information. Some laws specifically address the security measures that must be taken to protect customers' personal and financial information. Among these are Regulation P, Privacy of Consumer Financial Information; Interagency Guidelines on Information Security; Interagency Guidance on Internet Authentication; the Children's Online Privacy Protection Act; the Right to Financial Privacy Act; state requirements protecting Social Security numbers, and the Red Flag Rules under the Fair and Accurate Credit Transactions Act. The Bank Protection Act requires banks to install and maintain certain bank security systems. The Bank Secrecy Act and USA PATRIOT Act help detect and deter financial crimes, including money laundering and potential terrorist financing activity.

SELF-CHECK AND REVIEW

Learning Check

1. What are some security features banks use to protect customers?
2. What are the three ways to authenticate high-risk transactions? Give an example of each.
3. What is phishing?
4. More laptop computers and other mobile devices are now used in banking than desktop computers. Discuss the implications of this for bank fraud.
5. What are some methods of stealing information to commit identity theft?
6. What are a bank employee's responsibilities with respect to ethical behavior?
7. How should a bank employee respond during a robbery?
8. What are some ways banks help federal authorities protect the country against terrorism?
9. Why should banks become involved in local emergency management processes?

Answers to Self-Check and Review

Chapter 1
Banks as Service Providers

1. *How do banks contribute to their communities?*

   In addition to providing deposit and credit services to individuals and businesses in the community, banks contribute time, talent, and funds to build, restore, and enrich their communities. Bank employees have a history of service to charitable organizations, and banks sponsor many community events and financial education programs.

2. *What five government agencies regulate bank activities?*

   - Federal Reserve System (Fed)
   - Office of the Comptroller of the Currency (OCC)
   - Federal Deposit Insurance Corporation (FDIC)
   - Consumer Financial Protection Bureau (CFPB)
   - State banking departments

3. *Why is the National Bank Act of 1863 important in relation to dual banking? Does dual banking still exist today?*

   The dual banking system came into being in the 1860s when the National Bank Act of 1863 allowed banks to elect a national charter. Thus, banks may be chartered by either a state government or the federal government. The dual banking system still exists today.

4. *What were some of the causes of the Great Depression that began in 1929?*

   There were many causes of the Great Depression, including: banks' involvement in underwriting securities and lending money to purchase those securities; inadequate margin requirements that allowed investors to borrow much of the money to purchase securities; no protections for depositors when banks failed; and stringent Fed rules that prohibited lending troubled banks enough reserves to remain open.

5. *Explain why easy credit, as exemplified by subprime lending, led to tighter credit, both of which helped trigger the Great Recession that began in 2008.*

   The Great Recession began with a housing bubble, largely created with relaxed credit standards and a proliferation of subprime loans. When the bubble popped and housing prices fell, the risky mortgages that had been packaged and sold as mortgage-backed securities declined in value, which led to companies that traded in those securities and financial institutions that invested in those securities to suffer huge losses. This, in turn, affected the ability of financial institutions to extend credit. With worries of a deepening recession and the ability of borrowers to repay debt, banks and other financial institutions restricted credit further.

6. *What are some trends in banking today?*

   Trends in banking include an ongoing evolution in the regulation of financial services that banks offer; continued expansion of the financial services offered to customers; more intense competition in financial services; innovations in technology for product delivery and operations; more innovative delivery of services, through smaller branches for example; and more precise targeting of customers via social media and online marketing.

Chapter 2
Banks as Businesses

1. *How does the Federal Reserve manage the money supply?*

   The Federal Reserve manages the quantity of money in circulation to ensure that credit is available in the amounts and at interest rates consistent with specific economic objectives. The methods the Federal Reserve uses to manage the money supply include reserve requirements, discount operations, and most important, open-market operations managed on its behalf by the Federal Open Market Committee and implemented by the Federal Reserve Bank of New York.

2. *Why does the Federal Reserve need to manage the money supply?*

   A nation's money supply is the sum of all the funds individuals and businesses have immediately available for spending in the domestic economy. Careful management is necessary to ensure that the money supply doesn't grow too fast and result in inflation or too slowly and result in a recession.

   To ensure that the deposits banks create are not too much or too little for the needs of the economy, the Federal Reserve controls the amount and cost of reserves available to banks. It buys and sells government securities in the open market, raises and lowers the amount of reserves banks must hold, and sets the target federal funds rate banks use when they lend to each other. These actions in turn become the basis for the interest rates banks offer their customers on both loans and deposits.

3. *Some banks have experienced losses while others have remained profitable. Who ultimately is accountable for a bank's poor financial performance?*

   Although executive management, led by the bank president and CEO, makes the day-to-day operating decisions, the board of directors ultimately is responsible for financial performance and must answer to the shareholders. The board of directors has the power to appoint the bank's senior officers.

4. *What is a bank's largest asset? Its largest liability? Its largest income and expense items?*

   A bank's largest asset is loans, which generate the majority of revenues. The largest liability is deposits, which provide funds for making loans. The largest income item is the interest received on loans, and the largest expense is the interest paid on deposits. An increasingly important source of revenue is non-interest fee income. Other large expense items are salaries and employee benefits.

5. *Why is accurate financial data so important to bank shareholders and investors? To federal and state regulators? To customers?*

   Shareholders and investors consider accurate financial data a predictor of growth potential. Federal and state bank examiners evaluate financial reports to determine a bank's true financial condition and ascertain whether it has sufficient capital. Customers are concerned about the financial stability of their bank.

6. *What would be the consequences if a bank overemphasized liquidity to the detriment of other factors in funds management? What would be the consequences of overemphasizing safety at the expense of liquidity and income?*

   If a bank emphasized liquidity only, keeping large supplies of currency in its vaults in case of increasing customer demands for funds, the percentage of deposits available for lending would shrink. The drop in loanable funds would impair the credit function and reduce income. If a bank tried to achieve absolute safety, it would never assume any risk in putting deposits to profitable use, and the potential to maximize loans would not be reached. This situation would result in lost income opportunities and failure to serve the credit needs of its community.

7. *What is the difference between the discount rate and the prime rate?*

   The discount rate applies to short-term credit extended by the Federal Reserve to banks. The prime rate is a base rate that reflects how a bank evaluates such factors as cost of funds, overhead, loan portfolio risk, and profit objectives.

8. *What is the net worth of a bank that has the following assets and liabilities?*

	(thousands of dollars)
Cash on hand	$45,400
Investments	$76,600
Loans (net of reserve for loan losses)	$224,300
Fed funds sold	$35,800
Fixed assets	$18,900
Other assets	$12,200
Deposits	$312,700
Fed funds purchased	$68,600
Other liabilities	$4,300

Assets = Liabilities + Net worth
or
Assets – Liabilities = Net worth

Assets = $413, 200 ($45,400 + $76,600 + $224,300 + $35,800 + $18, 900 + $12, 200)
Liabilities = $385,600 ($312,700 + $68,600 + $4,300)

$413,200 – $385,600 = $27,600

Net worth = $27,600

9. *What is the net profit or loss of a bank reporting the following revenues and expenses?*

	(thousands of dollars)
Interest and fees on loans	$253,700
Interest and dividends on investments	$22,100
Interest paid on deposits	$158,800
Salaries, wages, and benefits	$70,300
Taxes	$11,000

Net profit = Revenue – Expenses

Revenue = $275,800 ($253,700 + $22,100)
Expenses = $240,100 ($158,800 + $70,300 + $11,000)

$275,800 – $240,100 = $35,700

Net profit = $35,700

Chapter 3 Deposit Accounts

1. *Why are deposits important to banks?*

   Deposits from checking, savings, and money market deposit accounts and certificates of deposit provide a majority of the funds banks use to lend and invest.

2. *What are the basic differences and similarities between a checking account and a savings account?*

   Checking accounts are transaction accounts. Deposits made to noninterest-earning checking accounts are payable on demand. Usually the customer intends to withdraw checking account funds in the near future to pay bills and meet expenses.

   Customers generally place funds in savings accounts to set aside money for future needs and to earn interest. Technically speaking, savings account funds are not immediately available to the depositor. Although banks rarely do so, they can require seven days of notice before a withdrawal from a savings account.

   Checking accounts and savings accounts do not have maturity dates. Deposits and withdrawals can be made on any day. Thus, unlike a time deposit account, such as a certificate of deposit, no interest penalty is imposed for withdrawal from a checking or savings account.

Also, under Federal Reserve Regulation D, transaction account deposits are subject to reserve requirements. Savings account deposits are not.

3. *How do automatic transfer services benefit a customer?*

   With automatic transfer service (ATS), customers can write checks that exceed their checking account balances, and the bank by prior arrangement (preauthorization) will move funds automatically from their savings accounts to cover the checks.

4. *What deposit account would you recommend to a customer who wants to earn interest and would like the option of writing a small number of checks (no more than six) every month?*

   A money market deposit account (MMDA) offers higher annual percentage yields than savings accounts. This type of account also allows a limited number of monthly check and other preauthorized transfers to third parties (six per month). Withdrawals made in person are unlimited.

5. *How can customers make deposits into their accounts without going to the bank?*

   Without visiting a bank branch, a customer can make a deposit by electronic fund transfer (EFT), automatic transfer service (ATS), remote deposit capture, automated teller machine (ATM), computer and mobile banking, wire transfer, Internet banking, direct deposit, deposit by mail, deposit by payroll card, and courier and armored car services.

6. *How do account transactions differ for joint accounts held in joint tenancy versus those held as tenants-in-common?*

   With a joint tenancy with rights of survivorship account, each account holder may make transactions, and only one signature is required. When one account holder dies, the funds in the account typically pass to the surviving account holders in accordance with state law and without need to establish an estate.

   Tenancy-in-common accounts often require the signatures of all account holders for transactions. From the bank's perspective, tenancy-in-common accounts need more monitoring. If the bank pays checks with only one signature when it has agreed to require the signatures of all the account holders, it could be liable to those account holders who did not sign the check. Upon the death of one account holder, the remaining holder is entitled only to his or her share in the account. The decedent's share may be inherited by a third party.

   Most banks require joint accounts to be established as joint tenancy with full right of survivorship.

7. *When a deposit account is opened, why is it important for a bank to establish the authority of the customer to use the account? What three steps does the bank take to accomplish this?*

   When an account is opened, the bank enters into a contractual relationship that gives customers the ability to extend credit themselves, gives them a means to convert checks and other instruments into cash, and creates other situations that could result in a loss to the bank. Three steps that a bank takes to open an account are to (1) establish the identity of the person opening the account, (2) determine that the person has the legal capacity to open the account, and (3) ensure that the person has the authority to open the account.

8. *What types of deposit transactions are covered by Regulation E?*

   Regulation E covers, for example, direct deposits of paychecks and Social Security payments, ATM transfers, debit card purchases, telephone bill payment services, and banking transfers initiated through the Internet, including making deposits, transferring funds between accounts, and paying bills.

9. *Connie has a single checking account containing $10,000, a single savings account containing $30,000, and a single certificate of deposit in the amount of $35,000. She also has three joint accounts containing $200,000, $110,000, and $90,000, respectively. Because there are two owners for each of the joint accounts, her interest is half of those balances. What is her insured amount? How much is uninsured?*

   Connie has a total of $75,000 ($10,000 + $30,000 + $35,000) in insured accounts in her name only. She also has a total of $400,000 ($200,000 + $110,000 + $90,000) in joint accounts with one other person. Her half interest in the joint accounts is $200,000. All of the $75,000 in her individual accounts is fully insured. Her full $200,000 interest in the joint accounts is also fully insured because the FDIC insurance limit is $250,000 for each type of ownership category (individual and joint ownership).

Chapter 4
Payments: Cash and Checks

1. *What law governs the requirements that make a check negotiable? What are those requirements?*

   Article 3, Negotiable Instruments, of the Uniform Commercial Code (UCC) establishes check negotiability. For a check to be negotiable it must be: (a) payable to bearer or to order, (b) an unconditional order to pay, (c) payable for a specific (fixed) amount of money, (d) payable on demand or at a definite date, (e) in writing and signed by the drawer.

2. *Who are the parties to a check?*

   The parties to a check are the drawer, the payee, and the drawee. The drawer writes the check. The payee is the one to whom the check is written. The drawee is the bank that holds the drawer's account and pays the check.

3. *What is the difference between a blank endorsement and a special endorsement? Discuss when each is used.*

   A blank endorsement consists simply of the signature of the payee or other holder of the instrument. A blank endorsement can be used for any purpose and allows flexibility and ease of transfer. However, it essentially turns the check into a payable to bearer document and, with it, the risk that it can be cashed or deposited by anyone. In a special endorsement, the holder both signs the instrument and names the party to whom rights to the instrument are being transferred. It is used when the endorser is mailing the check to another party.

4. *What are the differences between a cashier's check, a teller's check, a certified check, and a traveler's check?*

   Cashier's checks are issued by a bank and drawn on that bank. The bank is both drawer and drawee. Teller's checks are issued by one bank but drawn on another bank. The issuing bank has the same obligation for teller's checks as for cashier's checks.

   A certified check is a customer's check previously accepted by the bank on which it is drawn. A traveler's check functions like cash (and is thus useful when traveling in places where other forms of payment are not accepted) because it is payable on demand to the payee. A traveler's check does not require the holder to present it to the bank on which it was drawn for payment.

5. *What are some examples of checks that might be rejected from the normal posting process and require handling as exception items?*

   Checks may require special handling as exception items because, for example, the funds available in the account may be insufficient to pay the check, an uncollected balance may not leave a sufficient balance in the account to pay the check, there may be a stop payment on the check, or there may be a hold placed on the account.

6. *What is dual custody? Provide an example of when it is used.*

   Dual custody (dual control) is a security technique that uses two or more individual parties operating together to protect sensitive functions, information, or assets. Both parties are equally responsible for physically protecting materials in vulnerable transactions. Currency is prepared for shipment and received using dual custody procedures.

7. *What are at least three signs of a fraudulent check?*

   Any three of the following apply:

   - Check lacks perforations, is stained or discolored, or has an odd "feel." Most check paper has the same weight and texture.
   - Check number is either missing, does not change, or is low, between 100 and 500. Ninety percent of returned checks have low check numbers. Low check numbers indicate a recently opened account and, therefore, a potentially more risky check.
   - Additions to the check are handwritten.
   - Customer's address or bank's address is missing.
   - There is evidence of erasures or alterations.
   - MICR numbers are missing or are shiny. Fraudulent checks often substitute regular toner or ink for magnetic ink.
   - MICR encoding does not match the check number, the bank district, or the routing symbol in the upper right-hand corner of the check.
   - The word "VOID" appears across the check.
   - The check lacks an authorized signature.

Chapter 5
Electronic Banking

1. *How do virtual banks operate?*

   Virtual banks operate only online; they have no physical branches. Customers make deposits primarily through direct deposit and automatic transfers from accounts at other financial institutions. Withdrawals are made online, by telephone transfer, or by card.

2. *How are electronic fund transfers (EFTs) and Automated Clearing House (ACH) services related?*

   Banks use EFTs to borrow from each other, invest surplus funds, settle clearing balances in the check collection process, and provide fast and efficient transfer services for depositors. ACH services are the channel through which banks perform these services, forwarding information from their own customers in batches to either the Federal Reserve or the privately owned ACH, which processes, distributes, and settles the transactions electronically.

3. *What are Fedwire, CHIPS, and SWIFT?*

   Fedwire Funds Service is an EFT settlement system used for transfers of reserve account balances of depository institutions and U.S. government and federal agency securities, and certain third-party payments—usually those that are large-value and time-critical—to bank customers. CHIPS (Clearing House Interbank Payments System) is a member bank-owned system for clearing mostly large-value payments. It is the focal point for payments in the international dollar market. SWIFT (Society for Worldwide Interbank Financial Telecommunication) is a worldwide network by which messages concerning financial transactions, such as letters of credit, payments, and securities transactions, are exchanged among banks and other financial institutions. It also encompasses corporate and market support systems for payments, securities, and trades.

4. *How do contactless payment cards work?*

   Radio frequency identification (RFID) technology transmits information a few inches from a card carried by a customer to a card reader at a retailer or service provider. The customer does not have to swipe the card (although most contactless cards also can be swiped), let go of it, sign a receipt, or input a personal identification number. RFID transfers are used mostly for small-ticket items such as fast food purchases or parking fees.

5. *How is check imaging used, and what are the benefits to a business?*

   Paper checks received by a business in payment for products or services it supplied to a customer can now be scanned to create an electronic image, which is then transferred as an electronic file for collection. Many businesses now make deposits using check imaging, also called remote deposit capture (RDC) or check truncation, using scanners that capture both sides of the check. Check imaging makes it possible for businesses with outlets in different localities to consolidate their accounts at a single bank and reduce the need to have accounts at different banks in different localities. For small businesses, RDC also offers the convenience of depositing checks without having to visit the local bank branch.

6. *What federal regulations apply directly to electronic banking?*

   Regulation E covers Electronic Funds Transfers, Regulation CC implements the Expedited Funds Availability Act, and Regulation J applies to check collection and funds transfers. The E-Sign Act makes electronic signatures and e-contracts equivalent to paper signatures and contracts. Other regulations that apply to traditional banking methods also apply to electronic banking, as do the federal privacy laws.

Chapter 6
Lending

1. *Why is the lending function so important to banks?*

   The lending function is important to banks because:
   - Of the three cornerstones of banking—the deposit, payment, and lending functions—the lending function represents the most significant source of income.
   - Lending is one of the most traditional elements in the relationship between a bank and its customers.
   - Under the Community Reinvestment Act, banks are evaluated and given a public rating on their record of helping to meet the credit, investment, and service needs of their communities, including individuals, small businesses, small farms, and low- to moderate-income consumers.
   - The quality of a bank's loan portfolio often is critical to its survival.
   - Lending is essential to the functioning of a healthy, growing economy.

2. *What is the difference between open-end and closed-end credit? Give some examples of each type of consumer loan.*

   Open-end credit is a revolving line of credit on which a customer may draw for a specified period. The balance may fluctuate from zero to a set maximum. Two examples of open-end credit are home equity lines of credit and credit cards. Closed-end loans involve an agreement with the customer specifying the total amount of the loan, the maturity date, the number of payments, and the dates on which payments are due. Automobile and home equity loans are examples of closed-end loans.

3. *Why are home equity loans and home equity lines of credit popular?*

   Interest paid on these loans may be tax-deductible. Also, the interest charged is typically lower than for other loan products because the loan is secured by the customer's residence.

4. *If a business wants to purchase a piece of equipment, what loan type is appropriate—working capital or term loan? Why?*

   A long-term loan is appropriate because the funds are for long-term use of the equipment. These loans have maturities of up to five years. Working capital loans are short-term (typically 90 days) and generally are used to purchase raw materials or finance other immediate needs.

5. *Why do applications for business credit typically require a more thorough investigation than applications for consumer credit? What sources of information can be tapped to provide this more thorough level of investigation?*

   Commercial loan requests are usually for larger amounts of money, and more factors may affect loan repayment. For example, in the case of a consumer loan, the applicant's income and credit score are critical factors in judging creditworthiness. In the case of a commercial loan applicant, business income is less predictable, being influenced by economic conditions, supplier relationships, accounts receivable aging, and many other factors. Consequently, the "credit score" of a commercial loan applicant must be arrived at by using many resources, including credit files, credit agencies, annual reports and financial statements, and contacts with suppliers and others who have business dealings with the applicant.

6. *What kinds of payment protection are available to consumers?*

   Payment protection may be an insurance or fee-based product. Credit insurance is issued by an insurance company and may cover life, disability, or loss of income. Fee-based credit protection and bank products include debt cancellation and debt suspension agreements.

7. *What are some activities involved in loan administration?*

   Loan administration activities include:
   - Mailing regular statements
   - Receiving and posting specified payments
   - Keeping address information current
   - Ensuring that the bank's security interest is recorded, filed, and returned to the bank
   - Answering customer inquiries
   - Reporting the loan to credit reporting agencies
   - Maintaining documentation for examination by internal and external auditors and regulators
   - Closing the loan and taking it off the books when the final payment is received
   - Releasing any security interests in collateral

8. *What is the function of loan review?*

   The loan review area examines loan documents to ensure accuracy, completeness, and conformity with bank loan policy and with state and federal laws and regulations. It gives bank management and directors assurance that:
   - Loan officers are staying within their authority
   - Lending policy, procedures, laws and regulations are being followed

- Investigation and analysis are adequate
- All necessary documentation on each loan has been properly obtained and filed

9. *What roles does the bank board of directors play in the lending function?*

   The bank's board of directors represents the highest authority on lending policy. The directors' responsibilities include:
   - Determining the types of loans to be made
   - Tightening credit standards when warranted
   - Establishing and monitoring legal lending limits and minimum loan amounts
   - Setting loan policy
   - Assigning credit authority
   - Authorizing all loans above a stipulated amount
   - Reviewing the loan portfolio to ensure that the bank is meeting local credit needs and complying with CRA
   - Conducting periodic reviews and audits

10. *What are some laws with which a loan officer must comply when making a mortgage loan?*

    The Equal Credit Opportunity Act, Truth in Lending Act, Community Reinvestment Act, Home Mortgage Disclosure Act, Real Estate Settlement Procedures Act, and the Dodd-Frank Act are among the laws that affect home mortgage lending.

Chapter 7
Personal Financial Planning

1. *Why do many Americans have reason to be concerned about their financial affairs?*

   The personal savings rate of Americans as a whole has declined steadily for two decades, with only a modest improvement beginning in 2009. Further, a recession in 2008 that extended into most of 2009 hurt accumulated wealth, leaving most Americans with a lower net worth on their personal balance sheets. Many Americans carry too much debt, with young Americans, in particular, saddled with burdensome student debt. As a result of failing to adequately save early in life, older Americans often have not accumulated enough assets to complement their pension plan benefits in meeting all their financial needs. The result is that many Americans are having trouble meeting their financial obligations, and some older Americans have been forced to delay the date when they can retire.

2. *What are a bank financial planner's ethical responsibilities?*

   Financial planners must behave ethically by providing objective information, without consideration of whether one financial product might be more profitable for the bank than another. Bankers must be careful not to stray into areas beyond their professional expertise and licensed qualifications, such as giving specific legal advice that is more appropriate coming from a lawyer or tax advice that is more appropriate coming from a certified public accountant.

3. *What factors and effects must be taken into account in financial planning?*

   Financial planning must take into account the customer's financial needs and goals, life stage, and risk tolerance level, and recognize the potential effects of inflation, appreciation, interest, and the time value of money. When selecting investment options, the risk/return trade-off also must be taken into account.

4. *What are the preliminary steps in financial planning?*

   The financial planning process begins with an analysis of the customer's current position, or net worth, and then his or her financial needs and goals. With this information, cash flow and investment strategies are developed and incorporated into the plan. Then the customer and required experts put the plan into action. The plan should be reassessed, usually annually, for needed modifications.

5. *What is the purpose of life insurance, and who needs it?*

   Life insurance replaces the income the policyholder contributed to the family before he or she died. Single people with no dependents usually need only enough insurance to cover funeral expenses and unpaid debts. Adults with dependents may need more insurance to ensure that their dependents' future living expenses, including care giving, are covered.

6. *What are the three basic investment strategies and motivations that influence investment choices?*

   The three basic investment strategies are conservative, moderate, and aggressive. The customer's risk tolerance level, which is defined by life stage, personal circumstances, and financial plan goals, determines the investment strategy. Common motivations are to safeguard or increase principal, produce income, or pursue high returns.

7. *What are the two basic types of personal trusts?*

   Testamentary and living trusts are the two basic types of personal trusts. Testamentary trusts are created under the terms of a decedent's will. As trustee, the bank is responsible for managing assets turned over to it by the executor or administrator and for making payouts to the beneficiaries as specified in the will. Living trusts are trusts created by living individuals who execute a trust agreement and transfer property to the trust. Individuals who set up living trusts often want to avoid the details of probate or keep transfers private.

8. *How are banks structured to deliver investment and brokerage products? Through what channels are these products delivered?*

   To deliver investment and brokerage services, banks set up full-service brokerage companies either as subsidiaries or through affiliates in their financial holding company. Some banks make arrangements with a third party or a broker-dealer, or establish a joint venture with these third parties, to offer investment services.

9. *What are the requirements for the sale of retail nondeposit investment products?*

Banks selling investment products must take a number of precautions, including:

- Marketing nondeposit investments in a way that does not mislead or confuse customers about the products or the risks, including separating retail deposit-taking and retail nondeposit sales functions
- Prohibiting bank employees, such as tellers, from offering investment advice
- Refraining from offering uninsured retail investment products with a product name identical to the bank's name
- Conspicuously disclosing that investment products are not FDIC-insured, are not obligations of or guaranteed by the bank, and carry the risk of possible loss of principal

10. *List some bank deposit, insurance, investment, and trust products that can help meet customers' basic retirement needs.*

Some bank products and services that can help customers achieve their retirement needs include:

401(k) plans
Traditional IRAs
Roth IRAs
SEP IRAs
Spousal IRAs
Annuities
Living trusts
Life insurance
Health insurance
Disability insurance
Long-term care insurance

11. *What law and bank organizational structure allows banks to be full-service centers for retirement planning? What regulatory principle operates to ensure that the nondeposit functions in banks are regulated and examined for compliance?*

The Gramm-Leach Bliley Act (GLBA) allowed banks to offer a full line of financial services, including underwriting and selling insurance and dealing in securities. The primary structure allowed by the law that made this possible organizationally is the financial holding company, which is deemed to be legally able to engage in any activity that is "financial in nature."

The GLBA also established the functional regulation system. This regulatory principle requires certain authorized banking activities, such as the sale of insurance and securities, to be subject to the authority of the appropriate federal and state regulators other than the federal bank regulators.

Chapter 8
Business and International Banking Services

1. *What types of cash management services help a corporate customer optimize the interest earned by deposits or reduce the interest expense of loans?*

   Controlled disbursement and zero balance accounts help businesses optimize day-to-day cash management by establishing an automated link between different disbursement or zero balance accounts and a cash concentration account or a line of credit. When there are more funds than needed in the disbursement or zero balance accounts, they are automatically transferred to a concentration account, usually an interest-earning or investment account, or are used to reduce the balance on a line of credit. Cash concentration services allow a business that has accounts at numerous banks to pool surplus balances in a concentration account that can then be invested at a higher rate of return than the business could otherwise earn on separate smaller accounts.

2. *What check imaging advance is rapidly gaining acceptance in the business community and changing the way banks deliver cash management services?*

   Remote deposit capture, also known as point of purchase (POP), accounts receivable conversion (ARC), and back office conversion (BOC), is changing the way banks provide cash management services. With this service, a business can convert payments into check images or ACH data at either the point of purchase or off-site locations such as an accounts receivable office in company headquarters or a third-party processing center, including those run by banks. The check data proceeds through the ACH system for collection and payment. For businesses, the service reduces collection time, expedites returns, and reduces payment processing costs.

3. *How does key person insurance differ from directors and officers liability insurance?*

   A company purchases key person insurance on employees whose loss, by death or from disability, would financially hurt the company. Executives and other employees with managerial or technical expertise usually are insured. Proceeds from a key person policy can be used to recruit and train replacements, help replace lost profits, and reassure creditors and suppliers about the continuity of the business. Directors and officers (D&O) liability insurance also insures key business people—that is, directors and senior managers who make the decisions in running the company—but in this case the purpose of the coverage is to protect those key people from liability arising from actions connected to their corporate positions. D&O insurance pays damages resulting from settling claims against directors and officers and reimburses them for defense costs.

4. *What types of customers need capital market services? What are some examples of capital market services that banks provide?*

   Capital market services are useful to corporate customers who need money to finance operations and growth. Banks help such companies access public and private equity and debt markets. Capital market services range from specialized lending to underwriting, structuring, and distributing corporate debt.

5. *What corporate trust services do banks typically provide?*

   Banks offer corporate agency services (safekeeping, transfer, registrar, and paying agent services); employee benefit services, such as employee welfare programs (insurance and payments for sick leave, vacation, disability and training) and pension programs (defined benefit and defined contribution plans).

6. *What organizational structures can banks use to facilitate delivery of international banking services?*

   Organizational structures banks use for international banking include:
   - *Edge corporations*—subsidiaries of national banks used for either foreign trade-related banking or foreign investment
   - *Foreign branch*—a branch in another country that is approved by both the Federal Reserve and the host country and abides by the laws of both the United States and the host country
   - *Shell branch*—a special-purpose overseas branch without a physical location, used for investment purposes such as Eurodollar deposits
   - *International banking facility (IBF)*—set up to allow a domestic bank to accept deposits and offer loans to foreign customers. The accounts of the IBF are separate from the parent bank's accounts. Federal Reserve approval is not required, but the Fed must be informed, and the banking facility must abide by its regulations
   - *Foreign representative office*—an office located in another national capital that does not provide as many services as a foreign branch. Representatives build business that is handled by a foreign branch of the bank
   - *Foreign subsidiary*—a foreign company in which the U.S. bank has a majority ownership interest or another form of control. It is used when foreign branches are not allowed
   - *Foreign joint venture*—a foreign company in which the U.S. bank shares ownership and management with other banks

7. *How does a letter of credit protect the interests of both the buyer and the seller of goods?*

   A letter of credit guarantees that the exporter (seller) will be paid if all the terms of the contract are met, and that payment on behalf of the importer (buyer) will not be made until the contract has been fulfilled.

8. *Your Japanese company is importing semiconductor parts from the United States. Each part costs 30 U.S. dollars. The currency exchange rate at the present time is 104 yen = 1 U.S. dollar. How much does each semiconductor part cost in yen?*

   Foreign currency (U.S. dollars) x foreign currency exchange rate (in Japanese yen) = Japanese yen

   30 U.S. dollars x 104 = 3,120 yen

9. *What does UCC Article 5 govern? What are some sample rules? Is there an international law similar to UCC Article 5?*

   UCC Article 5 sets out rules governing letter of credit transactions, including the agreement of the parties to the transaction, rules for its enforcement, the issuer's payment responsibility, and what happens if there is wrongful dishonor.

The international rules for letters of credit that support and supplement Article 5 are the International Chamber of Commerce's UCP 500, Uniform Customs and Practices for Documentary Credits.

Chapter 9
Building Relationships: Marketing, Sales, and Customer Service

1. *Do employees who rarely interact with bank customers have a role in building customer relationships? Why or why not?*

   Yes. Employees who perform jobs where there is little direct contact with customers still have an important role in the relationship-building process. Bank employees who are responsive to requests from coworkers are providing customer service and supporting relationship building. Meeting delivery standards is providing customer service and building relationships. A bank will have difficulty convincing customers that it cares about their business when back-office personnel regularly make errors.

2. *What are some of the ways a bank employee can demonstrate responsiveness to customer needs?*

   Demonstrating responsiveness includes acknowledging customers as they approach, being present, being ready to help them, listening carefully to understand their needs, taking responsibility for the problems they present, working as a team member with coworkers to solve problems promptly and accurately, and resolving special problems in a friendly and caring manner.

3. *How does marketing fulfill a social responsibility? Why is this good business practice as well?*

   It is easy to understand why marketing its product and services is desirable and beneficial for a bank; the public is well served also. The Community Reinvestment Act requires that banks be evaluated on how they meet the credit needs of their communities. Advertising loan products is one way of ensuring that, when there is a need for credit, low- and moderate-income customers turn to their local bank. When a bank provides financial support for philanthropic activities or its employees become involved in the community, it is good public relations, which is a form of advertising, and also fulfills the bank's social responsibility. The banking industry is also engaged in ensuring that all members of the American public are financially literate. By supporting educational initiatives directed at good savings and borrowing practices, banks help reduce the number of unbanked and underbanked Americans, which is a social necessity, and also create potential new customers.

4. *What are the benefits of cross-selling and referrals?*

   A bank that effectively cross-sells additional products and refers business to other departments or affiliates expands its customer relationships, helps customers meet their financial goals, and sells more products, both immediately and over the long term. When employees cross-sell and make referrals, customers are given the impression the bank values their business and has their financial interests in mind. Customers who use multiple products and services are more likely to maintain long-term relationships with the bank.

5. *What are some of the things customers do in anticipation of making a purchase?*

   In anticipation of purchasing a product, customers often look through newspaper advertisements and Internet websites, talk to other people, and read information pamphlets and promotional brochures. When contemplating a loan, a customer may request a loan application. Often a prospective customer will call the bank or approach an employee in person to solicit information about particular financial products. A teller who notices that a business customer makes deposits every day may suggest remote deposit capture or refer the customer to cash management.

6. *What is the difference between a product feature and a product benefit?*

   A product feature is a characteristic of the product; a product benefit describes how the product will meet customer needs.

7. *What steps are involved in bringing a new product to market?*

   Bringing a new product to market entails multiple steps under the direction of a product development team. The process begins with market research and the profiling of customers, the market, and the bank's competitors. The product development team solicits and screens new product ideas, tests the concept, performs a business analysis, creates the product, test markets it, introduces it to the market, and evaluates its performance.

8. *A bank advertisement for a home equity loan promoting the special interest rate of 3.25% catches Patty's eye because home equity loans offered by other lenders are around 4%. The ad says the loan is subject to a credit check and house appraisal. Patty applies for the loan and is approved. At closing, the loan papers state that the interest rate is 3.75%. When Patty points this out, the loan officer tells her that to receive the 3.25% rate she must open a deposit account with the bank so that the amount due on the loan each month can be automatically withdrawn. What is Patty the victim of? Explain. Why does the bank's ad fit the FTC's definition of a deceptive act?*

   Patty is the victim of a bait-and-switch. The bait is an interest rate that is lower than that offered by competitors. The switch is a higher-priced product. The ad omitted conditions for qualifying for the low interest rate, thus it was misleading to Patty, who meets the definition of a reasonable customer. The misleading ad affected Patty's choice of product. By the time she realized the loan was not as advertised, it was too late to change her decision without incurring a substantial loss, including the money she spent on a home appraisal.

Chapter 10
Safeguarding Customers and the Bank

1. *What are some security features banks use to protect customers?*

   The most common security features banks use to protect customers are:
   - Automatic session expiration
   - Automatic account lockout
   - Direct deposit
   - E-alerts
   - Unique security numbers and passphrases
   - Online bill payment and statements

2. *What are the three ways to authenticate high-risk transactions? Give an example of each.*

   The three ways to authenticate transactions are by:
   - Something the user knows
   - Something the user has
   - Something the user is

   A password or personal identification number (PIN) are examples of something the user knows. An ATM card and smart card are examples of something the user has. A unique physical characteristic, such as a fingerprint or a voice or facial scan, are examples of something the user is.

3. *What is phishing?*

   Phishing involves sending a customer an email request directing him or her to a phony website. The email appears genuine because often the bank's name, logo, or other graphic appears on it. The email asks the victim to provide account numbers, a Social Security number, or password. The illegally obtained confidential information is then used in identity theft and credit card and Internet-based frauds.

4. *More laptop computers and other mobile devices are now used in banking than desktop computers. Discuss the implications of this for bank fraud.*

   Mobile devices are more easily stolen than desktop computers. If the stolen device belongs to a bank employee or a customer who banks online, the loss far exceeds the replacement cost of the computer because of the potential that personal or financial information could be accessed to commit bank fraud, particularly identity theft. Laptop computers (as well as other mobile computer devices) are also responsible for the growth of locations that offer Wi-Fi access. This, in turn, has spawned the relatively new crime of wireless hacking, where identity thieves frequent Wi-Fi hot spots looking to obtain confidential personal and financial information from unsuspecting customers banking online.

5. *What are some methods of stealing information to commit identity theft?*

   Criminals use both low- and high-tech methods to exploit a person's assets and credit. Some of the methods of obtaining confidential information include dumpster diving for receipts, bills, personal records, or other paper with personal and financial information; skimming credit or debit card numbers when these cards are processed; phishing; diverting billing statements to another location by falsifying a change of address form; stealing wallets and purses, mailed bank and credit card statements, preapproved credit offers, and new checks or tax information; bribing employees who have access to bank information; and hacking into personal records.

6. *What are a bank employee's responsibilities with respect to ethical behavior?*

   Bank employees are expected to adhere to the bank's code of conduct, which spells out expectations for ethical behavior. Bank employees also have the responsibility to report ethical violations and misconduct.

7. *How should a bank employee respond during a robbery?*

   When a bank robbery is taking place, appropriate behavior includes remaining calm, assuming that the robber has a weapon and that it is real, doing exactly as the robber instructs, following the bank's robbery procedures, never trying to overpower or out-think the robber, being observant, forming a good mental picture of the robber's appearance, carefully observing the robber's speech or mannerisms, and retaining evidence such as a note.

8. *What are some ways banks help federal authorities protect the country against terrorism?*

   The many ways banks assist federal authorities include:

   - Implementing policies and procedures against money laundering, in compliance with the Bank Secrecy Act, such as filing currency transaction reports (CTRs) on transactions exceeding $10,000
   - Filing suspicious activity reports (SARs) on suspicious transactions with FinCEN
   - Abiding by the customer identification requirements of the USA PATRIOT Act
   - Blocking accounts and freezing assets of individuals, organizations, and countries that appear on the OFAC's sanctioned list, which is on its website

9. *Why should banks become involved in local emergency management processes?*

   In times of emergency, banks need to work together to share cash reserves, facilities, and communications systems. They can also partner with other local industries and local, state, and federal emergency management agencies to provide a coordinated emergency relief effort. The more banks and other entities plan in advance, the more likely it is that recovery periods can be shortened.

A to Z Glossary

abandoned call—A telemarketing call that is not connected to a sales person within two seconds after the recipient answers the telephone and completes a greeting.

accounts receivable—An amount owed to and not yet delivered or accepted by a company.

actuarial calculation—The mathematical determination of rates and premiums for life insurance, disability insurance, and pension benefits based on tables detailing the frequencies of mortality (death) and morbidity (disability).

adjustable-rate mortgage—(ARM) A mortgage on which the rate is subject to periodic adjustment. The rate usually is tied to a widely published market index or rate of interest.

advertising—Any form of communication paid for by a sponsor for the purpose of informing and persuading consumers to buy goods, ideas, or services.

affiliate—A business organization sharing with another organization some aspect of common ownership and control, such as interlocking directorates, stock ownership, or parent company.

agent—A person or company that acts for another person or company (the principal) by the latter's authority.

agreement corporation—A corporate subsidiary of a bank engaged in international banking and finance.

altered check—A check on which a material change, such as the dollar amount, has been made.

amortization—The periodic reduction of the principal amount due on a mortgage or other term loan. When the full amount is repaid, the loan is fully amortized. An amortization schedule is a table listing how much of each loan payment is applied to the principal and how much is applied to the interest.

annual percentage rate (APR)—The cost of credit on a yearly basis. Expressed as a percentage, APR results from an equation that considers three specifically defined factors: the amount financed, the finance charge, and the term of the loan. The APR is usually expressed in terms of the effective annual simple interest rate.

annual percentage yield (APY)—A rate reflecting the total amount of interest paid on a deposit account, based on the interest rate and the frequency of compounding for a 365-day period.

annuitant—The beneficiary of an annuity; the person insured under an annuity plan and on whose life expectancy annuity payments are based.

annuity—An insurance product that provides a systematic payment for a specified period, usually a number of years. Payments typically are made monthly but can be made quarterly, semiannually, or annually.

appreciation—The increase in the value or usefulness of an asset.

asset-based financing—A financing method usually focused on the cash flow of a particular asset or asset group for return on an investment or loan.

ATM card—A plastic access card that enables the cardholder to withdraw cash through an ATM and that, in some retail locations, can be used for point-of-sale transactions after a personal identification number (PIN) is entered. The cost of the transaction is debited from the cardholder's bank account.

audit—An official examination and verification of accounts and internal controls, usually by an independent accountant, to determine whether financial information is accurate and prepared in conformity with generally accepted accounting principles (GAAP).

authentication—(1) Determination that a message comes from a source authorized to originate the message; (2) a measure designed to protect against a fraudulent transmission by establishing the validity of a transmission, message, station, or person.

automated clearing house (ACH)—A clearing facility operated for the convenience of banks in a particular region, generally through the regional Federal Reserve Bank. An ACH electronically processes interbank credits and debits.

bait-and-switch—Advertising a product or service at an attractive price (bait) and then informing a consumer who is ready to purchase that the product or service is not available or is of lesser quality and encouraging the consumer to purchase (switch) to a higher-priced product or service.

bank holding company—A corporation that owns or controls one or more banks.

banknote—Currency issued by a bank promising to pay the amount of money designated on its face when the note is presented to the bank.

beneficiary—(1) The party legally entitled to receive the proceeds of an annuity, insurance policy, letter of credit, trust fund, retirement account, or will, either from an appointment, assignment, disposition, instrument, or contract; (2) in the context of electronic fund transfers, the term used in Article 4A of the Uniform Commercial Code to refer to the person to be paid under the payment order.

benefit—The value the product's or service's features gives to customers to meet their needs, such as earn money, save money, save time, provide convenience, or provide security.

bill of lading—A document given by the shipper of goods to the recipient acknowledging receipt of shipment and the terms of delivery.

biometrics—Automated methods of identifying a person based on a physiological or behavioral characteristic, such as a voice, fingerprint, or typing pattern.

board of directors—The governing body of a corporation ultimately responsible for its financial performance, consisting of individual directors elected by the shareholders.

book entry—A method for electronically registering and keeping a record of securities ownership without issuing physical certificates to owners. Securities are not in printed form but exist on the books of the issuer's agent. Transfer is by electronic debit and credit.

business contingency plan—A plan for maintaining or resuming business operations should unexpected events occur. Also known as business continuity plan.

business loan—A loan to a business to meet short-term or long-term needs. Also known as a commercial loan.

buying on margin—Using borrowed funds to buy assets such as stock.

call—The right of a corporation to repurchase a bond obligation or stock.

captive finance company—A finance company owned by a manufacturer to finance dealer inventory and/or to make loans to consumers for the purchase of its products.

cash—(1) Money in the form of bills or coins; (2) money on hand or in the bank.

cash letter—An interbank electronic or paper transmittal form, resembling a deposit slip, used to accompany cash items sent from one bank to another.

certified public accountant (CPA)—An accountant licensed to practice public accounting. To earn this title, a person must pass the Uniform Certified Public Accountant Exam and meet other requirements established by each state for education and experience.

charter—A document issued by a federal or state supervisory agency granting a bank or other financial institution the right to do business.

check—A draft on an account in a bank that the owner of the account signs to direct the bank to pay a certain amount to the payee.

check debit card—A plastic access card that enables the cardholder to purchase goods or services or withdraw cash online through a point-of-sale terminal and offline upon signing a receipt. The transaction cost is debited from the cardholder's deposit account. The card, which may be used for ATM transactions as well, may carry a VISA or MasterCard logo.

civil money penalty (CMP)—A fine imposed by a civil court on an individual, business, or organization that has profited from illegal or unethical activity or has violated a law or regulation. Also known as civil monetary penalty.

closed-end fund—An investment fund that allows only an original prescribed number of shares to be distributed. It raises substantially all of its funds at the time the fund is established. The fund is traded like a stock on an exchange. Compare to open-end fund.

code of conduct—A formal set of guidelines approved by the board of directors that represents a company's policies for corporate governance and individual conduct.

collateral—Specific property or other assets pledged by a borrower to secure a loan. If the borrower defaults, the lender has the right to sell the collateral to liquidate the loan.

commercial paper—Negotiable, short-term, unsecured promissory notes in bearer form issued by major corporations with unquestioned credit standing as a means of borrowing.

Community Reinvestment Act—A federal law mandating that federal bank regulators regularly evaluate how financial institutions help meet the credit needs of their communities, including low- and moderate-income sections of the community, and publicly rate the bank's performance.

consumer loan—A loan extended to consumers, either individually or jointly, primarily for the purpose of buying goods and services for personal use.

Consumer Price Index—A measure of the average change over time in the prices paid by consumers for selected goods and services. It represents whether prices are rising or falling in the U.S. economy and, thus, whether there is inflation or deflation.

corporate governance—The manner in which directors, management, and auditors handle their responsibilities to shareholders.

corporate resolution—A document filed with a bank that defines the authority given to the corporation's officers and specifies who may sign checks, borrow on behalf of the corporation, and otherwise conduct business and issue instructions to the bank.

corporation—A business organization treated as a legal entity and owned by a group of shareholders (stockholders). The shareholders elect the directors, who serve as the governing body managing the corporation's affairs.

correspondent bank—A bank, often a larger bank, that maintains an account relationship or engages in an exchange of services with another, usually smaller, bank. Sometimes called upstream correspondent bank. The bank that uses the services is the respondent bank.

credit risk—The risk that the borrower cannot or will not repay a loan with interest as scheduled.

creditworthiness—The ability and willingness to repay a debt, largely demonstrated by the borrower's credit history.

cross-selling—A sales practice whereby a customer is invited to purchase additional products and services that are related to the product or service acquired.

daylight overdraft—(1) A negative balance created in an account when payments made during business hours exceed incoming funds actually received; (2) an overdraft in a bank's reserve account at a Federal Reserve Bank during business hours.

deferred compensation—The contractual postponement of payment for services rendered until a future date; commonly used with respect to retirement benefits (qualified or nonqualified) to be paid in the future.

defined benefit pension plan—A pension plan that guarantees the payment of a specified benefit at retirement.

defined contribution pension plan—A retirement plan fund that takes in employee contributions, which may be matched by employer contributions, and then invests the contributions into one or more investment alternatives determined by the employee.

demand deposit—Funds that a customer may withdraw from a bank with no advance notice, usually by writing a check or using an ATM.

de novo bank—A bank that has been in operation for five years or less. Commercial banks operating for five years or less that convert to Federal Reserve membership are subject to the de novo bank application and supervision standards.

dependent—A person, such as a child, who depends on another person, such as a parent, for care and financial support.

depositary bank—The bank in which a check is first deposited. The bank also may be the drawee if the check is drawn on, payable at, or payable through the bank.

depository institution—A financial institution that obtains funds mainly from deposits by the public. Commercial banks, savings and loan associations, savings banks, and credit unions are all depository institutions.

depreciation—The decrease in the value or usefulness of an asset.

direct deposit—A process by which funds are deposited electronically to bank accounts. Commonly used for payroll and Social Security payments.

discount operations—A tool of monetary policy in which banks borrow funds from the Federal Reserve. These loans, priced at the discount rate, help reduce liquidity problems for banks and maintain stability of financial markets.

diversification—A method of decreasing the total risk of investments by investing funds in different kinds of assets.

dividend—Payments made by a corporation to its stockholders. The payments are based on a percentage of the corporation's after-tax earnings and are usually made quarterly.

doubtful loan—A loan that probably will not be collected in its entirety and poses default risk.

draft—A signed order by one party (the drawer) addressed to another (the drawee) directing the drawee to pay, at sight or at a definable time in the future, a specified sum of money to the order of a third person, the payee.

dual banking system—The banking system in the United States today in which a bank may be chartered by either a state or the federal government.

dual custody—A security technique that uses two or more individual parties operating together to protect sensitive functions, information, or assets. Both are equally responsible for physically protecting materials in vulnerable transactions. Neither party may access or use the materials independently. Also known as dual control.

Edge Act corporation—Established under the Federal Reserve Act, a corporation that is a bank subsidiary for either foreign trade-related banking or foreign investment.

electronic benefit transfer (EBT)—A system for electronic payment of government-sponsored benefit programs using plastic cards and point-of-sale (POS) technology.

electronic check—An electronic version of a paper check that includes the date, payee name, payment amount, and signature. Checks bear a digital signature security code proving payment was authorized by the account holder.

electronic fund transfer (EFT)—A transfer of money from one bank account to another that is initiated through an electronic terminal, telephone, computer, or magnetic tape.

embezzlement—A crime involving the fraudulent use or keeping of money or other property that has been entrusted to one's care. Also known in banking as misappropriation of funds.

employee benefit program—A program established or maintained by an employer, employee organization, or both to provide employees with a certain benefit or set of benefits, such as pensions, profit-sharing, stock bonuses, and life, health, accident, and disability insurance.

endorsement—A signature (other than the signature of the maker, drawer, or acceptor) typically made on the back of the instrument, such as a check, for negotiating the instrument, restricting payment, or transferring liability of the instrument to another party.

equity—The investment interest of all shareholders in a corporation, equaling the excess of assets over liabilities and including common and preferred stock, retained earnings, surplus, and reserves.

established business relationship—A commercial relationship in which the consumer has purchased, rented, or leased the seller's goods or services or conducted a financial transaction with the seller within the 18 months immediately preceding a telemarketing call; or has inquired about, or applied for, a product or service offered by the seller within three months immediately preceding the call.

estate—The assets (property) a person owns such as real estate, cash, stocks, bonds, and all other personal property, and the person's liabilities (debts) and other legal obligations. Often used to describe the property of a decedent.

ethics—Principles of conduct and judgment that affect business practices.

Eurodollars—Deposits denominated in U.S. dollars at banks and other financial institutions outside the United States. Although the name originated because large amounts of such deposits were held at banks in western Europe, similar deposits in other parts of the world also are called Eurodollars.

executor—A party, often a bank, trust company, attorney, or even an heir, who is appointed in a will to carry out the terms of the will.

external auditor—An auditor who is independent of the bank, usually reporting directly to the internal auditor or the board of directors or audit committee.

feature—A characteristic of the product or service, such as the interest rate or the term.

federal funds—Excess reserves that banks deposit at Federal Reserve Banks and are made available for other banks to borrow, generally for a very short period of time such as overnight.

Federal Register—A daily publication of the federal government that contains, among other material, proposed and final regulations adopted by federal agencies.

federal savings association—A thrift institution that is chartered by the federal government to provide deposit services and extend credit for homes and other goods and services.

fiduciary—An individual, bank, or other party to whom specific property is turned over under the terms of a contract and who acts for the benefit of another party on a basis of trust and confidence.

financial intermediary—A financial institution that facilitates the exchange of funds between savers and spenders by taking in funds from savers and then lending those funds to borrowers and investors.

financially literate—Having a basic understanding of financial matters, especially as it pertains to personal finances, such as making wise savings and borrowing decisions.

fiscal year—The 12-month period selected by a business or government as an accounting period, at the end of which the books are closed and profit or loss determined. It may correspond to the calendar year.

fixed assets—Assets used by a business for its long-term conduct of its enterprise, such as building, machinery, and furniture.

foreclosure—A procedure to obtain legal title to property, typically for the purpose of selling the property to recover loan amounts.

foreign exchange—The trading in or exchange of foreign currencies for other foreign currencies.

fraud—An intentional misrepresentation made by one person to another who, believing the misrepresentation, takes some action and suffers a loss of property or a right to the first person. The elements of common law fraud are: (1) a false representation, (2) with respect to a material fact, (3) made with knowledge of its falsity, (4) with intent to deceive, and (5) with action taken in reliance on that representation.

functional regulation system—A regulatory principle incorporated in the Gramm-Leach-Bliley Act that requires certain authorized banking activities to fall under the authority of federal and state regulators other than the principal federal bank regulators (this was somewhat modified by the Dodd-Frank Wall Street Reform and Consumer Protection Act of 2010).

grace period—The period of time before the payment due date during which a credit card account holder is allowed to pay off the monthly bill without having to pay additional interest.

heir—A person who inherits property.

hold—A restriction on the payment of all or any part of the balance in an account.

holder—A person who is in possession of a negotiable instrument and who is entitled to receive payment of the instrument.

identity theft—A crime involving the possession of identifying information not lawfully issued for the possessor's use, or the attempt to access the financial resources of another person through the use of illegally obtained identifying information.

incident response program (IRP)—A comprehensive plan for reacting to threats to the security of a bank's data, systems, employees, or facilities.

indemnification—An action taken to compensate or reimburse someone for losses or damages incurred.

indenture—A contract underlying a bond issue, signed by the issuing corporation and the trustee, who acts for the bondholders. It sets forth the rights and responsibilities of the corporation, trustee, and bondholders and the terms of the issue.

information security program—A plan for ensuring that data and technology systems are not accessed by unauthorized users.

insider fraud—Fraud perpetrated by someone who works inside an organization.

insolvent—A position where liabilities exceed assets, resulting in the party being unable to meet its debt obligations.

internal auditor—An auditor who is employed by the bank, regularly working with all levels of management.

intestate—Derived from the Latin word *intestatus*, meaning one who dies without having made or left a valid will.

investment banking—The marketing of new security issues, usually through an investment banker or underwriter.

irrevocable letter of credit—A letter of credit that, once issued, cannot be cancelled and can be modified only with the consent of all parties to the credit, including the beneficiary (often an exporter).

keystroke tracking—The practice of monitoring the keys struck on a computer keyboard, often done covertly to obtain passwords and other protected information.

large-cap stock—Generally, stock of companies whose market value is greater than $10 billion.

lease financing—A specialized area of finance dealing with renting property owned by a lender, financing the leases of a company engaged in rentals, or financing the purchase of an item to be leased out by the borrower.

liquidity—(1) The ability of a business to meet its current obligations or to take advantage of new investment opportunities, such as a bank's ability to cover withdrawals, pay for operating expenses, or make loans; (2) the quality of an asset that makes it readily convertible to cash without significant loss.

loan review—The function of examining loan documents to ensure they are accurate, complete, and conform to laws and regulations and the bank's loan policies and procedures.

long-term loan—A loan of a fixed amount that is repaid according to a specific schedule over a period of several years, typically one to 30 years.

loss loan—An uncollectible loan or a loan that is not an appropriate asset for the bank.

magnetic ink character recognition (MICR)—Numbers printed in magnetic ink near the bottom of the front of a check to facilitate automated processing. The position and content of the MICR line are governed by industry standards. MICR encoding includes the bank's routing number, the customer's account number, the number of the check, and often the amount of the check.

malware—Derived from a combination of the words "malicious" and "software," it broadly applies to viruses, Trojan Horses, worms, and any other software programs designed to damage computers and computer systems.

market risk—The risk that the market value of a security or other asset will decrease because of interest rate changes and other market conditions.

market share—One seller's portion of the total sales of a product, usually measured as a percentage. In the financial services industry, market share is typically expressed as a percentage of deposits.

marketing customer information file (MCIF)—A software program that can sort and analyze customer information and serves as a customer information database.

matched funding—An asset and liability management technique in which assets are financed with liabilities of the same maturity or duration.

medical information—Under the FACT Act, which amended the FCRA, information, oral or recorded in any form, created by or derived from a health care provider or a consumer that relates to the past, present, or future physical, mental, or behavioral health or condition of an individual, the provision of health care, or payment for the provision of health care.

medium of exchange—Currency or other financial instrument used to facilitate transactions between parties.

mid-cap stock—Generally, stock of companies whose market value is between $2 billion and $10 billion.

monetary policy—The management of a nation's money supply by a central bank, such as the Federal Reserve, to ensure the availability of credit in quantities and at interest rates consistent with specific economic objectives.

money laundering—Moving large amounts of illegally obtained cash through many bank accounts or to other legal investments or assets in order to hide the source of the money.

money market deposit account (MMDA)—A type of savings account created in 1982 that pays a market interest rate and gives account holders limited check-writing privileges.

mortgage-backed security—An investment instrument that is backed by mortgage loans as security.

mortgage servicer—A company that collects mortgage payments from the borrower and performs other services, such as paying insurance and taxes from the borrower's escrow account.

multifactor authentication—Authentication by two or more of the following: something the customer knows, has, or is.

national bank—A bank that is chartered by the federal government to provide financial services (as opposed to a state bank).

negotiable instrument—An unconditional written order or promise to pay a certain sum of money. The document must be easily transferable from one party to another by endorsement and delivery or delivery alone. Every negotiable instrument must meet all requirements of Article 3 of the Uniform Commercial Code.

net worth—The difference between total assets and total liabilities as calculated for an individual or business.

nonbank financial company—A financial institution that does not have a banking license but is allowed to provide most banking services.

nonbank subsidiary—An entity owned by a bank holding company that offers nonbank products and services.

nondeposit investment product—Any financial product with an investment component that is not a deposit product and thus not insured by the Federal Deposit Insurance Corporation (FDIC). Stocks, bonds, insurance products, and government and municipal securities are examples.

noninterest income—Income a bank derives from sources other than interest, for example, fees and service charges, trading income, and investment securities gains.

nonsufficient funds—An expression indicating that a check or item drawn against an account exceeds the amount of funds available in the account. Commonly called an "NSF" or overdraft.

notary public—A public officer who acknowledges or otherwise attests or certifies documents as authentic, usually under an official seal.

NOW account—An interest-earning transaction account against which check-like instruments (negotiable orders of withdrawal) may be drawn. This transaction account is not a demand deposit account: the bank must reserve the right to require the depositor to give seven days advance notice before withdrawing funds (a requirement that is rarely imposed).

official advertising statement—Mandated by FDIC regulation, a statement that must be included in all advertisements (unless specifically exempted) that the bank is a member of the FDIC. Specific requirements apply as to the wording, size, and placement of the statement.

on-us check—A check deposited or otherwise negotiated at the bank on which it is drawn.

open-end fund—A mutual fund that sells new shares directly to new investors and redeems shares at the market price when investors wish to sell. Assets in the fund increase or decrease as investors move money into or out of the fund.

open-market operations—The purchase and sale of U.S. Treasury and federal agency securities by the Federal Reserve to influence the growth of the nation's money supply. They are the principal means by which the Federal Reserve implements monetary policy.

opt out—Explicitly choosing not to do something, such as to not receive bank product literature. As opposed to opt in, which is explicitly choosing to do something.

originating depository financial institution (ODFI)—The term adopted by NACHA—The Electronic Payments Association to refer to the bank that receives payment instructions from the originator and then forwards those instructions (entries) to the automated clearing house (ACH) operator.

overdraft—A negative (minus) balance in a customer's checking account resulting from the paying (posting) of items for an amount greater than the account's available balance.

pandemic—A disease spread over a large geographical region and affecting a large proportion of the population.

partnership agreement—A legal agreement stating the contributions each partner has made to the business, the nature of the business, and the proportions in which each partner will share in profits or losses.

partnership resolution—A document containing language certifying that the name of the partnership is exactly the same as the one provided to the bank and listing who is authorized to write checks and sign for loans on behalf of the partnership.

payment protection—Products that are sold in conjunction with loans so that the loan can be paid if the customer dies, is injured or disabled, or loses a source of income.

peer group—In banking, a statistical grouping of banks that have similar characteristics, such as asset size. Each bank is compared to other banks in the group.

perfection—The process by which a secured party protects its security interest from third parties by taking possession, holding certificate of title, controlling, or filing or recording documentation of the security interest in local or state public records.

point-of-sale (POS)—A device used to transfer funds from a bank account to a retailer to pay for purchases.

portfolio—The assets owned by one organization or person and managed as a collective whole to reach specific investment goals.

positive pay—A bank service that pays a business's checks only if they match the check data on an electronic list of issued checks that the business sends to the bank.

power of attorney—A legal document that authorizes a person named as an agent (attorney-in-fact) to act on behalf of another person (the principal).

premium—(1) The payment for insurance coverage in either a lump sum or installments; (2) the amount or percentage above face value at which securities are bought or sold.

pretext calling—Attempts to use the phone to gain access to another's account information by pretending to be the account holder or an authorized signer on the account.

primary market—The market in which an issuer sells new securities to investors. Among middlemen who aid in the sale of a company's securities are investment bank underwriters, brokers, and dealers.

prime rate—The interest rate a bank offers its most creditworthy customers and the base rate used to set interest rates for other loans.

principal—The person or company that appoints another (an agent) to act on his or her or its behalf.

probate—A judicial procedure whereby the validity of a will is proved and a decedent's estate, in accordance with a will if it exists, is administered.

profile—In marketing, identifying relevant characteristics of customers to gain insight about the need for a product in the marketplace.

promissory note—A written document with the customer's (maker's) promise to pay a certain sum of money to the bank (the payee), with or without interest, on demand or on a fixed or determinable future date.

proxy statement—A document intended to give shareholders the information they need to vote knowledgeably on matters brought up at shareholder meetings.

purchase decision—In the buying process, the culmination of prepurchase activity, in which a customer first assesses information gathered to reduce the risk associated with a decision about a product and then makes the purchase.

pyramided reserves—The reserve patterns of banks before the Federal Reserve System was authorized. Smaller banks would place their reserves in larger banks, which would then place their reserves and those of the smaller banks in money center banks such as those in New York City.

radio frequency identification (RFID)—An automatic identification method that relies on storing and remotely retrieving data using devices that can be attached to, or incorporated into, products such as tags or transponders.

ratio analysis—A technique for analyzing a financial statement that examines the relationships between certain values reported in the statement.

receiving depository financial institution (RDFI)—The term adopted by NACHA—The Electronic Payments Association to refer to the bank that receives automated clearing house (ACH) entries from the ACH operator and then posts them (either as credits or debits) to the accounts of its depositors, the receivers.

recession—A period of significant economic slowdown, often defined as a decline in the gross domestic product over two or more consecutive quarters.

redlining—Excluding potential loan customers because they wish to finance real estate located in a certain geographic area, regardless of whether they are depositors or meet all other criteria of creditworthiness.

referral—Directing a potential customer from one area of the bank, such as consumer lending, to another area, such as insurance, to help the customer obtain information about or purchase another product or service.

regulation—An official rule or set of rules having the force of law. Regulations are issued by government agencies and are based on, and designed to implement, a law enacted by a legislature.

remote deposit capture (RDC)—A service that allows consumers or businesses to scan checks and transmit the scanned images or automated clearing house data in an encrypted form to a bank for posting and clearing.

repurchase agreement—A sale of securities with a simultaneous agreement to buy back the same securities at a stated price on a stated date. It is the most common form of overnight investment for corporate funds, supported by securities (usually U.S. Treasury bills) from the bank's (or broker's) inventory.

reserve requirement—A mandate that each bank set aside a portion of its cash assets against its outstanding deposits. Today reserve requirements are managed by the Federal Reserve as part of its monetary policy duties and apply only to the deposits in transaction accounts.

revocable letter of credit—A letter of credit that may be withdrawn by the issuer at any time without prior notice to the beneficiary.

right of survivorship—The right of surviving tenants to take full possession of specific assets, such as account funds, upon the death of other tenants, without establishing an estate but subject to state laws.

risk/return trade-off—The relationship between an investment's risk and its potential return; the lower the investment's risk, the lower the return, and vice versa.

sales promotion—Any activity, other than advertising, publicity, and personal selling, that provides incentive to the consumer to purchase goods or services; for example, offering premiums and having in-branch displays.

savings and loan holding company—A corporation that owns or controls one or more savings and loan associations or savings institutions.

savings bank—An institution that primarily accepts interest-bearing time and checkable deposits for investment in mortgages and high-grade securities. A savings bank may also make loans to businesses and consumers.

secondary market—A market for the resale of securities (such as the dealer market, a stock exchange, or the mortgage-backed securities market) where ownership is transferred from one owner to another. The first sale of any security is in the primary market; all subsequent sales are in the secondary market.

secondary mortgage market—Transactions involving selling and purchasing mortgages. Mortgage loans originate in the primary mortgage market. Bundles of those mortgage loans may then be sold to investors in the secondary market.

secured loan—A loan for which the customer has pledged some form of collateral to protect the lender in case of default.

securities—Financial instruments such as stocks (equity securities) or bonds (debt securities) that have value and are easily bought and sold between parties.

securitization—The pooling of debt, such as mortgage loans, and selling the consolidated debt as securities to investors. In the case of loans, the loans are then no longer assets of the lending bank, although the bank may continue to service them.

security interest—The right a lender has to obtain possession of the collateral, sell it, and retain the proceeds (up to the amount of the remaining debt) if the customer is unable to repay the loan.

security token—A physical device that communicates with a computer, either by direct attachment or wireless communication, to confirm a person's identity for the purpose of performing authorized transactions.

settlement—The conclusion of a transaction, including completing all necessary documentation and making the necessary payments; the point at which claims and obligations are satisfied.

share draft—A bill payment device offered by some credit unions. Members of a credit union can write these check-like instruments against their savings share accounts.

sight draft—A draft payable on demand when presented to the drawee.

small-cap stock—Generally, stock of companies whose total market value is less than $2 billion.

smart phone—A mobile phone enabled to access the Internet.

spam—Unsolicited junk emails sent to a large number of people to promote products or services or to spread computer viruses.

spyware—Computer software that collects personal information about users without their informed consent. (Anti-spyware is computer software that blocks and prevents the use of spyware to invade a personal computer, computer server, or data processing system.)

state bank—A bank that is chartered by a state to provide financial services (as opposed to a national bank).

stop payment—An order by a depositor to the bank (the drawee) to not pay a previously issued check or item.

subprime loan—A loan made to a borrower who does not qualify for prime market interest rates because of credit problems or other deficiencies. A subprime loan charges a higher interest rate and/or greater fees.

substandard loan—A loan whose risk is high given the collateral and the loan's structure.

substitute check—A paper reproduction of the original check drawn from an electronic file that contains an image of the front and back. It bears the full MICR line as allowed by industry standards for such checks, conforms in paper stock and dimensions to the standards, and can be processed through automated check systems.

tablet—Handheld computer devices, with screens typically larger than smart phones but smaller than laptop computers, and using a touchscreen rather than a keyboard and mouse.

time draft—A draft payable at a fixed or determinable future time.

truncation—The process of removing the physical paper check from the processing flow.

trust—A fiduciary relationship in which one party (a person or a corporation) holds title to property for another party based on a legal agreement and the fiduciary principles of law.

unbanked—People who do not have a relationship with a bank or similar financial institution and generally rely on cash or money orders to receive or make payments.

underbanked—An individual who may have a checking or savings account but relies heavily on alternative financial services, such as payday loan providers, rent-to-own businesses, or pawn shops.

underwrite—To assume a risk for a fee, such as for insurance or investments. Insurance underwriting guarantees cash payment if there is a loss or casualty.

Investment underwriting guarantees the purchase of new offerings of corporate stock or debt securities of a corporation or government entity by purchasing the entire offering and then selling it in the market.

Uniform Commercial Code—A set of laws adopted by states to govern commercial and financial transactions between parties. Many states add their own amendments to the basic code.

unsecured loan—A loan for which the borrower has not pledged some form of property as collateral in the event the loan is not repaid in full.

value—The worth of a product or service that is expressed in money (price) or a quantity of another product or service. It is also the quality that makes something desirable or important.

virus—A software program capable of reproducing itself that usually causes great harm to files or other programs on the same computer.

whistleblower—An employee who reports fraud or other wrongdoing within a company.

Wi-Fi—Short for wireless fidelity. Wireless fidelity is a radio frequency standard that is used to connect devices, such as computers, together using a wireless connection.

Wi-Fi hot spot—An area that allows computers equipped with wireless fidelity (Wi-Fi) to receive Internet connection.

wrongful dishonor—Failure of the drawee to pay a properly payable check.

A to Z Index

C

D

E

F

G

H

I

J

K

L

N

O

P

S

T